Building a Pragmatic Data Platform with dbt and Snowflake

AF691664

Roberto Zagni and Jakob Brandel

Technics Publications
SEDONA, ARIZONA

TECHNICS PUBLICATIONS

115 Linda Vista, Sedona, AZ 86336 USA
https://www.TechnicsPub.com

Edited by Steve Hoberman
Cover design by Lorena Molinari

All rights reserved. No part of this book may be reproduced or transmitted in any form or by any means, electronic or mechanical, including photocopying, recording or by any information storage and retrieval system, without written permission from the publisher, except for brief quotations in a review.

The authors and publisher have taken care in the preparation of this book but make no expressed or implied warranty of any kind and assume no responsibility for errors or omissions. No liability is assumed for incidental or consequential damages in connection with or arising out of the use of the information or programs contained herein.

All trade and product names are trademarks, registered trademarks, or service marks of their respective companies and are the property of their respective holders and should be treated as such.

Without in any way limiting the author's exclusive rights under copyright, any use of this publication to "train" generative artificial intelligence (AI) technologies to generate text is expressly prohibited. The author reserves all rights to license uses of this work for generative AI training and the development of machine learning language models.

First Printing 2026
Copyright © 2026 by Roberto Zagni and Jakob Brandel

ISBN, print ed.	9798898160494
ISBN, Kindle ed.	9798898160500
ISBN, PDF ed.	9798898160517

Library of Congress Control Number: 2026930086

To the four females in my daily life:
my wife, who supports me every day,
my daughters, who keep me grounded in reality,
and our dog Lily for the sparkles of love and happiness
that she spreads around every day.

To my mother and my late father who
-through their sacrifices and support-
allowed me to become what I wanted to be.

I love you all.

Roberto Zagni

To the bright and curious data engineering students at Hyper Island and Nackademin,
who challenged early ideas in this book and helped sharpen the thinking.
To the business leaders who shared their time, experience, and real world lessons
through the case studies.

To my loving and steady husband Tobias,
to my kids Freja and Adrian, who keep my priorities clear,
and to our Bernedoodle Luna, who adds joy to every ordinary day.

I am grateful to you all.

Jakob Brandel

Preface by Ludwig Sewall

Working with Jakob and Roberto

During my career, I've had the privilege to work closely with both Jakob Brandel and Roberto Zagni, two individuals widely recognized as some of the most respected and influential professionals in the modern data space.

I first worked with Jakob as a customer, during the early procurement and adoption of Snowflake, where I experienced firsthand what it means to successfully guide an organization through large-scale platform transformation. I've never seen someone build as much trust, alignment, and goodwill within an organization as Jakob. His ability to drive change, combined with empathy and a deep understanding of technology, was invaluable in building our data platform.

I witnessed Roberto's contributions to the analytics industry long before we worked together, as we were both active at leading analytics consultancies in the Nordics before later getting to know each other through advisory boards and industry events. More recently I had the opportunity to work closely with Roberto through my role at dbt Labs, where he was a key enterprise customer.

I'm excited to see Jakob and Roberto working together on this book, as they each bring decades of experience from different parts of the value chain. In Building a *Pragmatic Data Platform with dbt and Snowflake*, they have channeled that collective expertise into a definitive guide for the industry.

Customer, Consultant, and Product Perspective

Over the years, I've experienced modern data platforms from multiple perspectives:

- A customer procuring and implementing both Snowflake and dbt,
- A consultant helping organizations execute migrations and transformations
- My current role at dbt Labs, where I guide our largest customers through platform transformation.

I've been deeply involved in the Snowflake Data Superhero community and have also driven the Swedish dbt community. Today, I lead strategic customer engagements at dbt Labs as the only Solutions Architect in the Nordics, partnering with many of the region's largest enterprise organizations on platform strategy and modernization initiatives.

Across my career, I've implemented multiple end-to-end analytics architectures, advised on more than 20 migrations as a consultant, and overseen more than 50 customer environments in my role at dbt Labs. Even with that experience, I still continuously learn from both Jakob and Roberto, and this book reflects many of the practical lessons that matter most in real-world platform implementations.

Enduring Architecture Principles

Too often, discussions around data platforms become trend-driven or focused on idealized architectures that are difficult to operationalize in real organizations. Pragmatic Data Platform instead focuses on practical implementation patterns, architectural tradeoffs, and hands-on examples from real customer environments.

The technologies shaping the analytics landscape will evolve over time, but the principles of simplicity, scalability, and maintainability will continue to define successful data platforms.

This is particularly valuable because many organizations today face similar challenges: balancing governance with agility, scaling teams without losing control, selecting the right architectural patterns, and avoiding unnecessary complexity. The chapters in this book help connect those challenges to practical implementation choices, making the reasoning behind each approach clear instead of simply presenting theoretical best practices.

A Practical and Valuable Guide

Even with my own extensive background in Snowflake, dbt, and modern analytics engineering, I found this book highly valuable. The combination of clear architectural reasoning, practical implementation guidance, and examples grounded in real-world experience makes this an unusually actionable resource.

Whether you are a data architect, analytics engineer, engineering leader, or someone beginning the journey toward a modern data platform, this book provides a strong foundation for understanding not only how to build scalable solutions, but also why certain patterns succeed in practice while others fail.

In a space often dominated by hype and overly complex frameworks, Pragmatic Data Platform stands out as a grounded, experience-driven guide for building data platforms that actually work in practice.

Contents

Figures

Introduction

We have designed this book to be of value to a diverse audience of data professionals, including Data and Analytics Engineers, Data Architects, and Business Managers.

Our approach is **pragmatic**: we champion simple, effective solutions accessible to most organizations, avoiding overly complex solutions that demand specialized skills and extensive resources. At the end of the introduction, we describe the simple, yet realistic project that is the skeleton of the book.

Modern data management demands more than writing SQL; it requires clear, structured processes and the adoption of software engineering best practices.

This book bridges the gap for data teams, offering practical, SQL-friendly DevOps techniques to move past outdated workflows into tried-and-tested, scalable, collaborative systems that drive better decisions. All the while staying simple and SQL first. We help you to elevate your development process **from Art to Industry!**

Why read this book

In this book, we are trying to collect in a single place the best practices, customer experiences, and practical examples that should be at the base of every data project:

- How to organize your project and teams to identify and fulfill the business needs.
- How to build an architecture that starts from the current needs and evolves with your organization.
- How to enable your team to deliver day-to-day, month-to-month, producing a platform that is easy to work with, well understood, and maintainable.

In our many years of combined experience, we have seen that successful projects require stakeholders to have a level of understanding of what others are doing and mutual respect for each other's needs.

Projects are made by people, and success happens when people work well together and are empowered to focus on the clear goals they have committed to.

In this book, we provide the information useful to the key roles that drive the development of data projects:

- **Data Managers** – they are the stakeholders in charge of finding a solution (technical and organizational) for the current and future data needs of an organization and fulfilling them in a timely and cost-effective manner. A single person can embody this role, but it is often covered by a few roles, such as Head of Data, BI Manager, Project Managers, and so on.

- **Data Architects** – they are the stakeholders tasked with designing a technical solution that fulfills the identified data needs of an organization, considering available resources and constraints on time, money, and know-how. Even in this case, the role can be fulfilled by a single person or by a team of people with titles such as Data Architect, Enterprise Architect, Data Engineer, and more.
- **Data Engineers** – they are the stakeholders tasked to implement the most technical details and bring to fruition the vision designed by the Data Architects. They used to cover the full spectrum, from infrastructure setup to data modeling and the delivery layer, to provide the desired information to consumers. Today, the role is more focused on infrastructure, automation, data movement, and the delivery of information, with the transformation part falling under the Analytics Engineer role.
- **Analytics Engineers** – they are the stakeholders tasked to model the data and implement the Business Rules inside the planned design. This is also known as transforming the source data into business information. It is common for people with diverse skill sets and titles to collaborate under this general role, bringing the competencies and knowledge to produce meaningful information for business users.

It is important to consider that while these roles and their responsibilities are often well defined, the boundaries of their interactions should be soft, and their collaboration as far-reaching as possible. After all, collaboration thrives on mutual support and deteriorates under rigid sign-offs. To blur these boundaries even further, it is quite common for Data Architects to participate in the implementation of their own designs, taking on the roles of Data Engineer or Analytical Engineer. Also, the distinction between these two roles is recent, with the role of Analytical Engineer coming to denote the part of traditional Data Engineering focused on the transformation from data to information.

Thanks to the low friction of modern development tools like dbt Cloud, other key stakeholders, like BI developers and analysts, or anyone with SQL competence, can also become part of the project and contribute first-hand to its development.

In most of the book, we will concentrate on the three major roles of Managers, Architects, and Engineers, using the terms Analytics Engineer and Data Engineer as general synonyms, with the eventual nuance that the former mostly relates to the transformations done with dbt and Snowflake, which is the focus of this book, and the latter to highlight a wider role. At the same time, we will not discount the fact that there are other important roles in every project, such as sponsors, business experts, and BI developers/analysts, without whom no project will ever come to life.

Resources for data managers

In our experience, Data Managers place great importance on ensuring the viability of projects under their responsibility and on reducing risks across dimensions such as time, money, know-how, key people, the future-proofness of the solution, and more.

The first resource we offer Managers is our pragmatism: prioritizing experience, proven technologies, best practices, and a general no-nonsense approach over any other consideration or product we might like and use at any moment. The second resource is our focus on the overall process of building a data platform, where topics like team organization, way of working, access to domain experts and governance can be as important for success as the quality of the code in the platform. The last, but maybe most important, resource we offer is an array of real-life experiences from other companies when dealing with similar goals and set of tools. Understanding what other organizations have done, where they succeeded, and where they struggled can meaningfully reduce the risk of new projects and steer them in the right direction before they hit the same issues.

All these resources are concentrated in the first part of the book, which covers Chapters 1 to 7, with special emphasis on the first four chapters that introduce the architecture of the Pragmatic Data Platform (PDP), the project setup, platform governance, agile development, and data mesh. Last, but not least, Chapter 7 introduces the use cases. Feel free to contact us if you need more information on the use cases.

Resources for data architects

Data Architects have the arduous task of balancing a solution that fulfils all the organization's needs and wishes while staying simple and small enough to fit within budget and calendar constraints, and as developer-friendly as possible. They must choose robust ways of working, powerful yet simple tools, and apply the right patterns and best practices to keep project complexity at bay and maintainability over the long run high.

We think we can help them by offering an opinionated architecture, a simple yet powerful way of working, and a proven set of patterns and best practices implemented in tried-and-tested macros. All this comes with the conscious effort to build on the shoulders of giants and keep things as simple as possible, leaving more complex solutions for cases when they are really needed. To help with understanding and practical use of our ideas, we provide a sample project that we start outlining in the first part, covering governance, deployment, security, and way of working. We will continue to develop and fully flesh it out in the second part, where we cover all the layers of the Pragmatic Data Platform.

We expect that Data Architects will be interested in most, if not all, of the chapters, as their role requires a thorough understanding of the general principles outlined in the first part and a good command of the most technical topics detailed in the second part.

Resources for engineers

The roles of Data and Analytics Engineer can range from ingesting source data to transforming it into usable information by building data models with SQL or Python, creating data marts to power reports using a star schema, and sometimes producing the reports themselves.

Modern payloads augment these needs with additional requirements, such as exporting data to files to power high-volume interfaces, performing feature engineering to support ML and AI payloads, and even providing data to serve API calls for external applications. We help Engineers first and foremost by advocating for simpler solutions and ways of working that maintain flexibility and control, allowing them to focus on solving real problems rather than fulfilling shallow platform requirements or writing boilerplate code. We also strive to provide the simplest ways to automate or speed up as much as possible the repetitive tasks that each data platform development throws at us, be it ingesting files, renaming columns, generating composite keys, storing historical data, or building facts and dimensions.

Our proven solutions come from real experience on big projects, but no one-size-fits-all, so we expect not everything we suggest will work for you. The general ideas and most of the code we provide should be fine as-is or very easy to adapt to different needs.

Throughout this book, we provide patterns and ready-to-use code, sometimes collected into larger packages, to speed up your development. Still, we will always strive to present and clarify the underlying principles so that you will be in complete control of what your code does and able to adapt it or its use to your specific conditions. To illustrate how to use our code and patterns, we provide a sample project that covers all layers of the Pragmatic Data Platform. In its development, we strive to present alternative ways of doing that might be better in different cases, rather than a single "golden solution".

We expect that Engineers will concentrate their efforts on understanding and dissecting the code presented in the second part of the book, layer by layer, carefully assembled in the sample project. We believe that the first part will provide valuable insights into the higher-level topics that hold a data platform together and will prove useful for day-to-day work and for a better understanding of opinions or decisions reflected in our code.

Sample project, code samples, and prerequisites

This book comes with a sample dbt project that is available at: **https://github.com/pragmatic-data/stonks**. You can start looking at it, even if in this intro, we are not yet writing code.

We will start writing code in Chapter 2. Inside the repository of the sample project, you will find the code samples discussed in a specific chapter under the `code_samples_by_chapter` folder, which is divided into a sub-folder for each chapter, named `chapter_XX`. Please note that in these folders, you will see the code samples as they are at that point of the book, while in the folders of the dbt project, like `models` or `macros`, you will find the final version after all the eventual changes discussed in the book.

There are no special hardware or software requirements to work with the sample code, as the three tools we will use in the project (dbt Cloud, Snowflake, and GitHub) are SaaS tools that work in any browser and offer free plans or at least a free trial period. On the competence side, across all chapters of this book, we assume a basic understanding of data engineering, data warehousing, and SQL concepts.

PART I

Building a Pragmatic Data Platform

This first part lays the essential groundwork for building a modern data platform.

We move from high-level architectural strategy and governance principles to the hands-on setup of your project establishing the **Pragmatic Way of Working** from day one.

Our goal is to equip you not just with the "**what**," but also with the "**why**" and the "**how**," ensuring you have the foundational principles clearly in place and a fully configured dbt and Snowflake environment ready to tackle the implementation details discussed in Part 2.

We begin in Chapter 1 by introducing the **Pragmatic Data Platform (PDP) Architecture** and comparing it with other popular styles, such as Medallion and Data Vault, to highlight its unique advantages in simplicity and maintainability. We then establish the core **DataOps and software engineering principles** that are central to our approach. In Chapter 3, we define the governance framework that guides our projects, including practical strategies for implementing a data mesh and handling sensitive PII.

Chapters 2 and 4 provide a hands-on guide to getting your project off the ground. We walk through the automated setup of your environments in Snowflake and dbt Cloud, covering our pragmatic approach to security, roles, and user management. You will learn to configure your project, manage the entire release cycle using Git, and automate deployments, establishing a robust CI/CD workflow before writing and executing your first line of transformation code.

To ground our work in reality, Chapter 5 introduces the **"Stonks" sample project** that serves as our hands-on example throughout the book.

Finally, Chapter 6 provides invaluable context by reviewing **eight real-world case studies**, showing how companies successfully implemented data platforms with dbt and Snowflake, aligning with the PDP principles to solve critical business challenges.

CHAPTER 1

A Pragmatic Data Platform

In the introduction, we explained that we have designed this book to be of value to a diverse audience of data professionals, including Data and Analytics Engineers, Data Architects, and Business Managers. This chapter introduces the general architecture of the **Pragmatic Data Platform** (**PDP**), including its layers, signature elements, and advantages. The rest of the book will guide you from fundamental principles to the intricacies of each architectural layer. In this journey, we will cover both the initial development and the evolution needs typical of long-term projects like data platforms. We will discuss the similarities and differences among the PDP, Data Vault, Medallion Architecture, and major classical architectures, providing you with a range of options and guidance for reconciling these approaches with the diverse needs that arise in data projects. We then present our core beliefs about data engineering and describe the software engineering principles that we consider most important in a data platform development project.

We use the **pragmatic** name for our approach to highlight our aim at practical, effective solutions that most organizations can adopt without the need for rare skills and extensive resources. The topics that we are going to cover in this chapter are:

- **The Pragmatic Data Platform Architecture**: Learn the layered, pattern-based design of the PDP that promotes simplicity, maintainability, and rapid value delivery.
- **Comparison of the PDP Architecture with other major data architectures**: Understand how the PDP aligns with and differs from popular architectural frameworks.
- **DataOps and Data Engineering best practices**: Introduce the core software engineering principles and techniques to build a reliable and scalable data platform.

The pragmatic data platform architecture

The Architecture of the **Pragmatic Data Platform** (**PDP**) is a proven architecture based on simple, well-established patterns and strategies for building an enterprise-grade, general-purpose data platform tailored to modern cloud databases such as Snowflake, Databricks, BigQuery, and others.

The **Pragmatic** in the name means that we want to provide enterprise-level solutions to common needs that start simple and can be easily and naturally extended to fulfill even more complex requirements, adding extra complexity only when it is really needed.

We believe that, while it works well, **less is more**, and that any extra tool, pattern, layer, or bit of complexity should be added only if really needed or if it provides so much value to offset the cost of that complexity. We will try to keep the infrastructure and governance complexity to a minimum while providing a flexible platform that works well in enterprise settings with dozens of projects and many teams and units, offering ways to extend this core setup to address more complex needs. Similarly, we will adopt a data architecture that is very simple to get started with, that uses a modular domain-driven approach, and that can naturally evolve into a soft mesh or even a full-fledged data mesh, allowing your teams to work in the most natural way depending on their organization and the needs of your use cases.

*The overall goal of the Pragmatic Data Platform is to enable your teams to go "**from art to industry**": developing with less improvisation, more best practices and uniform ways of working.*

High-level Architecture

We take a pragmatic approach using what we think is the best from the available architectural styles, such as Data Vault, Inmon, Kimball, and data mesh, to use the full power of the available tools, while keeping the expertise requirements as simple as possible.

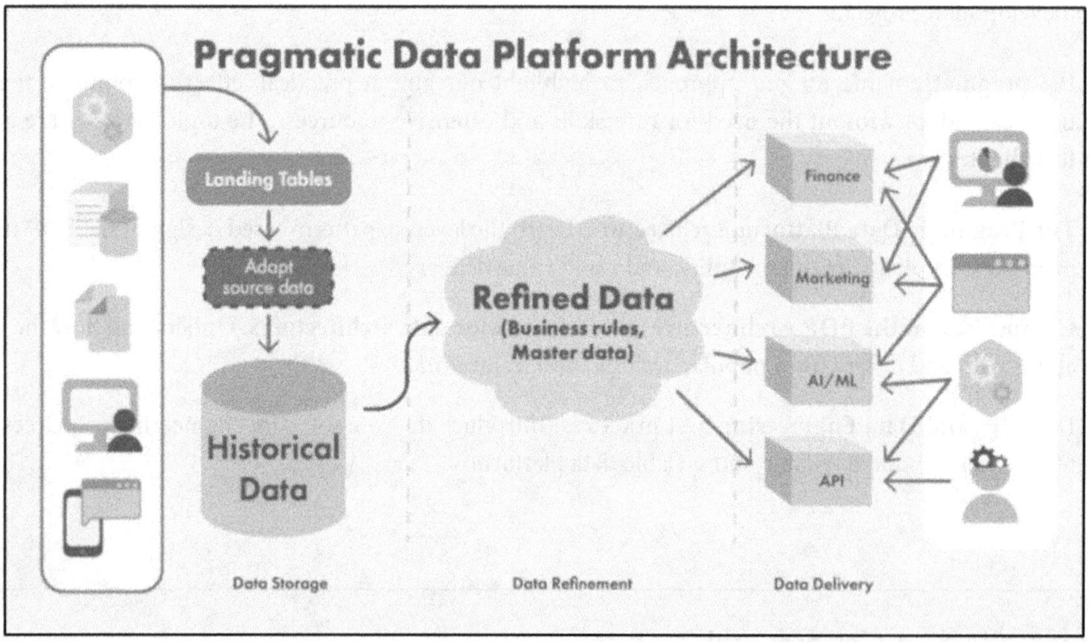

Figure 1: High-level view of the Pragmatic Data Platform Architecture.

Looking at Figure 1, we see the following high-level parts:

Data sources. On the left, we can see that the inputs for modern data platforms are disparate, ranging from machine-generated data to data from ERP systems, reports, and data extractions from partners and third parties, as well as web and application data. Nowadays, semi-structured and non-structured data are also becoming increasingly important, thanks to AI tools that allow the extraction of useful metadata and information.

Data storage layer. This is the layer responsible for the ingestion and storage of the source data received from the data sources. Data extraction can also be part of this layer. In this layer, the **Landing Tables** receive the raw source data during the **data ingestion**. The staging models adapt and make this data easier to use. For example, parsing dates and timestamps or converting to the UTC zone. Every new version of the data is detected and saved in the historical table. Finally, the versions are formatted to provide a uniform interface with many useful metadata, making the downstream use of the history simpler.

Data refinement layer. This is the layer where historical data is transformed into complete and usable information by applying the necessary transformations, including master data and business rules. Thanks to idempotent models that rely on state only for performance, but not for correctness, this layer can be recreated at any time from historical data, making evolution, maintenance, and code fixes much simpler than in traditional data warehouses. The modular design and domain-driven approach that we suggest allows for the implementation of long-lasting business concepts, with clearly named models organized in an easy-to-understand lineage, where each model clearly exposes its purpose thanks to its name and position. This makes the projects simpler to manage and more accessible to all the stakeholders.

Data delivery layer. This is the layer that finalizes and exposes the curated data sets for the downstream clients that implement the desired use cases. We organize this layer in data marts that have the goal of delivering data in the best format and the most suitable data model for each client. Common examples are facts and dimensions according to Kimball star schemas, wide tables for reporting or AI/ML workloads, data exported in files in the desired formats, or operational style tables to serve interactive APIs. In this layer, we have (usually a few) transformations that are specific to the data mart, in contrast to those that are general in nature and belong to the refined layer, and the final models that expose only the necessary data for the use case with the desired names and types. The final models are the public interfaces of your platform and you must manage them like any other public APIs, with explicit contracts, versioning, and governed access to the data.

Clients. The traditional clients for data platforms are BI tools and advanced analytics, but their range is growing quickly as data platform capabilities expand. Nowadays, they include high-volume applications such as AI models, search services requiring quick point access, and various APIs to power user- and machine-facing applications. A modern data platform must allow for easy response to new needs and power new types of clients. This can happen if the underlying data platform continues to evolve in response to market changes and if the data and tools used to manage it adhere to data engineering best practices, ensuring the resulting platform remains extendible without compromising existing use cases.

If you feel like this is nothing revolutionary, we are very happy, as our goal in drawing the Pragmatic Data Platform architecture is to maximize the benefits that we can attain while reducing the new things to learn for data professionals.

---

*We refer to **idempotent models** with a relaxed meaning of the concept, referring to models that can be run again and again without causing problems. Therefore, we are fine with models producing substantially the same results, even if some details, such as timestamps in metadata, may differ on occasion.*
For example, it is acceptable if a full refresh of a table produces the same rows as a normal incremental load, but with new load times.

In the next section, you will find a brief overview of the major advantages we aim to achieve, and in the following section, we will compare the Pragmatic Data Platform architecture with other major architectural styles, enabling you to better contextualize our advice with your experience and the existing body of knowledge.

We believe **there is no silver bullet**, and no situation is exactly like any other. It is great to have a solid set of principles and practices to refer to, knowing they are proven, anyway we cannot claim that everything we propose will work well for your specific case. Therefore, our suggestion is to understand the options you have, the needs you must satisfy, and be pragmatic in choosing the best option that fits the needs and how to apply it.

The first part of this book will cover the more general aspects of building a data platform, including governance, deployment, data quality, and Agile development in the Pragmatic Data Platform, along with other general topics such as macros and tests. We will also introduce use cases from companies that have already adopted the dbt and Snowflake toolset.

The second part of the book will delve deeply into each layer of the platform, moving to hands-on coding using a sample project that will run alongside the book, from governance to delivery, to introduce real code leveraging the macros, patterns, and ways of working of the Pragmatic Data Platform in a realistic yet simplified setting.

By the end of this book, you will have more tools in your hands to tackle the issues you will confront and be able to select the right tools for your specific use cases.

Key features of the Pragmatic Data Platform

- **Ingestion into landing tables** is pattern-driven, highly automatable, and high-performance. Ingesting data from files in all formats supported by Snowflake or your preferred cloud platform is a solved problem, and landing the data in the Landing Tables should be a simple, painless, and repeatable process that leverages as much automation as possible without compromising on process control.
- **Staging, historicization, and version management** are pattern-driven, highly automatable, high-performance, and low-storage. Going from the source data in the Landing Tables to all the changes correctly historicized and ready to be used in the refined layer is also a solved problem. While this is a more complex and variable problem than ingestion, we also aim to make it a simple, painless, repeatable, and automatable process that you can tailor to your specific needs. The use of best practices like **insert-only historicization** will provide you with a high-speed process that reduces the amount of data stored while making your process auditable. The use of Hash Keys and Hash Diff columns will allow you to clearly define the identity of your entities and how you monitor their changes (i.e., versions).
- **Bi-temporality and auditability** of source and history data are at the foundation of the data platform. Efficient permanent storage of both the technical timeline and the business effectiveness timeline provides confidence in building the downstream layers and applying the relevant business rules. Clear patterns for ingesting and historicizing simple entities and complex multi-entity inputs (such as ERP reports) enable you to select the appropriate level of auditing for the data and metadata of your data platform with minimal effort.
- **Macros for automation and platform extension.** One of the greatest advancements of dbt is the ability to bring multiple layers of code reuse in the SQL realm, allowing complex pieces of code to be encapsulated in simple-to-use macros that work as expected. This allows us to eliminate most of the boilerplate code

that typically makes up a significant portion of a data platform's code; it also enables us to automate many repetitive tasks that consume a substantial amount of time. Last, but not least, encapsulating complex code into well-described macros allows less experienced colleagues to contribute to the platform development even without the seniority in dbt and Snowflake needed to code the macros themselves, in the same way that we do not need a mechanical engineer to drive our cars.

- **Test automation**. Another great advantage brought by dbt is the ability to easily write and apply tests to verify that the input data conforms to your expectations, that the transformations produce the expected results, and that the data you are delivering fulfills the agreed-upon contracts. Automated tests save a huge amount of time and provide the data team confidence in the code they write and in the data that they deliver, allowing them to spend less time firefighting issues and providing more confidence to refactor and improve the platform, reducing the technical debt and delivering new features.
- **Modular and Domain Driven Design**. The models that build the refined layer of your data platform will construct your Business Concepts in a modular, step-by-step, and reusable manner, avoiding loops. This allows you to write code that is much simpler, without complex and unexpected side effects. No more multiple pieces of code interfering with the state of your tables. This makes it simple to produce code that is idempotent and can transform either just the last batch of data or your entire data set. The further application of domain-driven principles to organize teams and code, keeping closely related concepts and models together, improves the quality and consistency of the code while reducing the cognitive effort of team members.
- **The data and state reside in the storage layer**. The essential state for the platform is maintained in the storage layer, primarily in the history tables that are built through automation and according to well-established patterns. The reliability of the code, patterns, and way of working, combined with the slow pace of change in the inputs, makes for a very stable foundation of the data platform. We often also keep a raw copy of the source data in the landing tables and/or the source files. From these, we can rebuild also the history tables. The cost would "only" be different process metadata, but same data.
- **Refined and Delivery layers that are effectively stateless**. The refined and delivery layers are built with idempotent models that can use state (like incremental loads) to improve performance, but their correctness does not depend on preserving the state; therefore, they can be recreated at any time. This, together with the modular code, enables developers to write well-isolated models that have few reasons to change and can be easily modified and reapplied to all historical data when the business rules need to be updated. This removes the need for complex and risky backfilling and reverse engineering operations to apply changes in the past. These simplifications reduce the cognitive load for developers, empower the data team to fix issues and evolve the business logic, and provide a quicker time to market for new features.
- **Flexible and well-governed delivery data layer**. The delivery layer is organized into as many data marts as needed, with each data mart serving a particular use case. Separating the refined layer, where the generic and reusable business concepts are built, from the data mart allows us to better serve each case. Data marts serve as containers to hold the code and data specific to a use case, providing tailored names and models, and a clear integration point where security and governance can switch from the general to the specific use case needs.
- **Integrated DevOps with CI/CD**. One of the topics that often receives less attention but plays a significant role in how a data team delivers is the development and release process. Using a version control system that has evolved into a collaboration platform, such as GitHub, marries automation with collaboration.

With dbt Cloud in the Pragmatic Data Platform, we build a process that is highly automated, simple, and well audited, allowing us to reduce the time and effort needed to deliver our code and perform safe deployments. This also enables great visibility and the ability to comment on changes within the team. Setting up a CI/CD process is also very simple and greatly reduces the risk of issues being released or ending up in production. You can achieve the same level of automation with dbt Core and open-source tools, but you will need to have the required competencies and invest more time in the setup.

This is not an exhaustive list of all the benefits that can be achieved by correctly adopting dbt and Snowflake to build your data platform, but these are the ones that stand out in our minds and are easy to achieve with the Pragmatic Data Platform.

Bi-temporality is the ability to store and use data across two timelines: the technical timeline, which indicates when the data platform received the information, and the business timeline, which indicates when something happened in the real world. We generate the technical timeline in the platform, so we always have it. The business timeline must be present in the source data and is useful when the order in which we receive the data differs from the order in which events occurred, or exact business times are important.

In our opinion, the ability to segregate the necessary state in the storage layer, allowing the other layers to be recreated at will, is the real game-changer. Still, all the listed advantages get compounded to provide a modern, efficient, and fulfilling way of working for your data teams.

In the Pragmatic Data Platform, data and metadata are permanently stored in the history tables within the storage layer, and the refined and delivery layers can be recreated from these tables. This means that, in principle, the refined and delivery layers could be entirely built using views, providing the maximum possible flexibility in development and allowing updates to the history tables to be transmitted immediately to the consumers. In practice, it often makes sense to speed up operations and reduce costs by using modular and idempotent incremental loads for larger tables and materializing the models used to serve the data, while retaining the flexibility to rebuild everything when and if desired.

In the next section, we will provide a simple comparison of the Pragmatic Data Platform versus other commonly referred-to data architectures.

Comparing PDP to other architectural styles

The Pragmatic Data Platform (PDP) builds on the shoulders of giants and selects the best ideas from various available architectural styles. The PDP keeps complexity at bay and provides a reusable set of patterns and practices that you can easily apply to your organization.

In the following sections, we will examine the major architectural styles that contribute to the Pragmatic Data Platform. You will see that we share some commonalities, as well as differences, with these architectural styles. We will highlight the reasons for our choices for or against some practices, so that if you are in a different situation, you can consider taking a different decision.

Note that each of the following subjects is covered by multiple books, so we will not go into detail here. The goal is to provide you with a starting idea and discuss some of the features we have introduced in PDP, as well as the problems we have attempted to address. At the end of this chapter, a list of books is provided for those who wish to explore these architectural styles in more detail.

Kimball classical data warehouse architecture

The most ubiquitous design style in the data warehousing world is the **dimensional model,** made popular by Ralph Kimball, which has become the de facto standard for representing data in **Business Intelligence** (**BI**). The signature feature of the dimensional modeling design style is to produce a data model structure called a **star schema**, which is the expected input for most BI tools.

In a star schema, one **fact table** containing the events or records with the measures of interest is surrounded by several dimension tables. A **dimension table** is a denormalized table that contains the descriptive data at the lowest level of detail that you want to access and should not contain measures (in the original Kimball definition and many BI tool implementations) to avoid the fan trap issue. A **measure** is a number that you want to use for calculations in your reports. Figure 2 shows a typical star schema organized around an **Order** fact.

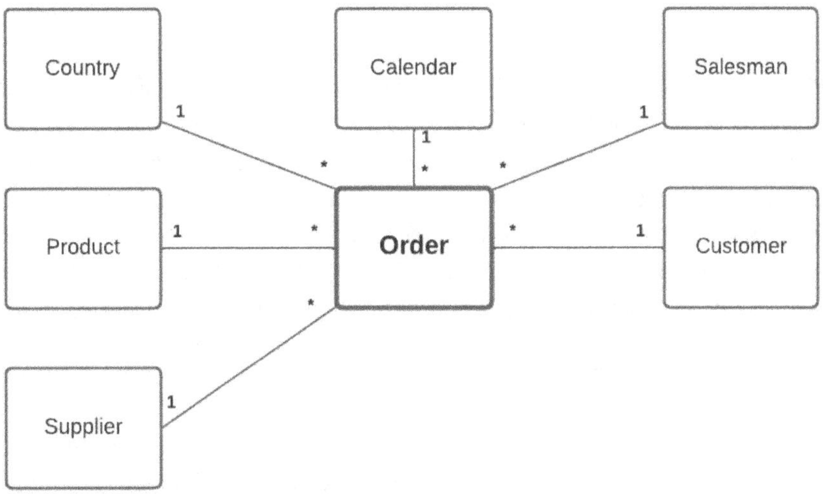

Figure 2: Example of a star schema with an order fact and multiple dimensions around it.

The main advantage of a star schema is its simplicity, which makes it easy to query and understand, even for non-technical users. Given its simple structure and exclusive use of many-to-one relations from the fact to the dimension, it is also very performant for querying and well-suited to provide data for interactive reporting. In principle, every fact could have its own set of dedicated dimensions, but this would immediately introduce the problem of having multiple copies of similar but different dimensions, such as customer or product, which would be needed for most facts.

The concept of a **conformed dimension** is used to avoid the multiplication of dimension tables and to integrate the data from different systems. A conformed dimension is just a dimension, but it is designed to be used by all or at least most of the fact tables that are interested in such descriptive data. It must therefore be at the smallest granularity needed and must contain all columns of interest in all reports that have to be built on all facts that use the dimension.

The Kimball data warehouse methodology utilizes a spreadsheet, known as the **enterprise bus matrix**, with business processes/events in rows and dimensions in columns to plan the data warehouse content and track the relationships between conformed dimensions and facts that describe a business process. The following small example clarifies how simple yet powerful this matrix is.

BUSINESS PROCESS	DELIVERY PRIORITY	DATE	PRODUCT	PROMOTION	CUSTOMER	EMPLOYEE	WH
ORDERS	1	X	X	X	X	X	
FORECASTS	3	X	X	X	X	X	
PURCHASES		X	X				X
INVENTORY	2	X	X				X
RETURNS		X	X		X	X	X
SHIPPING		X	X	X	X	X	X

The X sign in the rows of the table indicates what dimensions, named in the column headers, must be connected with the fact(s) that represent the business process described in the row. Once all facts and dimensions are created through ETL or ELT transformations, access to the prepared data for clients, such as BI tools, is provided through data marts.

---

*A **data mart** is a collection of data, generally a subset of all the available data, that is selected to satisfy the BI needs of a specific business area, such as a department or use case.*

A Kimball data mart is composed of a handful of facts and their dimensions, effectively providing one complete star schema per fact, which is used to analyze the connected business process. The idea is to provide a limited number of tables, which makes it easier for analysts to find the desired data and produce accurate reports, as they use the same conformed dimensions and names. The collection of available data marts serves as the primary external interface for accessing the data platform, making it extremely important that the names and semantics of the available tables and attributes are clear.

The data processing in a Kimball data warehouse is based on transforming the incoming source data to build the needed conformed dimensions and facts. The transformations are performed directly from the data sources to the facts and conformed dimensions, with the facts and dimensions serving as the long-term storage structures for the data in the data platform. The source data is not stored.

The major problems in a Kimball warehouse stem from the fact that this network of facts and dimensions serves as both the central data model and the storage mechanism. A star schema, which by design lacks fact-to-fact relations, has less representative power than a general relational schema; in fact, it loses information by having to coalesce all descriptive data into a limited set of conformed dimensions and facts that must adhere to all the current business rules. This overlapping of storage, business rules, and data loss creates a situation where most of the code has often reasons to change.

In the Pragmatic Data Platform, we adopt the Kimball style as the default way of delivering data for reporting, and we consider facts and dimensions as an acceptable final representation of business concepts in the refined layer. On the contrary, we will not try to store the data as facts and dimensions.

Let's dig a bit deeper into the downsides we see in the original Kimball architecture.

The process of loading and storing data from data sources is deeply intertwined with the implementation of business rules, as conformed dimensions and facts are both the goal of business transformations and the primary storage for all data. This causes the code to have a high level of complexity and many reasons to change, as any change in a data source or a business rule may require reworking all the transformations between the data source and the final tables, including fixing existing data. This can easily spread to connected facts and dimensions, resulting in a very high rate of code changes compared to business needs. This becomes even more acute as the project becomes bigger, because more facts connected to one dimension create more potential for that dimension to change.

Having the main data storage in the facts and dimensions, which are derived from multiple sources with various technical and business transformations, makes it practically impossible to determine what the original data looked like. It is risky, as it may be impossible to undo the application of a wrong or incorrect business rule to correct it or apply a new business rule to the existing data. Storing the history of changes for a dimension is not easy when multiple sources need to be integrated, and it becomes extremely complex when the dimension must also incorporate business rules. Therefore, very often, dimensions simply store the current values.

According to the original Kimball definition, there must not be measures in dimensions, because if you have them and you use them for calculations involving the connected fact, you always have a **Fan Trap** that makes calculations based on the metric wrong. Not having or not using important metrics, such as the price in a product dimension, is very limiting. Therefore, in practice, we have measures in the dimensions; therefore, users should be aware when a Fan Trap is triggered. Another big limitation according to the Kimball rules is that facts are only connected to dimensions, not to other facts. However, some of the most interesting analyses are built by using data from multiple facts, such as orders, deliveries, or returns.

Kimball star schemas do not work with multiple facts, so you either write your own SQL to produce the composite fact for these interesting analyses, while avoiding the **Chasm trap**, or you need to look at other methodologies, like the Unified Star Schema.

Finally, the Kimball method is bottom-up, oriented towards local quick wins limited to the business processes identified in the enterprise bus matrix, usually by a department, not to build a comprehensive data view of the enterprise. Despite the enterprise name, the facts and conformed dimensions described in the matrix might not handle other reporting needs besides the ones listed in the matrix, even if the source data would have done. Put another way, storing your data according to the Kimball architecture means you will have a significant loss of information compared to the raw source data. This stems from the focus on the facts and dimensions described in the matrix, the need to consolidate data from multiple systems in the conformed dimensions, and the fact that a star schema can represent less information than a generic relational model.

At this point, it should be clear why we will not attempt to store our data in facts and dimensions; however, it is a good idea to produce them at the end, in data marts, as use-case-specific artifacts to support reporting with BI tools. In the Pragmatic Data Platform, we will maintain data in a business-oriented relational model without forcing it into facts and dimensions before the delivery layer.

Related to relational models, like star schemas, there are two common data problems. The Fan trap happens between a fact and a dimension if you use a measure coming from the dimension.

A Fan trap is a common problem in relational models with one-to-many relationships, such as a fact to a dimension. If you join the two tables and take a measure (a number) from the one side (the dimension), then you will find it replicated many times, multiplying the measure by the number of key matches between the fact and dimension. When a BI tool aggregates on some columns and sums up the other columns, you will have completely unreal and inflated numbers. This is the reason why, in a pure Kimball model, you should have no measures in dimension tables.

The Chasm trap instead happens between two facts with a common dimension.

A Chasm trap is another common problem of relational models with two one-to-many relationships on the same key, like two facts pointing to the same dimension (and hence same FK). In such a case, if you join the two facts on the common key, you end up with a key-by-key Cartesian product, where all the rows for one key on one side match all the rows with the same key on the other side. In this case, we are using a non-existent many-to-many relation, as two facts having a common dimension do not explain how the two facts are related. The result will be a huge multiplication of the rows, making the query wrong, slow, and with totally incorrect results.

Inmon classical data warehouse architecture

Bill Inmon is considered the father of data warehousing, and, together with Ralph Kimball, he has shaped most of the way data warehouses are built. While Kimball was working bottom-up to satisfy the (mostly departmental) need for reporting, Inmon tried to build a repository of data that describes the organization and its business processes, providing a company-wide single source of truth.

The signature concept of the Inmon design style is the **ambition to create a corporate-wide, integrated, and interoperable data repository**. The goal is therefore to identify the **business concepts** that describe the company and how it works, taking the input source data and turning it into homogeneous data under the correct concept. To avoid redundancy and maximize expressive power, the data is normalized to Third Normal Form (3NF), and all interesting relations between the desired concepts can be captured.

Third Normal Form (3NF) is a database modeling strategy that reduces information redundancy, thereby saving storage space. The idea is to extract all entities (or groups of columns) whose values are repeated many times in the data model into their own table, replacing them with a single column containing the identifier for each entity or group.

For example, if you have product names and descriptions in your invoices, you can replace them with the product ID; similarly, if you have streets or full addresses that are often repeated, you can create an address table and replace the addresses with their IDs.

The business concepts stored in the data warehouse can be very close to the facts and dimensions, or base components, used to produce the facts and dimensions we find in a Kimball star schema and data marts. Still, they would be divided into more tables, retaining the full range of relationships between facts and dimensions and the underlying business concepts.

Data for reporting needs is delivered through data marts built to satisfy the information needs of a specific business area. You can build a data warehouse according to the Inmon design, and then produce facts and dimensions pretty much as we have seen in the Kimball style, or you can produce wide tables that directly serve each reporting case without any further joining.

The main difference in this case is that the data warehouse layer stores a richer set of concepts and relations than is strictly necessary to power the desired facts and dimensions. As you can imagine, the goal of enterprise-wide data integration requires an enterprise-wide effort, with commitment from top management, over an extended period. An important advantage of the Inmon model is that the data warehouse built on enterprise-wide business concepts is highly resilient to changes in the business and in the technical source systems. Because it reflects the company's business processes, the Inmon data warehouse contains the data to answer most reporting questions, even those that were not initially identified.

The main drawbacks are the scale and complexity of the process, which require a highly skilled data modeler to split the data into 3NF and experts in data warehousing to code the ETLs, maintain the platform, and create/update the data marts when new reporting needs arise. A key drawback is that the main storage of the data is in the form of business concepts, after many transformations and the application of business rules, making it hard to return to the original data. This exposes the data warehouse to the need for rework because storage occurs after both integrating multiple data sources and applying business rules. It also makes it impossible to audit the original data, as only the transformed data is stored. This is a common issue with the Kimball design style, but the Inmon business concepts preserve much more information than the simple facts and dimensions of the Kimball style.

In the Pragmatic Data Platform, we aim to build business concepts similarly. Still, we will not force any normalization, and we will store the full history of the source data in the storage layer, building the business concepts downstream in the refined layer using modular steps, keeping the original data unchanged and auditable.

Thanks to advancements in performance and the drastic reduction in the cost of storage, we can address one of the major issues with Inmon and Kimball styles: we can decouple the storage of the data from the representation of the target data model and removing the need to use third normal form. This, in turn, simplifies the ingestion and storage of the source data to the point of almost complete automation and provides much greater flexibility and ease of coding business concepts. Code modularity reduces both the complexity and the reasons to change of most steps in the transformation, greatly reducing the platform's coding, evolution, and maintenance costs.

Data vault

Data vault (DV) is a data platform-building methodology invented by **Dan Linstedt**. The current incarnation, **Data Vault 2.0** (**DV2**), was released in 2013 and continues to evolve as technology, data platforms, and use cases evolve. The latest update, **Data Vault 2.1** (**DV2.1**), was released in 2023. The DV2 methodology encompasses an architecture, a model, a way of working, and an implementation, but the most famous and signature element is the DV model.

The central idea in DV is that all information is aggregated around the identified business concepts, and that data is integrated using the **Business Key** (**BK**). Concept definition and identity management are two important cornerstones of DV2.

The signature DV model is based on these three core elements:

- **Hub**: Contains all the unique instances of the BK for the concept described by the hub.
- **Link**: Contains all the unique instances of a relationship between hubs, as a tuple of the BK.
- **Satellite**: Contains the changes over time of the descriptive information of a hub or link.

While the core elements of DV are the three listed above, the DV methodology provides a multitude of specialized satellite types for use in specific situations, plus a few other elements, such as point-in-time and bridge tables, greatly increasing the total number of constructs and concepts to master.

Figure 3 shows an example of a simple DV model.

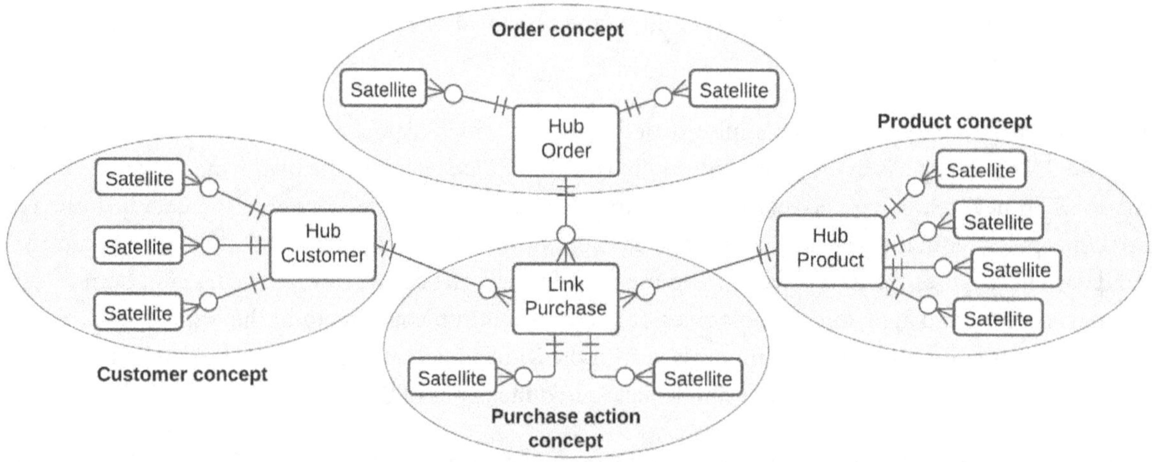

Figure 3: Example of a Data Vault model.

All the relationships in a DV are one-to-many, with a hub at one end of the two. The side of the hub always has cardinality exactly 1, as a key tenet is that all keys for a business concept are stored in the hub for that concept. Each link records only the existence of the relationship it tracks at some moment in time between the connected hubs, using their BKs, not all instances or the state of that relationship; that is demanded of the attached satellites.

The identities of the business concepts of the domain are stored in a hub dedicated to each concept, the relationships between concepts (hubs) are encoded using links, one for each relationship, and the descriptive data is stored in as many satellites as needed.

The DV model, by adopting links as the only way to connect hubs, always uses a many-to-many relation, making the data model more complex and difficult than it would be in the common case of a many-to-one relation, where the intermediate link table would not be needed. Anyway, the link provides flexibility, allowing a relation to evolve from one-to-many to many-to-many without any changes to the model or data loading code.

Satellites are containers for descriptive data that can be attached to a concept whenever we need to store new information. They just depend on the BK of the concept they belong to. On the one hand, this allows adding new data without touching anything in the existing model; on the other hand, using the new data requires a new join. Building and understanding a DV model requires a high level of training in data modeling and the specifics of DV to avoid potential pitfalls. The other key element that distinguishes DV from the previous modeling styles that we have seen is the DV architecture, illustrated in Figure 4.

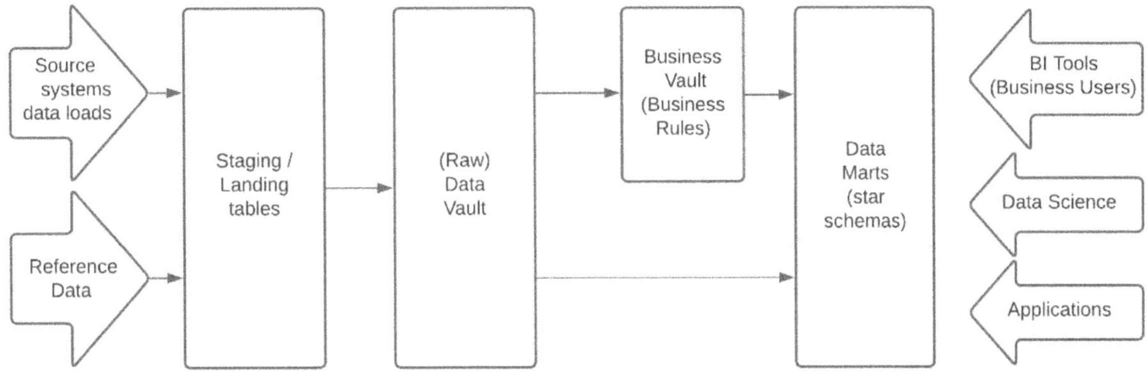

Figure 4: Data Vault architecture.

Notice the similarity with the Pragmatic Data Platform architecture. If you replace the Raw Vault with the History tables and the Business Vault with the refined layer, you can put together the first two blocks into an equivalent of the storage layer, and the analogy should be more apparent.

The core difference between the two systems is that while the Raw Vault/History and Business Vault/Refined layers have similar goals, they are built differently, they use a different modeling technique (plain relational for PDP), and therefore their contents are organized differently, even if in the end they convey similar information and can produce the same results.

The **Raw Vault** (**RV**) is the only place where all the history is stored forever. The load process uses patterns based on best practices, is highly parallel and automated, and is often automatically generated. This ensures speed of delivery and correctness of the code.

The data in the RV is still largely the source data and therefore auditable, but it has been organized and integrated by business concept using BKs. The absence of modifications is a feature, not a problem, as it enables auditing and allows us to go back to the RV layer and recalculate everything in accordance with current business rules.

The Pragmatic Data Platform works in a similar way, keeping the Storage layer even simpler by using a linear pipeline and standard relational modeling without splitting sources into hubs, links, and sats. Defining the HashKey has the same semantic power of defining the Hub and with modern data platforms it would be easy to generate it.

The business rules, the most specific part of the data platform, are applied in the **Business Vault** (**BV**), which takes the original data and applies all needed business rules to produce the refined versions of the identified business concepts. In this regard, the Pragmatic Data Platform aims to provide more guidance for the Refined layer, advising the use of a modular approach, building layered domains, and identifying model types by prefix.

The last step is taking the required data from the RV and BV to produce the **data marts**, where the data is usually organized according to the Kimball star schema, the USS, or whatever model your BI tool and use cases need, that is, data understandable by business users.

The following is a list of logical and technical reasons that we like in DV and also have in PDP:

- The greatest benefit of DV is the **separation of the storage of the historical data from the application of business rules**, which gives each part of the architecture only one reason to change, drastically reducing the need for rework to add or change a data source or to modify or add a business rule.
- The use of highly standardized core elements, hub, link, and satellite, allows a great level of automation in generating and running the loading logic.
- The use of **natural keys** (NK) or calculated surrogate keys (SK) instead of generated SKs, such as sequences, simplifies the ETL, as there is no need for SK lookups during the load, enabling highly parallel processing. Note that NKs can be used "as is" or hashed to build a single-field calculated SK, generally called **HashKey** (**HK** or **HKey**).
- The use of **Hashed Difference** (**HashDIFF**) fields to detect changes between versions of an entity instance greatly simplifies and automates loading patterns.
- The adoption of loading patterns that use **insert-only queries to store a complete and auditable history**, while not unique to DV and PDP, enables efficient manipulation of billions of rows by exploiting the scalability of new cloud-based platforms.
- The ability to handle bi-temporality, as in, when something happened versus when we got that information, is very important in some contexts, such as compliance departments.

The following is a list of what we do not like in the Data Vault, and we tried to avoid in PDP:

- Creating a DV platform requires skilled data professionals with training and experience in DV2, a hard requirement to meet in many situations. In PDP we use normal relational models.
- While the core elements are only three, any real DV implementation will use a multiplicity of specialized satellite types that require extensive knowledge to select the appropriate ones and advanced competence to implement them correctly. In PDP we use a few core macros and models for most use cases, using specialized models based on standard SQL for special needs.
- DV models require a huge number of joins to collate all the bits and pieces of data back in the correct form. This is generally beyond the comfort zone of most developers and certainly out of reach for analysts and business users. The result is that while data is there, it is quite difficult to use. In PDP we don't split the data unless strongly beneficial, avoiding extra joins caused by the loading process.
- Creating a proper DV requires a thorough analysis of the domain's business concepts, as the wrong choice of hubs can hinder the entire project. This requires sponsorship at a high enough level, enough time, the availability of experts on the business side, and someone who can put it all together. In PDP business concepts are also very important, but you have more leeway to fix them in the REF layer.

The DV methodology has been able to adopt the best from previous design styles while adding noteworthy improvements: like Inmon, it puts business concepts at the core of the DV organization, but preserves original data; it uses the de facto standard Kimball star schemas to deliver easy-to-use data marts for the users of BI tools; it innovates by separating the ingestion and storage of source data from the application of the business rules, to decouple the two most challenging aspects of building and maintaining a data platform.

We can say that the DV methodology is attractive in all cases where the size of the development, the complexity of the requirements, and the project's funding provide the availability of the highly skilled people required and the high-level sponsorship.

The creation of the Pragmatic Data Platform is the direct consequence of the fact that it is very difficult to have all the factors listed above to embark on a proper DV project, and that we feel better to do properly something simpler that provides most of the benefits than risking a bad and costly failure when the conditions for a proper DV project are not in place.

Data mesh

The hottest buzzword in the data world right now is **data mesh**. The data mesh approach was born in some of the most tech-heavy companies to address a common problem across the data engineering industry: data ownership. The pain is real and widespread: the people in charge of building the enterprise-wide unified data platform do not know the source data and have little connection with the real business people; they receive at best weak support from their colleagues that run the business applications and have little to no opportunity or ability to interact with the key people that really understand the business and how data is used and interpreted on the business side.

If the root problem is that different teams manage the source systems and the data platform, and that business departments and the IT department are not aligned, is there a way to fix this?

The solution in tech-heavy companies that have started to adopt the data mesh has been to use the approach that has worked for application software delivery. They took the microservice architecture and the DevOps way of working and applied it to the data realm, creating the data mesh.

The data mesh can be thought of, simplistically, as a microservice architecture in which each microservice is a micro-data warehouse or data product. Instead of trying to build a unified, centralized data platform, ***a data mesh is built from business-unit-scale data platforms that can interact through well-defined interfaces with clear semantics. The interaction in is managed by connecting data products.***

The individual domains of the mesh, or even each data product, can be maintained by different teams. The key point is that the team providing the data product is the same team that runs the other technological systems for the business unit, so it has data ownership of the source data or is the owner of the business concepts encapsulated in the data products.

What is a **data product**? In short, it can be:

- An application that allows doing something using the underlying data and business rules that you do not have but are in the system providing the product. An example could be verifying that a customer is active or authorized to place an order of a certain amount. Another could be a customer-facing application that requires an estimate of a house's value or a quote for car insurance.

- An interface that allows retrieving data with clear semantics. An example could be the marketing department providing recent customer actions or touchpoints, a production site making available the status of an assembly line, or the logistics department making available data on distance, fuel consumption, or CO2 produced by its trucks or associated with its deliveries.

- A data mart is a data product you are already familiar with. The effect is that the technicians building these data products have end-to-end control over the data and understand its semantics and the business rules they are dealing with. You also have proper alignment and motivation to deliver high-quality data, as it is the entire business unit's responsibility to provide and maintain the agreed business products.

It all sounds fantastic, but remember that *a distributed system is much more complex than a centralized one*, and it introduces many new problems that do not exist in a monolithic system. For example, the CAP theorem states that any distributed system can provide only two of the following three guarantees: Consistency, Availability, and Partition tolerance. Furthermore, the required skill set to manage Agile projects, provide reliable APIs, and keep many distributed data pipelines running might not be readily available in most traditional industries, even in tech-heavy companies and big e-commerce businesses.

Recognizing that the available competencies and the maturity level in data management in most companies might not match the required levels to start implementing a full-fledged data mesh spanning multiple different platforms and technologies, in the Pragmatic Data Platform, we focus on the data mesh insights that are easy to adopt and bring tangible benefits, such as:

- Focusing on data products, using clear interfaces, semantics, and versioning.
- Starting with a focus on source-oriented domains as the base data products, we can easily assign to the owners of the data sources and build almost automatically, with little overhead, while exploiting their knowledge of the data and source systems. This facilitates building clear and stable interfaces for the source data and their evolution.
- Assigning ownership of other data products to the relevant business unit (BU) so that the goals of business and development people become more closely aligned, developers know the data and business rules they work on, and have better access to businesspeople. This facilitates the coding, validation, and evolution of the business concepts.
- Aim at an interface-driven data mesh deployed on a single platform, possibly working on all data products with the same tools (dbt, Snowflake, and git), to avoid most of the problems of heavily distributed systems integrating different technologies. As an example, we will leverage dbt-mesh to enable multiple dbt projects to interact through clear interfaces, with data contracts, versioning, and tests, while providing a single lineage to trace data across transformations.
- Actively design (not hope) to integrate the individual data products and data domains, like a municipality builds a high-level Town Plan that splits the responsibility between individual zones, clarifying what services should be made available by each zone and how they connect.

As you can see, we remain pragmatic by selecting from existing architectural styles the concepts we can implement with a simple upskilling of existing competences, leaving it to your discretion to decide when and if to venture into advanced topics that require new competences and/or technologies.

Medallion architecture

Another hot buzzword in the data world is the **Medallion Architecture**, an architectural style or, better, a data flow pattern used to organize data transformations in data lakehouse platforms. Figure 5 provides a quick recap and a high-level comparison of the Pragmatic Data Platform and Medallion flow.

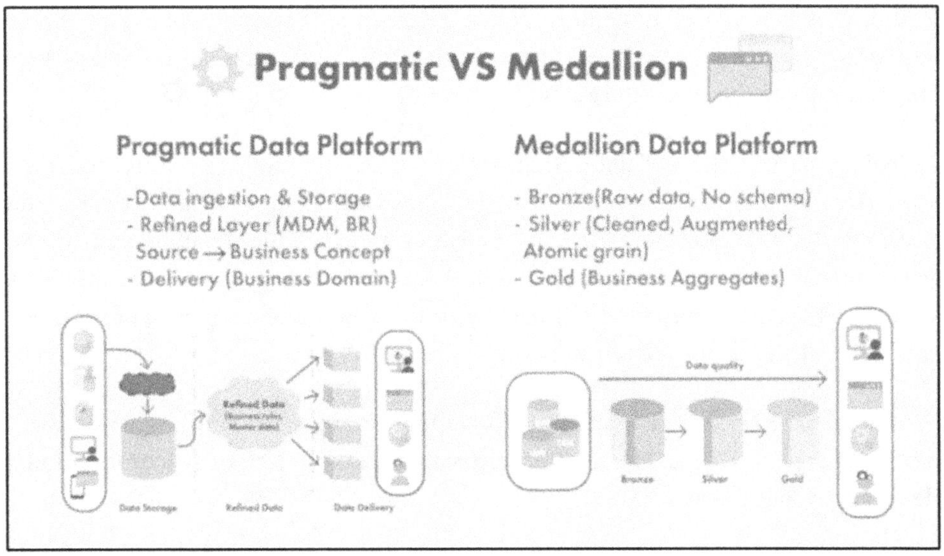

Figure 5: Comparison between Pragmatic Data Platform and Medallion flow.

The Bronze layer is very close to the data Storage layer, with the difference that in the Pragmatic Data Platform, we have the staging step where we apply the hard rules, with the result that the history that we store is auditable, preserves the semantics of the source system, and the stored data is already easily usable down the line with good names. If we really want the source data "as-is" we have the Landing Tables that can be preserved as needed for auditing and eventual history reload, instead of cleaning them up for performance.

> *With the **"hard rules"** concept, we refer to the set of data transformations that must be applied to incoming source data to make them usable in the data platform without altering their meaning. Some examples can be renaming a column to standards, parsing dates or numbers from text fields, extracting nested objects to make standard flat SQL tables, converting all timestamps to UTC to make them directly comparable, applying some transformations to handle PII information (like masking the last octet from an IP) or converting a column to uppercase to have uniformity across multiple systems (if the change in case does not change the meaning).*

The Silver layer has some characteristics of the Refined layer. Still, its scope is limited, as the goal is to achieve "just-enough" transformations and data cleaning to make the data usable down the line. Just-enough in the Silver layer means that data is matched, merged, conformed, and cleansed to build an Enterprise view of the major business concepts, without going into the details of the specific use cases and generally avoiding joins to enrich the data and aggregations. This layer prioritizes loading speed over complex business rules. This is more than what we do in the Storage layer of the Pragmatic Data Platform, but less than what we do in the Refined layer, as we try to build everything in the Refined layer that is not specific to a single use case and could therefore be reused.

The Gold layer is responsible for applying the final use-case-specific transformations and publishing them in an easy-to-use, readable, and performant format, which often means as a star schema. On the surface, this is close to what we do in the Pragmatic Data Platform's data marts. Still, in the Medallion flow, more transformations and business rule applications are left for the Gold layer. Add to this a heavier presentation layer where delivery often involves creating a specific database for each application of the Gold layer, and you can see that this can lead to code, rule, and data duplication and the loss of a single truth.

In PDP, we prefer to focus the data marts on the governance and personalization of delivery for the specific use case, including the creation of a limited, well-thought-out interface to simplify use and potentially expose the data mart as a data product. To us, implementing business rules and other transformations in the data mart makes sense only when they are clearly limited to the specific use case.

In our minds, the major issue with the Medallion Architecture is that... it is not an Architecture. It is a data readiness framework that provides a bit more guidance than the previous Data Lake idea (too often just dump data there, leading to data swamps), but that guidance is shallow, open to very wide interpretation, and, in practice, it doesn't really guide much on how to do the few things it says to do. Thus, not helping to avoid one of the major issues with traditional data warehousing, made even worse by data lakes: the creation of a big bowl of spaghetti code and data that nobody wants to touch after a few years.

The split nature of the Gold layer, where many transformations are repeated with slight changes, if not outright duplicated, is another source of trouble, like multiple alternative truths, a lack of synchronization, and a highway towards multiple spaghetti code bowls.

The freedom of interpretation of the steps in each layer is so wide that by taking the Landing Tables as the Bronze layer and moving the more specific transformation from the Refined layer into the data marts, one might even argue that the Pragmatic Data Platform is one incarnation of the general Medallion data flow, but providing much more detailed guidelines and ready-to-use code.

After this introduction to the Pragmatic Data Platform and its relationships with the most common architectural styles, let's continue by discussing our core ideas about Agile development under the name DataOps, and data engineering best practices.

Data engineering best practices and DataOps

Building a data platform with modern analytical databases and tools like dbt is similar to building software: SQL queries are treated as code and managed with version control systems, pull requests are opened to discuss the changes, tests and continuous integration are run to find as many problems as soon as possible and deployment automation simplifies and speeds up the release process, at the same time ensuring consistency and repeatability.

Understanding DataOps

The approach to building a data platform that empowers teams to follow the above best practices is called **DataOps**, and it is the transposition into the data development practice of the **DevOps** movement, which has brought great improvements in software development, helping teams become more productive and satisfied with their jobs.

In short, the core ideas of DataOps are to provide the team with the tools it needs, as well as the authority and responsibility for the entire development cycle: from coding to Quality Assurance (QA) to releasing and then running production operations. The cornerstones to achieving this are the widespread use of automation, such as in release and testing, the reliance on proactive monitoring, and the team's shared ownership of the code.

> *Typical examples of the DevOps mentality are the four-eyes principle, requiring each piece of code to be seen and approved by at least two people (through pairing, pull requests, or code walkthroughs), and the boy scout rule, which prompts to leave the code you touch in a better shape than it was before you touched it, independently of who wrote it, therefore improving the work over time.*

Another important concept is the active management of technical debt. It is fine and normal that some parts of the code base might be released initially even when they're not yet up to standard, but this must be for a real contingent reason, and the team must repay that debt by fixing the lower-quality code once the contingent reason has passed.

The **Analytics Engineer** is the professional figure at the center of DataOps. He organizes data transformations and their dependencies just as a software engineer designs an application, using reusable patterns, building modular models, and applying the separation of concerns to minimize the need to change a model for many different reasons.

The analytics engineer's job is not just to write the SQL that does the required transformations from raw data to information, but also to apply patterns to break down, structure, and organize the transformations in a meaningful and repeatable way, using clear naming, so that everybody in the team knows what to expect from each step of these transformations. This is the goal, but the hard reality is that people still staff many data teams without a software engineering background who grew up working on legacy data platforms. This is one of the major reasons for writing this book: to help these teams adopt modern software engineering techniques under DevOps in a pragmatic, SQL-friendly way.

In the following subsections, we discuss some software engineering best practices that help data teams work more effectively, and this book is dedicated to all teams that want to adopt this modern, improved way of working with data.

Version control

Having a central repository with all code stored and organized for everyone to access, with a clear understanding of the versioning sequence, is already an improvement over situations where SQL files were saved to shared disks and versions were maintained by file or folder name. The situation with worksheets and notebooks is still not far from that "heroic" stage where all falls on the shoulders (and brain) of a few developers.

The ability to create branches to work independently and then merge changes with little to no effort enables parallel feature development and a safe way to experiment with changes.

Adopting a version control system, such as Git, goes beyond these practical benefits because it enables many other positive processes, becoming the integration hub that can trigger collaboration and automation processes, such as the following:

- **Pull requests**: This powerful feature lets the team review proposed changes from developers, comment on them, request clarifications, and propose improvements, all while getting up to speed on the latest changes. This is a major way to break down knowledge silos and enable competence development within the team.
- **Automation**: When new code is checked in, many types of automation can be triggered, from code quality tools that analyze it to automated tests, and all the way to continuous integration, data contract validation and continuous deployment.
- **Configuration management**: Being able to clearly identify each discrete release and label them with semantic numbers enables tracking and managing which features were present or changed at any time in a single project or along a chain of projects.
- **Authorization**: In bureaucratic or heavily regulated environments, the version control system can work as a recording tool for approvals, making that required step trivial.

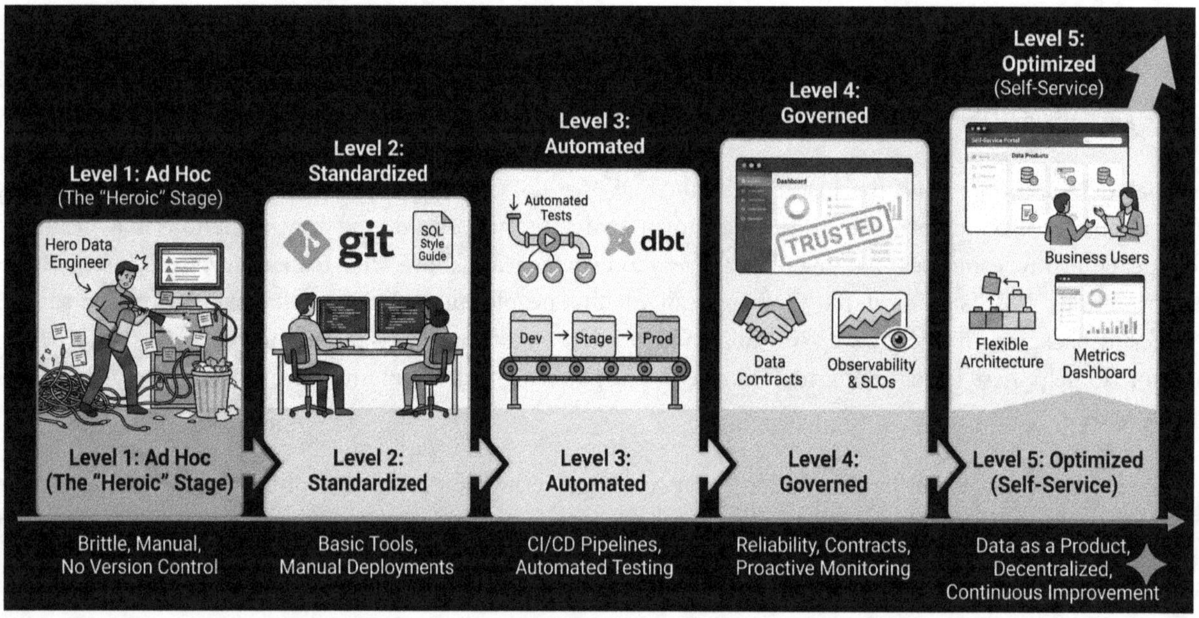

Figure 6: DataOps maturity stages. Generated by Gemini.

Quality assurance

The three cornerstones of DataOps organizations are:

- **Ownership**: The team owns the product, the code, and its way of working.
- **Freedom**: The team is free to choose the right tools and processes for its work.
- **Responsibility**: The team is responsible for developing and maintaining the product, writing, and supporting it in all aspects.

This organization relies on the team having all the competencies to do its work and on a solid quality assurance process being in place. Some competences can be from support teams. The best way to ensure that code in production works is to have automated tests that run whenever new code is released or new data is loaded. Trust, but check. With such a process in place, it is possible to move away from the reactive/firefighting stance of most data teams and focus on value-creating activities with the data.

As a developer, you should think about tests and quality assurance efforts as your ticket for sleeping well at night. As a bonus, you will be recognized for providing trusted data and experience fewer interruptions in your daily work fixing data issues. Being able to catch bugs and data issues before they hit production is invaluable, as it saves the data team and its clients a lot of time, provides better service to business users, and, most importantly, elevates and sustains trust in the data.

You cannot have a data-centric organization if people do not trust the data they work on.

Modularity of the code base

One of the most problematic aspects of many data platforms is the amount of code repetition required to do the same thing. Code is often copied and pasted from one place to another, or even developed slightly differently by different people, as they do not work as a team but as isolated siloes.

The most important change in writing code in modern analytics is the ability to use functionalities that were once available only in proper languages. The reduction in boilerplate code helps focus on good business logic code. Modern tools provide features such as functions for encapsulating reusable code, conditionals, loops, meta-programming, and testing that were not possible or easy in plain old SQL. What was available with stored procedures or user-defined functions (UDF) is very limited in comparison, like a station wagon or a pick-up truck would be compared to a proper truck.

Another cornerstone for simplifying and modularizing the code is reducing the use of incremental loads, freeing us from dealing with their complex state. In modern data platforms, we can easily, quickly, and cheaply recalculate all values according to the current business rules, avoiding the effects of past ETL runs and previous business rules.

dbt provides, as first-class objects, the desired programming functionality on top of SQL and the ability to modularize code. This, together with the speed, scalability, and massively parallel architecture of cloud DWs, makes it possible and more efficient to transform huge amounts of data from scratch than to update existing data. When you factor in the significant simplification of the logic and the productivity gains for developers, it is a win-win scenario. Taking advantage of these new possibilities offered by dbt and cloud DWs requires a mind shift within the data team. The analytics engineer should aim to write clean, reusable code and produce models that are always up to date with the latest business rules.

The data team must go from lonesome data artisans to a highly productive team operating at scale, building layer upon layer and minimizing rework. ***From Art to Industry!***

How many times are you going to develop "the" customer or product concept and the resulting dimension? What about the invoice or order concept? Are you going to refine each from the raw data every time, with slightly different rules every time you need one in a report or data mart?

The modern data stack allows you to build reusable models so you can code the customer only once, perhaps by combining lower-level models that represent the online customer, the store customer, and the wholesale customer. All of them are useful, refined models that can be reused across multiple contexts and as components of a higher-level concept. The key here is that developers and the business must align to define the relevant business concepts, and the technology then helps to implement them, reducing code duplication and promoting the use of stable interfaces.

Personal development environments

What is both the most precious and most expensive resource of a (data) department? The people!

To enable your development team to quickly iterate on code, develop and test new features, every developer must have their own environment where they can work without waiting or needing to synchronize with others, and without fear of breaking something for others. Being free to run your code when you are ready, run tests that give you trusted answers in seconds, or break and recreate your environment in minutes are essential abilities that the modern data stack provides. These, in turn, enable developers to focus on writing good, clean business code rather than on support or side tasks, let alone just waiting.

On the contrary, when developers must test their code in production, they cannot afford to make errors, as failing can cause serious issues. The result is little testing, fear of changing any piece of code and releases that take forever, as every little change must be thoroughly considered and weighed against its consequences. Even in the case where there is only one shared development environment or a few that are slow or expensive to create and therefore must be shared and well-maintained, the result is similar: fear of change and demotivation because of time lost waiting for an environment or from misleading results because the dev or test environment does not reflect the production environment. After all, this should not be very surprising, as most people do not like waiting in a queue and are even less keen on walking on a cable suspended high up, with or without a safety net. Personal development environments are a key enabler for quickly developing and testing new functionality. How can you release daily or even multiple times a day if each developer waits half a day to try out their code on a shared environment?

Continuous integration is the next step in increasing speed and trust in the development process, ensuring that all individual features work well together. It provides another, stronger level of confidence, reinforcing the awareness that all the code being released has been tested, reviewed and discussed by the team. Continuous deployment or continuous delivery provides the final step, allowing code tested in the integration environment to be released to production. That can be done automatically (continuous deployment) or upon manual code promotion (continuous delivery).

Designing for maintainability

Another key best practice is to be mindful of the future, that is, to consider evolution and maintenance. This does not mean trying to predict the future, premature optimization, or bringing forward potential future work; these are actually bad things.

Data platforms are some of the longest-living enterprise applications, so while you are writing one, you can be assured it will be in use for a long time. This means that over time, there will be many changes in data sources and business rules, and even more questions will arise about the data. That, in turn, means that a lot of people, including yourself, in the next months and years are bound to come back and reread that code. This makes the case for writing code that is easy for humans to understand. This is so important that the next section will dig deeper into this topic.

Writing code that just works is not enough; just as putting a key button half-hidden in a difficult-to-use place is not good design. Design your code so that the next person to touch it will thank you for putting the button where it is easy to see and use. Writing maintainable code means writing code that is easy to understand and change for your fellow human colleagues:

- Avoid long and complex queries by breaking down your logical steps into individual Common Table Expressions (CTEs) so that you can provide proper naming for each step and create clean, readable code.
- Keep your models under 100 lines and the number of joins to two or three, unless a model has the single purpose of joining many tables. In this area, the evergreen book Clean Code by Bob Martin and the articles by Martin Fowler on architecture, refactoring, and agility will be great guides; even if the code samples and the main discussion focus on Java and application software, the ideas apply to every programming context.

Performance and correctness are a consequence of well-architected, clearly expressed code; they are never an excuse to write obscure code or overly complicated logic. Remember, the less code there is, the fewer bugs there will be. The fact that we use SQL or Python-based scripting to express our logic does not mean that we should settle for anything less than clearly expressed business logic.

If the code is easy to understand, it is also easy for humans to verify its logic and for automated tests to confirm that it does what is expected; that is not the case if the code is obscure, or the business logic is not clearly understood or mixed across many cases. The other key part of writing maintainable code is making sure that your code does not need to change every other day and that when you do need to change it, it is easy to do so. For this, we can resort to the entire body of knowledge in software engineering, with particular regard to the SOLID principles of object-oriented programming.

The following are some SOLID-inspired principles that are easy to use in data projects:

- **SRP**: The **single-responsibility principle** says that a model should have one, and only one, reason to change. In practice, this means a model should focus on doing one thing, do it well, and make its purpose obvious. This means the opposite of the huge query that does everything at once, and more if possible.
- **OCP**: The **open/closed principle** says that a model should be open for extension and closed for (interface) modification. This means that the models we use as connecting points between systems and projects should be stable in the interfaces they expose and easily extensible. In the data world, this is easily accomplished by choosing good, business-proven names that can stand the test of time and by using views to insulate consumers from potential changes to the tables that store the underlying data.
- **LSP**: The **least surprise principle** says that a model should do what seems obvious it would do from its name and position in a project. You should be able to guess correctly what it does and not be surprised by it after reading its code. Without this principle, you cannot trust any piece of code without rereading it every time, making work a pain. For example, you would not expect a view in a data mart to read from a raw data source, nor would you expect a model that applies a master data mapping to also calculate an unrelated metric.

- **ISP**: The **interface segregation principle** says that a client should not depend upon an interface it does not use. Seems trivial, but we all have seen customer dimensions with over 100 columns. Again, it is quite simple to adhere to this principle in the data world by using a view that provides access to the underlying refined data, exposing only the required information, not everything available "just because." In this way, we limit the "blast radius" of eventual changes that make some fields unavailable or change semantics.
- **DBC**: The **Design By Contract** approach states that clients and providers should define a precise, verifiable specification of the interface used for communication. In the data world, this is easy to accomplish by implementing the interface with a view that uses well-specified column names, data types, and semantics. A dbt data contract will ensure you follow it.

In discussing these principles, we have already tried to adapt the wording and the examples to the data world, so you might find them slightly different from the equivalent definition for application software development. In the list above, to maintain the SOLID acronym, we have replaced the Liskov Substitution Principle with the Least Surprise Principle and the Dependency Inversion Principle with the Design by Contract approach, as we see them as better fitting for data projects.

Besides these overreaching principles, there are other software engineering concepts, such as abstraction, encapsulation, and inheritance, that while not described here provide good inspiration, such as using views to define an abstraction (think of a generic interface such as a basic customer or product dimension that can be in many general-purpose data marts that do not need all the details) or encapsulation (by exposing a subset of the columns of a big table with an appropriate name). Lastly, a lot of a project's understandability and maintainability depends on even simpler actions, such as adopting agreed-upon conventions that make it easy to find a model or understand what it does, as the LSP suggests.

Another important topic for maintainability is documentation. Mind that overly detailed, manually created documentation tends to become stale very quickly, becoming worthless or even misleading. Here, we want to stress that if you want up-to-date documentation, the low-level documentation should be automatically generated.

The stable parts, such as the high-level architecture, the Town Plan connecting business concepts, the model descriptions, the semantics of important columns, and the core descriptions of reports and dashboards, are sufficiently stable and valuable to be created and maintained by humans.

Writing code for humans

In the previous section, we introduced the idea that writing code that is easy to understand is good for a project. In this section, we will explain why it is essential.

Some people believe that when coding, you just write new code, but the reality is that to write one row of new code, you often must go back and check what you have done in multiple places, which means reading tens of model names and dozens or hundreds of rows of code. This becomes more evident as a project ages and the number of people involved grows, because you will not know or remember what each piece of code does. We have seen in previous sections that there are patterns to minimize and keep this issue in check, but remember that size is one dimension of complexity, and we can only do so much to manage it. Removing duplicated or copied-and-pasted code is the top priority, as it reduces the project's size, enables evolution, and makes maintenance much easier.

Other important things that we can do to keep complexity in check are as follows:

- **Reduce the need to re-read code**, applying the Least Surprise Principle (LSP). To do so, use meaningful model names, prefixes, and suffixes; use a good, layered architecture; and apply patterns consistently (and as few as possible) so that models behave as you would expect from their name.
- **Make the code that you write easy to re-read/understand.** To achieve this, use good Common Table Expression (CTE) names, clear column names, and put everything that is not standard at the top of the file, so that every "deviation from expected" is easy to spot as soon as possible.
- **Keep the models that you write focused and limited in dimension.** One model should do one thing, do it well, and communicate it well with its name. This is the Single Responsibility Principle (SRP), which leverages intermediate steps and builds simpler concepts to be used within more complex ones, while avoiding creating a single model that does everything. Here, low model complexity and low project size are at odds, so err on the side of keeping your models simple and focused while still having them do meaningful work.
- **Keep dependencies ordered and flowing in only one direction**, from one layer to the next in the architecture. The expected flow of data and direction of dependencies is as follows: source systems => landing tables => storage => refined => delivery (marts). Avoid at all costs jumping across multiple layers or, even worse, creating dependencies in the wrong direction. Luckily, in such a case, dbt will most likely error out because you will create a circular dependency; in any case, it would be a major issue in your project, making it hard to understand.
- When you see an improvement, **refactor your models to keep them current.** Consistency is a key factor in keeping a big project and multiple people working well together. If you have the right tests and the correct architecture in place, you can apply refactoring at low cost, even in data warehousing. This will keep your project workable for pretty much forever, rather than having to rebuild every few years. Does this ring any bells? Have you ever done evolution, revolution, and re-evolution projects?

When your project is new and has little code, there is little risk of calling the same things by different names or of general confusion by poor naming choices. Yet the points highlighted above are real concerns in any decent-sized project, and they matter so much more for its success than most people think.

We know it will be very difficult to achieve a 100% rate of naming things consistently in every place in a big project, or to get only good names, but the benefit is already worthwhile if we get close to it. The closer the better.

Chapter review

Congratulations, you now have the seeds to build great data platforms!

This chapter provided an overview of the Pragmatic Data Platform's architecture, emphasizing the key themes explored throughout this book. We also defined the core roles within a data project (Data Managers, Data Architects, and Data Engineers/Analytics Engineers). We outlined how this book supports each role's specific needs and challenges. Furthermore, we compared the Pragmatic Data Platform to other prevalent data architectures (Kimball, Inmon, Data Vault, Data Mesh, and Medallion Architecture), clarifying its distinctions and the rationale behind our architectural decisions. We closed the chapter introducing the core DataOps and Software Engineering principles, built in the core of the Pragmatic Data Platform to enhance code quality and team productivity.

In the next chapter, **Pragmatic project setup**, you will learn how to set up a modern data platform and be introduced to the sample project that will accompany us on this journey. Its goal is to explore realistic use cases to write more meaningful code than the usual Hello World.

Recommended resources

Dbt and Snowflake introduction

- Roberto's first book on dbt and Snowflake, presenting the first iteration of the Pragmatic Data Platform. It provides a wide, entry-level introduction to data engineering, dbt, and Snowflake.
  Roberto Zagni, **Data engineering with dbt: A practical guide to building a cloud-based, pragmatic, and dependable data platform with SQL**. Packt Publishing, 2023, ISBN 978-1803246284.
- The pragmatic data blog presents the core principles of the Pragmatic Data Platform and contains articles discussing data topics, often establishing a connection to how it can be done following the principles of the Pragmatic Data Platform. https://www.pragmatic-data.net/.

Kimball data model

- The self-declared definitive guide from the creator itself: Ralph Kimball & Margy Ross, **The Data Warehouse Toolkit**. Wiley, 2013, ISBN 978-1118530801.

Inmon design style

- The foundational book from the father of data warehousing: W. H. Inmon, **Building the Data Warehouse**. Wiley, 2005, ISBN 978-0764599446.

Data Vault

- A great introduction to modeling and the DV: John Giles, **The Elephant in the Fridge: Guided Steps to Data Vault Success through Building Business-Centered Models**. Technics Publications, 2019, ISBN 978-1634624893.
- A concise, practical introduction to DV, ideal for a quick intro: Kent Graziano, **An Introduction to Agile Data Engineering Using Data Vault 2.0**, ISBN 978-1796584936.
- The most complete and up-to-date book on Data Vault 2.0 available. At over 600 pages, it is long and a great reference for those who already know DV2 basics. Quite steep if you are starting from scratch, but it will get you to the top of DV competencies. Patrick Cuba, **The Data Vault Guru, a pragmatic guide on building a data vault**. 2020, ISBN 979-8691308086.
- The DV2 bible, from its inventor Dan Linstedt, even if it is a bit old and does not reflect some of the most recent and important changes in the standard: Daniel Linstedt & Michael Olschimke, **Building a Scalable Data Warehouse with Data Vault 2.0**. Morgan Kaufmann, 2015, ISBN 978-0128025109.

Unified Star Schema

- The book that introduced the USS, an improvement toward self-service reporting of the Kimball style. Even if we did not introduce this book from Francesco and Bill is a good source of information about model issues encountered in reporting, such as fan and chasm traps. The first part is an updated vision of the Inmon style, from Bill Inmon himself: Bill Inmon & Francesco Puppini, **The Unified Star Schema: An Agile and Resilient Approach to Data Warehouse and Analytics Design**. Technics Publications, 2020, ISBN 978-163462887.

CHAPTER 2

Pragmatic Project Setup

This chapter introduces our default technology stack: dbt, Snowflake, and Git. This chapter also guides you through setting up the sample project used throughout this book.

Security is also a key focus: we'll cover how security operates in dbt Cloud and Snowflake, present the goals of our initial setup, and show how to flexibly extend it to meet your needs. Finally, we will start writing code using our open-source Snowflake Admin dbt package for an efficient setup and explore alternative environment configurations. The topics that we are going to cover in this chapter are:

- **The Pragmatic Data stack**: Define the core technologies—**dbt**, **Snowflake**, and **Git**—that form the foundation of our data platform.
- **Environments and the Development Cycle**: Establish a clear workflow and the necessary data environments to support agile and robust development practices.
- **Deployment and security with dbt Cloud and Snowflake**: automate code deployment and implement security with the native features of both **dbt Cloud** and **Snowflake**.
- **Users, Roles, and granular Data access**: Design and manage user permissions using a robust **Role-Based Access Control (RBAC)** model within Snowflake to ensure data security.
- **Automated project setup**: Use the dedicated Snowflake Admin dbt package to efficiently and consistently provision the necessary database objects.

Sample project and code

The sample dbt project is available at: **https://github.com/pragmatic-data/stonks**. The code samples for this chapter are in the sub-folder `chapter_02`, under the `code_samples_by_chapter` folder. Please note that, to better fit the limited space on the printed page, we omit most comments and change the formatting of code blocks compared to the files.

The pragmatic data stack

Given the title of this book, it is quite simple to guess that our stack is built on dbt and Snowflake, but it also needs a third component, a git provider. What is not so immediately apparent is why we prefer this set of tools and what the major differences are with the available alternatives.

Evolution of the analytical stack

Data engineering encompasses a huge set of competencies and tools, covering the data life cycle from start to end, ranging from security and scripting and programming to infrastructure operations and data visualization. In the **legacy data stack**, using transactional DBs and basic ETL tools, it was quite difficult for a single person to cover the complete data lifecycle with a thorough understanding, let alone having the time to develop and manage it all.

The advent of cloud-based data warehouses like Redshift in the mid-2010s marked the turning point from legacy to what would become the **modern data stack**. A huge amount of cheap storage and processing power became available, removing the need to buy capacity upfront. This enabled the rise of cloud data movement tools like Fivetran, Airbyte, and Matillion, which made it quick and painless to load data into these standard cloud DWs from the most common systems, such as traditional DBMSs, established ERPs, operational software, and new SaaS applications. This enabled companies to load vast amounts of data into these cloud Data Warehouses (DWs) and process it much faster and more cheaply. Spending a fraction of the cost of on-premises systems also reduced the need for the most complex and time-consuming data engineering tasks: extracting and locally transforming data.

Having a data extraction tool with SaaS experience that you set up quickly and delivers data to your DW in hours made it possible for a single person to own all or most of the data life cycle, at least for the source systems that could be managed with data movement tools. It also solved the need to study and keep up to date with these rich, but often-changing, APIs of source systems like ERPs and CRMs. That problem is now solved by the developers of the data movement tool.

Nowadays, you create ad hoc pipelines only as a last resort when no tool exists to automate data movement, or when someone (often mistakenly) believes that the time to build an in-house, basic solution will cost less than using a readily available one. Having the raw data readily available prompted the next question: How can we improve the transformation phase and make it more effective? How do we engineer the data?

This is what dbt was created to help with and what is at the core of this book.

*The term **modern data stack** has come to identify the collection of tools that embrace cloud-based technology, are centered around a scalable cloud database, and allow the building of an efficient, scalable, and maintainable analytical data platform, facilitating a DataOps way of working.*
*This was named to contrast with the **legacy data stack**, which contains pre-cloud tools.*

*By now, all major products had to embrace the cloud or die, so the distinction is not as important for tools anymore, and we can just talk about an **analytical stack**.*

When we talk about **analytical tools** and **ways of working**, we will assume that the available tools belong to the cloud-enabled generation and that the way of working embraces DataOps practices. We will continue to use the term *modern* when we want to highlight the difference from legacy, pre-cloud tools and ways of working. This is especially true about practices still in use in many organizations.

In the following sections, we will discuss the organizational changes resulting from the shift in focus within data departments.

Why analytics engineering?

With the advent of post-cloud tools, focus shifted from data extraction, transformation, and loading into the DB of transformed data, due to limited DB performance, to loading raw data into the DB and transforming it into refined information for the business, leveraging the flexible power of cloud databases. This is often referred to as a shift from the **ETL (Extract-Transform-Load)** to the **ELT (Extract-Load-Transform)** paradigm, with the T now also easily performed in SQL. With this shift in focus, the term **analytics engineering** has emerged to describe the central part of the data life cycle, spanning from access to raw data to making refined information available to BI reporting tools. It is not a coincidence that this is the life cycle part covered by cloud platforms and dbt. And it will be the focus of this book.

In the current analytical data stack, we divide the data life cycle into the following steps:

- **Data collection**: Collecting all the data in a single place by using ready-to-use or low-code tools and rarely resorting to ad hoc data pipelines, like you might need with SAP or other legacy or proprietary data sources. This can also be called data movement or loading.
- **Analytics engineering**: Transforming the raw data into refined, usable, trusted data. This is what you do with dbt, using your preferred data platform, which is Snowflake in our case.
- **Data analysis**: Using the refined data to build reports, dashboards, ML & AI apps, and more. This is the work you do to make data accessible to business users.

A major revolution for data professionals using a modern data platform is the adoption of DevOps. Thanks to Git and deployment automation, data professionals can work as a team instead of working in isolation with poor development practices. The focus is now on applying software engineering best practices to make data transformation development as reliable as building software. You might have heard about DevOps and DataOps.

The data life cycle in the modern data stack has clear boundaries that align well with modern tools, with good consequences for data teams.

The roles in the modern data team

The data teams that have adopted the modern data stack and the DevOps way of working have different needs from those of the previous teams. This brought a shift in the mix of professional figures that collaborate in data teams using dbt and a cloud DW:

- **Data engineer**: The "traditional" data engineer, armed with scripting/coding and deep infrastructure knowledge, is still very much valuable, especially when not all sources can be managed by modern data-loading tools. Even when all can be easily landed in the cloud DW, complex scheduling, security, and a myriad of other topics still require the expertise and focus of a data engineer, but less than before.
- **Analytics engineer**: A new figure from old competencies. Firmly focused on knowing the data in the platform and the business, to transform data into useful information. Less involved in data movement, she is instead focused on making the data well-modeled, usable, available, and trusted. This has always been needed, but now more professionals on the data team have the time and the right tools to focus on it.
- **Data analyst**: This is an extended version of the traditional data analyst. Now he can understand and even help build foundational data models and drive the development of data marts. He also has an unprecedented ability to access a wider array of well-governed datasets than the legacy data platforms. In this book, we will not focus on BI tools and data analysts, but they should be interested in at least the topics we discuss, as they can become powerful actors.
- **Data architect**: Besides the big responsibility of having a wider perspective and the competencies to integrate the data platform into the rest of the enterprise's technical infrastructure, the data architect often also performs the tasks of a data engineer, focusing on infrastructure and governance, and sometimes also those of an analytics engineer.

While it makes sense to clearly distinguish these roles, it is important to note that they overlap significantly despite the array of names, with the core competency being SQL and data literacy.

Best tooling for a pragmatic data platform

Our Pragmatic Data Platform (PDP) is more of a design philosophy than a fixed technology stack. Still, we recognize that some tools on the market are much better than others for building a Pragmatic Data Platform. Earlier, we introduced the modern data stack in general terms. Here, we will present our tools of choice and explain why we prefer them over alternatives.

The guiding principle for PDP is simplicity. The goal of the data team is not to write code, but to provide up-to-date, easy-to-use data for business users and to quickly add or modify features when the business needs them. The second non-negotiable principle is the **ability to work as a team**, collaborating and using the Agile principles that we will describe in Chapter 4. The third cardinal principle is a future-proof solution that includes relying on **first principles** (in contrast with the latest technological hype) and adopting data **and software engineering best practices**, as data platforms are among the longest-lived enterprise investments.

The three Guiding Principles of the Pragmatic Data Platform:

***Simplicity**: The art of avoiding complications without benefits.*

***Team collaboration**: The only way that your project will stay healthy over time.*
***Future proof(ness)**: Principles and best practices to keep doors open to evolution.*

The truly differentiating components for building a modern data platform are the database platform, which must be analytical and cloud-based, and the data transformation tooling to write, test, deploy, and orchestrate the code to be run on top of the database. Let's review these two categories.

Database platforms

Regarding the cloud database, the following are common candidates:

- **Google BigQuery (BQ)**: It is a highly scalable database that is now using standard SQL and is surrounded by a developer-friendly ecosystem of integrated tools. With a big footprint in the Marketing ecosystem and its high scalability and automated performance tuning, BQ is a good solution that can be operated with ease, though it has two major downsides. One is its billing based on the amount of data processed by its queries, making the cost unpredictable. Secondly, Big Query operates exclusively within the Google Cloud Platform (GCP) ecosystem. This exclusivity can be restrictive for organizations seeking a multi-cloud strategy or those preferring other cloud providers.
- **Databricks**: They position themselves as the Data Intelligence Platform, which has led to widespread adoption in data science applications based on Python. They have since moved towards providing full-fledged support for data warehousing with SQL, but they are still deeply rooted in working at a quite low level and explicitly with files. This is an advantage for experts looking to deeply optimize a few big operations, but it can be a death by a thousand cuts when you are running a big platform and do not want to spend a lot of time just configuring the tool and optimizing hundreds of queries.
- **Data Fabric**: Fabric stands out for its deep integration with Microsoft's ecosystem, including PowerBI, and Azure Synapse. However, non-Microsoft tooling is not as well integrated, which makes cross-cloud data collaboration more challenging. Architecture is still a bit up in the air, as Data Fabric is new, and it seems to be just a cloud-coated version of a 25-year-old MS SQL Server, a pre-cloud row-based engine not built for analytics. Performance is not proven, with few benchmark tests (in itself a giveaway).
- **Snowflake**: It is synonymous with simplicity, as a cloud-based analytical database designed to have no tuning knobs, with the promise that it just works well without indexes and optimizations. It allows you to focus on writing business code and delivering data to the business, even across the enterprise, as it has always focused on securely sharing data with minimal effort. To keep up with the rise of ML and AI, Snowflake has added many services, greatly increasing its capabilities to a comparable level with Databricks while maintaining its focus on operational simplicity and aiming for the initial "no tuning knobs, it just works" experience.

Nowadays, there are many cloud data platforms, but we have named the three that, in our opinion, are currently the best, with the addition of Microsoft Fabric, because it is widely known and sometimes a forced fourth option.

Our preference goes to Snowflake mostly because of its simplicity and "just works" philosophy, and its ability to easily and safely integrate data across companies and cloud providers. It is an important feature for data-centric companies that want to integrate with their ecosystems.

Data transformation tools

Regarding tooling for working with the data, we consider dbt the best tool, providing data developers with the ability to work like a team of software engineers in a comfortable way and with integrated DevOps capabilities. This is the second revolution in Data management we talked about earlier!

We exclude low-code and GUI-based platforms because they inevitably compromise the ability to work as a team of software engineers. Also, these tools provide a graphical user interface that initially helps with basic development tasks, which anyway can be handled by automation and patterns, while making anything else a painful treasure hunt for the right switch or parameter.

Having decided to use dbt as your development tool, you are still faced with a choice:

- **dbt Core**: This is the open-source software created by dbt Labs, developed in Python, that you can freely download and run locally from the command line on many operating systems, including Windows, Mac, and Linux. It provides all the core functionalities of dbt and can be used for commercial projects.
- **dbt Cloud**: This is the commercial software created by dbt Labs on top of dbt Core, offering a Software-as-a-Service (SaaS) experience that wraps dbt Core in a web interface. It makes it easier to use dbt Core functionalities, plus adds many extra features that are useful when running a real-life data project in an enterprise setting.

Given Pragmatic Data Platforms' focus on simplicity and team productivity, we prefer the dbt Cloud version because it is delivered as a Software-as-a-Service application, making it easy to get started. It also adds many features designed to make development, maintenance, and operations simpler, quicker, and more productive, even in large projects!

The following is a partial list of the main additions of dbt Cloud over dbt Core:

- A powerful web-based IDE, with online compilation and execution of models.
- A guided git workflow, integrated into the web IDE, including support for pull requests.
- The creation and maintenance of development environments, including the self-update of the dbt version.
- The creation of execution jobs to run multiple dbt commands reliably, with the ability to orchestrate the execution of a chain of jobs across projects.
- The scheduling, monitoring, auditing, and alerting of job execution.
- The monitoring of data source freshness.
- The publishing of generated documentation for each dbt project.
- The use of the dbt Explorer also allows non-developers to interact with dbt projects, find information, and traverse it across dbt project boundaries.
- The ability to use dbt Mesh and access data across projects.
- The full features of the Semantic Data Model.

In this book, **we have decided to use the dbt Cloud development environment**, as it makes it easier to work with dbt projects, requires no installation, and looks and works the same for everyone, regardless of the operating system on your computer.

Git providers

The last core component of our setup is a cloud-based Git provider. All the common ones, like GitHub, GitLab, DevOps, or Bitbucket, provide the core functionality we use (git basic ops and pull request collaboration), so for the core functionalities you can pick the one you prefer. We are going to use GitHub both because of its good integration with dbt Cloud and because it is our usual git provider. The others work almost as well.

Now that we have introduced the analytics stack, the data life cycle, the composition of modern data teams, and explained the tools of our choice, it's time to look at what we need to get a real dbt project started. We will first introduce environments and then users, roles, and security in a Snowflake and dbt project. We will then look at the code to set that up, using our open-source dbt package to easily create a dbt project setup in Snowflake.

Initial platform setup

Before we get started writing code, we need to set up the accounts for the tools we will use. Luckily, they are all SAAS products that you can get started with in a few minutes by creating a new account if you don't have one. Let's get through them:

- **Snowflake account**: You can go to https://signup.snowflake.com/ and start a 30-day free trial.
- **dbt account:** You can go to https://www.getdbt.com/signup and start a 14-day Team plan trial. After that you will have a free forever Developer plan.
- **GitHub account:** You can go to https://github.com/signup and create a new account that can host both public and private git repositories for free.

We will not go into the details on how to create the three accounts here, but once you are ready with them, we can get started creating our first project. You will find all the steps in the **Automatic project setup** section later in this chapter.

Before getting our hands really dirty with coding, let's cover some key concepts about environments, users, and roles, and their setup, so you will know what you'll be doing in the code.

Environments

Every data project needs a set of resources, software, and configurations to make it work in the way that best suits your case. In our case, this generally consists of a Snowflake account, one repository in a git provider, one project in dbt Cloud, and the configuration to connect them.

Code is seldom born perfect on the first attempt. You need to test and evolve it until it works as expected. If you have multiple people working on the same project, you also need to validate that their independent developments work well together. To do this, you need the ability to run your code in multiple, independent versions. You do this in dedicated environments. An **environment** is the set of resources needed to run one specific version of the code and data of your platform.

In the Pragmatic Data Platform, an environment is usually made up of one dbt environment in your dbt Cloud account, one database in your Snowflake account, and one branch in your git repository. The dbt environment defines a user impersonating the desired role in the database and the environment's eventual schema prefix.

You create an Environment in dbt Cloud by providing the configuration for these resources. Running your code in one environment means that dbt will use the selected role of the user to run the code of the branch using the configured DB as the deployment target. A foundational decision for every project is which environments will exist, how to manage them, how to develop code, and how to promote it from one environment to the next. This is usually called the **project way of working**.

At a minimum, you want to have the following environments:

- `Development`, DEV, where you can write code and experiment.
- `Production`, PROD, where code is stable and runs to serve your business.

Such a minimal setup is fine only for the smallest cases, if you have only one or two people working on code and never working in parallel.

The most common setup is to have both a development and production environment as seen before, with the addition of one or more intermediate environments, with one named CI (Continuous Integration) or QA (Quality Assurance), but historically called TEST, being the common choice.

Their function is to provide an environment where the multiple parallel works of the developers are merged with the current code, and the resulting integrated code is tested before release to production (CI role) and/or used to validate data and downstream dependencies before a release in production (QA role). Testing new and changed code must happen in DEV, so please do not call this environment TEST; choose between CI or QA depending on which role you feel is more relevant. We often opt for QA to emphasize validation of the integrated code.

In complex situations, when some developments cannot be released immediately upon development, there might be additional environments, one for each specific future release. They are usually called release candidates and allow development for each release to accumulate in its own branch, while allowing immediate release of fixes and improvements to existing features using the CI/QA environment.

Our pragmatic default setup, designed to work very well out-of-the-box in most real-world cases, uses one `development`, one `CI/QA`, and one `production` environment. We will generally refer to them as **DEV**, **CI/QA,** and **PROD** terms, even if you can name them as you wish. You can easily add release candidates, if needed.

We will discuss security in the next section.

Users, roles, and granular data access

In the previous sections, we discussed environments and noted that it is usually required to govern access to data. In this section, we will first discuss how data access works in Snowflake and dbt Cloud, and then show how to set up access between your projects. At the end of the chapter, we will discuss how this general environment design is flexible and can evolve into an advanced setup if you have sensitive data that developers cannot access.

Data access in Snowflake and dbt Cloud

When we work with dbt and Snowflake, we have many moving parts regarding security, making it look more complex than it needs to be with a well-thought-out setup. In this section, we break this down into two roles: controlling Snowflake's actual access and providing the correct Snowflake identity for dbt. In the next section, we will show the code to make it happen.

Snowflake controls physical security

First and foremost, we must always remember that physical access to the data is controlled by Snowflake security. Snowflake security is based on privileges assigned to roles, and roles can be assigned to users or to other roles to make a role hierarchy. A user can be assigned multiple roles, giving him access to potentially disjointed hierarchies of roles that, in turn, grant him all the privileges of those roles.

Access and operation on data are based on the privileges available to the user running the query. This boils down to checking if at least one role available to the user, through the roles directly and indirectly granted to him, has the required privileges. The only special case in Snowflake is resource creation, as it also grants ownership of the created resource. This will be important for our setup, as dbt needs to create schemas, tables, views, and sometimes additional objects. Snowflake has the notion of **primary role**, that is, the role impersonated by the user at a certain time. A user impersonates one of its available roles by issuing a `USE ROLE` command or by setting a default role in the connection string used to connect to Snowflake or in its Snowflake profile. This is important as the primary role -not the user- will own the created object.

To create a Snowflake object, only the hierarchy of the primary role the user impersonated at the time of the `CREATE` query is searched for the required privilege. A key aspect of Snowflake security is that only the object's Owner role can delete it, either by issuing a `DROP` command or through the user interface. Creation privileges through the primary role, access through any other role, and owner control of deletions are key concepts you need to understand to design a role strategy for your dbt projects or to work well with Snowflake. Another important difference between Snowflake and other databases is the organizational hierarchy and the boundaries between the objects within it.

Snowflake organization hierarchy

Most database management systems have only the concepts of a database and a schema, with different databases being disjoint entities that you must work hard to make then work together. That is not the case in Snowflake. These are the levels in the Snowflake organization hierarchy:

- **Organization**: This is the broader administrative boundary that can control how multiple accounts interact with each other and with other accounts. For example, it controls replication across zones and manages objects across accounts.
- **Account**: This is the primary administrative, legal, billing, and technical boundary where all resources are contained. User accounts and the "normal" roles are account-level resources. It is the smallest instance of Snowflake you get.
- **Database**: It is very similar to the database definition in most DBMSs, serving as the top-level organizational container for technical objects. At the same time, it is just an account object whose privileges can be assigned to account roles.
- **Schema**: It is the smallest organizational container whose role is to directly contain most technical objects related to data, such as tables, views, stages, file formats, and the like. Privileges can be assigned to account or database roles.

Looking at this list, it should be clear that in Snowflake, users and roles do not exist within a database; they are within an account, so they can easily have privileges across multiple databases. Security in Snowflake is managed at the account level, mainly by providing privileges to (account) roles and assigning them to (account) users. This, in turn, makes it very easy for Snowflake users to operate and collaborate across databases. Schemas are useful for finer-level organization and access control.

*In Snowflake, a **database** is a top-level logical (soft boundary) container for organizing and segregating data, containing multiple schemas and objects such as tables and views. A **schema** is a subset of a database that groups related objects to further organize data within the database.*

Please don't confuse or mix account roles with database roles, which are roles restricted to a single database and were recently introduced by Snowflake to allow sharing roles across resources shared with different accounts. Both types of roles exist to grant privileges and make them available to users, but they are different. You need slightly different syntax to work with them, and database roles have many limitations… so when you are working inside an account, just use normal = account roles. Keep database roles only for their use case in shared resources.

Dbt Cloud provides the correct Snowflake identity

Understanding how data access, object creation, and deletion work in Snowflake is crucial for our dbt setup, as the user and roles we will use in dbt need to be able to create and delete the desired objects and read from the desired sources while enforcing proper data security.

When we run a data pipeline, we configure dbt Core or dbt Cloud with the desired user and the primary role we want that user to impersonate. Dbt connects to Snowflake with the provided user and sets the primary role through the database connection.

In the environment configuration, we configure a service user and the appropriate primary role for deployment environments such as `PROD` and `CI/QA`. The developers instead use their personal Snowflake credentials to work in their personal development environment, eventually using OAuth for Single Sign-On rather than passwords.

A key feature of dbt is its ability to determine the execution order of SQL commands to maximize parallelism while respecting dependencies, so that many threads can run simultaneously to achieve the best possible performance from our Snowflake warehouses. We do not want to have to issue `USE ROLE` statements because, besides not being easy to do at the right moment in a multi-threaded environment, they will also feel clumsy and go against the spirit of the tool. Therefore, we need a primary role that can create and delete all necessary objects, such as schemas, tables, and views, in the target environment. To create and delete objects, we need the primary role to own these objects. In contrast, the roles we inherit provide access to all the resources we need, whether managed by other dbt projects or not. To achieve our goal, it is enough to select a primary role with the ability to create schemas in the target environment's database. Once our role creates a schema, it becomes the owner and can create tables, views, and other objects within that schema. Being the owner, it can also delete all such objects. We usually call the service user used by dbt something like EXECUTOR. It will be used by dbt to execute our SQL commands, impersonating the correct primary role for each environment, keeping them separated and safe. For each environment, this user needs a role that can access the environment's database, use a warehouse for compute, and create schemas within the database.

The initial setup, in the next section, will describe the roles we are going to create, their hierarchy, intended usage, and the privileges provided to each role.

Pragmatic Data Platform core role setup

In this section, we will describe the initial role setup for Pragmatic Data Platform projects. The next section will cover the setup in more detail, not just the roles, and provide the code to perform the initial setup for your projects. This role setup has also been tried and tested in large projects and ensures easy, successful governance of data access. This initial setup covers the objects that exist in each environment from the beginning. It will gradually become complete with the addition of specialized roles to govern access to the data marts. You can create these roles after creating the relevant data marts. This will be covered in the dedicated section of the next chapter.

Goals of the initial setup

Let's lay out the goals for our initial setup:

- **Works well in any project**: it is low-maintenance and covers all the usual platform needs, providing a simple solution for other, less common needs.
- **It is future proof and flexible**: we can run it before committing to future details, like the names of data marts or the layout of schemas and handle them as we learn more.
- **Provides consistency and structure:** offers a guided, easy way to manage privileges, roles, and users, regardless of how many environments we choose to have.
- **Well-engineered security**: a **technical role** controls access to resources in a given environment by assigning the correct privileges. It is never granted directly to users.

- **Makes user management simple**: an **organizational role** groups technical roles across environments for a specific class of users. It is granted to users to assign them the required privileges for their class.
- **Sound security setup**: give the least privilege needed by each role, and the ability to easily craft new organizational roles with the desired profiles for new classes of users.
- **Structured role hierarchy**: an Admin role that owns the databases and is the head of all roles in a project. This provides for strong control of DBs and easy monitoring of the role hierarchy.
- **Focused roles**: roles are segregated by environment to enable finer shaping of organizational roles and avoid automation mishaps/mix-ups across environments.
- **Enforce use of automation**: provide developers with full access to development and only read access to upper environments to improve environment reliability by forcing code and automation to deploy changes instead of manual operations.

To accommodate the most common use cases by default, we use three environments (DEV, QA, and PROD) and three organizational roles: **developer**, **reader**, and **dbt executor**.

Figure 7 illustrates the default initial role setup of the Pragmatic Data Platform. In the image, we can note:

- We have three environments with one database each, named **DEV**, **QA,** and **PROD**.
- The Admin role "ADM" owns all three databases and serves as the head of the hierarchy for all project roles (hierarchy not shown).
- We have two technical roles for each environment: RW (read-write) and RO (read-only):
  - The **RW role** for each environment owns the environment's schemas and all other objects, and can create and delete them, because it has been granted the ability to create schemas and owns the objects it creates. This is the role dbt impersonates, using the correct RW for each environment.
  - The **RO role** for each environment has read-only access to all objects in the environment's database, such as schemas, tables, and views. It is suitable for data catalogs, monitoring, and early reporting until you create data mart-specific roles.
- There are the three organizational roles of **executor**, **developer,** and **reader** that are assigned to users to provide the right level of access to the project. They provide your users with the correct, transparent, cross-environment access.

This setup is both simple and complete, providing everything you need to keep running many projects forever while assuming close to nothing about your project.

One expected evolution is the addition of data mart-specific roles to provide read-only access to a single schema in PROD. They make sense only once you create the data marts and only if your BI users access your DB directly. In such a case, you should use Snowflake roles to manage access to different data marts. If you use your BI tool, like Power BI, to read the data via a BI service user and cache it for your BI users, so you read the data once and they do not access Snowflake directly, then you would implement your access in the BI tool. In such a case, you might not even need the data mart-specific roles.

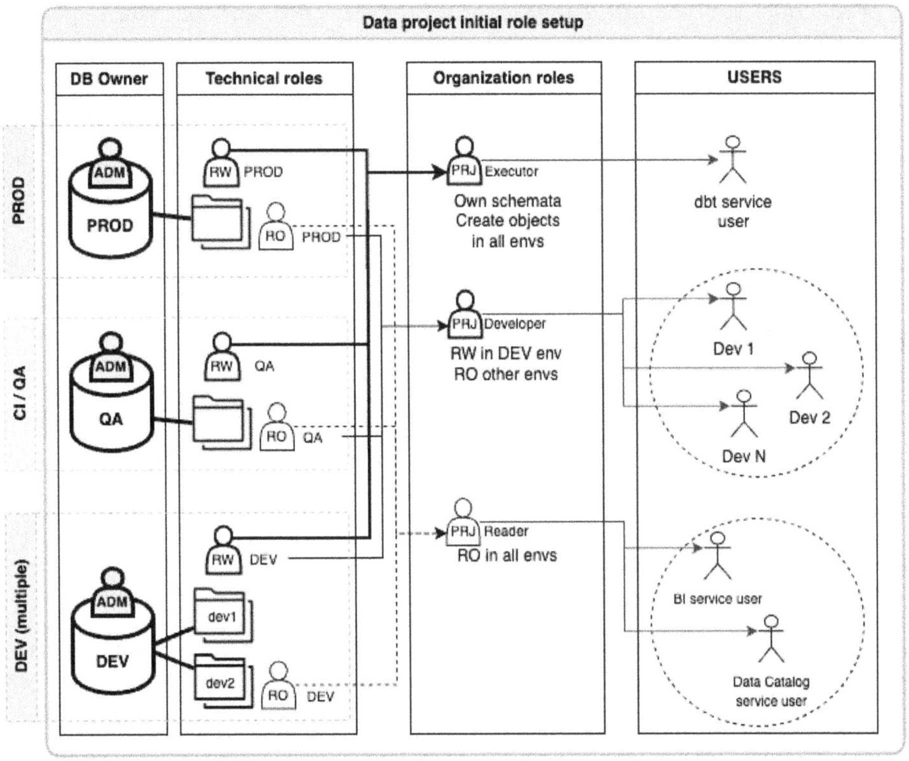

Figure 7: Default initial role setup for Pragmatic Data Platform projects.

Default setup naming convention

Our Snowflake Admin dbt package, which we will use in the next section to code and automate the setup, uses a simple, straightforward naming convention for all project objects, from databases and warehouses to roles.

> *The general naming convention is* `<project>_<environment>_ <function>`.

As an example, we suggest that the **ADM** role be named `MY_PROJECT_ADMIN`, the PROD database `MY_PROJECT_PROD`, and the RO role for the DEV environment `MY_PROJECT_DEV_RO`, which clearly identifies their project, environment, and function as appropriate.

According to Snowflake's best practices, we assign the project admin role to the Snowflake `SYSADMIN` role to provide administrative access to the project for account-level administrators. This admin role should be granted to few people, used only for admin tasks, and never in normal operations.

We highlight that it is crucial that dbt impersonates the `RW role` of the environment dbt is working on, as the ability to delete objects depends on their ownership, which in turn stems from the creation of the object. This, in turn, provides strong guarantees that if, by error, you try to run in one environment while impersonating the role of another, it will cause little or no harm, as the role will be unable to read, write, or delete anything from environments that are not its own. The usual example is some code in your development environment trying to write by error to production: you will just get an error, as the `DEV_RW` role that you impersonate in the DEV environment has no privileges in the PROD environment.

In the next section, we will show the code and technical details to set up the environments, define the roles, and manage users. It will also cover how to create the eventual data mart roles and manage users for them, too.

Automated project setup

In this section, we will take the principles from the previous sections and turn them into actual code that generates the SQL commands to run in Snowflake to materialize the desired setup.

Project planning

The first step in creating a new project is planning how it should look. We must decide things like names, the number (and names) of environments, the number of warehouses, and so on.

Pragmatic data platform blueprint setup variables

In earlier sections of this chapter, we presented the Pragmatic Data Platform setup for role organization and general naming conventions. By following that blueprint, we are left with few choices, as most will be derived from it or have defaults. Let's go through the choices for the sample project we will follow along with this book and the major derived values:

Project name: `STONKS`

The project's short name is the primary input, as it serves as the basis for our naming convention. It must respect the rules on identifiers, as it will be part of many. All the following inputs have valid defaults, so they are optional.

Environments: `['DEV', 'QA', 'PROD']          -- this is also the default`

In our project, we will use the default three environments with the PDP default names, opting for QA as the name of the intermediate environment to avoid overloading CI with both the environment and the CI process.

Owner role: `STONKS_SYSADMIN                  -- the default is SYSADMIN`

Instead of using the default `SYSADMIN` role, we opted for a specialized role that will be granted all the project's roles. The correct Snowflake setup is preserved by granting the `STONKS_SYSADMIN` role to the `SYSADMIN` role.

Snowflake warehouses: only one shared warehouse `-- only one WH is the default`

This is the default setting, and the name of the shared warehouse will be `STONKS_WH`, generated by the naming convention. The alternative is one warehouse per environment, with the environment in the name.

With this very small set of choices, all optional except for the project's short name, we can complete and run the project setup script, as we will see in the next section. Our choices for the setup values will be stored in dbt variables defined in the `dbt_project.yml` main config file of our project.

Blueprint database objects

As an example, let's look at what gets created in the DEV environment by the execution of the setup script from the Pragmatic Data Platform blueprint with the inputs defined in the previous section:

- **Database**: `STONKS_DEV`. This is the database for the DEV environment. Created by the SYSADMIN role, granted ownership to the STONKS_SYSADMIN role.
- **Warehouse**: `STONKS_WH`. This is the initial warehouse for the DEV environment. Created by the `SYSADMIN` role, granted ownership & all privileges to the `STONKS_SYSADMIN` role.
- **Writer role**: `STONKS_DEV_RW`. This is the role dbt will use to execute SQL commands in the `DEV` environment. Created by the `USERADMIN` role and granted to the `STONKS_SYSADMIN` role, to fulfill the Snowflake best practices on role hierarchies. This makes `SYSADMIN` able to operate on DEV.
- **Reader role**: `STONKS_DEV_RO`. This is the role that may be used to read data from the `DEV` environment. Created by the `USERADMIN` role and granted to the `STONKS_SYSADMIN` role.

The same objects are created in each environment, with obvious name adjustments.

Blueprint technical roles

For each environment, the script sets up the required privileges for each role to perform its tasks. For example, the **writer role** has access to the database and warehouse in the environment, ownership of the existing schemas (usually only `PUBLIC` exists), and the ability to create schemas in the environment database. Similarly, the **reader role** has usage on the database, warehouse, and schemas of the environment, and SELECT access to all views and tables. It also receives usage and SELECT on the future schemas, tables, and views.

It is important to clearly recognize the importance of the **writer role**. This is the role that you will **configure as dbt role**. It will create and own all database objects created with dbt jobs and run-operations. The creation of securable objects and technical RW and RO roles for all environments is the foundation of our governance, and we should not assign these technical roles directly to users.

Blueprint organizational roles

The setup process also generates the organizational roles to assign the appropriate level of access to individual users. Their naming, with our inputs and their default definition, is as follows:

- **Executor role**: `STONKS_DBT_EXECUTOR_ROLE`. The role that will be granted to the service user for dbt. This role provides access to the **writer** role (RW) in each environment, so we can use a single dbt service user (often called EXECUTOR) that impersonates a different role in each environment. This effectively enables reading from but prevents creating or deleting objects in other environments.

- **Developer role**: `STONKS_DEVELOPER`. The role granted to the SF users of the developers. This role provides access to the **writer** role (RW) of the DEV environment and to the **reader** role (RO) of other environments. It guarantees that developers can easily manage their own development environment, but can only read from other environments. The inability to manually alter the higher environments forces them to always use the automation to produce changes. The lack of manual changes guarantees the correct alignment between environments.
- **Reader role**: `STONKS_READER`. The role is to provide read-only access to all layers of an environment. This role is suitable for monitoring or other use cases requiring access to all layers and/or across environments. In the next chapter, we will see how to create roles to provide access to a single schema/data mart.

Later in this chapter, we will see how we can use these roles to easily configure the desired access for our Snowflake users with a simple YAML configuration.

Roles needed to run the setup macros

Code running in dbt pipelines should always run as the role configured in dbt for the environment. In the Pragmatic Data Platform, it is always the writer role (RW). It is our primary task, when wearing the architect hat, to design the platform so that the role dbt impersonates can perform all the operations we expect it to, and no more!

Minimizing the privileges assigned to all users, including service users, is a security best practice that ensures any operation performed by code executed by dbt occurs only within the intended perimeter and within the allowed range of operations. Examples in the Pragmatic Data Platform design include the fact that each environment has a different writer role, so that code running in one environment cannot interfere with code running in other environments. Or the fact that we can't drop the database of the executing environment, even by error, because the writer role does not have ownership of the database. Anyway, there are situations when macros have good reasons to change the primary role and explicitly pick a specific role to use the privileges required to perform their job. This is what our setup macros need to do.

The best practice is to keep these special macros clearly apart and never mix them with normal ones, as the most likely outcome would be an error rather than the expected result. Successful execution of such "security aware" macros is possible only to users who can impersonate the higher roles required by the specific set of macros. In the case of the environment setup macros, the user running them must be able to impersonate these roles:

- `SYSADMIN` – to create warehouses and DB objects.
- `USERADMIN` – to create users and roles.
- `SECURITYADMIN` – to set up future grants for the reader role.

Some other macros to set up more specific objects or perform other operations, like creating a `STORAGE INTEGRATION` or enabling replication, might require even higher roles, such as ACCOUNTADMIN, or granting the needed privilege to another role. Separating concerns between the setup operations, which require a plurality of higher-than-usual privileges, and the normal pipeline operations is very important to keep everyday operations simple and working correctly.

Conventional macros, the ones used in transformations, must not change the role being impersonated.
They should execute operations in the current role, as set by dbt according to the configuration.
Any deviation from this standard should be made very clear, and the relative macro should be kept separated from the normal ones. In general, macros cannot assume that the user running the SQL can impersonate any role other than the one configured in dbt for the current environment.

The desire to keep the setup macros clearly separated and restrict access to them is a good reason to have a separate dbt "SF Admin" project. It would contain only these "security aware" macros, like the setup ones, for one or more projects. This simplifies providing access to the project administrators or other users delegated to perform configuration operations and who have the required roles.

In the next session, we will create our first dbt project by connecting Snowflake, dbt Cloud, and a GitHub repository. To keep the setup to a minimum, we will "bootstrap" the dbt project by hosting the setup macros in the project itself. However, in a mature organization, it is much more effective to dedicate a specific dbt project (often named SF Admin) to host the setup macros for all the dbt projects. This will also provide a natural place to handle cross-project access, configuration and data movement needs.

Bootstrapping of dbt project

In this section, we get started with our sample project, which will accompany us throughout the book, by setting up the database object and the roles needed to work on the project. To configure the macros, generate, and run the setup script, we need a working dbt project.

Creating your first dbt project

Creating a new dbt project is a three-step process:

- **Have a user with enough privileges in Snowflake.** The first step to creating a new dbt project is to ensure you have a user in your Snowflake account with access to the roles listed in the previous section, "Roles needed to run the setup macros." The user that you create when making a free trial account is fine, maybe even a bit overpowered, as it can impersonate all initial SF roles, including ACCOUNTADMIN. For the setup, this user is fine, but later, you should create another user with the minimum required roles to work on the project.
- **Have an empty repository.** The second step is to create a new private repository in your GitHub account to host the code for the new dbt project you are creating. Please keep the repo totally empty so that dbt Cloud offers us the option to initialize the repo with the dbt standard initial project, which is perfect for laying out the folder structure and validating that everything works. Pick a name for your repository. We picked `stonks`, so the URL for our repository is going to be `https://github.com/pragmatic-data/stonks`.
- **Configure a new dbt Cloud project.** The third and last step is to create a new project in your dbt Cloud account and configure it to use your Snowflake account and the new repo.

The dbt project creation is a three-step process supported by a wizard. First, provide the name of the new project and the eventual folder in the repo to serve as the dbt project root. Use `STONKS` as the name in dbt, like what we have in GITHUB, with no sub-folder, making the repo root also the dbt project root. This is the most common setup. Next, pick a connection or create a new one for the development environment. And then, to create a new one, you are sent to a new browser page to select the database type, Snowflake in our case, and provide the data to connect to your account: account, database name, warehouse name, and a role. For now, you can leave the role empty and enter anything as a database or warehouse.

For the Snowflake account, use the initial part of the URL to connect to your Snowflake account. The part before "`.snowflakecomputing.com`". It will generally look like `<account-code>.<region>.<cloud-provider>` (try it without the cloud-provider part for AWS, or read the Recommended resources section at the end of the chapter for all details).

Once you select a connection, you can enter your development credentials. Select "username and password" or "key pair" and enter them, then provide the "schema" (I changed it to `RZ` or similar) that is the unique prefix for schemas in your development environment. Enter 'dev' as the target name, and four to eight threads. Test the connection and save if it works, fix the params otherwise.

Connect to the git repository holding the code for the project. To select the repository we created earlier, pick the right git provider, then authorize and configure the dbt integration with it. Once you have configured the Git integration, you can finally select the repository from the list available through the integration. If you are using a git provider that is not listed, pick Git Clone, and you will need to configure access to Git with URLs and access keys (usually SSH keys). Once you have completed these three steps, you will find yourself with a new empty project in dbt Cloud.

The next step is getting the repository initialized with the dbt default project. To make it happen, select **Cloud IDE** from the **Develop** entry in the left menu. Once the IDE (Integrated Development Environment) has loaded, you should see the **Initialize repository** action button in the Version control area of the IDE (top left). Click it and dbt will create the default folder structure with a couple of sample models under the `models` folder. Make your first Commit to save the generated code. You will also have to pick a name for the branch to be created, so pick something along the lines of `initial-setup`.

Forbidding commits directly to the main branch and requiring the creation of a feature branch to host changes is an important best practice that the dbt Cloud IDE enforces automatically for users. The logic is that changes must go through the integration process (a Pull Request with human review and automated CI) before becoming part of the main branch and being deployed to other environments.

---

*To validate that the connection to the database is working, you can open an empty file (hit the plus sign in the top-right of the IDE), enter `SELECT 1`, and hit the **Preview** button in the lower part of the IDE. Close and discard once tested.*

Please note that if this is the initial setup and we are doing a bootstrap from an empty Snowflake account, you do not have any DBs or WH in Snowflake that you can configure in the connection/development environment, so you can't run much more. That is why our next step is to install the dbt package to automate the generation of SQL commands for creating all the necessary objects in the Snowflake account and completing the setup of our environments in dbt Cloud.

Installing the Snowflake Admin dbt package

The SQL code to get us started with three environments is not that much. However, we are still talking about a few hundred lines of SQL with a handful of moving parts in the configuration and a few subtleties we need to remember to apply consistently, from future grants to creating the correct ownership chain for roles and objects.

To ensure a simple, consistent application of the Pragmatic Data Platform guidelines and design principles, we have created the SF Admin dbt package. Providing the few inputs we discussed in the previous sections, and having the code generated accordingly, is quicker and much safer than copy-pasting a setup script and replacing/altering the code each time we need to set up a new project.

The peace of mind that comes from knowing all projects are reliably created using the same blueprints reduces errors and facilitates collaboration across projects.

Installing the package in your dbt project requires just a few lines of YAML.

Create the `packages.yml` file in the root folder of your dbt project (the same folder where the `dbt_project.yml` file is) and add the following content:

```
packages:

  # Pragmatic Data Platform—Snowflake Admin package
  - git: https://github.com/pragmatic-data/sf-admin
    revision: main
    warn-unpinned: false
```

The first line declares that we are listing the packages that we want to import into the project, and the rest of the file provides one entry for the SF Admin package:

- The `git` attribute imports a package from a git repository.
- The `revision` attribute pins the import to a specific version (tag) or branch.
  It is important to pin a specific version or commit to avoid issues from unexpected changes. We suggest following the URL in your browser and looking under **Releases** in GitHub to find out the most recent version.
- Setting the `warn-unpinned` attribute to false suppresses the warning that would be raised when a `revision` does not point to a fixed commit in the repo, like we did.

Once you save the file with a new package or a change in the content, any recent version of dbt Cloud will recognize that a package needs to be installed and will automagically run the `dbt deps` command. You will see that a `package-lock.yml` file has been created or updated in the root folder. It tracks which versions of which packages are installed in your project. You will also see that the package code has been copied from the git repo under the `dbt_packages` folder. The SF Admin package is under `sf_project_admin`. Both folders are greyed out because the `dbt_packages` folder and its contents are ignored by default, as specified in the `.gitignore` file.

Opening the command history window (the ^ button at the bottom left of the IDE, left of the command line) you will also see an entry for running the `dbt deps` command. You can see whether the result was successful, and on the right side of the windows, you can access the System Logs for a detailed log of what was done. If the command was not run automatically, or if you need to fix something and re-run the command, you can do so by typing `dbt deps` in the command line at the bottom of the IDE and pressing Enter. For more information on the dbt Cloud IDE and how to install packages, you can read the materials listed in the Further Readings section at the end of this Chapter. For a more detailed, step-by-step process, you can look at the README.md of the sample project.

If you have the dbt Cloud Enterprise version, you can create the same content of the `packages.yml` file in a file named `dependencies.yml`. In the dbt Enterprise edition, using the new name enables you to declare also other dbt projects in the same dbt Account as dependencies.
More on this in the section dedicated to the dbt Mesh feature in the next chapters.

In all other editions, you have dependencies only on packages, so the file is still called `packages.yml` as it has always been before the introduction of the dbt Mesh feature.

Now that we have the SF Admin package installed, you can make another commit to the setup branch, and then we can start using the package to generate our setup SQL.

Snowflake setup with the pragmatic data platform blueprint

In this section we will configure the setup variables and use the Pragmatic Data Platform blueprints defined in the `project_initial_setup__sql` macro to create the desired databases, warehouse and roles to deploy the project according to our design.

At the end of this section, we will update the environment definitions in dbt to use the objects and roles we created. The only requirement for this setup is to run the development environment with a user who has the necessary privileges to run the required commands. See the previous section, "Roles needed to run the setup macros," for more details.

Let's get started with the practical work!

1 Getting started with the setup blueprints

To get started, we will have two steps: duplicate the setup blueprint and define the setup variables in the config.

1.1 Duplicate the file with the blueprint of the setup

While we could start from scratch writing the setup macro, we can get a head start by cloning the default one from the SF Admin project, which we already have under the `dbt_packages/sf_project_admin` folder. Duplicate the `project_initial_setup.sql` file (inside the SF Admin project in `/dbt_packages/sf_project_admin`, under `integration_tests/macros` folder) to the macro folder of your project

(/macros). You can copy it directly there, but we suggest creating a subdirectory named project_setup to keep all the setup scripts together. An even better choice is to create the setup folder directly in the root folder, but then you need to add it to the list of macro folders in the dbt_project.yml config file.

1.2 Define the setup variables in your config

Copy the variables from the config file (dbt_project.yml) of the SF Admin package (inside the SF Admin project, in integration_tests/dbt_project.yml) to the variable section of your project's config file in the root folder.

```
vars:

  project_short_name: XXXXX
  owner_role: SYSADMIN # <<-- YOUR_PRJ_SYSADMIN if you want
  environments: ['DEV', 'QA', 'PROD']
  useradmin_role: USERADMIN
  creator_role: SYSADMIN
  single_WH: True
  dev_env_names: ['DEV']
  shared_dev_wh: COMPUTE_WH
```

These are the default values for the variables that are used in the SF Admin package. We will edit some of them further down. You can find a copy of our dbt_project.yml config file in the repository in the code_samples_ by_chapter/chapter_02/sample_project folder. By defining these variables in your project, you can override the value used in the SF Admin macros without the need to pass the desired value in every macro call.

2 Edit the blueprint to fit your project design

Now that we have duplicated the blueprint from the package into our project, let's edit it to work for our project. To provide a "real project" feeling first rename the first macro in the project_initial_setup.sql you cloned from; run_create_sample_project to run_project_setup, then the second macro from create_sample_project to project_initial_setup__sql. Next, we will edit the variables in the dbt_project.yml config file and the second macro to generate the SQL code for our project.

2.1 Define the project configuration

Edit the macro/vars to include at least the three mandatory configurations: project name, list of environment short names, and the role that will own the project's resources. Edit your dbt_project.yml config file to define the three key variables:

```
vars:

  project_short_name: STONKS
  owner_role: STONKS_SYSADMIN
  environments: ['DEV', 'QA', 'PROD']
```

By setting the variable here, we can also reuse these definitions in the other setup and management scripts that we will cover in this and the next chapter, so we suggest setting them. You can leave the other variables as in the blueprint or just remove them. By editing the variable and the script, you can tailor the setup to your needs. Next, let's edit the `project_initial_setup__sql` macro.

2.2 Getting the configuration into the setup macro

We start with the three key settings. You have three alternatives:

- Keep using the variable and remove the default value, so that if you don't set the variable, you get an error. This is the best option if you choose to set the variables. We will go with this option.
- Keep using the variable and set its default value (the same as the variable) to avoid an error if you don't set it. This is not a great idea, as you might be easily misled if you don't keep the variable and default aligned.
- Replace the use of the variable with the value, as in the following example:

  ```
  {%- set prj_name = 'STONKS' -%}
  ```

  That is very easy to read and is needed if you choose not to set the variables. It is not the preferred choice as it requires manual synchronization of these values across the setup and management scripts. Avoid, unless you find a good reason, like using a global SF Admin project.

Going with the variables without the setup value, so that we get an error if the config is removed, this is how the first rows of the setup macro will look:

```
{% macro project_initial_setup__sql() -%}
 {#---- CONFIGS YOU MIGHT WANT TO CHANGE... #}
 {%- set prj_name = var('project_short_name') -%}
 {%- set environments = var('environments') -%}
 {%- set owner_role = var('owner_role') -%}

 {#---- CONFIGS YOU MIGHT WANT TO LIVE WITH THE DEFAULTS #}
 {%- set creator_role = var('creator_role') -%}
 {%- set useradmin_role = var('useradmin_role') -%}
...
```

We have included the last two local variables because we defined them in the config file, but if you want to go with the defaults, you can remove or comment them out so the macros get none and use the default from the package.

2.3 Creation of the role to own the top-level objects of the project

If we have decided to create a new role that will own the top-level objects of our project, such as the databases and warehouses, then the next step in our setup macro is to create that role. We do that with this code:

```
...
{{ sf_project_admin.create_role(
     owner_role,
     comment = 'Sysadmin like role...',
     parent_role = 'SYSADMIN',
     useradmin_role = useradmin_role
  ) }}
...
```

Let's analyze the interesting parts of the previous code:

We are calling the create_role macro in the sf_project_admin package, so we must fully qualify the name of the macro. We use the owner_role local variable to pass the name of the role to create. We have hardcoded SYSADMIN as the parent role. This makes sense as it is the only place where we use this logic, and SYSADMIN is almost always the best choice. Another value makes sense only if there is an intermediate role that will own the owners of a set of projects (like department, data product, country). We set the useradmin_role parameter as the local variable with the same name. If you have not set the local variable, you can even remove this line.

With this simple call to the macro in the SF Admin package, we have created a new role to own the project's objects. This is the advantage of macros and packages. If we have configured SYSADMIN to own the project's objects, we have nothing to do, as the role already exists in Snowflake.

2.4 Creation of the initial warehouse(s)

Now that we have the config and the role to own the project's objects, we can start creating the first objects. We start with the creation of the warehouses, as it is very simple. If we have decided to use a single warehouse for all environments to minimize cost, we are done with the following macro call:

```
{{- sf_project_admin.create_warehouse(
        prj_name = prj_name,
        single_WH = true
  ) }}
```

We just pass the project name and set the single_WH parameter to true when calling the create_warehouse macro of the SF Admin package. The default naming for a single warehouse is <prj_name>_WH. If you want to create one warehouse for each environment, you can use the full functionality of the create_warehouse macro and pass all the parameters you need. The default naming is <prj_name>_<env_name>_WH. Please note that to use the environment name, you must set the single_WH parameter to false.

The object naming is done by specialized macros, like get_warehouse_name(...), in the naming.sql file in the core folder of the SF Admin package. You can call the macro to create individual warehouses and pass whatever you want as env_name. Still, the most common approach is to wrap that call in a for loop over the environments to create one warehouse for each environment.

2.5 Creation of the environments

The next step is to create and configure the individual environments. To get that done, we will create a for loop over the environments and inside it call the needed macros (one or two) for each environment, like in the following snippet:

```
/* == Create ALL environments, one at a time == */
{%- for env_name in environments %}
  ...
{%- endfor %}
```

Most of the job is performed by the create_environment macro:

```
{{ sf_project_admin.create_environment(
    prj_name = prj_name,
    env_name = env_name,
    owner_role = owner_role,
    creator_role = creator_role,
    useradmin_role = useradmin_role,
    future_grants_role = 'SECURITYADMIN',
    single_WH = true
) }}
```

This macro does the heavy lifting of the environment creation:

It creates the database for the environment with the creator role. The default naming for the DB is <prj_name>_<env>. It transfers the database ownership to the owner role, grants all privileges on the DB to the owner, and allows the owner to create new schemas.

It creates the technical **Read/Write role** to be used to write to the environment and grants it to the owner role (usually SYSADMIN or similar). The default naming for the **RW role** is <prj_name>_<env>_RW. It grants the RW role the necessary permissions: the use of the database and the warehouse for the environment (or the only one), ownership of existing schemas, and the ability to create new schemas.

It creates the technical **Read Only role**, used to read from the environment, and grants it to the owner role (usually SYSADMIN or similar). The default naming for the **RO role** is <prj_name>_<env>_RO. It grants the RO role the needed permissions: the use of the database and the warehouse for the environment (or the only one), and the use of the schemas in the database, select on all existing views and tables, plus usage on future schemas and select on all future views and tables.

Please note that Snowflake allows owners to grant privileges on existing objects, while granting privileges on future objects is a powerful feature reserved for `SECURITYADMIN`, a powerful admin-level role second only to `ACCOUNTADMIN` and appointed, as the name implies, to manage security. Only if you set the variable `future_grants_role`, that role (by default, `SECURITYADMIN`) is used to grant future objects, and you need to run the script with a user that can impersonate it. If future objects are not granted, you must grant access to the RO role using the dbt **grant** feature. As you can see, there is much going on in this macro that effectively creates the DB and the roles to work with the DB objects. If you have multiple projects and your developers work a bit here and a bit there, it might be useful to define a shared warehouse for all development work, so that you effectively get any overlapping queries run by your developers for free. In such a case, you might create the shared WH with the same command we used in the previous chapter:

```
{{- sf_project_admin.create_warehouse(
      prj_name = 'SHARED_DEV_WH',
      single_WH = true
  ) }}
```

And then grant access to it for the RW roles with the following macro:

```
{{ sf_project_admin.grant_shared_wh_to_writer_role(
     prj_name, env_name, owner_role,
     shared_dev_wh = 'SHARED_DEV_WH'
)}}
```

In the previous call, you need to provide `prj_name` and `env_name` to build the RW role name, the WH owner to grant usage, and `shared_dev_wh` to provide the name of the shared WH. An alternative way to provide the name of the shared WH is to set the variable `shared_dev_wh` in the dbt_project.yml file.

At this point, we have everything we need to run our project: the DB, the WH, and the roles, but we would need to manually manage these low-level roles. To make it easier, we will create the organizational roles in the next section.

2.6 Setup of the default organizational roles

As we have seen in the **project planning** section, we want to create three organizational roles: dbt executors, developer users, and reader users, to encapsulate the appropriate RW and RO role assignments for these users. We generate the SQL to create and configure these roles with the following macro call:

```
{{ sf_project_admin.setup_default_org_roles(
     prj_name,
     environments,
     owner_role,
     useradmin_role
) }}
```

We need to pass the project short name and the list of environments to determine which technical roles exist, and the owner role to determine who to grant the newly created roles to. Last, but not least, the user admin role is used to do the work. With this step, we have completed the discussion of our blueprint, but -of course- can personalize further the setup script to create additional resources.

3 Inspect and execute the generated SQL for the Snowflake setup

Now that we have entered the setup variables and completed editing the blueprint, it's time to review the generated code and, if all looks good, execute it. The easiest way to verify the SQL generated by a macro is to open a new model, paste the code that generates the SQL from the macro, and click compile. To inspect the snowflake setup SQL, enter the following code in a new model:

```
{{ project_initial_setup__sql() }}
```

Once you click the **Compile** button, dbt will run the macro and write the generated SQL to the output. You can keep adjusting the setup variable and the macro code, and recompiling, until the generated SQL is as you want it. You cannot run this SQL using the Preview button, because the generated SQL is wrapped in a SELECT command. Once you are happy with the generated SQL, you can run it in dbt as a **run operation**. You can run it in the command line of the IDE with the following command:

```
dbt run-operation run_project_setup
```

The `run_project_setup` macro uses our `project_initial_setup__sql` macro to generate the SQL code, then runs it with the `run_query` macro, which takes the SQL text, runs it on our database, and fetches the result. In this case, we ignore the result, as we are just interested in the side effect of the execution, that is, the creation of the DB objects and roles, but in other cases, we use it.

A common alternative for the first project is to take the generated code and run it one query or block of queries at a time using the Snowflake UI, so that you can view the output and effect of every query.

Update dev env configuration

Once the project setup is deployed according to our blueprint, we can complete the configuration of our DEV environment, using our Snowflake user in DEV. To update the DEV env, we need to update the connection to use the database, warehouse, and roles we just created.

Under the **Deploy** menu, pick **Environments**, then click the **DEV environment** from the list and the **Settings** button in the top right. Under Connection, click **view connection details**. In the new browser page that opens, check and eventually edit the following values for the connection:

- Database = `STONKS_DEV`
- Warehouse = `STONKS_WH`
- Role = `STONKS_DEV_RW`

Once you are done with the connections, you might also want to verify that your DEV credentials are correct under the Credentials menu in the Your Profile section of the account **Settings** menu. To complete the dbt project setup, we also need to create the dbt executor service user. This will be done during the user setup in the next section.

Alternative management of the project setup

In your first dbt project, it's common to use a bootstrap setup, which runs the project setup scripts directly from the dbt project itself, as we just did. It can be done for all projects, but in organizations where there are multiple projects and not all users have the privileges to run the setup script, it is often useful to create a dedicated "Snowflake Project Admin" dbt project that will contain all the setup scripts for all projects, including the user management from the next section and other scripts.

Putting all setups in one project is useful because access to this project can be limited to administrators who oversee the setup and have the privileges to run the setup scripts. This does not pose any problems because the setup process is completely separate and independent of the project's operation. In such a project, it is customary to create one folder for each project, containing the config and setup scripts for that project. The result is that all setups are collected in a single repository, so it's easier to administer all projects, automate tasks, and share a common experience, creating a pool of experienced administrators, which is always a good thing. Such an administration project also provides a natural place for cross-project setup scripts.

User setup

Now that we have created the database objects and roles, it's time for the last two steps of the initial Snowflake setup: creating a service user that dbt will use to run the deployment environments and assigning the organizational roles for the project to users.

Getting started with the blueprints to manage users

Both goals can be accomplished by editing some YAML definitions in the blueprint file `manage_users.sql`, which you can duplicate from `integration_tests/macros` in the SF Admin project, as you did for the setup blueprints. Duplicate it into your setup macro folder (`/macros` or `/project_setup`) and replace the `XXXXX` placeholder in macro names with the unique name for your project. We will use `STONKS`, so this is what you will see in our macro names. Developers and readers in the `manage_users.sql` file you change to fit your needs. This file contains a block of YAML text that is assigned to the `users_dict_yaml` variable, which is parsed into a Python dictionary and passed to a few macros that perform common user management operations, but -of course- your need might be different. You can both change the existing macros and add new ones.

Initial user setup

The role of the YAML text in the `manage_users.sql` file is to associate users with the different roles that you will have in your project. Initially, you will have only the three default roles that we created in the Snowflake setup, which we will associate with the three default attributes: `dbt_executor`, `developers`, and `readers`. The names should be self-explanatory. In the future, you will add here other roles you create, with the actual role name, and list which Snowflake users should be granted that role. For the `dbt_executor`, you are expected to pass a single username, while for the other roles, you can provide a list of names.

1 Edit the user management YAML block

The following code exemplifies what an initial version of the YAML could look like:

```
{% set users_dict_yaml -%}

dbt_executor: STONKS_DBT_EXECUTOR

developers:
 - ROBERTO_ZAGNI_ADMIN              # high privilege user
 - ROBERTO_ZAGNI_DEVELOPER          # limited privilege user

readers:
 - STONKS_READER        # read only user to STONKS data

{%- endset %}
```

Rename users to the names you need, delete the users you don't need, and comment out other parts of the configuration that aren't used yet. Now that we have entered the setup, let's make it real in Snowflake.

2 Create the executor service user

The first thing we can do is to create a new service user to run this project. To achieve this, we can simply run the `create_dbt_executor_user___STONKS_project` macro with the following command in the dbt command line:

```
dbt run-operation create_dbt_executor_user___STONKS_project
```

This will generate the SQL to create a user and run it, producing a Snowflake user with an initial password set by the `initial_pw` setup variable, which needs to be reset at first use. Using username and password is not enough for a good service user. To properly set up a service user, you should use key-pair authentication.

You do that with the following steps.

Generate a new SSH key pair, that is, one file with the public key and one with the private key. You can look at the pages referenced in the **Recommended resources** section or search online for how to create and configure a key pair in Snowflake for your operating system.

Add the public key for the service user in Snowflake, with this code:

```
USE ROLE USERADMIN;

ALTER USER XXXXXXXX_DBT_EXECUTOR SET
  TYPE = SERVICE
  RSA_PUBLIC_KEY='MIIBI...'
;
```

In the SQL command in Snowflake, please omit the public key delimiters. When we configure the dbt environments, you will need to enter the private key (and passphrase if you added one) in the configuration for the env. Once you are done, you will be able to use the executor user with the key-pair.

3 Grant the organizational roles to your users

The last thing we do is to grant the roles for the project to the users we already have.

You can also use the user management YAML to create the users that you specify if they do not exist. It is quite common for large organizations to create Snowflake users through general user management systems, such as Active Directory or equivalent systems, and enable Single Sign-On for dbt and Snowflake. The SSO setup is beyond the scope of this book, and you can find excellent video and documentation from dbt Labs at https://learn.getdbt.com/ and in the dbt docs. To create the users configured in the YAML block, you can run this command:

```
dbt run-operation create_users___STONKS_project
```

You might not want to run dbt projects in your dev environment with the all-powerful user that you are using for the setup. This would be a good time to create another user with access only to the needed roles (the developer role and maybe the project admin role) and configure your dev environment in dbt to use it.

Be mindful that if, for your dev env, you use a user without access to higher roles, you will no longer be able to run the setup scripts without changing the DEV user. That is why mature teams move to a separate SF Admin project: you can run the normal dbt project with normal developer users, and configure the admin project with more powerful personal users that can execute the necessary setup operations.

Once you have all the users you want to configure in your file, you can run the following command to assign the roles according to the YAML configuration:

```
dbt run-operation refresh_user_roles___STONKS_project
```

As the name of the macro implies, this command refreshes the roles assigned to users, so you can run it as many times as you wish, and it will add the desired roles to any newly added user. Please note that this command only adds roles according to the configuration; it never removes any role from any user, let alone removing roles when you remove the user from the relevant list. This behavior is consistent with our experience that roles are never really removed from anyone in a project unless they leave the project, which usually means completely removing the associated user. If you want to remove users with the macros, you can just add the names of the users to remove under the `users_to_delete` attribute in the YAML and run:

```
dbt run-operation drop_users___STONKS_project
```

If you want to remove a role from a user, you can manually run the command:

```
REVOKE ROLE <name> FROM USER <user_name>;
```

If you need to do that on many users you can look at the code generated by the macro `refresh_user_roles___STONKS_project` and adjust the SQL. If you need more sophisticated user management, you should implement SSO and use groups from your user management tool to handle dbt and Snowflake users and roles.

Completion of dbt project setup

At this point, you have all that your project needs in place in Snowflake:

- One DB for each environment.
- One warehouse for all environments (or one for each environment).
- One writer and one reader role for each environment.
- Three organizational roles: DBT_EXECUTOR, DEVELOPER, and READER.
- Users have been assigned the desired organizational roles
- All these resources and roles are under the ownership of the role that you have designated as OWNER of the project (potentially created by the setup script).

Now that we have run the project setup, created the executor service user, and granted the project roles to your users, we have finally in place all the elements we need to complete the configuration of our dbt project: the deployment environments and the job that will run the code in each environment.

Creation of deployment environments

In the previous section, we already updated the development environment's setup with the correct database, warehouse, and role name (RW) for the DEV environment. Now you will create the QA and PROD environments.

These are the steps to create the QA environment:

In the **Deploy** menu, select **Environments** and then the **Create Environment** button

Enter the name, like `QA` or `Quality Assurance`.

If you can work with production data, leave the deployment type to General so deferrals and cross-project references resolve against production. Otherwise, select **Staging** if you use test data that is different from production data. Do not select a custom branch so that we will use `main` for the QA environment.

Select the same connection that you have in the DEV environment. Update the connection settings with the correct role name (`STONKS_QA_RW`), database (`STONKS_QA`), and warehouse (`STONKS_WH`) for the QA environment. In the Deployment credentials section, select key-pair, then enter the private key and passphrase for the STONKS_DBT_EXECUTOR service user (in dbt, you must include the private key delimiters). If you did not create the key-pair, select username and password, but it's not the best, future-proof setup. Enter a schema prefix for the QA environment. As we have created separate databases for QA and PROD, we can set the same prefix, like `STK` or `STONKS`, for both environments so that the schema names are identical and the only difference in the connection string is the database name.

Test the connection and save the configuration.

To create the production environment, you go through the same exact steps, but you provide a name like `PROD` or `Production` for the environment, pick Production at point three, and at point four, you check the custom branch box and enter the name of the branch that you want to use for production. We generally use `PROD` or `production`. At point five, you set the names for the production environment. At points six and seven, you enter the same user, credentials, and schema as in QA, then you can test the connection and save.

Please remember to create the branch for your production environment in your repository.

You have now defined the environments, but nothing is happening there yet.

Creation of the core full build jobs

To really run your code and deploy the generated SQL to your database, you need to create dbt jobs, which are pretty much equivalent to a list of dbt commands to be executed in a specific environment, with eventual scheduling. To create a job, you select **Jobs** from the **Deploy** menu, then the **Create job** button. Here we will create only the base job for each environment with the following steps:

1. Select the **Deploy job** template from the **Create job** button.
2. In **Job settings,** enter a name like `<env>—Build all`, a description, and pick the environment for which you are creating the job.
3. In Execution settings, check **Run source freshness** and **Generate docs on run** checkmarks, leaving unchanged the default `dbt build` command.
4. Leave deactivated **Schedule** and **Job completion** under **Triggers**. Save.

Rinse and repeat for the other environment.

Now you have a base job that can deploy your code to your environments. In the next chapters, we will add more jobs, including one to trigger a Continuous Integration build when we start a Pull Request and another to run ad-hoc commands.

Chapter review

In this chapter, you've successfully embarked on your journey to building a Pragmatic Data Platform.

We've explored the power of the modern data stack, centered around dbt and Snowflake, and discovered how these tools are revolutionizing the data world by bringing software engineering best practices to data management. We've also taken a practical approach, setting up our sample project using the Snowflake Admin dbt package. This involved configuring essential components such as Snowflake, dbt Cloud, and GitHub, and understanding how they work together to build a robust data platform. Security was a key theme, and we dived into how to manage users, roles, and granular data access in Snowflake and dbt Cloud, ensuring your data is both accessible and protected. Finally, you learned how to automate your project setup with our open-source Snowflake Admin dbt package, making the process efficient and repeatable.

In the next chapter, **Data Governance**, you will learn how Data Governance helps you to define and manage the standards for your data platform. We will explore the Data Mesh pattern and how Data Products help in managing complex platforms.

Recommended resources

SF Admin package

- The package is on GitHub: https://github.com/pragmatic-data/sf-admin. The README.md on the home page has some detailed instructions to set up new projects.

dbt Cloud

- All that you need to know to configure package and project dependencies in your projects: from dbt Hub to private and public repositories. https://docs.getdbt.com/docs/build/packages.
- The official documentation about the dbt Cloud IDE. https://docs.getdbt.com/docs/cloud/dbt-cloud-ide/develop-in-the-cloud.
- How to find out the right URL to connect dbt to your Snowflake account: https://docs.snowflake.com/en/user-guide/admin-account-identifier#non-vps-account-locator-formats-by-cloud-platform-and-region.
- How to configure the key pair auth for Snowflake in dbt and SF docs: https://docs.getdbt.com/docs/cloud/connect-data-platform/connect-snowflake#key-pair.
- https://docs.snowflake.com/en/user-guide/key-pair-auth#configuring-key-pair-authentication.

CHAPTER 3

Pragmatic Governance

Data governance is about adopting principles, practices, and technology to manage data throughout its lifecycle, from ingestion, transformation, usage, and eventual retirement.

This chapter provides a comprehensive introduction to data governance for modern data platforms, focusing on the essential considerations for Chief Data Officers, Data Architects, and cross-functional stakeholders.

Furthermore, we will discuss the evolution of data governance to support data mesh architectures and the use of data products. The chapter concludes with guidance on complying with privacy regulations, such as GDPR, and references a decision-making checklist available at https://technicspub.com/Pragmatic-Data-Platform.

In the first part of the book, we will establish a robust and pragmatic governance framework by detailing:

- A pragmatic integration of Snowflake's security features with dbt's way of working.
- Strategies for development environments and cross-project dependencies.
- Streamlined development workflows for continuous integration and delivery.

Our approach emphasizes a practical implementation, avoiding bureaucratic bottlenecks while ensuring data is secure, accurate, and readily accessible to authorized users. This chapter will cover the following key topics:

- **Pragmatic Data Platform Governance**: Establishing effective governance principles and practices for modern data platforms.
- **Data Mesh and Data Products**: Implementing decentralized data architectures and managing data as a product.
- **Handling Personally Identifiable Information (PII)**: Strategies for managing sensitive data in compliance with privacy regulations.
- **Data flow across data projects:** We discuss the degree to how environments are connected influences the way teams work and their effectiveness.

Sample project and code

The sample dbt project is available at: **https://github.com/pragmatic-data/stonks**. The code samples for this chapter are in the sub-folder `chapter_03`, under the `code_samples_by_chapter` folder. Please note that, to better fit the limited space on the printed page, we omit most comments and change the formatting of code blocks compared to the files.

Pragmatic data platform governance

I would be hard-pressed to find people enthusiastically talking about government, taxes, and bureaucracy. Filling out the tax return is one of the saddest days of the year!

At the same time, everybody enjoys living in a place where justice and all other public services work. Reality is that you can't have the latter without some effort in the former. Building a data platform is an effort to balance providing access to an ever-increasing range of sources, results, metadata, data models and documentation, ensuring that access is as intended. Data platforms have needs similar to those of society: we must put rules in place to enable the platform to achieve its goals and work well for all stakeholders. The data lakes that turned into data swamps have proved that a Wild West approach does not work.

Good governance is essential for effective data management, which in turn is crucial for any organization that relies on data to operate, innovate, or make decisions. It fosters improved performance, compliance, and competitive advantage. In the rest of this section, we will cover what you should consider in your governance efforts, while in the rest of this chapter, we delve into how to implement parts of it.

What is governance?

Governance is the set of activities under which the goals and rules for a data platform are established, monitored, and enforced.

Governance should be a collaborative effort among interested stakeholders, so that all needs are accounted for, responsibility is allocated where it makes sense, and the burden is shared and softened through automation. The Pragmatic Data Platform is trying to balance the least effort with optimal results. We view Governance positively, seeing it as the groundwork that drives better results for the broader audience of our work. Not as a necessary burden!

The pillars of governance

The data ecosystem (data, metadata, data models) in a modern enterprise is complex:

- Input comes in from many different sources, with different technologies, from different applications, with different formats, and at different speeds.
- It is stored on different, weakly connected cloud and on-premises locations, in different databases and storage clouds.
- It is consumed in different ways too: internal users and applications, ML and Gen AI models, and also external users, such as customers, business partners, or other enterprises in the same value chain.

Governing such a complex ecosystem would already be complex without the added challenges brought by regulations and security needs. To tackle the Governance challenges, we can divide them into five areas:

- **Compliance**: Making sure that data and processes around it abide by regulations and do not expose the company to legal and financial consequences.
- **Security**: Ensuring that data objects are accessible only to designated people, both internally and externally to the company, and blocking unauthorized access.
- **Privacy**: Ensuring that sensitive data, at the business or personal level, is accessible only to designated users. This is on top of the rules enforced by compliance and security.
- **Data quality**: Making sure that data is fit for its purpose. This can be further divided into multiple topics, such as consistency and integrity.
- **Access**: Ensuring data can be accessed and used when needed. This can be further divided into multiple topics, such as availability, usability, and interoperability.

Let's go through each of these pillars to show how Snowflake and dbt Cloud can help you achieve an effective and efficient Governance model.

Governance features in the pragmatic data platform

Governance in the Pragmatic Data Platform (PDP) is not a separate software module or a tool you buy; it is the natural result of combining **Snowflake's** infrastructure, **dbt Cloud's** development workflows, and **PDP** methodologies. Rather than viewing governance as a theoretical overlay, we implement it directly through the tools you use every day, leveraging the native strengths of our stack:

- **Snowflake** handles the heavy lifting of infrastructure security (Encryption, MFA, Failover) and granular access controls (RBAC, Dynamic Masking).
- **dbt Cloud** enforces process governance through Version Control, CI/CD, and Testing.
- The **PDP** provides the architectural patterns —such as the strict separation of environments, the use of Service Accounts for deployment, and "Insert-Only" storage models— to ensure that the tools are used securely and consistently.

To achieve **Compliance**, we combine the strengths of the entire stack. We rely on Snowflake's built-in certifications (such as FedRAMP and SOC2) and its business continuity features to handle the infrastructure compliance. On the process side, dbt Cloud's tight integration with Git ensures every change is version-controlled and traceable, while its lineage capabilities prove exactly how data is transformed. The PDP methodology complements this by enforcing an "Ingest All Data" and "Insert-Only" strategy in our storage layer, creating a comprehensive, auditable history that allows for forensic analysis and report reproduction at any point in time.

For **Security**, we adopt a defense-in-depth approach. Snowflake handles the granular controls through Role-Based Access Control (RBAC) and default Multi-Factor Authentication (MFA). We extend this into the development lifecycle using dbt Cloud's project-level RBAC and User Management. Crucially, the PDP methodology enforces a strict separation of environments: developers work in personal sandboxes, while deployments to QA and Production are handled exclusively by Service Accounts. This ensures that no human has direct write access to production data, maintaining strict operational integrity.

Privacy goes a step further than security by controlling visibility. We utilize Snowflake's Dynamic Data Masking and Data Clean Rooms to ensure sensitive PII is only exposed to authorized roles. The PDP supports this with a lightweight PII framework that tags and handles sensitive data as soon as it enters the platform. By moving sensitive pipelines in separate dbt projects accessible only by specific users, we ensure that privacy is baked into the code, not just the database.

To guarantee **Data Quality**, we move beyond simple monitoring. While we can use Snowflake's dashboards and Time Travel to detect and revert anomalies, the PDP shifts quality left into the development process. We use dbt's automated testing and Data Contracts to enforce schema integrity before code is ever merged. Furthermore, our "Four Eyes" principle (mandatory code reviews) and standardized testing guidelines for each layer ensure that quality is a cultural standard, not just a technical check.

Finally, regarding **Access**, the goal is high availability and usability. Snowflake's multi-cloud replication and auto-scaling compute separate storage from execution, ensuring that heavy ingestion or complex queries never block user access. dbt Cloud automates the delivery of these assets via CI/CD pipelines and generates documentation to make data discoverable. The PDP ensures this ecosystem remains manageable by organizing the platform around clear interfaces, making the data easy to navigate and interoperate with other systems.

Deep Dive: For a detailed technical mapping of specific Snowflake and dbt Cloud features to each of these five governance pillars, please refer to the **"Appendix - Implementing Governance with Snowflake and dbt"** included in the book repository.

In this section, we have presented what Data Governance is and its many facets, along with how the different components of the Pragmatic Data Platform can help you with it. In the next sections of this chapter, we will discuss how you can split up and organize bigger projects with the concepts of Data Mesh and Data Products.

Data mesh & data products

Data Mesh and Data Products are two facets of the same medal used to organize data projects that span multiple sources and development teams. They are important in Governance as they help to organize your data platform and consume its results.

Data Mesh is both an organizational and a technical approach.
To work well, an organization must be leading and technology supporting. Not the other way around.

The core idea is that by dividing the use case into smaller, well-defined domains, it becomes easier to develop each part because it is technically simpler, and it can be assigned to people who know and care about it more than a generic do-it-all data team.

A domain is a sphere of knowledge, influence, or activity. The subject area to which the user applies a program is the domain of the software. More on this later in the chapter.

The key tenet of the data Mesh approach is to decentralize ownership so that teams own their own data, data pipelines, and all the processes associated with operating their domain. A Central team provides support with tooling and cross-project **federated governance**, but the domain team is in charge within the domain. Figure 8 provides an overview of a data mesh architecture.

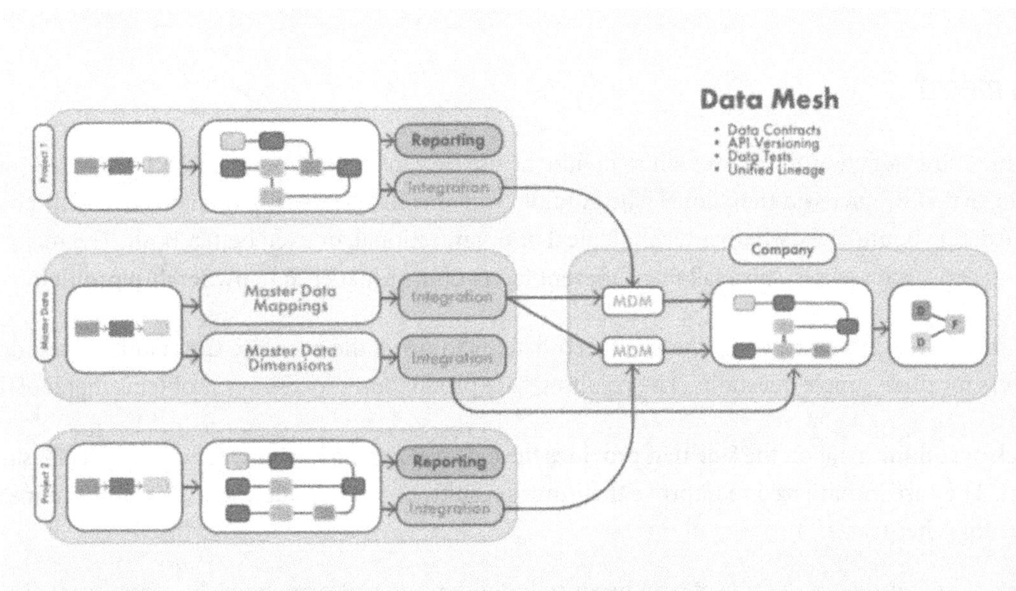

Figure 8: Data Mesh architecture with the Pragmatic Data Platform.

In the image, each domain is implemented in its own dbt project and exposes one or more data products through integration data marts, and it can have other data marts.

A smaller, better-known, and clearly specified project is surely simpler to build than a larger, more ambiguous one. Anyway, we must not forget that to operate reliably a mesh by connecting many islands, it is more complex than operating a monolith. Those who have been studying or working on data mesh or micro-services, the technology that provides the foundational idea of data mesh, know well that the operational problems become even harder when the islands are different and far apart.

The projects in a data mesh, in principle, could be done with different tools on different platforms. Our suggestion is to harvest the benefits of the mesh and limit the downsides by aiming for a "**soft mesh**" built on as much homogeneous technology and governance as possible. For each project, we can use our usual Pragmatic Data

Platform setup and architecture. Integration data marts are used to provide a well-governed API to connect projects, as we already do for other dependencies. The combo of dbt Cloud and Snowflake is ideal for this: Snowflake provides the flexibility to organize your data as you wish, making it almost trivial to securely share data across domain boundaries. Dbt empowers us to use good software engineering practices and to abstract away most of the plumbing. Dbt Cloud also provides the dbt Mesh feature, which we can use to handle these connections more simply.

A common setup is to use different databases and distinct, but similar, role hierarchies in the same snowflake account for each mesh project. It is also possible to use a shared role hierarchy to abstract away mesh details and make it feel more like a single project, while still maintaining well-defined ownership areas. In advanced setups, each project might be in a different Snowflake account, sharing data through shares or internal listings across different regions, to take the data mesh idea to its upper bound in larger organizations while limiting technical complexity.

These are basic technical considerations. In the next topic, we will discuss how the data mesh idea is as much an organizational idea as a technological one.

Why data mesh?

In the data mesh introduction above, we said to divide the use case into smaller parts, which we called well-defined domains, but that is simpler said than done! The guiding principle for identifying domains to divide your projects is to follow existing boundaries, whether technological or organizational, or even better, both. The major problems the data mesh approach seeks to solve fall into different facets of the broader **data ownership problem**.

Who owns the source data, who owns the produced data, who owns the process? Companies often do not have useful answers for these simple questions. The resulting data production process has problems that look like this:

- Lack of commitment on the side that provides the data, typically a business function or its IT support part. They are incentivized to improve their unit's results, not to provide useful, correct, and meaningful data for other teams.
- Lack of knowledge on the side of who needs to build the data platform, typically a data team. They have limited access and no competence with the data they receive.
- Lack of involvement and minimal understanding of the needs of the final users of the data, which can be as diverse as the full company.

A central data team seldom understands the purpose and intended uses of the datasets they provide. They also struggle to find time to do meaningful work with domain experts to improve this situation, with both sides often claiming they have no time. Lack of trust and fear of the unknown do not help the situation. These are not technical problems, but organizational ones.

The Data Mesh approach aims to address these problems by applying the concepts of domains and product thinking to split the software engineering task of building a cross-company data platform into connected data products built within domains.

Domain-Driven Design (DDD)

In the **DDD Reference**, Eric Evans, the inventor of the **Domain Driven Design** (**DDD**) discipline, describes it as an approach to development of complex software that:

- Focuses on the core **domain**. A domain is a sphere of knowledge, influence, or activity. The subject area to which the user applies a program is the domain of the software.
- Explores models in a creative collaboration of domain practitioners (business) and software practitioners. Speaks a **ubiquitous language** within an explicitly **bounded context**. A ubiquitous language is structured around the domain model and used by all team members within a bounded context to connect the team's activities to the software.

A bounded context is a description of a boundary (typically a subsystem, or the work of a particular team) within which a particular model is defined and applicable. A central aspect of DDD is that the domains and their language are discovered and maintained as a joint effort by technical and business practitioners. The result of DDD is that, instead of trying to build a huge monolithic application, you will build the pieces following the identified domains and bounded contexts.

The contents and the naming inside each component are defined by the bounded context it belongs to. You connect components across contexts and domains using explicit mappings and translations to avoid mistakes. The general map defining the global view and connecting the domains in DDD is called the Context Map. It defines the boundaries, how data flows between them, and the concept mapping.

DDD is born for software development and applies well to data projects, which are just a special kind of software project and face the same problems as all software. If you look at how companies work with data, you notice that units tend to operate within their context, using a stable set of data to produce specific information. This should provide initial hints about the domains you might have in your data platform and the features of the data products that fulfill their needs.

Data domains

We usually find three types of domains in data platforms:

- **Source-oriented domains**: They provide the events and entities that describe the reality of the business. They are very close to the operational systems. These are the most common and easiest to identify, as they are centered around the sources of data. Examples can include providing customer or product information, the deliveries made, the invoices paid, or the level of accounts from one specific system. These are best known by the people who work every day and operate the system of record that originates such entities. They might already provide some operational reporting to "nearby" teams or management, but it is seen more as a nuisance than a core responsibility. The approach suggested by data mesh is to assign ownership of the source domains to the people who produce their data and run the systems that handle it, making them responsible for providing the truth of their part of the business to the rest of the organization. The difference can be between just providing an "as is" data export of Products when it works, versus an easily set up, immutable, consistently up-to-date, and trusted source of current and past Products, with all their changes.

- **Consumer-oriented domains**: These domains are very much aligned with the business use of the data. This is the information businesses use to do their jobs. These are also easy to identify, as they closely satisfy related business needs and are typically used directly by the business. They often result from initiatives requested by others to the central data team, such as data marts, sales activity reports, KPIs for upper management, or product availability. The approach suggested here is to assign the ownership and the ability to build these domains to the consumer teams themselves. Who has a better knowledge of their needs and business rules? They have the ability and a real incentive to keep the data product as close to the business reality as possible, as their work depends on it. With the best possible understanding of their needs, control over the business rules, and access to the sources available through beautiful data products, they can build the best solution for their business.
- **Aggregate and shared domains**: These are the domains that remain "halfway" between source- and consumer-oriented. They are using other source-oriented domains as the primary source of their data, and they are not intended to be directly used by consumers but to serve as common or more manageable input to other domains. Their role tends to be to aggregate data, implement complex business rules that would otherwise need to be implemented in many places, or a mix of both, such as calculating live or periodic metrics used across many areas. Examples include aggregating website visits into sessions or calculating the correct exchange rate or internal price to use in different situations. The approach suggested is to assign them to the team that owns the most complex rules that justify the domain's existence, as they are the ones who know both the rules and when and why they need to change to serve the business.

When the focus is more on aggregating or summarizing data than on implementing complex business rules, a good owner is the major user of the final data set. Once you have identified the domains you plan to split your platform into, it is the product thinking that will help you define the features and priorities of the data products that you will build.

When designing your domains, be customer-centric and err on the side of consumer ownership. Outside of source-centric domains, push ownership towards the consumers. They know their work, and they can build what they need better than others, given the resources, which often include data people and the source-centric domains provided by other teams.

Data products

Figuring out your domains and the teams that will own them provides an initial subdivision of the main features of your data platform. This is just the initial task. To build, run, and evolve your data platform, you need a cross-functional team to discover, design, and build what you need in the right way, so that the domains work well together and your teams are delighted.

Don't start thinking about months spent on detailed data modeling! To start, we need what John Giles calls a Data Town Plan, that is, an alignment tool using common data patterns to describe the business concepts that interact in the organization and must be implemented by the data products.

Cross-functional teams

Building the features that compose the domains in your platform is not just an execution exercise. It is as much a path of discovery as building what you have found along the way. Your destination is seldom known in advance, unlike a static address on a map. Often, you just have a general direction, some clearly understood needs, and many more unknowns. More like we need to find "a bookstore with historic books" or "a company with many cars to service". To get there, a map or a car alone won't be enough. You need a team that can incrementally find the right direction and identify what to do to get to the destination. This is what product teams have been doing for a long time.

By identifying the domains, you have moved ownership to the people working to build your data products, ensuring they have the attention and time of their customers. Next, you need to bring product thinking, which provides customer orientation to identify the right features to build, into their data engineering practice. With both in place, you figure out what you need and build it the right way.

Data product thinking

Appointing a product owner and engaging with customers is just a start; the whole mentality of the data platform must be product-oriented. Many organizations still run the development of their data platform as projects. This usually means volatile teams assembled for the specific project with limited resources and time. That is at odds with thinking of your data platform as a set of data products.

When you develop a product, you have a core team assigned to it in a stable way, with the resources to keep it running and the ability to evolve the product along the vision crafted together with the rest of the company. The team might grow and shrink over time as the need for new features or available resources changes, but until your product exists, there is a core team that keeps working on it and develops its vision.

Another important point is that data product ownership does not necessarily imply data source ownership. The owners might be different persons or teams, but for source-centric data products, they should be under the same umbrella that owns the domain and is responsible for both in front of the rest of the company. This is the only safe way to ensure that the two areas work willingly together and to provide a quick way to sort out priorities and the practical issues real life is made of.

Data product qualities

These days, there is a huge hype around data products, and many books and resources on the subject, so we will provide you with simple guidelines to help you understand whether you are going in the right direction, as a full discussion is beyond our scope. First and foremost, we suggest getting inspiration from successful software products you know. Code libraries and REST APIs are good examples of software products designed to interact with other components and make the lives of their users better and simpler. APIs have a lot in common with data products. Delivering data is usually an important part of their role. Think of what makes them good or bad when you are in doubt about your domains and data products.

Second, your domains should be easy to find. Ideally, you will have a catalog of your business concepts, mapping them to the domains and data products. To make them accessible, you should also provide:

- Discoverable documentation with the semantics of your entities and providing good examples of how to use them.
- Clear naming conventions or patterns for accessing the resources you provide, such as database and schema names, and naming patterns for key columns.
- Clear access controls, along with the process for obtaining access. Think what role, who, and how.
- Usability, make your domains easy to find, simple and trusted for their content.

Third, your products should be easy to use. Make them usable by all departments, providing:

- Data contracts, to ensure that column names and types do not change.
- API-like versioning, so that your product and the ones that depend on it can evolve independently without friction.
- Good data quality, both through strong test coverage of your models and by providing quality KPIs like error rates, availability, and performance.
- A test sandbox for your users to get familiar with your data product. You can provide a sample dbt project with source declarations, sample models, sample analyses, and anything else that would help your customers.
- KPIs to measure adoption and dependencies on your product.

Some points in the above list are directly connected to how you develop with dbt and Snowflake, while others are more organizational in nature. Building your domains as good data products is not just a data engineering endeavor. Another important piece of advice is to avoid the proliferation of toolchains and the duplication of effort in building data pipelines. This is a common risk when you distribute the ownership of the data platform components. Mandating by rule seldom works with skilled people. It is much better when they do things of their own will, because they are convinced it is a good way of working.

Provide them access to a common infrastructure and way of working that helps them without tying their hands. The Pragmatic Data Platform is a good candidate, as it provides simple, clear governance while offering freedom in many implementation choices. This minimizes duplication and maximizes interoperability at both the logical and code levels.

In the next section, we look at a very common problem that requires clear, explicit governance: the handling of Personally Identifiable Information (PII).

Handling Personably Identifiable Information (PII)

Data privacy regulations, such as GDPR, CCPA, and HIPAA, and general good privacy hygiene suggest that Personally Identifiable Information (PII) and Protected Health Information (PHI) should be handled with care and made accessible only to those who need them. For example, a production manager looking at a report does not need to know the names of people who returned products or were critical in product focus groups or reviews. He benefits from knowing if there are so many complaints to become concerned or the comments received, to pick up suggestions, but not the identities of the authors.

In this section, we emphasize the need to handle PII and sensitive data with care, providing a high-level framework for handling them appropriately for a Governance-level discussion.

Let's start with some best practices for managing PII:

- **Minimize PII collection**: Collect and store only the required PII. By default, store only an anonymized version. Store the original PII only if really needed.
- **Access control**: Keep the original PII segregated from the rest of the data and limit access to it for only required use cases.
- **Use masking and anonymization**: Protect the PII by storing and disclosing only safe derivatives when the actual PII is not strictly needed, or by working with aggregates.
- **PII lifecycle management**: PII should be stored only for the time specified in your policies, in accordance with the reasons for retaining it. Enable automated deletion when deadlines or deletion requests arrive.
- **Monitoring and auditing**: Know where your PII is available, and monitor and audit its use to detect potential unauthorized access or data breaches.
- **Education and awareness**: Educate team members about your policies and the importance of identifying and handling PII and other sensitive data with care.

Most of these best practices apply generally to all PII and sensitive data that any organization wants to protect, whether mandated by rules or internal policies. You can take selective hints from the following framework and the code in Chapter 10 to handle any type of data that requires additional security beyond standard access controls. Please do not forget that a few people need access to everything, and most only to a few data marts.

A pragmatic PII framework

How can we, in practice, follow the best practices we discussed above? Can we do it in a simple, pragmatic way? Yes, we can. It is not even that difficult, with the most difficult step often being recognizing PII in the incoming source data. Figure 9 shows the Pragmatic Data Platform PII handling framework.

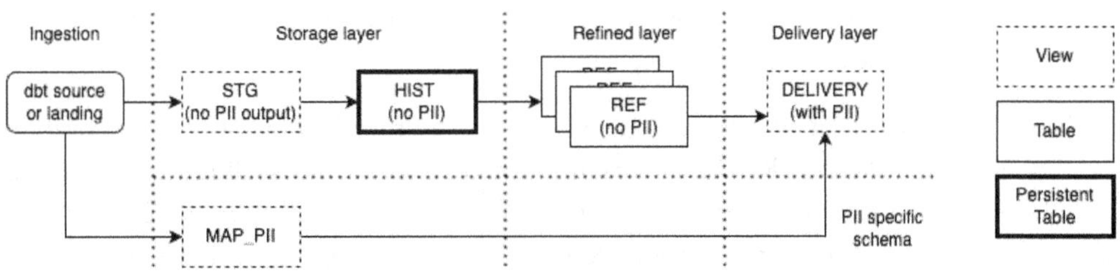

Figure 9: PII handling in the Pragmatic Data Platform.

The highest-level idea is to never store the actual PII in the tables of your "normal" data platform pipelines, shown in the upper part of the picture, so that they can live all eternity without any need for change due to PII. We want to keep the actual PII in only one place, usually the landing table or any other third-party table we read from, so that once we purge that place, the PII is no more.

To make the original PII available only in the selected locations where it is really needed, we create a view that maps the hashed PII to its readable form. It is possible to go back from the hash to the actual PII until the PII is in the source table. In the history tables and all derived tables in the refined and delivery layers, we will store a hashed version of the PII that we can keep there forever. Only the few delivery-layer models that need the PII will look up the hash and return the actual PII. Even then, only authorized users have access to the unmasked PII. For performance, the view can be replaced by a table that is re-created often enough for our needs, so that only the PIIs still in the source appear in the mapping table.

Building the mapping table is as simple as creating a second staging model that gets materialized in the correct segregated schema and contains both the actual PII and its hashed version, but only for the PII columns you really need in their original form. Do not add PII to the map until you need it in its original form somewhere. By keeping the PII in only one place, we have simplified our PII lifecycle management:

If we read from a third-party table, we delegate PII handling to that table. Once they purge the rows containing PII or anonymize it, we are fine, since our map table will no longer match the hashed version of the actual PII. If we read from our landing table, we have a single place to manage the PII lifecycle, with actions depending on the metadata we get from the source.

We close this section with a few practical suggestions to apply the best practices:

- **Minimize PII footprint**: Hash all PII in the STG tables; add to MAP_PII only the PII needed for the final reports.
- **Access control**: Keep the MAP_PII segregated; create specific versions of the data marts with and without PII; use data masking in data marts with a larger audience.
- **Masking and anonymization**: Whenever you provide the actual PII, add role-based masking in the database and BI tools, or create data marts with PII restricted to show the actual PII only to the people who need it.
- **PII lifecycle management**: Maintain only one copy of the PII to make it easy to manage.
- **Monitoring and auditing**: Catalog the data mart tables containing PII; analyze PII table usage and volume; create a KPI dashboard for PII use.
- **Education and awareness**: Have clear policies, keep them simple, and use them; consider PII work since the beginning to set aside the extra time needed.

We have gone through the GDPR introduction in the EU in 2017, and the best practices and governance setup of the Pragmatic Data Platform acknowledge the importance of managing PII, dispelling the notion that it must be difficult or complicated. While the more technical details can vary, we feel it is important that the compliance and privacy needs for PII and sensitive data are incorporated into the data platform governance from the outset.

Data flow across data projects

In this section, we discuss how data flows across data projects. The way environments are connected heavily influences the way teams work and their effectiveness.

The hell of legacy

Not long ago, teams were releasing to production every month or two. That was a slow tempo for releases! To develop features for which fast time-to-market was important, you could not wait for upstream dependencies to reach production and then start working on the finished dependency to develop your feature in your project. There was little choice but to live in the hell of working with unfinished, ever-changing work from DEV or TEST environments of upstream projects. Connecting dev to upstream dev, test to upstream test, and prod to upstream prod was needed to look ahead at what was being developed upstream, adapt to its changes, and be ready to take it into use as soon as possible after it was released. Working with bad data and changing code was not nice, but we had no real alternative to keep cross-project release times from exploding, so that was the default setup.

Welcome to modernity

Luckily for us, most teams have moved to more Agile ways of working, as we do in the Pragmatic Data Platform, releasing daily or at least weekly. Waiting for a few quick releases is no longer a big deal, so we can stop working on unfinished upstream features. Now we can wait until they are finished and released into production, without killing the overall time-to-market of cross-project features.

This reduces development time and cost by eliminating two major issues in the legacy setup: absorbing upstream code changes and release synchronization. Being able to wait for releases to go to production also means that, unless there are hard requirements to avoid it, we can finally work everywhere with the good data from production. This removes the third major issue: working with low-quality test data and poorly maintained intermediate environments.

Finally, in dev, we can already work on the same data that will flow through our pipelines in production. This means working with higher-quality data than in the past and being able to see the devil for what it is from the beginning. No more firefighting in PROD. By spending less time on each feature, the team can do more and with higher quality.

A modern general-purpose setup

Figure 10 on the next page illustrates our standard setup.

Each stage of our process now just depends on the PROD stage of the upstream project. Each project has a simple dependency on the upstream project, and all intermediate environments suddenly become private to each team. This reduces team workload, as they need to keep only PROD running to satisfy their dependencies, and they can even remove unnecessary environments. To highlight that the data project depends only on upstream production, the image shows the other environments of other projects in lighter gray, as we are not really interested in them.

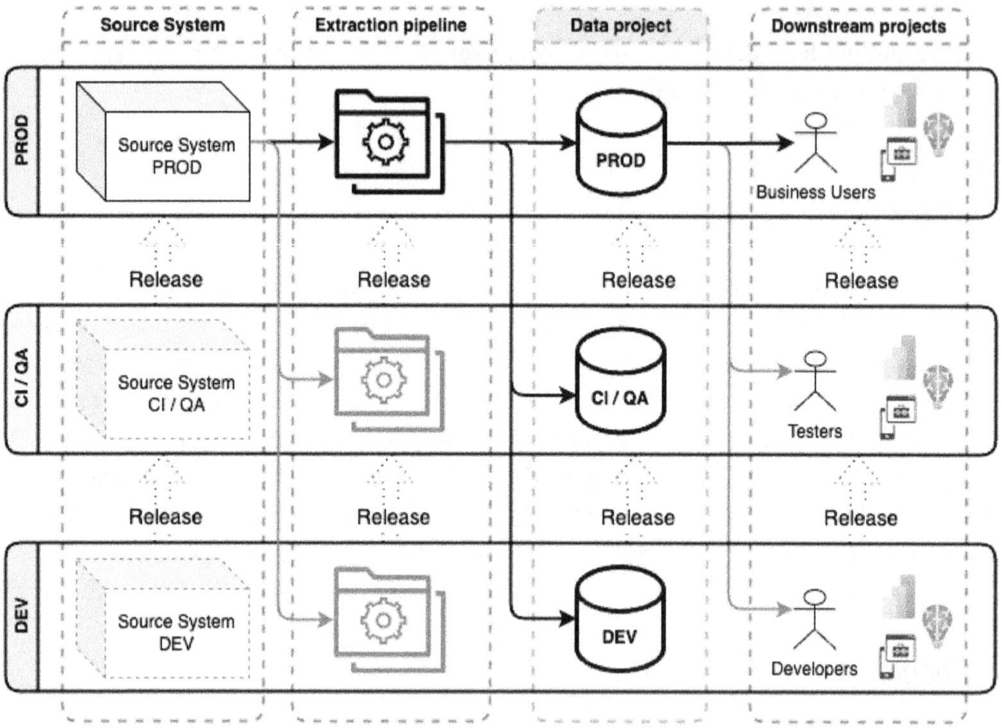

Figure 10: The Pragmatic Data Platform default cross-project setup.

This setup provides a scalable platform that can work in smaller organizations with few developers who seldom overlap their work, and in big ones with multiple people or multiple teams developing in parallel and releasing features as soon as they are ready. It will work equally well in a CI (continuous integration) or CD (continuous delivery) setup, assuming it is generally fine to release to production everything that has been released to CI/QA.

This PROD-only setup is so important and useful that, in dbt Cloud, you should label one environment as the "Production" environment. Doing so, the documentation and cross-project references, like those from dbt Mesh, will resolve against that PROD environment.

Handling special release needs

The assumption that we can release to PROD everything that has been released to CI/QA is generally valid, because eventually, you can always release code that is disabled or not (yet) in use in the production environment. When some features or larger changes take a long time to be released, it is impractical to restrict them to a single feature branch where only a single developer can work without hindrance, or to put all the changes in a place so that the feature/change is easily disabled.

In such cases, it makes sense to add a long-lived release candidate branch where the different lines of work for these features/changes can converge. At the same time, the other developments ready for production are merged into the CI/QA environment and then released to production. You can find more info about this topic in a series of articles we posted on our pragmatic-data.net blog.

Chapter review

This chapter has provided a comprehensive overview of data governance and its critical role in building a successful data platform. We've explored the five governance pillars and offered practical insights into key topics that require early, well-informed decisions. We have covered key topics like data mesh, handling PIIs, and data flow across projects, emphasizing that elements such as development environments, collaborative workflows, project scoping, and ownership are fundamental to the success of any data initiative. These factors extend beyond mere technical considerations into organizational structure and team politics, deeply impacting team performance, development velocity, and the ultimate value delivered to users and stakeholders.

In the next chapter, **Pragmatic Data Platform Way of Working**, we will delve into the practical application of these governance principles using dbt and Snowflake, guiding you through project organization, the release and deployment process, and the automation of database evolution with database migrations.

Recommended resources

Data Mesh and Data Products

- **How to Move Beyond a Monolithic Data Lake to a Distributed Data Mesh**, article by Zhamak Dehghani, the inventor of data mesh. https://martinfowler.com/articles/data-monolith-to-mesh.html#TheCurrentEnterpriseDataPlatformArchitecture.
- **A Guide to data Mesh**, e-book V2 by dbt Labs. A deep discussion of data mesh by dbt creators. Unsurprisingly, well aligned with our Pragmatic Data Platform way of thinking. Or the other way around. https://www.getdbt.com/resources/a-guide-to-dbt-mesh-download.
- **Products Over Projects**, an article by Sriram Narayan, deeply discusses working in product mode for software projects, but it resonates well for data products. https://martinfowler.com/articles/products-over-projects.html.

Domain driven design

- To get started on Domain Driven Design, look at the website by Eric Evans, its inventor, available at https://www.domainlanguage.com/ddd/.
- **Domain-Driven Design: Tackling Complexity in the Heart of Software**, by Eric Evans, published by Addison-Wesley Professional, ISBN 978-0321125217.
- **DDD Reference** is by Eric Evans, available as free PDF online at https://www.domainlanguage.com/ddd/reference/. Licensed under a Creative Commons Attribution 4.0 International License, available at http://creativecommons.org/licenses/by/4.0/.

Data flow across data projects

- **dbt Environments** is a 5-article series from the pragmatic-data.org blog that covers environment setup, branching strategies, and release management best practices. https://www.pragmatic-data.net/environtments-pt-1-the-hell-from-legacy/.

CHAPTER 4

Pragmatic Way of Working

This chapter dives into the heart of the Pragmatic Data Platform: how we work.

Effective governance is more than just rules; it's about shaping daily practices.

We'll explore the roles needed to read, write, and perform other actions, how code is tested, reviewed, and released to production, how to configure and name projects, and how to manage deployments across environments using Git branching strategies, building on the setup from Chapter 2. We will put this into practice by performing a full release from development to the intermediate and production environments using the sample project provided by dbt. We'll also cover essential maintenance operations performed through database migrations and address the less common but critical "extraordinary" operations that require elevated privileges. By the end of this chapter, you'll understand the complete workflow for building and maintaining a robust data platform. The topics that we are going to cover in this chapter are:

- Project Organization, Naming, and Configuration
- Deployment Strategies with Git Branches
- The Release Process: Walking through a full release cycle from development to production, including PRs, CI checks, and job execution.
- Database Change Management: schema evolution with Database Migrations.
- Extra-ordinary Platform Operations: Managing operations that require elevated privileges, such as setup tasks and user/role management.

Sample project and code

The sample dbt project is available at: **https://github.com/pragmatic-data/stonks**. The code samples for this chapter are in the sub-folder `chapter_04`, under the `code_samples_by_chapter` folder. Please note that for this chapter, the materials consist of diagrams and documentation. The data is under `chapter_09`.

Project organization and naming

A big initial topic for every project is how to organize and name its contents, from the project itself to the dbt models, along with all the intermediate structures like folders and databases. The main goals should be to make it easy for developers to find a model when they think about it and to allow meaningful deployment of tables and views into database schemas.

Project configuration

In dbt, a few project-level configurations are applied through the UI in dbt Cloud and through a mix of local git setup and values in the `profile.yml` file in dbt Core. These configurations are general in nature and pertain to the git code repository where the code for the project is stored, locally for dbt Core and configured with the UI for dbt Cloud, and the database connection details, telling what account, warehouse, database, schema, role, user credentials, and so on to use.

The general database connection details provide a starting point that can be overridden in full or in part for each environment. It also serves as the blueprint for every developer's connection, where the developer's own credentials are used to access the development environment. We have already seen in Chapter 2 how to connect dbt Cloud to our git repository, properly configure the DEV environment after creating the necessary objects in Snowflake, and create the QA and PROD environments. These steps are the only ones that differ between dbt Cloud and dbt Core. All other configurations in dbt are applied in the same way through code checked into your git repository.

General configurations in dbt are done through the `dbt_project.yml` YAML configuration file, while model-specific values are set in more specific YAML files, and these can be overridden by setting values with the `config()` JINJA function inside the model itself.

In Chapter 2, we already saw the `packages.yml` and `dbt_project.yml` files when we used the first to add the Snowflake Admin package to our project and the second to set the variables to configure it. The `dbt_project.yml` file is, in fact, the main configuration file that specifies the project's root folder and how to run the project. Besides the variables we added earlier, it also includes key project configurations such as name, version, and paths. For all the details, the dbt docs at **https://docs.getdbt.com/reference/dbt_project.yml** are the best and most up-to-date reference.

Let's set the name and version for our project by editing the top of the `dbt_project.yml` file, like in the following block of code:

```
name: 'stonks'
version: '0.1.0'
```

You can pick the name you want, but if you pick a different one you will need to adjust it whenever we use the project's name. A copy of this file, as of now, is in the chapter three folder in the book repo. In this chapter, we are not going to further change the path configurations (you might have added the `project_setup` folder to macro-paths in Chapter 2) or the target configuration. Still, we will add some general configurations for our models shortly.

While a few configurations must be applied through the `dbt_project.yml` file, most dbt object-level configurations can be applied in any `.yml` file, which can therefore be closer in place and/or name to the model, macro, or test it configures.

Configurations in the `dbt_project.yml` file are applied hierarchically, following the folder organization of our models, so that if you apply a configuration to a folder, all models inside it and its subfolders inherit that configuration, unless overridden at a more specific level, such as a subfolder or a specific model. Through this folder-based configuration inheritance, dbt code generation can be deeply integrated with your code's folder organization. By leveraging the folder structure, we can apply configurations with little effort to manage large parts of our project.

Folder naming and structure

For example, with a few simple configurations, we can specify how (materialization type) and where (database, schema) models are deployed based on the folder they are in. Broadly speaking, there are two major dimensions to evaluate in the context of organizing and naming folders and schemas in our projects:

- **The data source/domain**: How data is organized according to dimensions such as source system, geography, function, unit, or a combination of them.
- **Data refinement or model maturity**: The role and layer a model belongs to. The layers are storage, refined, and delivery (with individual data marts inside).

Our suggestion is to pick the one that is closer to how your teams and projects are organized as the primary dimension for organizing your models, and use the other as a sub-organization to complement how you want to deploy your code. For example, one potential organization would use data domains as the first dimension and refinement as the second, with folders like `domain01/storage` and `domain01/refined`, and, inside them, one folder for each concept we are going to manage.

Organizing deployment with custom schemas

In all but the smallest projects, the model organization in folders is also used to drive their deployment into database schemas. In dbt there are, in fact, two components that together generate the name of the schema where a model will be deployed:

- `target.schema` is the name specified as the deployment target in the mandatory `schema` configuration key in the environment for dbt Cloud and in the profile for dbt Core.
- `schema`, usually referred to as ***custom_schema***, is instead an optional configuration that further specifies the name of the schema a model must be deployed to.

By default, models are deployed in the `target.schema` defined in the environment or profile configuration. If a custom schema is provided (directly or through inheritance), the two are combined with the default result being as `<target.schema>_<custom_schema>`. For all the details, please see the dbt documentation at https://docs.getdbt.com/docs/build/custom-schemas.

In the Pragmatic Data Platform, we always use the custom schema to properly organize the models into deployment schemas, and we use the `dbt_project.yml` file to associate the custom schema configuration with the folders.

For example, looking at the configuration file in our new STONKS project, where we just have the models from the sample dbt project, we could configure the custom schema for the models in the example folder by adding the last line of the following block to the `dbt_project.yml` file.

```
models:
  stonks:
    example:
      +materialized: view
      +schema: example
```

In this code block we start with the first and second lines with `models:` and then `stonks:` as we want to configure dbt models in our "stonks" project (see the `name:` config at the top of the file), then we select the `example` folder and under it we provide two configurations: the first to materialize the models as views, and the second to create the models inside a schema with '`example`' as *custom_schema* value. If I set 'RZ' as the value of the (target) schema configuration in my credentials for the DEV environment, then the models will be deployed to a schema named RZ_EXAMPLE inside the (target) STONKS_DEV using my credentials.

In the Pragmatic Data Platform, we always use a custom schema, defined in the `dbt_project.yml` file. Therefore, the `target.schema` configuration entered in the environment/profile has the role of an environment-specific schema prefix, with all the schemas in one environment starting with the same `<target.schema>_`. The custom schema is the meaningful part of the full schema name.

Putting all these pieces together, we will organize the code in folders and subfolders with suitable names to make it easy for our people to find their way around and to attach a configuration to define the deployment of such models by hierarchically specifying and overriding the materialization and custom schema. You can find all the up-to-date details on model configurations in the dbt docs at https://docs.getdbt.com/reference/model-configs.

Deployment and git branches

In the previous section, we saw that we can decide where our models are deployed by combining the high-level environment configuration with the lower-level configuration provided in YAML or `config()` for folders or individual models. In this section, we will discuss which code should be used in each environment, as allowing a newer version of a model to replace an older one in a controlled way is a key feature of the release and deployment management part of Governance.

In dbt, we have two types of environments: one development environment (DEV) and any number of deployment environments (QA, PROD, and eventually more).

Development environment

You can configure only one development environment, but it is a special case: each developer gets a full environment, which is placed in the database configured for the development environment. Each developer, in principle, can create one copy of all schemas generated by the project, made unique for him using the `target.schema` value he had chosen when setting his credentials. Anyway, a developer seldom builds everything, and in general, development environments are quite sparse with respect to the entirety of the project, because a developer just builds/updates the few models around what he is developing, delegating (**defer to ...** button in the IDE) the rest to another full environment, QA or PROD, depending on the configuration. It is also a good practice to often clean up the development environment by dropping our own schemas, to concentrate on the work at hand and avoid working with an unpredictable mixture of old and new data and table definitions, built from different branches and at different times. That would bring more pain than value.

A key element of the dbt development environment is that each developer uses their own credentials, so they have access only to what is granted to their user, based on the roles and privileges assigned to their user. Another key feature of the development environment is that it is connected to the dbt Cloud IDE, so a developer can run or deploy in their DEV environment the code from any branch by selecting the desired branch in the IDE. This is extremely powerful, as it allows developers to easily switch between multiple branches over time to look at, preview, and build code from their development, other colleagues' work in progress, and pull requests to be validated. Cleanup is just a `drop schema` away.

Deployment environments

Development environments exist to provide developers with a sandbox that can be quickly deployed and reset to quickly evaluate any piece of code in a project, with little effort and without disrupting other project environments and the work of colleagues. Deployment environments are durable environments you carefully deploy and manage to perform a specific role. In a dbt project, you can create as many deployment environments as you wish, with one, two, or three being the most common cases.

In Chapter 2, we have created the QA environment and associated it with the `main` branch, and the PROD environment and associated with the `PROD` branch. This is the most common situation and our default setup. Please note that in the "git flow" process, the development branch is named `develop`, and the production branch is named `main`, while we use `main` and `PROD`, respectively. To use the git flow convention in dbt, you need to change your QA environment to use the `develop` branch and `main` (or an empty name) for the PROD environment. We preferred to use the branch names in a way that minimizes the dbt configuration.

A more complex setup involves creating another deployment environment to accumulate features developed for a future release. This extra environment is often called a "release candidate," as it is used to accumulate features that need to be integrated and tested together, but cannot be released immediately. They are candidate for a future release, usually waiting for something to be released in upstream projects before we can release our code.

Figure 11 illustrates how branches are created, worked on in the IDE using the DEV environment (boxes with colored backgrounds), and merged into the relevant branch. It is important to note that opening a feature branch from the CR branch and merging back to the CR branch are more advanced operations, as you need to perform a couple of actions in your git provider, rather than following the usual dbt-guided git process.

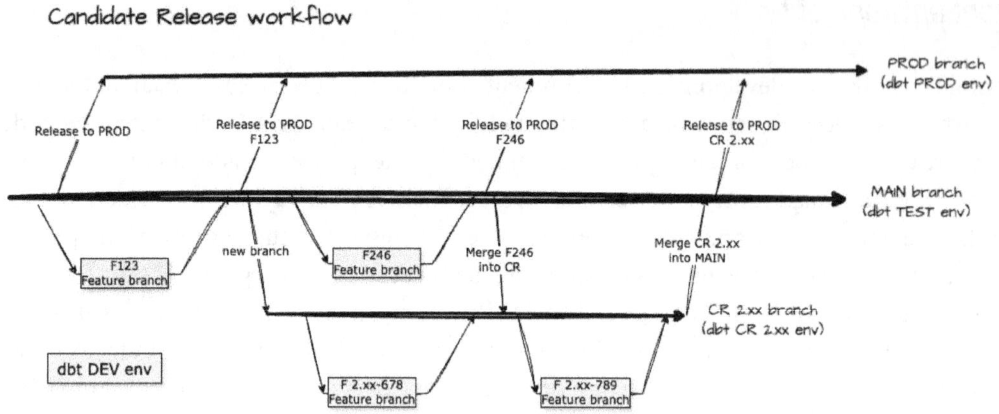

Figure 11: The branching strategy when using a release candidate branch.

When working with long-lived branches, such as Candidate Release branches, it is extremely important to keep them up to date with the development and patches released in the main branch.
Constant updates to the CR branches to keep up with the live project are the only way to avoid painful, last-minute catch-up work that could easily take longer than expected.
You can easily do this by merging the main branch into the long-lived branches, as shown in the image with the merge from main to CR labelled "Merge F246 into CR".

It is beyond the scope of this book to get into these details, also because if an organization finds itself in need of such an advanced process, it should have, or procure by hiring consultants, the competence to work with GIT beyond the basics. Now that we know how to pick which code to release and where it must be released, it is time to try out the release process using the sample project graciously provided by default when we initialize an empty repository.

The release process

This section describes the normal release process from development to production via the intermediate QA environment, using the sample dbt project and the environments we created in the previous chapter as examples. We will also complete creating the base jobs we want in our normal Pragmatic Data Platform setup.

The core of this process is code promotion across branches via Git-based Pull Requests and deployment automation via dbt jobs. To help you get familiar with the development and release process to QA and PROD, this section walks through the steps to release your code. We will run the sample dbt project in DEV and notice that it produces errors, so not all models are built. We will fix the models and note that if we had not built the project in DEV, we would have recognized errors only after the merge, leaving QA broken until the next release.

We will therefore add a CI job between DEV and QA, make some changes, open a new PR to QA, and see that it catches errors before they are merged into QA. We will fix the errors, commit, see that the CI is now green, and we can finally merge into QA and run the **QA – Build all** job that we created in Chapter 2 to deploy our code in the QA environment. We will then open a PR from main (QA) to PROD to release to production, and once merged, we will run the **PROD – Build all** job to deploy the code.

We added a bit of drama to the above process so you can see why we have it, but hopefully, most of the time, you will just open and merge a PR to main and run the job in QA. Then, when the feature is done, and you want to release one or more features, you will open a PR to PROD, and merge and run the job in PROD.

Building the sample project in your DEV environment

In this first practical step of the section, we will build the sample dbt project in DEV, identify an issue, and fix it. Let's get to a clean start. If you have made changes or deleted the sample project, you can find the code in its initial state under the folder `code_samples_by_chapter/chapter_03/sample_project/models/example__v1`. Let's also start with a clean branch, so commit everything you have changed to the branch you are in, then change the branch back to `main`. Create a new branch named `ch03-release-process`, and make sure you have the code for the sample project in place as it was initially. The important thing is that in the `my_first_dbt_model.sql` model, you have lines 14 to 16 that look like this:

```
    select 1 as id
    union all
    select null as id
```

Line 27 that is commented out, like in the code below:

```
-- where id is not null
```

And under the YAML file `schema.yml` you have the not null test enabled, with lines 10 to 12 looking like in the code box below:

```
  tests:
    – unique
    – not_null
```

To ensure your setup is as intended, build the project in your DEV environment, running the following command in dbt Cloud IDE command line:

```
dbt build
```

Upon execution, you will get the `not_null_my_first_dbt_model_id` error, with two steps executed correctly and three steps skipped. The result is that the table `my_first_dbt_model` has been created in your personal DEV environment, but the view `my_second_dbt_model` has not been created, as its model was skipped due to errors in an upstream dependency. Check it in Snowflake.

The reason to have a DEV environment is to build your work, verify that it works as expected, and keep fixing it until it does. Before committing, you want to be sure that your code is correct and ready to go to main. Sometimes, when you are working with a lot of models and there are a bunch of interconnected changes, or if you must leave a work half-done for a while, it is fine to make one or more work-in-progress commits to save where you are. It is a good practice to clearly label them as such, perhaps starting with "WIP—...".

For sure, before opening a PR and trying to release to main, you want to be sure that your code is working properly and does not produce errors. Anyway, we are all humans, so it happens —more often than we would like to admit— that, for one reason or another, code is committed to the repo and merged without being thoroughly built and tested.

It is bad and if we commit the code as it is now and then open a PR to merge it into main, the release process would just work. Then the QA environment would error when the model `my_first_dbt_model` is built, and skip building its dependencies.

Continuous Integration in dbt Cloud is here to help, so in the next step, we will add a CI job to our QA environment to avoid such a situation. For now, let's fix our code by uncommenting line 27 of the model `my_first_dbt_model`, making it look like the following:

```
where id is not null
```

Save the change and build again the project in DEV (with the `dbt build` command). Now everything should be fine, and you should have six green objects in the result panel. It is a good time to commit the code to the `ch03-release-process` branch, or whatever the name of the branch you are working in. Before opening a PR to release to main (our branch for the QA environment), we will add a CI job to the QA environment so we can see how it works when we open the PR.

Creation of a CI job

A CI job protects the environment it is attached to by building the code of any PR opened towards the target branch of that environment. The code is built into a temporary environment created for each new PR, with updates to the same PR being rebuilt in the same PR-specific temporary environment.

To create a new CI job for QA, follow these steps: In the **Deploy** menu, click the **Jobs** entry. Open the drop-down on the **Create job** button (in the top right side) and select **Continuous integration job** (notice the explanation "Run on pull-requests from git"). You will find yourself on the CI job page.

Under **Job settings**, enter a **job name** like `QA - CI job`. Select `QA` as **Environment**. Under **Git trigger**, leave the **Triggered by pull requests** switch active. Under **Execution Settings**, leave **Linting** and **dbt compare** off for now. Leave the command list unchanged with the command `dbt build --select state:modified+`. Change to QA the **Compare changes against an environment (Deferral)** drop-down. Under **Advanced Settings,** it is worth mentioning that you can chose a **target name** for the CI job execution, so that you could use it in some conditionals to do something different in CI, like using less data, the maximum number of **parallel threads** that dbt will ty to use and the version of dbt to use and a few other interesting options typically associated with environments. Once you have done your changes, save the CI, and we are almost done.

We have left the `--select state:modified+` code in the command run by the CI job. This means we are trying to run a "slim CI," a CI process that just tries out the models that have changed with respect to the target environment. To do that, dbt Cloud needs metadata about the contents of the environment. The model metadata is gathered when running normal **Deploy jobs.**

If you have never run the `QA - Build all` job, then you will get a notice "**QA has no runs to compare against. ...**" on a yellow background. By clicking the "**run a deploy job in that environment**" section of the notice, you will be taken to the QA environment page, where you can click the QA – Build all job, then, once inside its page, click the **Run now** button on the top right of the page. This will run the code already in the `main` branch and create the necessary metadata for dbt.

When your releases to QA are infrequent, a dedicated job to generate the metadata is created and run daily (or before opening a PR) with the simple command `dbt compile`. The goal of such a job is only to generate metadata so dbt Cloud knows which code is in the target branch of the QA environment before you try to merge any PRs. Such a job could have a name like `QA - Refresh metadata`.

Now that we have created a CI job and provided the baseline metadata, we are ready to open our first PR to promote our code from DEV to QA.

Releasing to the QA environment

In this step, we will make the first release to QA using the sample dbt project. Your dbt Cloud IDE should be in the `ch03-release-process` branch, and we have just committed the changes we want to push to QA, so we are ready to open a PR. After the last commit, the button in the Version control area should say "Create a pull request on GitHub." This is what we are looking for, so let's click the button.

A new page in your browser will open in GitHub (or the version control you are using) at the page to create a new **Pull Request** (**PR**) from the branch you had open in the IDE to the main branch (or whatever custom branch you have designated for your DEV environment).

The content will differ across git providers, but generally includes a list of commits since the two branches diverged and the changes to the files introduced by those commits. This helps you remember what was done and check that this is what you want to merge. Click the **Create pull request** button in GitHub, and you will be taken to a page to enter the title and description of the PR you are creating.

The title is usually concise and high-level, like "Release of sample dbt project," while the description is more detailed, listing the changes made and any needed caveats or breaking changes that the reviewer and/or the person merging the PR should know. It is common to use bullet points when there are multiple changes. For example, if a PR has changed the name of a model that was already released (exists in QA or PROD with the old name), it should list it and make it clear if a database migration to drop the old table is included in the release or not. We will discuss database migrations later in this chapter.

Enter something like `Fixed my_first_dbt_model by filtering out null IDs`, and once done, click the **Create pull request** button. Upon clicking, you will be taken to the PR discussion page, where there is also a box listing checks to be performed before allowing the PR to be merged. While initially green, after a few seconds this area will change to grey with a brown circle and the text **some checks haven't completed yet** as shown in Figure 12.

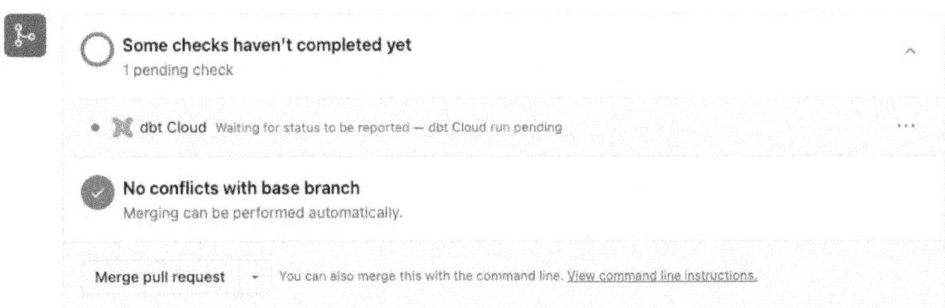

Figure 12: GitHub Pull Request – Check in progress.

While the checks are in progress, or after they finish, you can click the three dots on the dbt Cloud line and select **View details** to see the execution in dbt Cloud. Or the details of it once it is completed. If all checks go well, after less than a minute, the check area should return to green and look like the following image. Please **do not click** the **Merge pull request** button yet.

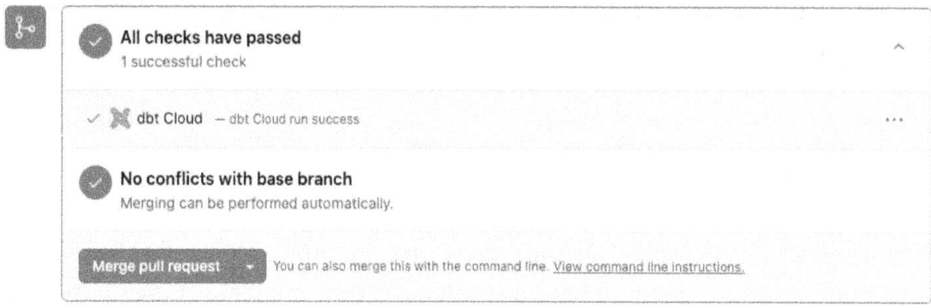

Figure 13: GitHub Pull Request – Checks done with success.

If you want to check what was done, how long it took, or similar, without using the three dots in the dbt row, you can always go to dbt Cloud, pick the Run history element from the Deploy menu, and you will find yourself on a page with all dbt runs. You should find a green run for the job `QA - CI job` that we created earlier. Figure 14 shows an example of such a job. Click it to inspect what was done in the job.

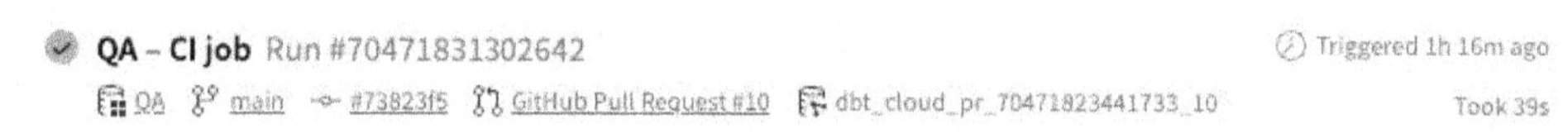

Figure 14: Example of a run result for the QA—CI job in dbt Cloud.

Looking at the result, you can see the target env you are merging towards (QA), the branch connected to it, the hash of the commit being tested, the PR connected to this CI run and the (target) schema used for this run (playing the role of schema prefix, as we discussed in a tip earlier in this chapter).

Clicking this job recap row and opening the details shows the actions taken and commands run during the job. It's worth noting that when you open the **Create profile...** step of the job, you will find a note that the connection schema was overridden to a value specific to this PR. Let's double-check what was done on the Snowflake side. Log in to your Snowflake account, and in the database object browser (on the left), open the database for the QA environment. You should see a schema whose name starts with DBT_CLOUD_PR, as in the first schema in Figure 15.

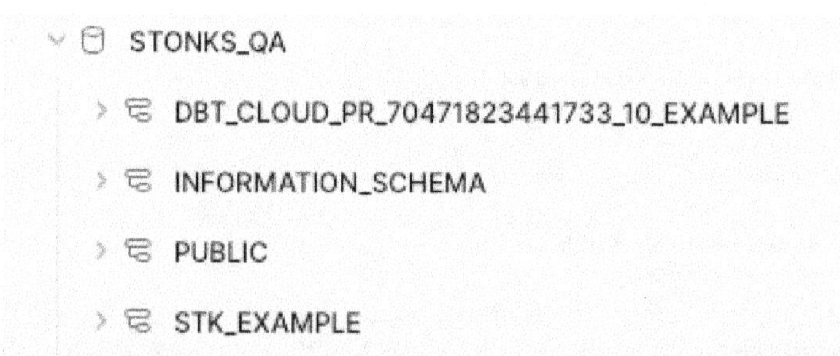

Figure 15: Snowflake—PR schema for CI job.

As you can see from the previous image from Snowflake, you should have both one schema with the name starting with the (target) schema used for this CI run and one with the (target) schema used for the QA environment, `STK` in our case. Both of these schemas end with the custom schema name `EXAMPLE` that we have set earlier for the example folder in the `dbt_project.yml` file.

If you wonder why we entered `example` in the `dbt_project.yml` file and we get `EXAMPLE` in the schema name, please note that Snowflake is case-insensitive for object names, unless you double quote them, and shows them in uppercase. Please never double quote names in Snowflake unless you are forced to. This goes against common practice, and it will be painful to always double-quote names and spell them with the exact uppercase and lowercase combinations. Don't do it!

Now that the PR checks are done, all is green, and we have verified what the CI job has done, it is time to solicit your colleagues' comments on the PR contents. If you have not added any reviewers during the creation of the PR, it is time to do so now. Once you have received the desired feedback, implemented eventual changes, committed the code, and verified that the last run of the CI job with such changes is still green, it is time to merge the PR, verify that the temporary CI schema is gone, and finally run again the `QA - Build all` job to immediately deploy to QA the latest code.

Go back to GitHub and click on the **Merge pull request** button. Improve or just confirm the proposed commit message with the **Confirm merge** button. You will get a confirmation that the merge is complete and a button to delete the now-obsolete feature branch you just merged. Click the **Delete branch** button.

Cool! Now the code from the PR is in the `main` branch and we can finally deploy it with the `QA - Build all` job. Go to dbt Cloud and click the **Jobs** entry from the **Deploy** menu. Click on the `QA - Build all` job, and in the detail page, click the **Run now** button. A new job recap row is added for this run, and you can click it to see the execution progress in 30-second intervals.

You can then move to the Snowflake UI and -after refreshing the database list- observe two things: first, the temporary schema for the CI job run in the QA database has been dropped once the PR has been merged. Second, the real QA schema for the example folder, `STK_EXAMPLE`, will contain the newly released version of the models once the `QA - Build all` job terminates without errors.

Now that the code has been merged into `main`, released to QA, and the old branch deleted, let's go to the `main` branch in the dbt Cloud IDE. Under **Version control**, open the drop-down on the button, select the **Change branch** entry, pick `main` as the branch, and click **Checkout**. Now that IDE is back to the `main` branch, click the **Version control** button that says **Pull from remote**. Doing this, we update the selected (local) branch of the IDE with the content of the same (remote) branch on the GIT server. Now also local `main` contains the new code we just merged from the feature branch. Our IDE is now almost up-to-speed with the GIT server, but it still has the local feature branch. To get rid of it, select **Prune branches** from the **Version control** button drop-down and then click **Continue**. We have now completed our release of a feature branch into the QA environment, merging the new code into the `main` branch of our GIT repository (server), and updating the local branches in our IDE.

This release process might seem long to you when reading each tiny action. Still, it is not in its essence, and it is quite quick to perform in day-to-day operations: open a PR, wait for checks to pass, gather feedback from colleagues, then merge and eventually run the deploy job, or let it run for its next scheduled run. In this run-through, we have explored many details that you normally do not pay much attention to, as they just go by with standard results, but we needed to make you aware of them.

Please note that the longest and most important part of this process is soliciting feedback from your colleagues on the code you are proposing to merge. This will have two major benefits. The first major benefit is that your colleagues will usually provide suggestions to make your code clearer for everyone to work with in the future, and sometimes will also find potential issues in the code (bonus goal). The second major benefit is that colleagues will be updated on the project's new content and current status, so what is being done is not just in your head. We are breaking knowledge silos apart.

> *People in great teams value PR benefits and prioritize this "community service," reacting promptly to PRs.*

Releasing from QA to PROD environments

In the previous section, we made our first release from a feature branch to master, the default branch connected to the QA environment. After a successful automated CI run, we have merged our code into master and run the QA job to do a full QA build. This is the same job that is scheduled to run daily to refresh all models. We also confirmed that the changes have been deployed to Snowflake. Now we have a mixed business and technical question: Should we release the last change to production right after releasing to QA?

For the business, it is usually great to get the latest changes, whether they are a fix or a new feature, unless they disrupt current reports or require special validation that can only be done in the QA environment. For technology, it is also better to get the latest changes ASAP, because smaller releases are less risky and can be fixed more quickly if anything goes wrong. The only reasons to wait would be the same for business and technology: breaking changes or extra validation needs beyond the usual automated testing from development and CI process. While it is better and we advocate for releasing small and often, it is not expected that releases to production match 1:1 those to QA. Still, the closer you are, the easier your job. Here, we will assume we are good to go to production, as is usually the case, and we will start our release shortly. In the following section, we will look at what to do if you are not going to release immediately.

Do you need more checks before releasing to prod?

Before getting started with the release to PROD, we need to make another decision: Are the tests done during development and the CI checks before merging into QA enough?

The question makes sense because we might put another CI process between QA and PROD, or automatically trigger a PROD run whenever we merge to PROD. Why do that? Because by running a CI process on top of PROD or running PROD itself, we would see errors immediately and not wait for the next scheduled run, often in the middle of the night. This would give us a chance to immediately fix issues before they reach PROD with the CI run, and on top of PROD with the merge job. These extra checks are useful, but they add time, costs, and complexity. They make sense if we believe that the checks that we already have in place are not enough, or we are happy to pay for double-checking.

By the way, enough for what? Enough to guarantee that production will continue to work without disruptions. How much is enough depends on the individual case, but in general, my feeling is that if you have good tests in your project and you are using production data in your QA environment, you should be fine to go to production without an extra CI job. Of course, if you have hundreds of people using your systems, and an error or older data in a few tables is not acceptable, or the consequences are very expensive, then it's better to add another layer of checks. You configure it the same way we have added a CI job to the QA environment, but adding it to the PROD environment. Please consider that a Merge job is more useful than a CI job if you are building something like a package, so you are running the project to validate it with some test data, or when you want to always have the data in your PROD environment immediately aligned with the latest version of the code, independently of the time of its release. In this matter, consider that in some cases, changes to reports during the day are not desirable.

Releasing to production

Now that we have decided to release to production, we will release everything that has been released to QA. This is done on purpose, to keep QA and PROD closely aligned. It is the only way to have a reliable QA environment, that is, a QA environment that intercepts issues effectively. It is also a very easy process for people who are not GIT gurus, as is common in the SQL developer community. This way, the project stays manageable and under control by the people running it.

If you need some of the features being developed not to go to PROD right away, you should NOT merge them to QA (main) and instead create a candidate release branch or another long-running branch to accumulate these features "for future release". Create an environment for it to build the code and check the data, as we discussed in the "Deployment environments" section earlier in this chapter.

The release process to production will again be a simple PR, this time from the `main` branch, representing the QA environment, to the `PROD` branch, representing the PROD environment. Please note that if you have not yet created the PROD branch when creating the PROD environment, just creating the PROD branch from the current main is equivalent to creating a PR and merging it.

If you have already created the PROD branch, follow these steps to do the release: go to the Pull Request page of your GIT provider and create a new Pull Request. Select the `PROD` branch as your target and the `main` branch as the source. Provide a title and description for the PR. Confirm the creation of the PR. We suggest always using "Release to PROD" as the title, with the list of features and fixes released in the description. This makes it very easy to see when a release has occurred in PROD. Also, add any special commands that need to be executed before or after the release, especially if they are not handled automatically by migrations. It's good to document what needs to be done.

If you have created a CI job, wait for it to complete correctly, or iterate by fixing and releasing to `main` until you fix it. If your process requires approval, the PR format is ideal, as you can add the necessary reviewers to confirm the release is ready to go to PROD. Once all is good, do the actual merge, and your code is now in production. If you have added the Merge job, it will start automatically upon merge. If you have not added it, starting the `PROD - Build all` job might be the next step if you want to immediately update the views and tables in PROD.

Great! You are done with your first release to PROD: just open a PR, wait for some checks, then click the merge button. Easy enough?

What if your release to production is blocked?

Now we have seen the sunny path: your development is complete, all necessary checks are complete, you are not breaking downstream clients, and the feature can go to production. It seems like an obstacle run, but luckily, the happy path happens most of the time. The other times, when you cannot release to production, are usually for one of these reasons:

- **Breaking changes**: Releasing your code would break something downstream in the dependency graph. This could be a report or some pipeline. If you are confident that the dependency can be fixed quickly because the same team controls it, or that it is ready to adapt to your changes, you can release or wait a short time to prepare the adaptation before releasing to prod. You might even keep the feature on its feature branch a bit longer to avoid blocking the release from QA to PROD. In general, the best way to handle breaking changes is through model versioning. You can look it up in the dbt docs, and we will get back to it when we talk about the delivery layer. It does not make a lot of sense for a single feature, but if it is coupled with the need for long-running extra validation or other actions, creating a release candidate branch and environment would satisfy both needs. If you have already released it in QA, check the suggestion under "Missing dependencies" on how to isolate and sterilize those changes.
- **Extra validation**: It is not uncommon that, for some deep changes or big features, extensive validation is required, maybe with the help of business, and that a stable version of reporting needs to be set up based on the new code. In this case, **if the validation is going to be quick** and you can keep QA blocked for that short time, the best solution is to use QA for the validation, keeping merges to QA on hold. A no-op is very efficient but has its own downsides. This is the typical case when a **release candidate** (**RC**) branch makes sense. Instead of merging the feature branches related to the big feature into QA for validation, you create a long-running branch that merges these branches and their fixes. By creating a dbt Cloud environment for this RC branch, you can deploy it. It is usually a good idea to have it in the same DB as the QA environment, with a different prefix. If the changes are limited to the delivery layer, where model versioning is always a good practice, then releasing the changes as a new version (without an RC branch) is an appropriate strategy. All clients will keep using the old version, which is still considered the current one. The only caveat is that it must be acceptable to deploy the new version to production before the end of validation.
- **Missing dependencies**: This is a common issue when working with non-production data in lower environments, and it should not occur if you use the same production sources across all environments. The problem is that if your sources in QA and PROD are not the same (or synchronized at the table and column level), you can develop your code in DEV and maybe even release it in QA, but if you would release it to PROD where a new table or column is missing or some name/type is different, then your code will not work in production, and the broken models' dependencies will not be refreshed. Avoiding release synchronization is the best reason to work with production data in all environments, but if you must work with non-production data, or sometimes look ahead to features not yet in production in your sources, you must deal with this case. The simplest way is to treat the non-production source as a different source and keep development using that source separated from development based on production sources. By isolating that code in a folder, you can put it into a private group and disable it outside of DEV (and eventually QA). In this way, you can keep releasing normally everything into production, even if you have code in your "non-prod" folder that depends on sources not yet in production. This works because such code will be disabled in the PROD environment.

The complete treatment of all complex cases you might run into is beyond the scope of this book, but you can start by looking at our blog for related articles and the dbt documentation and blog for the latest features and suggestions. We hope that, with the three solutions we quickly discussed here (model versioning, release candidate branches, and selective model enablement), we have given you good inspiration for designing an appropriate solution to your specific needs.

Database change management

In the previous sections, we have seen the workflow for the normal operations of your data platform: you develop models, test them, deploy to QA via CI, and then release to production. Nice and easy.

During deployment, the boilerplate for deploying your models is handled by dbt. Anyway, without special effects, your dbt models are limited to creating views and tables. All the views and most of the tables are recreated from scratch at every run, transforming data stored in a few permanent tables. Recreating objects from scratch makes handling ***schema*** changes for these ephemeral objects easy, as at every run, the view or table is created according to the current code.

Permanent storage in dbt occurs in incremental tables, which store content from one invocation to the next, like the History tables that we will introduce in Part 2 of the book. The evolution of the ***schema*** for incremental tables requires active management and is beyond dbt's capabilities.

*The word **schema** is way too overloaded in data engineering, and its meaning changes based on the object it refers to.*

Before we move on, let's try to give a quick clarification. For a table, view, or file, schema means its shape, that is, the column names and data types. For a database, a database schema is an organizational element used to divide it, like a folder for a file system. Database schemas form the second element of a fully qualified name, which has the form `<database>.<schema>.<table>`. In more general terms, a schema can refer to the set of tables and views, and their content, related to the subject of the discussion, like a data model, an application, or a database.

Evolution of incremental table

You have two ways to handle incremental table evolution: if the input and code allow you to recreate all the contents from scratch, you can request dbt to drop and recreate the table with the new schema by performing a full refresh, basically handling them as non-permanent tables. While this is done by dbt, it is not part of the normal run to build the models and must be explicitly asked for by you with a command like the following:

```
dbt build -s <model_name> -full-refresh
```

It is important to think well before doing this, because it can cause permanent data loss. That is why in many dbt projects, full refreshes are banned and that is enforced by the project configuration.

If you do not recreate the table from scratch, either to keep some data you cannot recreate or to avoid altering the loading metadata, you need to manually carve and execute the SQL commands to evolve your table. Incremental table evolution is an example of a maintenance operation that we will see next.

Common maintenance operations

The **run-operation command** is used to invoke a macro that executes general-purpose SQL commands that do not belong in dbt models. We have already used this command in the second chapter to run the macro that generates and executes the SQL to perform the setup. In that context, we have used the run-operation to perform extraordinary operations that require special privileges. The macro had to explicitly generate the SQL to switch to the required role to perform the operation, and we needed to call run-operation with a user that could impersonate the required roles.

To perform the common maintenance operations to keep your platform working, we use the same `run-operation` command, but as part of the normal deployment jobs. This means it will be executed by the same role that builds the models, and we cannot assume any special permissions beyond those granted to the dbt executor role. We must, therefore, limit our code to operations that can be performed with the user and role used by dbt in every environment. Governance at work. If you need to run extraordinary operations, such as the setup in Chapter 2, you can use the same ideas we will see here. Still, you should keep those macros separate from the common maintenance operations we will write as database migrations.

We will handle common maintenance operations, which are normal in any project and happen quite frequently, with database migrations. Their SQL is not part of the model execution, but must be part of the release process. In the next section, we will see how database migrations make this possible. Before going to see how to do them, let's have a look at common operations:

- **Dropping tables**, usually because you renamed your model after it was already released to QA or PROD. Dbt will never drop tables by itself, as they might contain useful data or still be in use outside of dbt.
- **Renaming or altering permanent tables** to add or remove columns. This is a common operation that needs our intervention only to evolve incremental models.
- **Full refresh of incremental tables**. It is the preferred way to recreate the data and/or schema of incremental tables from scratch. No need to write any SQL. Unfortunately, it is usually available only in the initial phases of a new project.
- **Handling grants** on platforms that don't support the dbt grant feature, like Fabric.
  This is better performed with the post-hook functionality if you need different grants for individual models, while it makes sense as a run-operation if you manage grants by full schemas.
- **Creating database objects** besides views and tables, like file formats and stages.
  A run operation with code generated by a macro is a powerful way to manage your platform, and you can also perform ingestion and export from and to files.
- **Performing bulk data operations.** While usually we do not want to alter any data, there are good situations when you want to run bulk operations, like re-hashing a table.

The general rule is that everything that can be done through SQL with the privileges of the role used by dbt, but does not fit into a model, can be written as a migration and deployed through a `run-operation` dbt command. Another common way to run generic SQL code is the `pre-hook` and `post-hook` functionalities of dbt, but their use is intended to execute SQL tightly connected to the specific model being run, not for general operations. The `run-operation` command is more general, as it can be invoked outside a dbt run or build, but on the other hand, it cannot execute SQL specifically related to the execution of a model.

Automating the maintenance operations

You might wonder: if you have to manually create the SQL, why not also apply it manually? The short answer is to avoid misalignment between environments. The way we have set up our governance, purposely, allows developers to run SQL commands manually only in their DEV environment. In higher environments, they need to run them through dbt automation, executing code that has been properly released. This is the only way to ensure that only vetted code is executed and that the environments stay aligned with the code in the repository and with each other.

The operations exemplified in the previous section can all be performed by writing simple SQL statements, such as drop table, alter table, and similar commands. We have also seen that developers should be allowed to run such SQL in their development environment, but not in higher environments like QA and PROD. When a resource is published in a shared environment, it becomes part of your data platform's public API. From this point onward, you must explicitly manage its evolution and eventual deletion. You also need to guarantee its alignment across environments and release its changes in sync with the code that expects it to be in a specific state, in each environment.

By creating SQL commands for changes in dbt macros and automatically executing them in the desired order, we will create an easy-to-use system to apply all the changes you need through simple SQL.

Database migrations

In our context of database evolution, a **database migration** is a set of SQL commands that, when applied, take your database from one (implicit) version to another. It is a discrete step forward from one database state to another. The consequence is that some part of the code that worked before might no longer work, and/or that part of the new code will not work with the previous version. This concept is widely used in application development, where the database must stay strictly in sync with the application code, and database changes are small, discrete, and always associated with specific application releases and versions. Database migrations are sometimes referred to as schema migrations to clarify the distinction from "full" database migrations, which are projects to move both data and schemas from one database to another. This latter meaning is not what we are after in dbt projects.

Many tools and frameworks exist to support database change management, and some, like Flyway, Liquibase, and Sqitch, are sometimes used alongside dbt Core.

In data warehousing, the database is constantly changing due to the code we run, but we still need to keep it synchronized with the code. When working with dbt, the tool takes care of most changes, but not all. Migrations are a simple and efficient way to apply the changes that dbt will not run on its own. We will show you how to handle database migrations only with core dbt functionalities, synchronizing the execution of your SQL commands with your code. We use a process inspired by Flyway, including the naming of the database migrations we will write. The working principle of our migrations is very simple: they are code, and they get released together with the rest of your code, so they are naturally synchronized with it. When the code looking for a new column or a different table name is released to QA, the migration that makes that change, being part of the same branch, is released together.

By keeping your code changes together with the migrations that perform the required alignment, the synchronization is automatic. To ensure that the migrations are applied before the newly released code hits the old version of the database artifacts, we will place the migration step as the first step in the jobs that perform the code deployment.

Idempotent database migrations

To allow us to release and run the jobs without having to babysit the migrations, we will write the migrations to be idempotent; that is, we can execute them an indefinite number of times and the result is always the same, without errors. Most SQL commands in Snowflake have the `IF EXISTS`, `IF NOT EXISTS,` and `CREATE OR REPLACE` options. This makes it quite simple to write SQL code that can be replayed any number of times without problems. When this is not the case, we can create helper macros that perform the same function by querying the database's information schema.

Please be aware that, even when using the `IF EXISTS` option, you will get an error from your SQL command if the schema that you are looking up the database object in does not exist. In general, you should be sure that the schema exists. If not, protect against it by using a macro like the `column_exists` macro we will see later. Being idempotent, a migration can stay active in master or any long-lived branch until it has been released and executed in all upper environments, including production. Once you are sure a migration has been applied everywhere, you will deactivate it, but it will remain in your repo to document what has been executed in the environments.

Writing database migrations

Putting together all the info from the previous sections, you have probably already figured out that we will write database migrations as dbt macros that will contain or generate the SQL commands to perform the required database operations. One key design principle is to keep separate the macro that contains or generates the SQL code, the core of a migration, from the helper macro that runs the generated code. To see firsthand how simple it is to write migrations, let's look at a couple of examples, focusing on the macro that generates the SQL commands.

The first example is the typical migration to clean up tables or views with old names, which is needed when we rename a model that has already been released beyond DEV. Create a file with the `V001_drop_example_table.sql` name in the folder where you have decided to keep the migrations with the following code inside:

```
{% macro V001_drop_example_table(
        database = target.database,
        schema_prefix = target.schema
) -%}

DROP TABLE IF EXISTS {{database}}.{{schema_prefix}}_EXAMPLE.TABLE_XXX;

{%- endmacro %}
```

This very simple macro already does two things:

- By default, it sets the two parameters, database and schema_prefix, to the values from the environment configuration. This ensures that, by default, the code adapts and works well in any environment, while still allowing us to override the values if the environment configuration is not what we want.
- It uses Jinja to dynamically generate a basic SQL command to drop the desired table if it still exists. The `EXAMPLE` section is the **custom schema** we discussed earlier in this chapter regarding deployment organization. That, and the table name, can be hard-coded, as the migration is a single-use object that - once released- will remain to document what was run.

You can edit this example and replace `TABLE_XXX` with `my_first_dbt_model` to drop the table from the sample dbt project we just ran earlier. You can also add a second line to drop the view `my_second_dbt_model`. If you want, you can replace both commands with a single command, dropping the entire `{{database}}.{{schema_prefix}}_EXAMPLE` schema. Please remember that you always need to end a SQL command with a semicolon (`;`) when you want to execute more than one SQL command in one go.

The second example is slightly more advanced as it uses more Jinja functionalities:

```
{% macro V002_drop_example_column() -%}

{%- set model = ref('MY_TABLE_ABC') %}
{%- set col = 'XXXXXX' %}

{%- if column_exists(model, col) %}

ALTER TABLE {{ model }}
  DROP COLUMN {{ col }};

{%- else %}

SELECT 1;  -- a cheap equivalent of a NO-op

{%- endif %}
{%- endmacro %}
```

This macro does the following:

- It uses the `ref()` function to get a handle, a relation object, to the desired model in the current schema, and assigns it to the `model` variable.
- Sets the `col` variable with the name of the column we want to check if it exists.
- Uses the `if` conditional to call the custom macro `column_exists(...)` that you can find in our sample dbt project, to check if the table still has the column that we want to drop.

If the column is still there, the code to drop it is generated, but it would be simple to add code to rename it or to do something else, like calculate a derived value and then rename the column. If the column is not there anymore, the SELECT 1; code is generated. It is a cheap operation that does nothing and can be run as a SQL command, avoiding the need for the caller to handle the returned SQL with special code.

We hope that, even with these two examples, we have shown how simple it is to code maintenance operations that are automatically tailored to every environment you have and synchronized with the code that needs them. With database migrations, your imagination and the ability to express it with Jinja and SQL are your only limits. For example, by combining the two examples, you can easily code a macro that drops a table only if it still has the old schema with a specific column name.

With great power comes great responsibility; use it wisely and don't get overboard.

The `column_exists` macro is in the sample project under the `migrations` folder. As we have seen for the `project_setup` folder, you can keep it under the `macros` folder or put it in the root folder and add it to the `macro-paths` config in the `dbt_project.yml` file, as we are doing.

Our `macro-paths` config in the `dbt_project.yml` file now looks like this:

```
macro-paths: ["macros", "project_setup", "migrations"]
```

Now that we know how to prepare SQL commands to evolve our database objects, let's see how we can execute them consistently across all environments.

Executing database migrations

Once we have the SQL to execute, thanks to the migration macros, dbt provides a simple way to run it: we just pass the SQL string to the `run_query()` function. As an example, you can create a macro like the one in the following code box to run the first example migration that we have discussed earlier.

```
{% macro run_V001_drop_example_table() %}
{% do run_query(V001_drop_example_table()) %}
{% endmacro %}
```

The macro above shows our general approach to running migrations with dbt: one macro to generate the SQL and another to execute it with `run_query()`. Please note that we have not passed the `database` and `schema_prefix` parameters to the migration macro, as they are optional.

Let's discuss two ways you can use to deploy any migration:

- Using a `run_XXXXX()` style helper macro allows you to manually deploy the migration. This is the only way to apply a migration if you can't find a way to make it idempotent. It can also be suitable when a migration does not need to be synchronized with code changes, but needs to be deployed ASAP. Examples include creating or updating database objects or working with data. This method should not be used unless necessary, as it works outside the normal execution and release process, relying on humans to apply the migration in all environments. As such, it is risky and should be limited to cases when you cannot run it the normal way or wait for it to run in the normal process.
- Apply the migration using the `run_migrations()` macro, which will automatically deploy it as part of the normal execution process at the beginning of each run. This is mandatory for migrations that must be synchronized with code changes, but should be the normal way to ensure that all migrations are deployed to all environments.

Our suggestion is to use the automated deployment. Anyway, to explain how migrations are run in dbt, it makes more sense to show the `run_XXX()` style macros and discuss manual deployment first.

Manual deployment of migrations

Adding a `run_XXXXX()` helper macro in the same file where you define the migration macro is an effective way to quickly run a migration manually, even outside the release process. By using the following run-operation dbt command, you can easily apply the example `V001_drop_example_ table` migration in your DEV environment:

```
dbt run-operation run_V001_drop_example_table
```

But what about higher environments? You cannot run dbt commands on other environments from your IDE command line. Also, we want that commands run in higher environments are logged and remain available for audit. To achieve both goals, we can create a dbt job to run ad-hoc dbt commands that do not belong to the normal project release and build cycle. This job will run to perform migrations and other one-off commands.

Creation of the ad-hoc job

By now, you are an expert in creating dbt jobs, and if you don't remember all the steps, you can look at the **Creation of a CI job** section earlier in this chapter. Create a normal deploy job with the `QA—Ad-hoc commands` name for the QA environment, a similar one for the PROD environment, and just enter the following command as an example:

```
dbt run-operation run_V001_drop_example_table
```

Do not enable freshness checks, doc generation, or a schedule. Check that under **Advanced settings,** you have the same **Target name** as in all other QA jobs. This will ensure that if your code is using the `target.name` variable, it will work as expected. This "ad-hoc" dbt job is special because you will edit its command(s) almost every time before running it, making it close to a command line in the desired environment, with the great benefit of logging execution and keeping it auditable. If you prefer, you can name the job `QA command line`, but I prefer the "ad-hoc" name, as it better expresses that we will use it to run the commands needed for any specific situation that does not belong in the normal release and execution cycle. Now that you have the "ad-hoc" job, which contains the run-operation command that will run your desired migration, you can deploy it by just hitting the **Run now** button.

Let's move to see how it is simpler to just let dbt and the normal execution cycle work.

Automated deployment of migrations

The best approach to deploying migrations is to run them with dbt as part of the normal execution cycle, as we show in this section. The underlying execution mechanism is the same as in manual deployment, but the difference is where the dbt `run_query()` function is called. Inside the `migrations` folder, create a `run_migrations.sql` file with the code:

```
{% macro run_migrations(
        database = target.database,
        schema_prefix = target.schema
) -%}

{% do run_query(
       V001_drop_example_table(database, schema_prefix)
 ) %}

{%- endmacro %}
```

Please note that, in practice, this is the same code as the `run_XXX()` macro, except that in this case we have the `database` and `schema_prefix` parameters both in the macro declaration and in the migration invocation.

The real improvement is that we now have a macro with a stable `run_migrations` name that lets you add any number of migrations you want to run, in the desired order, and it can be added to our normal execution cycle. To make it work as expected, you must add its invocation to the jobs that deploy code in every environment.

For us, it means adding the following code to both the `QA—Build all` and `PROD—Build all` jobs. Enter the following line as the first command of the jobs:

```
dbt run-operation run_migrations
```

Once you have added that command to these jobs, you can just add a migration invocation in the `run_migrations` macro, and it will be deployed at the next run of the job before the models are deployed with the `dbt build` command. No extra work for you, just simple automation.

This section has shown you the basic, no-frills way to automate database change management with migrations that are easy to write, work well, and everybody immediately understands. If you look at the sample project, you will notice that our `run_migrations` macro defers the actual migration invocation to another macro that uses more advanced functionality to automate logging and execution while minimizing errors from mistyping. You can probably learn a trick or two from that code.

Migration organization

Now that we know how to write and execute the migrations, let's have a quick look at how we organize them and their lifecycle. Figure 16 shows the initial state of the sample project, with the `run_migrations` macro and the two initial example migrations.

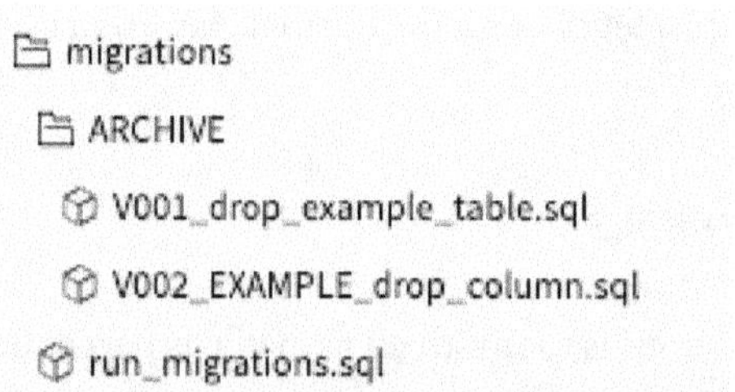

Figure 16: Initial organization of migration macros.

Please note that the two example migrations are inside a folder named `ARCHIVE`. The logic here is that the migrations are created and kept in the `migrations` folder until they are active, that is, while they are referenced by the `run_migrations` macro and run at every execution of the environments.

Once a macro has been deployed to all required environments, usually the day after its release to production, it is possible to deactivate it, that is, remove its invocation from the `run_migrations` macro so it is no longer run. At that time, it is a good practice to drag and drop the disabled migration into the `ARCHIVE` folder. Please do this to make it simple for us humans to see immediately which migrations are active and which ones are archived.

Please note that in the previous paragraphs, we meant active migration to be invoked by the `run_migrations` macro. From the dbt point of view, the migrations inside the `ARCHIVE` folder are still active macros that can be invoked at any time, for example, in a manual deployment using the `RUN_XXX` helper macro.

Extraordinary platform operations

The role of governance is not only to shape the day-to-day operations, but also to take a comprehensive approach to ensure that both ordinary and extraordinary operations, common and less common ones, are secure and follow the platform's goals and rules. In the Pragmatic Data Platform, we consider extraordinary operations those that require privileges not available to the dbt executor role used to execute dbt models and database migrations.

This distinction is very much a pragmatic organizational choice, as ordinary operations can be executed by every developer in their development environment and released to higher environments via the database migrations we just discussed. The extraordinary operations, on the contrary, can be run only by a selected group of users with access to the required high-privilege role(s). For this reason, they cannot be deployed to other environments and run as migrations. Anyway, they use the same migration architecture because, in dbt, the correct way to execute SQL operations outside models is through a macro invoked as a run-operation.

We have already seen an example of extraordinary operations in Chapter 2, when we set up our Snowflake platform. In general, all setup operations involving user and role management, such as creating data mart-specific roles, require special privileges. Another example of operations requiring special privileges is the creation of high-privilege objects, such as storage integrations to access files stored outside Snowflake, or **shares** to share data across Snowflake accounts. Similarly, creating a private or public listing and activating cross-zone data replication to make it available across regions are other operations that require typical privileges.

What are the traits specific to the creation and execution of these operations? Let's look at what is different with respect to database migrations.

Before any block of SQL commands, you need to explicitly start using the role necessary to perform the desired action with the `USE ROLE XXX;` command. The authorized users must invoke the run operation on the IDE command line, because that will use their personal user account, which can impersonate the required roles. These special operation macros must be kept well separated from database migrations, even if they look pretty much alike them.

The suggestion is to put them in a special folder, as we did for the project setup, or move them to a special operations dbt project, as suggested for the project setup as well. When you code these macros, you need to explicitly manage environments. To avoid hardcoding values or duplicating logic, you can use the helper macros we saw during setup. This reinforces the suggestion that these macros can be held together with or close to the project setup macros.

In the end, you can see these special operation macros as a special type of migration that requires a bit more complex handling.

Chapter review

Excellent work! You have already done your first release!

In this chapter, we've explored the core principles of the Pragmatic Data Platform's way of working, focusing on the crucial intersection of governance and daily practice. You've learned how to structure and configure dbt projects for effective deployment, including using custom schemas and environment-specific settings. We've walked through the release process, emphasizing the importance of CI jobs, code promotion via Pull Requests, and the management of deployment environments. Furthermore, you now have a solid understanding of database change management using dbt macros for migrations, ensuring your data platform evolves smoothly. Finally, we covered the handling of extraordinary operations, highlighting the need for secure and controlled execution of privileged tasks.

In Chapter 5, you will learn the basics of data modelling and how to represent data models.

Recommended resources

dbt Environments

- This 5-article series from the pragmatic-data.org blog covers environment setup, branching strategies, and release management best practices. https://www.pragmatic-data.net/environtments-pt-1-the-hell-from-legacy/.

dbt ref function documentation

- This dbt documentation explains how to use the ref function to reference models within your dbt project. https://docs.getdbt.com/reference/dbt-jinja-functions/ref.

dbt Relation object

- dbt's Relation class, which provides methods for interacting with database objects within dbt macros. https://docs.getdbt.com/reference/dbt-classes#relation.

CHAPTER 5

The Sample Project

In this short chapter, we introduce you to the sample project we will use in the book to tie together the development of the different layers of a data platform. We start by explaining why we have chosen this project, and then we will provide definitions for the core entities and the foundational data models around which the project revolves. Next, we present how the sample project will be fleshed out layer by layer in the rest of the book. Take this as a general roadmap drawn at the start of a project, not as a detailed table of contents telling you exactly what is done where. The topics that we are going to cover in this chapter are:

- Why have a sample project?
- The core elements of the STONKS project.
- The sample data provided with the STONKS project.
- Developing roadmap for the sample project.

Sample project and code

The sample dbt project is available at: **https://github.com/pragmatic-data/stonks**. The code samples for this chapter are in the sub-folder `chapter_05`, under the `code_samples_by_chapter` folder. Please note that, to fit the limited size of the printed page, we omit most of the comments and change the formatting of the code blocks compared to the files.

Why a sample project

I am a practical learner, and I feel I have really learned something only after getting my hands dirty, writing and running some code. Most of the developers I have known over the years agree with this approach, so if you are like us, I hope the sample project will improve what you will get from this book.

This book is about building data platforms mostly with SQL and Jinja macros using dbt Cloud, Snowflake, and git. The languages and core concepts we are going to use are not really new, but the tools and the way to generate and run the code are. Our sample project, therefore, will not try to show you all the possibilities of SQL or what macros you can write with Jinja, but will give us meaningful ways to discuss how the languages and tools can come together to build a good solution.

The sample project does not aim to be a perfect or fully finished solution, but enables us to discuss and expose you to multiple common needs and some realistic code found in current projects.

Why Stonks?

Stonks is a purposeful and playful misspelling of "stocks," intended as an informal, ironic way to refer to the investment world. It has assumed meme status after the 2021 GameStop short squeeze, when it became popular on Reddit and Twitter. As investors in public markets, we have a real interest in stocks and have been using dbt and Snowflake to track portfolios across multiple banks and brokers for a long time. Pretty much everyone has a basic understanding of how the stock market works and can relate to the information needed to manage a portfolio of stocks or other securities.

Over the years, we have been amazed by what a seemingly simple problem, tracking the value of securities, can actually become an unbelievably complex task. One would assume that, with securities clearly defined and official quotes on heavily regulated markets, it would be easy to track their values. They would be correct for the very basic cases. Still, the reality of how securities evolve, the wide array of ways brokers present data, and the inherent variability of free markets throw up many interesting problems. This is also common in professional projects where the setting seems simple, like tracking how much wood there is in a piece of forest. Still, the reality of how the data is collected and presented makes it more complex than one would initially think.

The combination of such a simple setting, coupled with the interesting problems that arise in managing the related information, makes for a great topic to build a sample project, but, trying to keep it light, I have preferred to use a light and playful name like "Stonks" instead of a more serious one.

The core elements of the Stonks project

In every data project, it is important to ensure that people have a clear, common understanding of the concepts and processes central to the project. This is the only way to align their work and reduce the friction caused by varying interpretations of concepts, models, and business rules.

With this book, we hope to help you run your data projects better across all dimensions, not just write good code or understand how dbt and Snowflake work. Clear goals, precise definitions, and simple high-level models are a must for every project, so we will do our part from the beginning.

This section will collect these foundational elements, provide the high-level goals and the definitions of the core concepts, and offer a general data model to help your initial understanding of the Stonks project.

Key objectives

The overall goal of the Stonks project is to build a simple investment-tracking platform that allows a user to track their ownership and the value of the securities held across one or more brokers over time, and analyze them in a single place. This goal can be split into three high-level technical objectives:

- Store the original information received from the different sources, so you can always pinpoint the actual source of all the data. This is a life saver in sourcing official information during tax audits.
- Build a refined layer populated with the business concepts needed to track and value the holdings.
- Facilitate the construction of multiple data marts that can be used for different purposes, from investment monitoring to tax declarations.

Glossary of key concepts

The following concepts are central to the understanding of the Stonks project:

Broker: A regulated entity that acts as an intermediary between buyers and sellers of securities. They execute trades on behalf of their clients, providing access to the market. Brokers may offer various services, including investment advice, research, and account management.

Account: A formal arrangement held at a financial institution (like a broker or bank) that allows an individual or entity to own and manage securities such as stocks and options, but also other financial products like mortgages and insurance. It serves as the formal registered entity telling who owns the financial products and at which institution they are held.

Portfolio: The collection of all the different investments held within an account. This can include a variety of assets, such as stocks, bonds, options, mutual funds, and other securities. A record of the holdings and their transactions.

Position: The specific amount of a particular security that is held within the portfolio, like a certain number of shares of a stock or a specific number of option contracts. The holding at a certain time of an asset in a specific portfolio.

Security: A tradable financial instrument that represents ownership in a public company (stock), a debt relationship with a governmental body or a corporation (bond), ownership rights (options), or other financial interests. It's essentially a certificate or record that signifies a financial value and can be bought or sold.

Transaction: Any action involving the buying or selling of securities, or the movement of funds in or out of the account. Includes activities like purchasing stocks, selling options, receiving dividends, depositing cash, or withdrawing money. Each transaction results in a change to a position's holdings, or to the account's cash balance.

Corporate action: An event initiated by a public company that can affect its outstanding securities and stakeholders. These actions can take many forms and include routine activities like paying a dividend, as well as rarer ones like a direct or inverse stock split, a spin-off, mergers and acquisitions, name changes, and eventually company delisting. Their effects vary widely and can usually be described in terms of one or more transactions, potentially involving more than one position.

Exchange: A regulated marketplace where buyers and sellers can trade securities in an organized and transparent manner. These platforms provide the infrastructure and rules for trading stocks, bonds, options, and other financial instruments.

The above elements define the key concepts we will work with in the Stonks project, but they remain quite high-level and generic. When we get into the real code and data, we will have to dig a bit deeper; therefore, the next detail sections will drill into some key concepts.

Securities

We have seen that a security is a generic tradable instrument that represents a financial interest and can be traded on an exchange. Let's list the most common types of securities that we will find in consumer portfolios:

Stock: Represents a fractional ownership in a public company, also called shares or equities. The term usually refers to common stocks, but other forms of stock exist, such as preferred stocks, which offer different rights and benefits.

Exchange-Traded Funds (ETFs): Investment funds that trade on stock exchanges, similarly to stocks, but own a basket of stocks.

Bond: A loan made by an investor to a borrower, which could be a corporation, government (federal, state, or municipal), or other entity.

Mutual Funds: Pools of money collected from many investors to invest in a diversified portfolio of securities. They are not traded on an exchange like stocks or ETFs, but are typically bought and sold at the end of the trading day based on their net asset value (NAV).

Option: The most common type of derivative, providing the owner the right to buy or sell a set of securities, usually 100 shares, at a certain fixed price on or before a certain date. Its value depends mostly on the underlying security, but also on factors such as remaining time and interest rates.

Other Types of Derivatives: Financial contracts whose value is derived from an underlying asset, index, or rate. Common types of derivatives are futures, forwards, swaps, and CFDs. Some are traded on exchanges, like futures, while others are privately negotiated between parties.

As you can imagine, all securities have some common features, but to treat them in more detail, each needs its own specialized information.

When it comes to identifying stocks, the ISIN code is probably the most effective, but it is seldom used and, unfortunately, not always exported by trading platforms. What most people commonly use, the stock symbol, is totally inadequate to clearly identify a security, as the same symbol (e.g., COG) could mean two completely different stocks traded on two markets. In fact, it happened to me to own both COG in Toronto and COG in London at the same time. Even just how this combination of symbol and exchange is expressed is not common at all, and to identify COG in London (traded on the London Stock Exchange, LSE), you could equally find COG:LSE or COG.L, but other formats might be found around, like LSE:COG.

When we are dealing with securities, there are a few other concepts that are worth describing:

Trade: A completed transaction involving the buying or selling of a specific quantity of a security at an agreed-upon price. It's the execution of an order placed by an investor through their broker on an exchange or other trading venue. A trade results in a change in the portfolio's holdings and a corresponding debit or credit in the account.

Listing exchange: The stock exchange on which a particular security is officially listed for trading. The listing exchange is the primary marketplace, although it might also be traded on other platforms.

ISIN code: Stands for International Securities Identification Number, a code that uniquely identifies a specific security, like a universal serial number for stocks, bonds, options, and other tradable securities. The ISIN provides a standardized way to identify securities across different countries and trading platforms, which is crucial for efficient clearing, settlement, and regulatory reporting of transactions. Each ISIN is a 12-character alphanumeric code comprising a country code, an issuer identifier, and a specific security identifier, followed by a check digit.

Symbol: Often referred to as a ticker symbol or stock symbol, it is a short alphanumeric abbreviation used to uniquely identify publicly traded shares of a particular stock on a specific stock exchange. Think of it as a shorthand code for a company's stock in a specific market. Stock often have different symbols on different exchanges.

Transactions

A **Transaction (TX)** is any operation that produces a change in a Position (buying or selling securities) and/or in the balance of a currency in the account. The transactions are divided into these three broad categories:

Trades: Trade TXs change one position and potentially the balance of one currency. They represent the account's interaction with the external world, resulting in a change in one position, whether or not it involves movement or changes in the account's balance. Examples include buying and selling securities, disposing of fractional shares received, or changing option positions due to option events such as expiration, assignment, or exercise.

Cash Transactions: Cash TXs change the balance of **one** currency. These TXs represent the account's interactions with the outside world, generating movement of funds without changes in any position, and only to one currency. They can be at the account level or be connected to a single position. Examples are interests paid or received (at account level) or dividends (at position level). The Cash TX does not change the eventual position associated with the TX.

Transfers: Transfer TXs represent the movement of currencies or securities between accounts. These TXs change either one position without affecting the balance of any currency or change only the balance of one currency without affecting any position. A special class of Trade or Transfer TXs occurs when the ASSET_CLASS is CASH, as they represent changes in the monetary amount in different currencies held on an account. A CASH Transfer TX represents the transfer of funds between accounts, while a CASH Trade TX is used to convert between currencies by buying and selling them on the FX market (hence the Trade designation).

High-level data model

To give you an overview of how these concepts are connected, Figure 17 provides a high-level conceptual model.

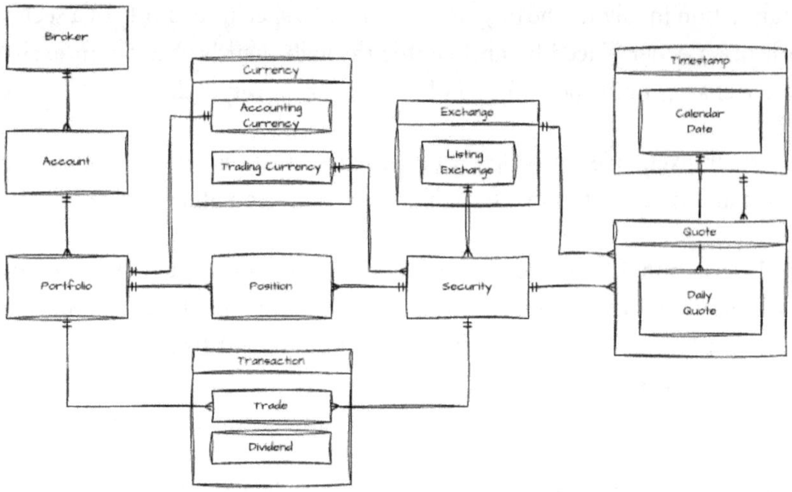

Figure 17: Initial conceptual data model.

Please be mindful that this is a conceptual model describing the world as we assume it to be. What you will get from your broker might be quite different, and consequently, you might need to adjust this model when implementing it. Two simple examples are:

- The Broker concept might be a full-fledged entity with a key and a table with several attributes, but in many cases, for the project's purpose it might just be a simple string with the name and no real table associated with it, or maybe just a reference table linking a few more descriptions to that string.
- Between Account and Portfolio at this level the distinction is often abstract or legal in nature. If you have only one portfolio, or if you have distinct portfolios that seem unrelated, there might be no visible identifier for the account. That is why we have linked the accounting currency to the Portfolio concept, not to the Account, despite the name.

Please consider that any model at this high level of abstraction targeting a generic field cannot be precise. Still, it is nevertheless useful for grounding reasoning on a common base, what John Giles would call a Data Town Plan. Good enough to know what goes where, and when we start looking at the real use cases, we will know how to make further assumptions. The role of business stakeholders in these early, high-level discussions is similar: describe the landscape and goals, providing the knowledge to pick a direction when these doubts arise. Remember that the real world -the data you get- might be different from the business rules/info provided by business people, especially the ones not working daily in the trenches. You will have to make the two sides come to terms, but it's difficult to argue against the data that you receive. In the next section, we will briefly introduce the data lifecycle and how it shapes the development of data platforms.

The sample data

This section introduces the raw data files we will use, their organization, and their logical data model.

While we've previously discussed conceptual business entities such as Accounts and Positions, this section will focus on the logical data model of the raw data exported from the source system. As always, when digging from high-level conceptual models into the reality of data, we will find it more complex and somehow different from the conceptual model. The Stonks sample project will use real data from the personal investment portfolios Roberto manages, just limited to a few stocks (AM, AR, CNQ, and TSLA). They cover the portfolio from the start of 2021 and do not include options, futures, or other types of securities. These simplifications are done to make the files easier to manage, keep downstream logic simple, and maintain some privacy for Roberto's investments. The data is from two Interactive Brokers accounts and brings the theoretical concepts of the Pragmatic Data Platform to life. You are welcome to use data from your accounts.

The data files

The Interactive Brokers export system provides a rich set of files and the ability to export data for selected periods or send it at a desired frequency. For this project, we will focus on four primary data sources that represent the core activities of a portfolio:

- **Trades**: This file contains a detailed record of every buy and sell transaction of stocks, options, and other securities. It is the most granular and critical data source for tracking portfolio activity.
- **Open Positions**: This file provides a snapshot of all securities currently held in the portfolio as of a specific date. It is a state-based file that complements the event-based Trades file.
- **Cash Transactions**: This file records all cash movements in the account, including dividends received, interest payments, deposits, and withdrawals.
- **Transfers**: This file contains the equivalent of transactions for securities transferred in or out of the account, rather than being bought or sold.

The last one, Transfers, is a bit special as it seldom has new data. It could be treated as a normal daily or periodic export, but in my case, it only has data for 2021, so we will load it only on demand.

Content and time coverage

All files, except the Open Positions one, contain transactions, so they provide you with all the granular information you need, regardless of the time of export or the period covered.

For the years 2021, 2022, and 2023, you will receive a single sample file containing all the data for that year, avoiding duplicates. Starting on July 19th, 2024, you have daily exports for Trades and Cash Transactions. Because of how the IB export works and/or was set up, they all cover the period from the start of the year to the export date. Restating everything from the start of the year every day is a bit excessive, but some overlap is common to provide a robust export. Given that our data set is quite small (a few thousand rows) and the PDP historization handles duplicates natively, it is good to be aware that there will be duplicates, even if they are expected and not a problem.

The Open Positions files instead contain snapshots of the account positions "as of" the end of the required export period, so the requested export date determines their content. This is also why Open Positions will be missing information about positions opened and closed inside the export interval. For the Open Position files, we have an initial export for the first three months of 2021, giving you the situation as of March 30th, 2021. After that, we have an export for each start or end of the month (or both) until the start of 2024. We have daily exports for the open positions since January 1st, 2024.

So, starting on July 19th, 2024, we have daily exports for the three major files. This means more granular data, but much more redundancy. Before that, we have all the transactions (Trades, Cash Tx, and Transfers) in yearly exports, without redundancy. Before Jan 2024, we had mostly monthly Open Positions; after that, daily. While this matters little for ingestion, it is very important when we need to code our business logic or when we need to evaluate the complexity of building features on our platform. In addition to these machine-generated files, we will use a fourth, small, and manually maintained data source for Corporate Actions, such as stock splits or mergers. This is both a necessity, as I haven't got my hands on a good export for these, so I need to manually enter the transactions, and it's a good opportunity to demonstrate how to handle static data with dbt seeds.

It is also quite common, the need to incorporate a process to manually add data to complement or fix issues in machine-generated data. This is a possible approach that is both simple and auditable.

Sample data organization

To keep our project organized and reflect a pragmatic approach to data management, in the `code_samples_by_chapter/chapter_09/source_data` directory of the sample project's repo, you will find the `sample_IB_files.zip` file containing the sample CSV files organized in a folder structure that reflects the entities described above and our ingestion process.

The dedicated folders for each file type (trades, open_positions, and cash_transactions) contain the files we will ingest first, including those exported up to July 22nd, 2024. Similarly named folders with a `_future` suffix contain the files exported from July 23rd, 2024, onward.

This organization is done to provide you with an initial load with substantial data (more than three years and half of data, that cover the older period when I do not have daily exports) while also giving you the ability to simulate the advancement of time by copying one or few files at a time from the _future folder to the normal one where the data is ingested from.

Sample data model

Figure 18 shows a conceptual data model that is a direct, yet simplified representation of the source system's export found in our source files. As you can see, the key concepts from our conceptual data model are there, but they are presented differently, embedded in the report we get. This is a common characteristic of customer-facing exports. Because they intend to be "self-standing" reports, they are wide and denormalized, containing information about the multiple related entities that are useful for explaining the single record. This contrasts with direct database exports, done by or for technical users and not intended to be used alone, which often contain only a single entity per file, making them easier to historicize.

In our case, the Trades file, for example, contains not only information about the transaction itself but also extensive details about the Security involved. This is the same for the other exports. Regarding the Account entity, they include the account ID, but also the account name. Logically, we treat the Account as an independent entity, as there are additional properties, such as base currency, owner, or start date, that make sense to add to this concept.

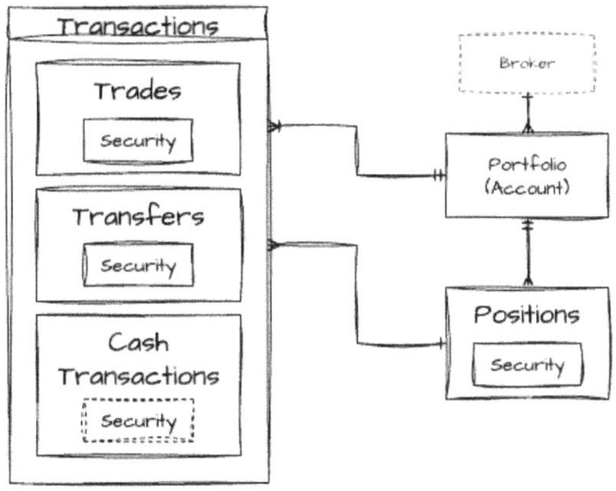

Figure 18: Conceptual data model example.

The presence of these multiple, often "nested" entities within a single wide report poses a challenge we will have to address in the Storage layer. There, our task will be to apply transformations to extract the separate entities, such as Security, from the exports into dedicated single-entity models and correctly store their history. This first level of extraction and enablement, the usability of the data – without changing its semantics – is crucial for correctly storing the base concepts we receive from the sources and making them ready for the next layers of the PDP. Understanding the raw data structures and what they contain is the first step in preparing the data for the next layers of the Pragmatic Data Platform. This is more complex than most exports in a corporate setting. Good training!

The storage data model

In the previous section, we introduced the idea that our source files contain not only the major concepts associated with the file, such as Trades, Open Positions, and Cash Transactions, but also data about nested concepts, such as Securities or Accounts. In the storage layer, we will store the major concepts as we receive them, and we will also extract the embedded Security concept from each to build a uniform, shared Security concept. The conceptual data model in the storage layer appears in Figure 19, on the next page.

As you can see in Figure 19, we consider both Security (from the IB export files) and Portfolio (Account) full-fledged entities. Security will be historized from source files, while Portfolio will be calculated in the refined layer, as there is little to historize. The Broker and Exchange are dotted, as we treat them as manually maintained references. Currency and Countries could be handled similarly.

For the sample project and the Pragmatic Data Platform macros, it makes little difference to consider them master data or reference data, with the difference being mostly whether you consider them part of your business concepts (that you control) or external data used to provide context for your business concepts (that you get, seldom updated).

In both cases, they can be ingested and historized in the same way, with the same macros. You can always opt for hashed or non-hashed primary keys (common for reference data, where internationally recognized IDs often exist) and the presence or absence of historization (less common, but useful and simple in PDP for reference data as well).

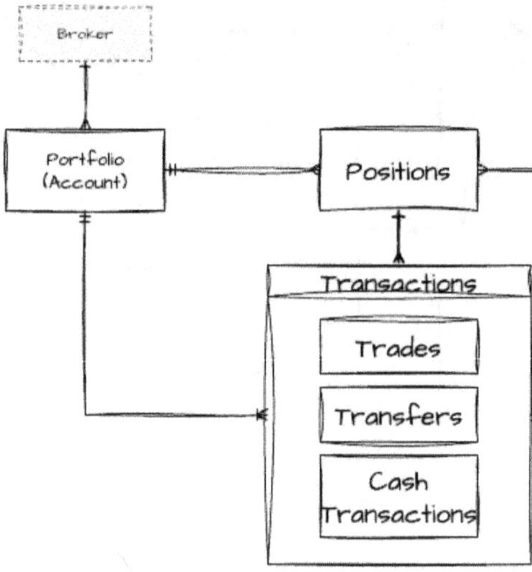

Figure 19: A conceptual data model in the storage layer.

Developing the sample project

This book is a journey from principles to practice.

We introduced the core concepts of the Pragmatic Data Platform (PDP) in the first part of the book, and then, in the second part, we use the "Stonks" sample project to bring those concepts to life. This project serves a dual purpose: it's a step-by-step guide to building a Pragmatic Data Platform and a ready-to-use reference project you can adapt for your real-world use cases. Unlike my previous book, **Data Engineering with dbt**, which started with a basic solution and then refined it, this book takes a different approach. Since dbt and the data community have matured, we've decided to target an audience already familiar with the basics of data engineering, SQL, and dbt. Our focus here is on building a robust, maintainable data platform with minimal effort and maximum automation, using specific patterns and the PDP macros. For these reasons, the sample project is developed throughout the book, building one piece at a time in its final form, following the layer discussed in each chapter.

A chapter discussing a single PDP layer is immediately followed by a chapter that builds out that layer in the sample project. This structure allows us to dive directly into advanced concepts and real-world examples, making the book a practical, layer-specific guide that practitioners can use as a reference when working on their own projects.

Roadmap for the sample project

Here's a guide to where you'll find the materials related to the development of the "Stonks" project in the book:

- **Chapter 1: A Pragmatic Data Platform.** We introduce the overall architecture of the Pragmatic Data Platform and the layers that the "Stonks" project will follow. This provides the high-level blueprint for our work.

- **Chapter 2: Pragmatic Project Setup**. This is where we discuss the **automated project setup** using the `sf-admin` dbt package to create a standardized environment with proper roles, users, and security settings for our sample project. Here you start configuring Snowflake.
- **Chapter 4: Agile Development**. This chapter sets up the dbt project for our sample project, configures the development and production environments, and automates the release and deployment process using GitHub pull requests and dbt Cloud jobs. You connect dbt and Snowflake, creating a working project that follows the PDP way of working.
- **Chapter 5: The Sample Project**. **The Sample Data**: We introduce the raw data files (`Trades`, `OpenPositions`, `CashTransactions`) that will serve as the foundation of our project. We lay out the raw data folder and file structure, demonstrating how to organize your dbt project for clarity and scalability. We also discuss their logical data model, highlighting its denormalized nature, with a nested entity such as Security within other entities.

  Developing the Sample Project: This section, which you're reading now, explains the project's role as a practical guide and how its development aligns with the book's structure.
- **Chapter 7: QuickStart and Implementation Patterns**. **Project Quickstart**: This chapter acts as a playbook for starting a PDP project. It ties together the foundational principles from Part I with a concrete implementation guide, providing a step-by-step process for getting your project up and running quickly. The section "Organization of raw data, macros, and models" provides a visual representation of how to organize the raw data files in your storage account (or in Snowflake), the macros, and the models in the dbt project.
- **Chapter 9: Coding the Ingestion Layer**. **Ingestion Setup**: We build macros to set up the Snowflake infrastructure (database, schema, stage, and file format) for ingesting our raw data.

  Ingestion Process: We write code to ingest raw CSV files from their respective stages into our landing tables. We also implement a single master macro to automate the entire process.

  Using a Seed for Manual Data: We introduce the corporate_actions seed to show how to handle small, manually maintained data, complete with data typing, documentation, and tests.
- **Chapter 11: Coding the Storage Layer**. Here, we take the raw data from the ingestion layer and apply our first limited transformations to make the data usable without changing its semantics or adding any business rules. We create the historized models for the entities we receive from the sources, ensuring we have a single source of truth for each entity from each source. We also extract entities nested within other source entities, such as Security, so they become first-class citizens of our data models.
- **Chapter 13: Coding the Refined Layer**. In this chapter, we will build out the core business logic on top of the immutable, rock-solid storage layer. We will create refined models that combine data from multiple entities to build our first curated datasets.
- **Chapter 16: Coding the Delivery Layer**. We will finalize the project by building the data marts and analytical models needed for business intelligence, reporting, and advanced use cases. This is where we create the final tables that our end-users will consume.

Chapter review

In this chapter, you've taken a significant step into the practical application of the Pragmatic Data Platform. We introduced the **"Stonks"** sample project, which will serve as our hands-on guide for building a complete data platform throughout the rest of the book. You learned about the three primary data files (Trades, OpenPositions, and CashTransactions) that form the foundation of our project and the logical data model they represent. We also provided a roadmap of how this project will be developed, chapter by chapter, in alignment with the PDP's layered architecture. By establishing the project's structure and discussing its role as a practical, scalable blueprint, we have set the stage for you to begin coding. In the next chapter, we will look at how real organizations have implemented pragmatic data platforms based on dbt and Snowflake. We will analyze several real-world case studies from various industries, providing you with a quick reference guide to see how the principles we discussed are applied in practice.

Recommended resources

Data Engineering with dbt

- For a broader, more introductory view of data engineering and the foundational principles of the Pragmatic Data Platform, you can refer to the author's previous book. The book provides an introductory view of data engineering and dbt, tailored for readers starting to build their knowledge about data platforms and dbt. It is a foundational book for the Pragmatic Data Platform way of working. Zagni, Roberto "**Data Engineering with dbt**", Packt Publishing, 2023.

The "Stonks" Sample Project

- The complete code for the sample project of this book is available for you to clone and explore on GitHub. It also has a folder, `code_samples_by_chapter`, with code and materials for each chapter. https://github.com/pragmatic-data/stonks.

Pragmatic Data Platform dbt package

- The macros used in the "Stonks" sample project are part of this open-source package from the same author of this book. You can find the code and documentation on GitHub. https://github.com/pragmatic-data/pragmatic-data-platform.

dbt Labs Documentation

- For detailed information on dbt projects, dbt Cloud, and general dbt best practices. https://docs.getdbt.com/.

dbt Project Structure

- For best practices on organizing your dbt project. https://docs.getdbt.com/docs/core-concepts/dbt-project-structure.

About Sources

- A key feature to access the raw data, dbt sources are how we reference our ingested files in this book. Learn more about them here. https://docs.getdbt.com/docs/build/sources.

Snowflake Documentation

- For comprehensive information on Snowflake's features. https://docs.snowflake.com/.

Getting Started

- A good starting point for Snowflake's core concepts. https://docs.snowflake.com/en/user-guide/getting-started.

Loading Data

- A comprehensive overview of Snowflake's data loading capabilities, including stages, file formats, and best practices. https://docs.snowflake.com/en/user-guide/data-load-overview.

Stages

- Learn about internal and external stages, which are central to how we ingest data in the PDP. https://docs.snowflake.com/en/sql-reference/sql/create-stage.

CHAPTER 6

Applied Data Platforms

Welcome to the practical heart of this book!

In the previous chapters, we explored the architectural layers and principles of the Pragmatic Data Platform. Now we shift from theory to practice, showing how real organizations across different industries have applied these ideas.

From telecom to retail, manufacturing to micromobility, the companies featured here faced very different challenges. Yet their journeys share common threads: a layered approach, the adoption of Snowflake and dbt, and a shift from firefighting to building sustainable data products. Each case study highlights the problems with legacy approaches, the decisions that led to modernization, and the outcomes they achieved. We've also included lessons learned, so you can apply the same thinking in your own context. If you recognize your own challenges in the stories of the leaders interviewed in this chapter, the Pragmatic Data Platform offers a proven path forward and provides a robust blueprint for success.

Sample project and code

The sample dbt project is available at: **https://github.com/pragmatic-data/stonks**. Please note that there is no dedicated code for this chapter, as the focus is on real-world interviews and case studies. If you would like to further discuss the use cases, get in contact with Roberto and Jakob on LinkedIn.

Case Study: Rebtel

"We knew that building a scalable system required more than just adopting new tools. It was about following best practices and creating a structure that could evolve with us." Chandan Singh

Rebtel, a Stockholm-based tech company. Founded to challenge the costs of international telecom services, the company evolved to offer a wide range of cross-border services. As Chandan Singh, Head of Data at Rebtel, explains,

"We were always about being rebels in telecom—hence the name Rebtel—and now we're expanding that spirit to solve problems for people moving across borders."

While Rebtel successfully diversified its offerings, its data infrastructure lagged behind the company's growing ambitions. Data incidents were frequent, and their team was spending more time fighting fires than innovating.

"We didn't have visibility on our data lineage, and we constantly worried about the accuracy of our data. Machine learning projects were on hold because we couldn't even trust the data we had.'"

Rebtel's Data Evolution:
A case for a pragmatic data platform

Industry: Telecommunications, Fintech

Headquarters: Stockholm, Sweden

Data Team:
1 Data Analyst/Scientist
2 Data Engineers
1 Head of Data

Tech Stack:
dbt Cloud, Snowflake, Stitch, Looker, AWS, GitHub

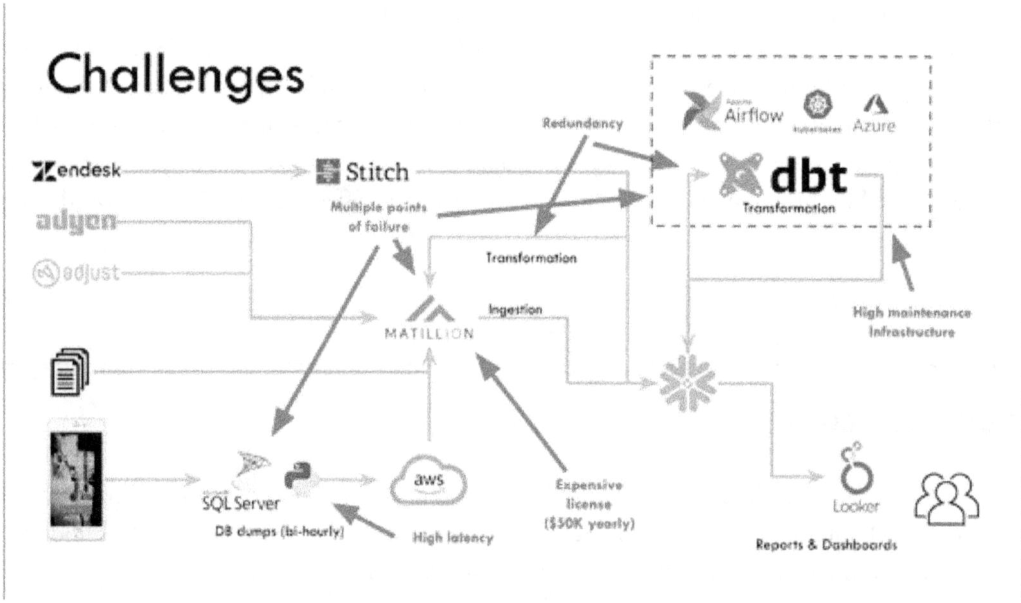

Figure 20: Rebtel challenges.

The problems with the legacy architecture

Rebtel's previous data infrastructure, while functional in earlier days, could no longer handle the growing complexity of the business. As Chandan noted, "We never knew if the data we were seeing was correct or even complete." This lack of transparency meant the data team often had to manually debug pipelines, a time-consuming and error-prone task. This unreliability created a ripple effect across the company. With frequent data incidents, teams were often in firefighting mode rather than focusing on innovation. Chandan elaborates: "Every time there was an issue, we'd have to spend hours debugging. It wasn't sustainable, especially with our goals to build more advanced analytics and machine learning models." The system also limited their ability to scale their machine learning capabilities, particularly in fraud prevention, a critical use case for Rebtel. Without confidence in the accuracy of their data, they couldn't launch new initiatives. "We had machine learning on the roadmap, but we couldn't move forward because we just didn't know if our data could be trusted," Chandan reflected.

The decision to modernize

Faced with these mounting challenges, Rebtel's data team knew they needed a change. Their solution? A cutting-edge stack powered by Snowflake, dbt Cloud, Stitch, AWS, and GitHub, with Looker added for business intelligence. This combination was chosen for its scalability, data governance, and cost-effectiveness. "We wanted something that could give us better visibility, reduce incidents, and most importantly, let us trust our data. We needed to move away from the black box," Chandan shared. The ability to generate clear data lineage and to incorporate testing, version control, and CI/CD (Continuous Integration/Continuous Delivery) practices, with GitHub integration, to empower the team. It wasn't just about improving processes but ensuring that the entire company could rely on accurate, up-to-date data. Snowflake, with its cloud-native, scalable platform, served as the foundation that enabled Rebtel to scale its data operations seamlessly. "The combination of Snowflake's power and dbt's flexibility gave us the infrastructure we needed to grow without constantly hitting walls," Chandan said.

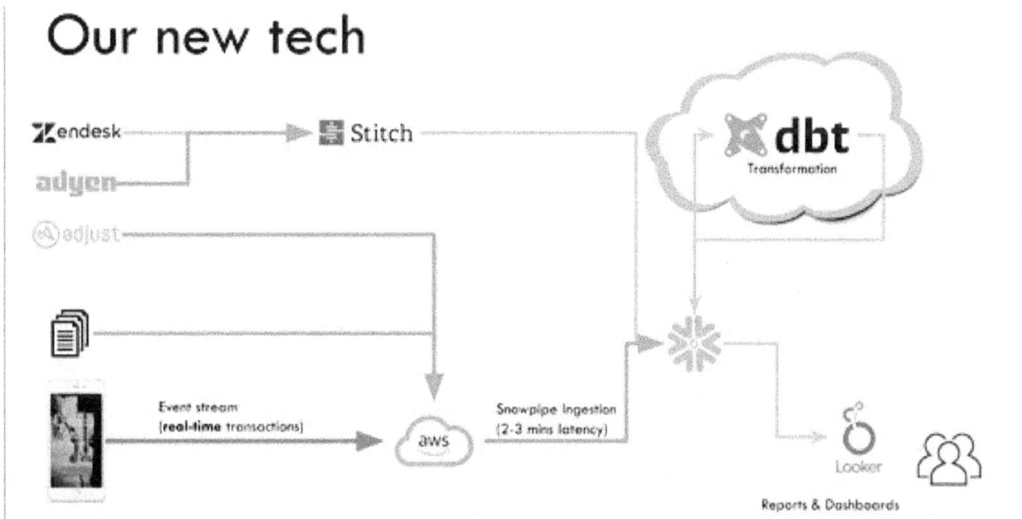

Figure 21: The new tech.

A new pragmatic data architecture

When Rebtel embarked on its journey to build a modern data platform, it wasn't just about solving immediate pain points; it was about creating a robust, scalable architecture that would support the company's future growth. As Chandan Singh, Head of Data at Rebtel, described it, "We knew that building a scalable system required more than just adopting new tools. It was about following best practices and creating a structure that could evolve with us." The foundation of Rebtel's new data platform rests on Snowflake for data warehousing and dbt for data transformation.

Layered data design: from raw to refined

One of the key decisions in Rebtel's architecture was to design clear data layers that aligned with its business needs. The team structured their data platform in layers:

- **Raw Layer**: Data is ingested as-is into Snowflake without any transformations. This raw data serves as the foundation for all subsequent transformations and is never directly queried by end users.
- **Stage Layer**: At this stage, data is cleaned and standardized, but still closely mirrors the raw data in terms of structure. This is the layer where most data transformations begin.
- **Intermediate (Int) Layer**: Here, the data becomes more business-oriented. Complex transformations and joins are applied to create intermediate models that are used across various analytics use cases.
- **Data Warehouse (DWH) Layer**: The final layer is where all business-facing data resides. This is the only layer accessible to business users and applications. "We made sure that all business queries go through this final, curated warehouse layer. It simplifies governance and ensures that users always work with the right data," Chandan emphasized.

Key practices

Rebtel built a mature, maintainable data workflow by enforcing dbt and software engineering best practices. Their team structured models into logical folders (stage, int, facts, dims, marts), implemented rigorous GitHub code reviews with SQLFluff checks, and automated testing:

- **Model Organization with dbt**: Rebtel's team followed dbt's best practices for organizing models, structuring them into folders such as `stage`, `int` (intermediate), `facts`, `dims` (dimensions), and `marts`. This approach ensures that the models are easy to navigate and maintain. "One of the key things we did was enforce a structure in how we manage dbt models. We organized everything into logical layers, from raw data to the final warehouse that business teams rely on," Chandan explained.
- **Code Review and Compliance**: Rebtel introduced a strict code review process using **GitHub**. Every commit underwent a review to ensure consistency and quality. They also enforced compliance with SQL best practices using **Sqlfluff**, which checks code against coding standards before code can be committed. "We enforced pre-commit checks with Sqlfluff to make sure every piece of code meets our quality standards before it gets merged into production," Chandan mentioned. This made their development pipeline more reliable, catching issues early in the process.
- **Commit Messaging and Documentation**: To ensure traceability, Rebtel required descriptive commit messages, often linked to JIRA tickets for easy tracking. Every new fact, dimension, or mart model built in dbt was also thoroughly documented within dbt itself. "Documentation was a big part of making the system sustainable. We didn't want to rely on tribal knowledge," Chandan said. This ensured that new team members could quickly get up to speed with the logic behind each data model.
- **Testing and Performance Optimization**: Rebtel considered testing a crucial part of their development process. They implemented both out-of-the-box tests (like unique constraints and null checks) and custom tests for specific business logic. "Every new model we build gets tests attached to it. It's not just about accuracy today, but making sure things don't break over time," Chandan explained. Furthermore, they review model runtimes and performance every six months, ensuring that the platform remains optimized even as data volumes grow.

Ingesting and managing data in Snowflake

Rebtel's data ingestion layer primarily relies on Snowpipe to stream data into Snowflake, ensuring new data is ingested in near real-time. Additionally, they use tools like Stitch to integrate various data sources, and AWS services such as Lambda and Kinesis for more complex data-fetching tasks. "We use a combination of tools to get data into Snowflake. For us, it's all about flexibility and choosing the right tool for the job," Chandan elaborated.

Integration of existing systems with Snowflake and dbt

Rebtel had several legacy systems and data sources that needed to be integrated into the new architecture. They used a combination of **Snowpipe** for real-time data ingestion, **Stitch** for extracting data from various SaaS platforms, and **AWS services** such as Lambda and Kinesis for real-time events. "The integration was a big challenge," Chandan admitted. "But by using a combination of tools and a clear strategy for where each piece of data should live, we managed to bring everything together into a single, cohesive platform."

Best practices for scaling and maintenance

To ensure their platform remains sustainable as it grows, Rebtel put in place several key best practices:

- **Regular Performance Reviews**: Every six months, the team conducts a review of its dbt models to optimize performance. "It's not a set-it-and-forget-it kind of deal. We constantly review and fine-tune our models to ensure that the platform can handle increasing loads," said Chandan.
- **Automated Testing and Monitoring**: With every new model, both generic and custom tests are created. Rebtel also monitors model runtimes to spot potential bottlenecks before they affect users.
- **Focus on Maintainability**: By enforcing documentation, code reviews, and commit hygiene, Rebtel ensures its platform is easy to maintain as new team members join and business needs evolve.

Immediate outcomes and long-term benefits

The impact of the new architecture was immediate. Within six months, Rebtel had successfully migrated its systems and even began prototyping a machine learning model for fraud prevention. This project had been shelved under the old architecture due to data inconsistencies. They have also successfully deployed another machine learning model that generates high-quality cross-selling leads for their marketing team. These new capabilities have a direct impact on the company's revenue and profit margins, an outcome that Chandan highlights as one of their biggest wins. "We could never have even started these machine learning projects with the old system," Chandan says. "Now, with Snowflake, dbt, and GitHub, we are confident in our data. We know it's correct, and that allows us to innovate."

The new architecture didn't just benefit the data team. Business users now had more trust in the data they were seeing. With better data governance and real-time insights, Rebtel's non-technical teams were empowered to make faster, more informed decisions. Additionally, by migrating from Matillion to dbt Cloud, Rebtel cut its licensing costs by 80%. But the benefits extended far beyond financial savings. The new architecture allows the team to focus on higher-value work rather than constant firefighting. As Chandan described, "We went from being reactive to proactive. Instead of fixing things, we're now building things."

The adoption of GitHub for version control and CI/CD pipelines also improved collaboration within the team. Analysts could now work on data transformations without depending on engineers, speeding up development cycles, and empowering more team members to contribute to data initiatives.

Lessons learned

Reflecting on the transformation, Chandan shared several lessons for other companies looking to modernize their data stack:

- **Transparency is Everything**: "One of the biggest pain points in our old system was the lack of visibility. With dbt Cloud, we can now see exactly how data is being transformed at every step. That's a game-changer." Clear data lineage not only reduces errors but also builds trust across the organization.
- **Scalability is Key**: Choosing Snowflake was a strategic move that allowed Rebtel to scale its operations without worrying about infrastructure constraints. "Don't wait until you've outgrown your systems," Chandan advised. "By the time you feel the pain, it's already too late."
- **Empower your Teams**: By implementing version control and CI/CD with GitHub, Rebtel fosters a culture of collaboration. Chandan emphasized the importance of giving teams the right tools: "Once people have the tools to do their jobs, they'll move faster, and you'll see results quicker than you expect."

Looking ahead

Rebtel's transition to a modern, pragmatic data platform with Snowflake, dbt, and GitHub has fundamentally reshaped how they work with data. It enables innovation, cuts costs, and builds trust across the organization. As Chandan Singh concludes, "We're not just building for today—we're building for the future. And now, we have the tools to take on any challenge."

Case Study: Voi & NordicFeel – Scaling data for urban mobility & e-commerce

When Fasih joined Voi, the fast-growing e-scooter company, he faced a classic challenge: how to turn rapid business expansion into sustainable data practices. "At first, we just connected a BI tool directly to our application DB Cloud SQL Postgres," Fasih recalled. "It worked for quick insights, but we knew that it was a temporary solution. As usage grew, cracks began to appear. We even ran into contentions and database locks because both OLTP and analytics were hitting the same system."

The team quickly realized that the ad-hoc setup couldn't keep pace with Voi's streaming data and analytics needs. The first major step was moving to BigQuery for analytics, which gave them more scale and streaming capability. But cost and flexibility soon drove them to Snowflake, where they could finally establish a layered, future-proof data platform.

<table>
<tr>
<td>Voi Micromobility

Voi Technology is a Stockholm-based micromobility company founded in 2018 that offers shared electric scooters across Europe.

With hundreds of employees and operations in many cities, Voi has grown rapidly as a leader in sustainable urban transport.

From the start, the company placed strong emphasis on being data-driven, using analytics to improve fleet operations, safety, and customer experience. This growth demanded a modern data team and platform capable of supporting both rapid experimentation and enterprise-grade governance.</td>
<td>Industry
Micromobility

Headquarters:
Stockholm, Sweden

Team:
13 data professionals across engineering, analytics, and science functions

Tech Stack
Snowflake, dbt, Tableau & Steep</td>
</tr>
</table>

Building a modern architecture

Fasih and his colleagues introduced a four-layer architecture:

- **Raw/Data Lake**: Direct dumps from backend services, 3rd party systems, and external APIs, staged in Google Cloud Storage.
- **Modeled Layer**: Cleaned, structured data sets.
- **Mart Layer**: Business-specific schemas and datasets, e.g., for finance, marketing, operations, etc.
- **Analytics and Metrics Layer**: Standardized definitions of KPIs, used across dashboards and tools.

The migration to dbt was a turning point. In the beginning, transformations were written as ad hoc SQL statements with limited structure and reusability. As the team adopted dbt, it became much easier for data analysts to create and manage their own marts while following centrally defined best practices. "During the transition, we opted for Matillion. But with Matillion, we lacked visibility and version control. We quickly scratched that idea and decided on dbt. dbt gave us a developer-friendly workflow that's still accessible to analysts. That democratization of data transformation using dbt was key in building a scalable data function," Fasih said.

Governance and the data academy

Voi's growth also required a cultural shift. Voi launched a data academy where Fasih designed and delivered SQL and analytics training. The purpose was to create a common language around data, enabling teams from operations, marketing, and finance to run their own queries and interpret metrics without relying entirely on engineers. The academy offered structured sessions on SQL fundamentals, data modeling concepts, and hands-on practice in Snowflake and visualization tools. It also included certification levels, so participants could gradually progress from basic querying to building their own data products. "If people don't understand how to ask the right questions, the best architecture in the world won't matter," he explained.

Combined with dbt tests, documentation, and ownership practices, Voi strengthened its governance foundation. Fasih points to these as best practices for any organization: define clear data ownership, automate testing to catch errors quickly, and maintain living documentation tied directly to transformations. "If you get these basics right from the beginning, you save enormous pain later on," he advised.

Looking ahead

Today, Fasih works at NordicFeel Group, a Nordic beauty retailer. Also, there he is using Snowflake and dbt to explore the next frontier: AI and natural language querying. See the picture of Architecture at NordicFeel below, where Fasih has built on his experience at Voi.

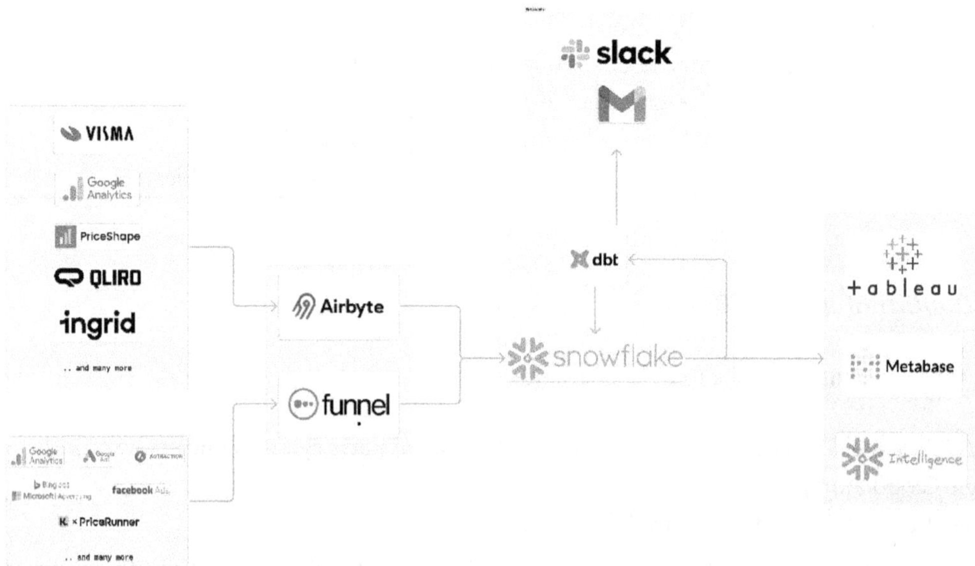

Figure 22: NordicFeel architecture.

He sees LLMs and semantic models as enablers of true data democratization. "The future is people asking questions in plain language and getting reliable, governed answers directly from the data," he said.

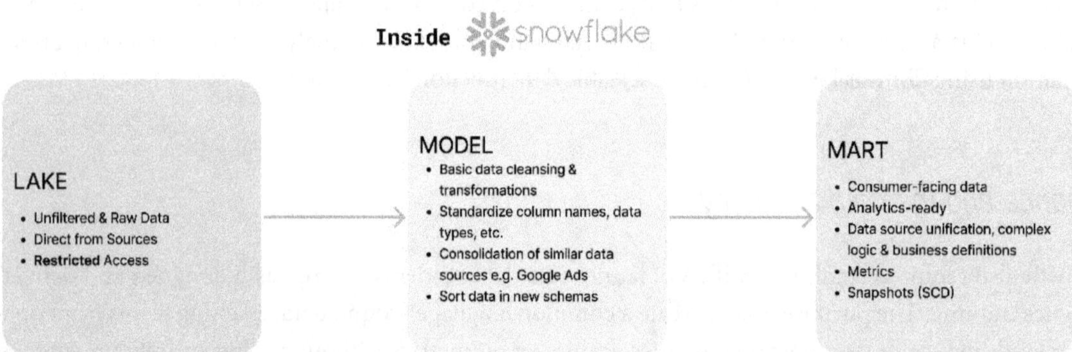

Figure 23: Details on the architecture.

Fasih is also excited about how dbt will become even more deeply integrated with Snowflake itself. Embedding dbt directly into the Snowflake environment will further lower barriers for data analysts, allowing them to build, test, and share models without switching tools or relying on engineers. Combined with advances in natural language interfaces, he believes this integration will unlock a new era of accessibility and collaboration across the data lifecycle.

He summed it up: "We're moving towards a world where analysts, engineers, and business users all work from the same governed platform. That's when true democratization of data happens."

Stena Fastigheter's Data Journey: From reports to predictive insights

"We wanted simplicity and scalability, not another complex system."
– Lars Johansson Blank

Stena Fastigheter: A Data-Driven Future for Sustainable Real Estate	Stena Fastigheter **Industry:** Real Estate
Stena Fastigheter, a leading Swedish real estate company, is recognized for its commitment to building sustainable and thriving communities. Stena Fastigheter, part of the Stena Group, manages over 26,000 properties across Sweden and has business interests in shipping, drilling, and ferry operations. Lars Johansson, Data Architect at Stena Rederi, has been a driving force behind the company's modernization of its data infrastructure. His experience, which spans over two decades of working with SQL Server and data warehousing, played a pivotal role in this transformation.	**Headquarters:** Gothenburg, Sweden **Data Team** Head of Data 2 Data Architects Sweden 3 Data Engineers Poland + Some Data Analysts Architecture was done in Sweden and development in Poland **Tech Stack:** Snowflake, Azure (Event Hub, Streaming Analytics, Data Lake Storage, Data Factory, DevOps, Functions), PowerBI, IoT, Custom Template/Code-generation

The initial data challenges

As with many well-established companies, Stena Fastigheter's legacy systems, including Azure SQL, created bottlenecks in an increasingly data-driven landscape. "Our old systems were functional for basic reporting, but they couldn't keep up with the need for real-time insights and advanced analytics," Lars reflects. The organization had numerous data silos that didn't communicate efficiently, delaying critical decision-making across departments, from property management to customer service.

Lars explains, "We had so many different systems that didn't talk to each other, and it took too long to get the right data into the hands of decision-makers." This fragmentation resulted in inefficiencies and missed opportunities for leveraging data to drive business outcomes.

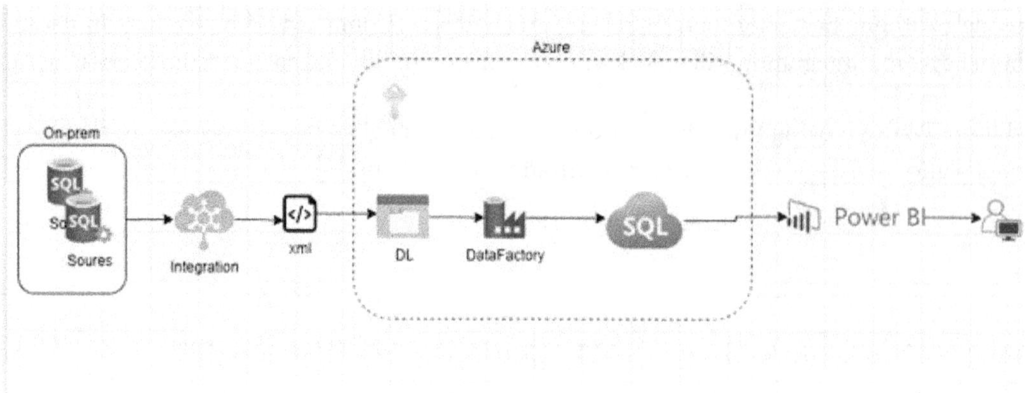

Figure 24: Stena Fastigheter architecture.

Embracing modern design principles

Stena Fastigheter embarked on a transformative journey by integrating Snowflake into its data ecosystem, guided by clear, well-defined design principles that emphasized scalability, transparency, and data integrity:

- **Immutable Data with an Insert-only Principle**: Inspired by Snowflake's inherent immutable data handling, Stena implemented an insert-only approach. Lars notes, "We almost never delete or update; we insert new rows for changes. This ensures full data traceability and simplifies error tracking." Updates, when necessary, follow strict SCD2 guidelines to maintain data integrity.
- **Robust Hashing Strategy**: Security and performance were enhanced by applying hashing to keys and sensitive columns, using MD5 to facilitate secure, efficient data operations. Lars explains, "Hashing gives us both security and a performance boost, essential for handling vast datasets."
- **Comprehensive GDPR Compliance**: Adherence to GDPR was pivotal. Sensitive information was either excluded or rigorously hashed with salt at extraction. Lars elaborates, "Privacy is crucial. Our sensitive data handling is meticulous, ensuring full compliance while retaining utility."
- **Metadata-driven Development**: Borrowing best practices from dbt, Stena automated code generation at development time. Lars emphasizes, "Automating via metadata means fewer errors, better governance, and faster onboarding for new sources."

Adopting a data mesh approach

Recognizing the limitations of a centralized data ownership model, Stena Fastigheter adopted a Data Mesh architecture to decentralize data management across business domains. Lars notes, "Data Mesh pushes ownership closer to business units, reducing bottlenecks and empowering teams to manage their own data while still maintaining central governance. It significantly enhances our scalability and responsiveness."

Data vault and layered data design

Stena Fastigheter's new architecture follows a layered data design, akin to the Data Vault methodology. This design was key to ensuring scalability, transparency, and consistency across the organization's data models. "We implemented a simplified version of the Data Vault approach, focusing on building robust and traceable layers of data," Lars shares.

- **Raw Data Layer (Land)**: Captures raw data from diverse sources, preserving original formats in Snowflake's transient tables, significantly cutting unnecessary storage costs.
- **Stage Layer (Stg)**: Data is standardized, cleaned, and consolidated. "This layer calculates hash keys and applies essential business logic," Lars notes, emphasizing the importance of ensuring consistent, high-quality data.
- **Data Warehouse Layer (DW_RAW and DW)**: Implements a DataVault-inspired model, maintaining traceability through hubs, satellites, and Point-in-Time (PIT) tables. Lars remarks, "Our structured approach here means every data point is traceable, making troubleshooting straightforward."
- **Data Mart Layer (DM)**: Adheres strictly to Kimball's STAR schema methodology. Lars underscores, "Our Kimball-style marts ensure users access accurate, business-friendly views of the data, supporting informed, strategic decision-making."

Leveraging data for sustainability

One of the key reasons for Stena Fastigheter's data transformation was to support its sustainability goals. "Data helps us track and improve the environmental performance of our properties in real time," Lars explains. By using advanced analytics, the team can monitor energy consumption, water usage, and even predict when maintenance is required, thereby reducing unnecessary waste. For instance, predictive models built on Snowflake data have enabled Stena Fastigheter to optimize heating systems across its properties, reducing both energy costs and its carbon footprint. "We've seen real improvements, especially in older buildings where we can now proactively manage energy use instead of reacting after the fact," Lars says.

Empowering teams through data

An unexpected benefit of Stena Fastigheter's data overhaul has been the empowerment of their teams. With modern tools like Snowflake, data is no longer confined to a small group of specialists. Instead, a wider range of employees can access and interpret data, accelerating decision-making processes across the company.

"We're no longer the bottleneck," Lars jokes, referring to his data team. "By giving more people access to real-time data, they can make decisions faster and with more confidence. It has transformed how we work." For example, property managers can now see tenant feedback data in real time, allowing them to act quickly to resolve issues, thereby directly improving customer satisfaction scores.

Lessons learned

Reflecting on the transformation, Lars shares several lessons for other real estate companies looking to modernize their data platforms:

Start with Trustworthy Data: "You can't build anything if you don't trust the data. Start by ensuring your data is accurate and transparent."

Empower Your Teams: "Don't hoard data. Make it accessible and useful to the people who need it."

Think Long-Term: "Data transformations take time, but the benefits—like improved sustainability and efficiency—are worth the investment."

Looking ahead

Stena Fastigheter is not stopping with just better reporting and analytics. Their new platform has laid the groundwork for advanced technologies like machine learning (ML). Lars and his team are already experimenting with ML models for predictive maintenance, allowing them to anticipate when systems like elevators or HVAC units will need repairs. "We're just scratching the surface of what's possible with machine learning. Once we trust our data—and we do now—we can start experimenting with more sophisticated models that will help us be even more efficient and sustainable," Lars shares.

Stena Fastigheter's journey to a modern data platform has transformed how they approach everything from tenant satisfaction to sustainability. By leveraging the power of Snowflake, they've built a scalable, future-proof architecture that will support the company's long-term growth and environmental goals. As Lars Johansson puts it, "We're not just collecting data anymore. We're using it to make our properties smarter, our tenants happier, and our company more sustainable. This is the future of real estate."

Lindex's data platform modernization: Breaking the monolith

"Those red traffic lights told us: it was time to change." – Anna Carlsén

LINDEX	
More than 70 years ago, Lindex started as a lingerie company in Alingsås, Sweden. Today, Lindex is an international fashion company with several different concepts. Lindex is one of the leading fashion retailers in the Nordics, with over 440 stores and 628.8 MEUR in turnover (2024) Lindex recognized the growing need for a scalable, efficient, and future-proof data platform and has been on a digital transformation journey to modernize its data platform.	**Industry:** Retail (Fashion) **Headquarters:** Gothenburg, Sweden **Employees**: 5,000+ **Data Team:** 1 Head of Data & Analytics, 2 Data Engineers (1), 3 Analytic Engineers (1), 3 BI Engineer (1) 1 Data Scientist **Tech Stack** Snowflake, dbt Core, Power BI, Azure, Sling, Airflow, Kubernetes, GIT

The challenges of a legacy system

For years, Lindex relied on a traditional data platform built on Oracle, Informatica, and SAP BusinessObjects. While this setup had served them well in the past, it struggled to keep up with the company's evolving data needs. Anna Carlsén, Head of Data & Analytics at Lindex, recalls: "Our platform was built for a different era. We lacked the ability to perform calculations on large amounts of data, and real-time analytics were simply not possible. Everything was batch-processed overnight, meaning we were always working with outdated insights."

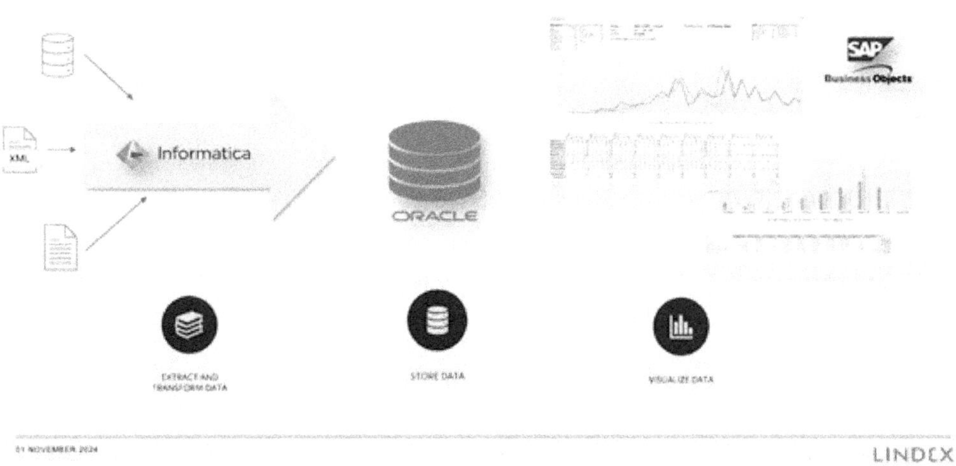

Figure 25: Lindex legacy architecture.

Beyond these technical limitations, the company faced several red flags in its existing architecture:

- **Visualizing Data from Different Sources**: "We relied on Business Objects, which was limited in integrating various data sources. It was frustrating for our teams who needed a holistic view."
- **Consuming Data in New Ways**: "Our ETL tool, Informatica, was designed for a different time. It wasn't flexible enough for modern business needs."
- **Performing Calculations on Large Datasets**: "Oracle could not efficiently handle the growing data volumes we needed to process, limiting our ability to scale."
- **Easily Sharing Data and Insights**: "Business Objects didn't allow seamless sharing across the organization, creating bottlenecks in our decision-making process."

"We spent a lot of time managing reports and trying to create solutions to meet the business's data requirements – requirements that weren't truly supported by the existing platform. It was a time-consuming process that rarely got us all the way, and we often had to make compromises instead of delivering the data and insights that were truly needed," Anna explains.

Adding to the complexity, integrating with Informatica was becoming increasingly expensive, particularly with the high cost of the Snowflake connector. Lindex needed a solution that was not only powerful and scalable but also cost-effective.

The decision to modernize

Recognizing the urgent need for change, Lindex embarked on a transformation journey. Their goal was clear: move from a rigid, legacy system to a flexible, scalable, and analytics-friendly data platform. The company chose Snowflake for data warehousing, dbt for data transformation, and Power BI for visualization and sharing.

"We didn't just want a new platform; we wanted a new way of working. We needed something that would empower our teams, reduce dependencies on IT, and democratize data across the organization," Anna emphasizes. One of the first steps was introducing Power BI, shifting decision-making from static, pre-printed reports to dynamic, self-service analytics. "This was a cultural shift as much as a technical one. Before, our stores relied on static reports that were already outdated when they arrived. With Power BI, we gave decision-makers the ability to explore data directly in meetings and act on insights instantly."

A dual-mode approach: Bridging the old and the new

Transitioning from a legacy system to a modern platform is never an overnight change. To ensure a smooth transition, Lindex adopted a dual-mode approach, where the legacy and new platforms ran in parallel.

"We knew we couldn't just rip out the old system and expect everything to work perfectly. So, we introduced the modern platform step by step while keeping the legacy system operational. This allowed us to migrate use cases gradually without disrupting the business," Anna explains. This approach also helped with organizational buy-in. Instead of imposing a new system, the data team worked closely together with business users to involve all key stakeholders in the process and run a PoC with different technologies.

"We didn't want to just present a 'finalized solution.' We worked together, creating internal ambassadors who championed the new platform. Change management was a critical part of the journey."

The architecture of a modern data platform

Lindex designed its new data platform with a layered architecture, ensuring clarity, maintainability, and scalability:

- **Landing Area**: Where raw data from multiple sources is ingested.
- **Transformation Area**: Where data is cleaned, enriched, and standardized.
- **Reporting Area**: Where business-ready, analytics-optimized data is stored.

This structured approach ensured that data was not only reliable but also easy to consume across departments. "A key principle was making sure we weren't just dumping data into Snowflake. Every layer had a clear purpose, and we built governance and best practices into the design from day one."

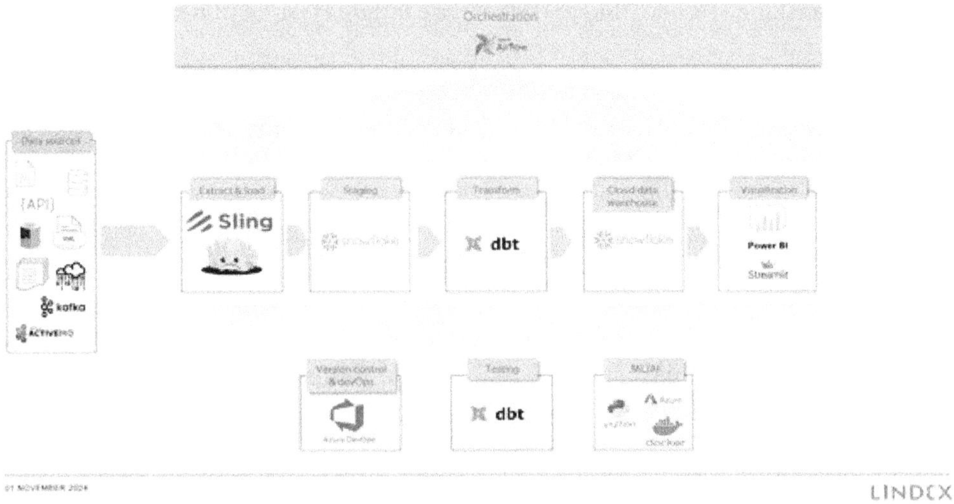

Figure 26: Structured approach.

From data silos to data democratization

One of the biggest shifts Lindex experienced was moving from centralized reporting to data democratization. With Snowflake and dbt, data engineers, analysts, and business users could collaborate more effectively than ever before. "Previously, analysts had to rely on IT to get access to data. Now, they can write their own SQL queries and build their own models. We've broken down silos and enabled true self-service analytics," says Anna. To further enhance adoption, Lindex launched an internal initiative called "Upskilling Analytics" to equip employees across departments with Power BI and SQL skills. "We saw a shift in mindset. Teams that previously depended on static reports started asking deeper questions and creating their own analytics. It was a game-changer," Anna reflects.

Lessons learned

For organizations looking to embark on a similar data transformation journey, Anna offers three key takeaways:

- **Start with the Business Need**: "Technology should solve business problems, not the other way around. Understand what teams need first."
- **Involve the Organization Early**: "Change is hard. The more you engage people, the smoother and more successful the transition will be."
- **Keep it Pragmatic**: "Don't overcomplicate things. Focus on building a platform that works for your company today but is also flexible, adaptable, and can evolve to meet your future needs."

With its new pragmatic data platform, Lindex is no longer just keeping up—it's leading the way in retail analytics, proving that with the right approach, even legacy-heavy companies can transform into data-driven powerhouses.

Looking ahead

Within months of launching the new platform, Lindex saw tangible improvements:

- **Faster Decision-making**: Teams could get self-service insights instead of just having access to IT-created reports.
- **Increased Collaboration**: Data engineers, analysts, and business teams worked together more seamlessly.
- **Cost Efficiency**: Moving to dbt Core and Snowflake reduced licensing costs while improving scalability.

Perhaps most importantly, Lindex positioned itself for future growth and advanced analytics, including machine learning.

"Before, we were just trying to keep up with reporting needs. Now, we're thinking ahead—about predictive analytics, AI, and real-time decision-making. The foundation is in place for us to innovate," Anna says. Looking back, Anna believes that the most critical factor in their success wasn't just the technology—it was the approach. "It's never just about the tools. It's about how you implement them, how you involve people, and how you create a culture of continuous improvement. That's what truly transforms a company."

Case Study: OutSystems: Building trust in data

"We've moved from data chaos to data culture." Pedro Sá Martins

"Before Snowflake, analytics was more about survival than strategy. We were querying replicas of production databases and stitching together answers manually. Today, we enable decisions, not just data." — Pedro Sá Martins, Manager, Data Engineering at OutSystems OutSystems, the global leader in high-performance application development platforms, thrives on speed. But rapid growth exposed weaknesses in their data infrastructure. Data was abundant but fragmented, difficult to trust, and cumbersome to access. Pedro Sá Martins and Bruno Moreira led OutSystems' journey toward a unified, trusted data environment. Their goal was clear: build a robust data culture empowered by reliable, certified datasets.	outsystems OutSystems has approximately 2,300 employees worldwide, with its headquarters located in Boston, Massachusetts. The data team comprises around 30 members: 10 Data Engineers (Canonical Models, Middleware, Pipelines, Data Experience) 15 Analysts and Data Scientists 1 Data Community Advocate 1 Head of Data They support around 700 active Power BI users and 250 Snowflake users **Tech Stack** Data Warehouse: Snowflake Data Transformation: dbt Business Intelligence: Power BI Orchestration: Apache Airflow ETL Pipelines: Fivetran, Snowpipe

From data friction to democratization

Initially, analytics at OutSystems relied on operational database replicas, leading to delays, frustration, and increased complexity.

"You could get the numbers if you knew where to look, but it wasn't scalable, and definitely not self-service." — Bruno Moreira, Data Engineering

Snowflake radically transformed its approach.

Legacy Platform

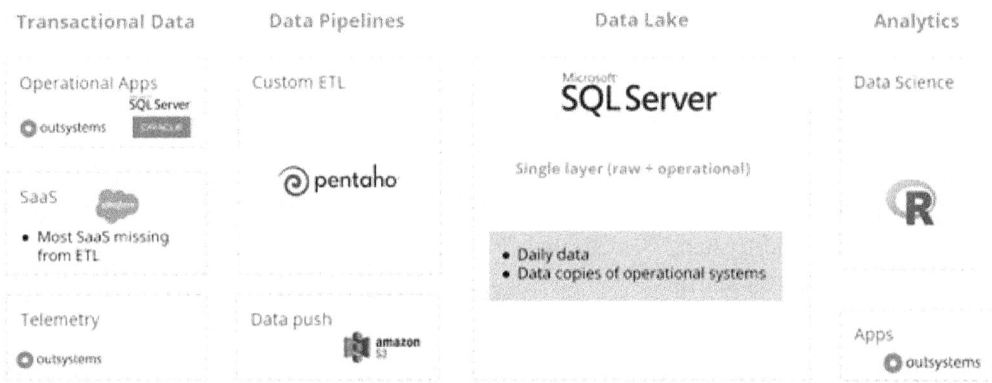

Figure 27: OutSystems architecture.

"Snowflake gave us a clean slate. Data wasn't locked away. Suddenly, everyone from engineers reading JSON telemetry data to sales teams analyzing account performance could use the same SQL language and tools." — Pedro Sá Martins

Yet democratization required new guardrails for data quality and security.

Canonical model: A trusted foundation

The cornerstone of OutSystems' modern data platform became the Canonical Model, a business-aligned data abstraction maintained by its Data Center of Excellence. In simpler terms, the Canonical Model is a standardized version of the most important business data, such as customers, revenue, and accounts, cleaned up, well-defined, and agreed upon across the organization. It serves as a common language for everyone at OutSystems when building reports, dashboards, or AI models. Instead of having each team define metrics in its own way, the Canonical Model ensures consistency and trust.

"Certification was key. If your Power BI dashboard pulled from the Canonical Model and met our standards, we stamped it as certified. Otherwise, it was just another spreadsheet with charts."— Pedro Sá Martins

Data layers: Structured for trust and scalability

OutSystems adopted a structured, three-layer approach in their Snowflake Data Lake, clearly defined by their business and compliance requirements:

- **Raw (Bronze Layer)**: Captures data directly from operational systems and third-party integrations (GDPR-compliant and CDC). Data is stored in its original format, ensuring traceability and data lineage.
- **Service (Silver Layer)**: Here, data undergoes preliminary cleansing, normalization, and transformation. It prepares operational and middleware data for analytical use, reducing complexity for downstream consumers.
- **Curated (Gold Layer)**: This highly refined layer represents the Canonical Model, consisting of certified business-critical metrics and datasets. These datasets are meticulously documented, contextually enriched, and closely governed.

Pedro Sá Martins highlighted the importance of this structured data pipeline clearly:

"Our layers aren't just technical classifications—they're purposeful stages of trust. Data moves progressively from raw and chaotic to structured and trusted. The Curated Gold Layer is the pinnacle of trust and is foundational for our certified reporting."— Pedro Sá Martins

New data platform

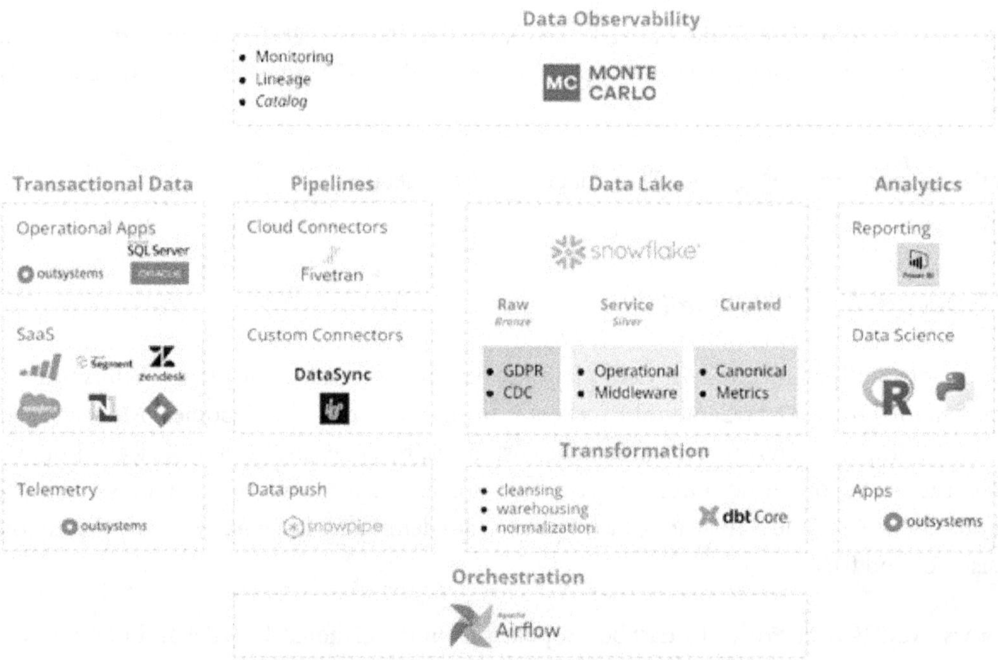

Figure 28: Shifting from Pentaho to dbt.

Initially, OutSystems used Pentaho primarily for SQL orchestration, but it soon proved challenging: "Pentaho felt like we were fighting the tool. dbt now feels like the tool is working with us." — Bruno Moreira

Moving to dbt significantly streamlined their processes. "Adding or removing a field is now just editing a SQL file. That's a revolution in productivity." — Pedro Sá Martins

The benefits were immediate:

- Simplified version control with Git.
- Built-in dependency management.
- Automatic documentation.
- Incremental models reduce development time.

"With dbt, deployments became safe, structured, and straightforward. We stopped fearing updates." — Bruno Moreira

Lessons learned

Implementing dbt was not without hurdles. Some advanced ETL functionalities required stored procedures or creative variable use.

"We sometimes missed features like metadata-driven looping available in Pentaho, but the simplicity and transparency of dbt outweighed those inconveniences." — Pedro Sá Martins

Despite challenges, the shift was overwhelmingly positive.

Looking ahead

With a robust data foundation, OutSystems continues to innovate. They are exploring further automation, enhancing data lineage, and expanding certification frameworks to AI and advanced analytics.

"We've moved from data chaos to data culture. People know where to go. They trust what they see. And they build confidently on top of it." — Pedro Sá Martins

OutSystems' journey illustrates how clarity, simplicity, and trust can transform data from an operational burden into a strategic asset.

Metso's data simplification: Making industrial analytics usable

"If it isn't easy to use, people won't use it." - Arttu-Matti Matinlauri

Metso Corporation is a Finland-based global leader in sustainable technologies and services for aggregates, minerals processing, and metal refining industries. With over **15,000 employees** operating in more than **50 countries**, Metso provides end-to-end solutions that help customers improve productivity, reduce environmental impact, and optimize resource efficiency. The company is listed on Nasdaq Helsinki and is known for its innovation in industrial automation, digitalization, and equipment lifecycle management.	**Industry** Minerals, Machinery, and Services **Headquarters** Helsinki, Finland **Employees** 15000+ **Tech Stack** Snowflake, dbt, Terraform. Streamlit, GitHub, Kafka, IoT Hub, Snowpark

When Arttu-Matti Matinlauri (VP Minerals Segment Digital) joined Metso he quickly realized the company's data platform was holding them back. Legacy systems, poor automation, and rising costs were not just technical inconveniences—they were business blockers.

"The design of the old Databricks platform was a mess," said Arttu-Matti. "It was easier to build a new house from scratch."

The breaking point: Why Metso had to change

Metso's legacy platform, built on Databricks, was plagued with architectural sprawl, inflexible automation, and soaring expenses. Developers struggled to manage the platform efficiently. Spinning up and down clusters was manual and error-prone, and a lack of data catalog and governance made it hard for teams to find and trust data. Cost was another major concern. The team found themselves spending €200,000 annually on tools like Semarchy MDM with minimal return. "We spent two months trying to get value out of Semarchy. With Snowpark and Streamlit, we rebuilt the same in ten days—for free," he said.

The new architecture: Simpler, faster, and smarter

In early 2024, Metso launched a modern data stack centered around Snowflake, dbt, and a modular cloud-native ecosystem:

- IoT Hub and Kafka for real-time ingestion.
- Snowflake for scalable cloud data warehousing.
- dbt for data transformation and modeling.
- Terraform for infrastructure-as-code.
- Streamlit for lightweight apps and UIs.

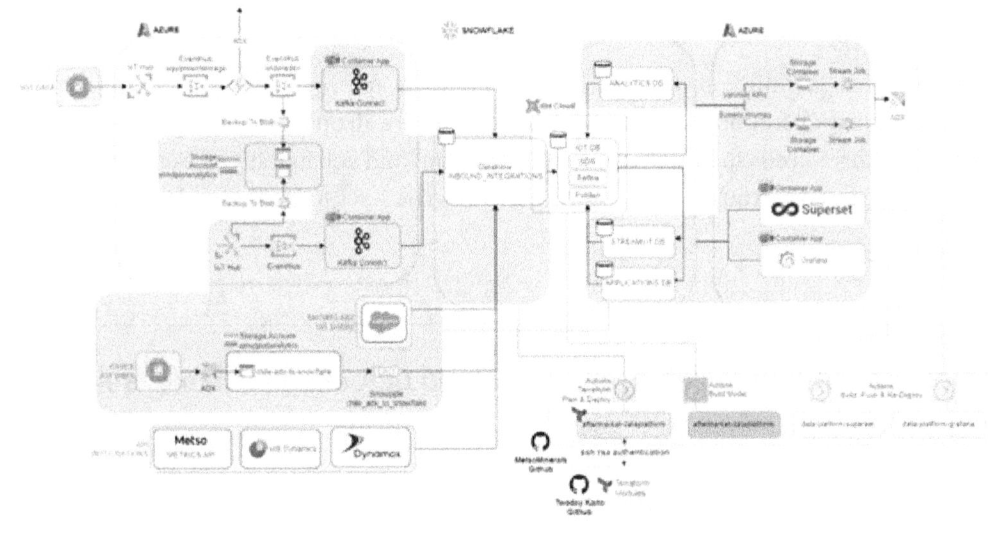

Figure 29: The new architecture.

Replacing Semarchy with a custom MDM solution built with Snowpark and Streamlit delivered immediate savings in both time and software licensing costs. "We saved months of development time and hundreds of thousands of euros in licensing fees," said Arttu-Matti. Their DevOps transformation was just as crucial. Leveraging GitHub and proper CI/CD pipelines, they moved away from fragile environments to a sandbox–test–production setup tailored for data.

Structured data layers and a common language for data

Inspired by modern architectural principles, Metso adopted a layered data architecture. Each layer represents a step in refining and validating data for real-world use:

- **Bronze**: Raw ingested data from machines and sensors.
- **Silver**: Cleaned, enriched, and validated data for operational use.
- **Gold**: Trusted, ready-to-use datasets for business intelligence and AI.

"We're making data visible with Snowflake. Operators and domain experts can now collaborate around the same truth," said Arttu-Matti. By organizing the data in layers instead of a multitude of tables, Metso ensures consistency across teams and systems, providing a shared foundation that everyone can build on.

Real-world impact: Faster innovation, lower cost

The new platform has already driven substantial impact:

- **Cost Reduction**: Estimated €200'000–300'000 in savings thanks to efficient processing and smarter analytics.
- **Faster Delivery**: Development cycles shortened from months to weeks.
- **Better Collaboration**: Cross-functional teams can now explore and use data independently.

Looking ahead

Metso's vision is grounded in futureproofing through continuous improvement and embracing AI and ML. Automated testing, AI-driven operations, and site-wide integration are all on the roadmap. "The number of sensors is growing. Our data platform needs to be autonomous, intelligent, and collaborative," said Arttu-Matti. "If you're not prepared to get fired every day, you're not living your dream. You have to challenge the status quo."

Stora Enso: How patterns, templates, and dbt cloud unlocked scalable, self-service analytics

"One of the big benefits of the new platform is scalability — we can scale up and down as needed." - Mattias Wigelsbo

When Mattias Wigelsbo joined the Forest Division of Stora Enso, all requests were handled by the central data and analytics team, creating bottlenecks, delays, and frustration.

Under the hood, the **technical foundation was fragmented.** The Forest Division had **multiple SQL Server instances** spread across business units and countries, including separate environments in Sweden and Finland—each with its own logic, schedules, and naming conventions. Integrations were mostly batch-based and lacked scalability. It was hard to trace data lineage, and even harder to reuse work across teams.

The result? Bottlenecks. Delays. Frustration.

Stora Enso knew they had to modernize.

"We couldn't be the ones transforming everyone else's data needs forever. It wasn't scalable."

Stora Enso had to rethink not just its tools but its entire data-**delivery model.**

Interviewee:
Mattias Wigelsbo, Data Architect

Industry:
Renewable Materials & Packaging

Headquarters: Helsinki, Finland

Employees: ~20,000

Data Team Size:
12–15 core members in the forest division with **up to 60** dbt developers across the company as a whole

Tech Stack: Snowflake, dbt, Power BI, SAP, Microsoft Azure, SQL Server, Data Factory

"We had reports and pipelines doing similar things in different places, but there was no single structure," Mattias noted. "If someone left the team, we often had no idea how something worked." This legacy setup made cross-country reporting, forecasting, and advanced analytics cumbersome and slow. And while demand for insights kept growing, the centralized team couldn't keep up. As part of the Precision Forestry initiative—a program focused on the digitalization of Stora Enso's Forest assets using geospatial data, imagery, and AI—the team adopted a federated model. "We now support others in becoming product owners. They build their own assets using the same platform."

The shift was both technical and cultural.

Laying the foundations with a pragmatic data platform

To support this federated approach, Stora Enso built a platform with **Snowflake** at its core. "We wanted a platform that's easy to use, doesn't need a dedicated admin team, and has infinite scalability," Mattias noted. **dbt Cloud** became their go-to transformation tool. Combined with Snowflake's simplicity and scalability, and a pragmatic way of working and patterns, it created an environment where domain teams could take ownership without needing deep engineering expertise. "Our transformation logic is in dbt. We've packaged it, added documentation, governance, contracts—it's all there."

A layered, transparent architecture

A key part of Stora Enso's platform design is a layered architecture that brings clarity for analysts and flexibility for engineers. "We have a landing zone in Azure Blob Storage where all raw data comes in," Mattias explained. "From there, we load it into Snowflake and apply transformations in dbt."

The structure is organized as follows:

- **Data Lake**: Raw files from SQL Server, images, logs—stored in Azure Blob.
- **Staging Layer**: Loaded into Snowflake with basic standardization (e.g., column types, names), but mostly untouched. Full history, no change in the meaning of data, no joins.
- **Transform Layer**: Used when the path to the refined model isn´t very straightforward, for example, when there was quite tricky logic that could be split into smaller "problems".
- **Refined Layer**: The curated layer is not limited to star schemas; it can be whatever is needed, for example, a "wide table" for ML use.
- **Mart Layer or Delivery Layer**: A subset of the Refined layer, used to deliver data for specific needs. For example, reports, machine learning, APIs, etc.

This design enables multiple business cases to pull from shared raw and transformation logic, while letting domains tailor their refined and mart layers to their specific needs. "Each refined model supports a specific business use case. But they can also be combined if needed," Mattias said.

Federated ownership where it matters

The shift to federated data ownership was not about handing off everything; it was about handing off the right parts. At Stora Enso, the mart layer is where domain teams have true ownership. This is where they build dbt models, design their own star schemas, and deliver insights via Power BI or other tools.

"We now support others in becoming product owners, building their own assets using the same platform," noted Mattias Wigelsbo. To make this work, the central team provided guardrails: dbt templates, naming conventions, and a common transformation backbone. Domain teams build on top of that foundation to create their own products.

The staging and refined layers, on the other hand, remain largely under the central team's control, especially for shared logic such as master data, calendars, and reference models. Domain teams can extend it when needed, but they do so within clearly defined structures. This split allows for scalability without chaos. Domains move fast in the curated layer, while consistency is preserved in the layers underneath.

How they got people onboard

The challenge wasn't building the platform—it was getting people to use it.

To accelerate adoption, Mattias's team used "starter kits", which are complete dbt project templates with standardized naming, access patterns, and logic for common operations. "We didn't just hand people new software and walk away," Mattias said. "We gave them ready-made templates, offered training, and supported them as they built. That's what really makes this work."

This was the first BIG-scale implementation of the pragmatic data platform. Roberto Zagni was directly involved, and the dbt macros you find in this book are the evolution of what was started in this project.

Use them to bootstrap your project: **https://github.com/pragmatic-data/pragmatic-data-platform**.

Governance without bureaucracy

Rather than heavy top-down control, Stora Enso focused on embedding lightweight standards into the platform itself. Stora Enso introduced simple agreements between the teams that generate data and those that use it. These data contracts, written in a human-readable format, help everyone stay aligned on what's being delivered. "It's not about enforcing strict rules," Mattias explained. "It's about starting the right conversations, so everyone knows what to expect."

The result? Faster delivery, fewer misunderstandings, and better collaboration between business and data teams. "We say: if you build a data product, it must include certain documentation. It must follow these naming conventions. If not, it doesn't go live."

This approach enables decentralized data ownership while maintaining consistency and trust across the platform.

Looking ahead

Stora Enso's journey isn't just about building pipelines. It's about enabling a data ecosystem. "People shouldn't think about how the data gets there. They should think about what value they can create with it," Mattias emphasized. His team continues to refine the balance between empowering domains and providing centralized support.

The goal is clear: a pragmatic, flexible platform that helps the business make better decisions—without IT standing in the way.

Traton's blueprint for data product ownership and collaboration

"We wanted a platform where business teams could take ownership of their data products" - Ramakishore Boda, Data Engineer, Traton Financial Services (Scania)

Traton Financial Services (TFS) is the financial arm of the Traton Group, which includes brands like Scania, MAN, and Navistar. At its core, TFS manages leasing and loan data for commercial vehicles—primarily Scania trucks and buses—across multiple regions, including the Nordics, South America, and Asia.

Though Ramakishore Boda is employed by Scania, he's been embedded in the TFS analytics team for over four years. His role? Design and maintain a modern cloud-based data platform that can serve diverse regional entities, simplify integration across brands, and centralize reporting.

The scope was clear: unify fragmented on-prem systems, move to a cloud-first architecture, and democratize data access—without sacrificing control.

Scania, Traton Financial Services

Industry	Automotive Financial Services
HQ	Södertälje, Sweden
Employees	50,000 (Traton Group) analytics team of 6
Data Team	5 data engineers, one data scientist
Tech Stack	Snowflake, dbt Core, Azure, Power BI, GitLab

Drivers for change

Before Snowflake and dbt, Scania's financial analytics ran on Cloudera's on-prem Hadoop stack. It was siloed and limited. "We had a data lake in Cloudera, but it was only serving one application and one country. There was no unified view across regions," Ramakishore recalls.

With growing demands from Scania Credit, CRM systems, and financial reporting units, the limitations of the old stack became apparent:

- It is difficult to scale or add new users.
- Inflexible for self-service analytics.
- Separate pipelines and data silos across regions.
- A shift was needed to something cloud-native, flexible, and developer-friendly.

Building the platform: A layered, scalable architecture

TFS adopted a modern ELT approach built around Snowflake, dbt Core, GitLab, and Azure:

- **Cloud Platform**: Azure.
- **Data Warehouse**: Snowflake.
- **Transformation layer**: dbt Core.
- **Orchestration:** GitLab Pipelines (previously Apache Airflow).
- **BI Tool:** PowerBI.
- **Version Control**: GitLab.
- **Source Systems**: SQL Server, mainframes, Dynamics 365, CRM, and others.
- **Ingestion**: Power BI Dataflows used as lightweight ETL to Azure Data Lake.
- **Loading to Snowflake**: Azure Data Factory (ADF) pushes raw data into Snowflake.

TFS followed a structured dbt project using:

- **Base Layer**: Raw ingestion into Snowflake, often called "staging".
- **Intermediate Layer**: Business logic and transformations, including unifying inconsistent schemas across countries.
- **Marts Layer**: Final curated data products ready for analytics and data sharing.

"Staging is the most critical layer. That's where we do all our data quality checks—schema evolution, column drops, type mismatches—we catch everything there," said Ramakishore.

To enforce quality and streamline development, they made heavy use of open-source dbt packages:

- dbt_project_evaluator.
- dbt-utils.
- dbt-constraints.
- dbt-coregen.
- dbt-pumpkin (created by one of their own team members).

These tools automate schema definitions, enforce tests, and simplify code generation.

Data mesh at work: Decentralized ownership with central governance

Though the platform is centralized in Snowflake, the team has embraced a data mesh-inspired model, organizing their architecture by data products:

- CRM Data.
- Dynamics 365 Financial Data.
- Scania Credit & Leasing.
- Regulatory Reporting.
- Audit Logs.

Each product area has its own dbt project structure and staging zone, mapped to business domains. "We let the product teams define the business logic. They know their data best. But the core engineering setup—we own that," explained Ramakishore. This hybrid model enables self-service modeling with business users who understand SQL to write their own dbt models in a dedicated GitLab branch. The data engineering team reviews and approves their work before merging it into production.

Enabling collaboration with GitLab

Instead of GitHub or Airflow, TFS chose GitLab pipelines for orchestration and versioning. "Since we already use GitLab for code versioning, it made sense to also run our dbt jobs there. No need to add more tools if GitLab could do it." They schedule daily jobs, track model changes, and support dbt snapshots for monthly historical data—a critical feature for financial reports.

Lessons learned

When asked about his main learnings from building the platform, Ramakishore didn't hesitate: "Dbt can look intimidating. People think you need to know Python, Jinja, or Git deeply. But if you know SQL, that's enough to get started." By decoupling the staging and logic layers, using community packages, and embedding data governance early on, the team created a flexible platform that scales with business needs.

One of the more advanced lessons? Involve your stakeholders. "We save a lot of time when the business teams model their own logic. We just guide them."

Chapter review

In this chapter, you explored real-world case studies from eight companies across industries—each facing its own version of the same challenge: legacy systems that were fragile, siloed, or slow.

By adopting Snowflake, dbt, and modern automation practices, these organizations built pragmatic data platforms that scale, integrate, and enable true self-service. **Their stories show how modern architecture unlocks speed, collaboration, and advanced analytics.**

They share a common foundation that reflects the core principles of the Pragmatic Data Platform (PDP). All rely on Snowflake and dbt as the technical backbone, organized into a clearly layered architecture separating ingestion, storage, refinement, and delivery.

They embed DataOps best practices—version control, CI/CD, and automated testing to ensure consistency and trust. Many are also evolving toward Data Mesh principles, empowering domain teams with ownership and federated governance.

Together, these stories demonstrate that while every organization is unique, the path to a pragmatic data platform follows a similar arc:

- Legacy bottlenecks eventually reach a breaking point.
- Layered design with Snowflake and dbt provides scalability and trust.
- Governance and automation reduce firefighting and increase confidence.
- Empowering teams with self-service analytics and modern practices drive cultural change as much as technical change.

Pragmatic Data Platform is not just a theoretical framework—it's a proven way of working that's already shaping how modern data teams succeed!

Recommended resources

Company websites & LinkedIn profiles

- **Rebtel**—https://www.rebtel.com/.
    - **Chandan Singh** https://www.linkedin.com/in/chandan-singh/.
- **Voi Technology**—https://www.voi.com/.
    - **Fasih Ullah** https://www.linkedin.com/in/fasihullah/.
- **Stena Fastigheter**—https://www.stenafastigheter.se/.
    - **Lars Johansson Blank** https://www.linkedin.com/in/larsjohanssonblank/.
- **Lindex**—https://www.lindex.com.
    - **Anna Carlsén** https://www.linkedin.com/in/anna-carls%C3%A9n-257a785/.
- **OutSystems**—https://www.outsystems.com/.
    - **Pedro Sá Martins** https://www.linkedin.com/in/pedro-sa-martins/.
    - **Bruno Moreira** https://www.linkedin.com/in/brunosousamoreira/.
- **Metso**—https://www.metso.com/.
    - **Arttu-Matti Matinlauri** https://www.linkedin.com/in/arttumatinlauri/.
- **Stora Enso**—https://www.storaenso.com/.
    - **Mattias Wigelsbo** https://www.linkedin.com/in/mattias-wigelsbo/.
- **Traton**—https://traton.com.
- **Scania**—https://www.scania.com.
    - **Ramakishore Boda** https://www.linkedin.com/in/ramakishore-boda-70844217/.

PART II

The Pragmatic Data Platform Layers

This second part discusses in detail each layer of the Pragmatic Data Platform.

We start with Chapter 7, providing a data platform playbook and a QuickStart to kick off your project in the right direction, and then we delve into each of these layers in the Pragmatic Data Platform:

- **The ingestion layer**. While Data Movement is mostly considered external to the data platform development, it is crucial to understand how it is done, and new features of Snowflake are bringing it within the scope of the data platform development. Data Ingestion is sometimes not considered part of the data platform development, or at least not in its core, but it is something dbt and Snowflake can do very well with high automation. As it is almost always needed, it makes sense to discuss it well.
- **The storage layer**. The Data Storage layer is the key layer for making a data platform quick and easy to create, and easy to fix and evolve. The core goal of the Storage layer is to centralize all states of the data platform (data and metadata), distill knowledge of upstream systems, and absorb and adapt their changes, reducing the need for overall rework in the data platform.
- **The refined layer**. The Data Refinement layer is the real brain of your data platform, where we shift our focus from storing data to transforming it into valuable, reusable business information built with your very own business concepts.
- **The delivery layer**. The Data Delivery layer is where you select what you have built in the Refined layer to present a complete yet easy-to-use data mart, wide table, or feature table for the different domains and use cases you have.

CHAPTER 7

Implementation Playbook

This chapter kicks off Part Two by providing a pragmatic playbook to help you build your data platform layers quickly and effectively. We aim to set you on the right path to start efficiently, while being ready to scale your platform with more data models, larger datasets, a growing team of developers, and an expanding base of users and consumers. We begin by anchoring our discussion in the data lifecycle, understanding how data is created, transformed, and consumed, and then detail the key activities across portfolio and project levels to ensure successful implementation and continuous improvement.

The topics that we are going to cover in this chapter are:

- The Data Life Cycle and Data Flow in a Data Platform.
- The Pragmatic Data Platform Playbook.
- File, Model, and Macro Organization.
- Project QuickStart.

Sample project and code

The sample dbt project is available at: **https://github.com/pragmatic-data/stonks**. The code samples for this chapter are in the sub-folder `chapter_07`, under the `code_samples_by_chapter` folder. Please note that, to fit the limited size of the printed page, we omit most of the comments and change the formatting of the code blocks compared to the files.

The data life cycle

Data engineering, at its core, is the discipline of collecting data from diverse sources and harmonizing it into a cohesive, understandable form that makes sense to business users and exceeds the value of its individual source components. Data engineers typically do not generate the raw data itself. Instead, they focus on the meticulous management and integration of existing data streams.

As Francesco Puppini, the inventor of the Unified Star Schema, aptly notes, the very etymology of "data" stems from the Latin "datum," meaning "given." The information we work with is bestowed upon us, making our role that of diligent and responsible stewards. The goal of data engineering is to distill this raw material into meaningful information, all while preserving the integrity of the original data and avoiding the introduction of noise or distortion throughout its journey.

Data flow for a data platform

The next few points introduce the general data flow at a high enough level that can be applied to pretty much every use case. The many, and often significant, differences between data platforms lie in how the steps are performed and in the results of each step. At a very high level of abstraction, the data flow is as follows:

1. **Data creation**: Data is generated in a source system when something work-related occurs. This is where the raw data is created.

2. **Data movement and storage**: Data from multiple source systems is extracted from the sources and moved to the data platform, stored with a desired time depth, and made available for analysis. The terms "source data", "raw data", "historical data", or simply "history" loosely refer to the different stages the data undergoes in this step.

3. **Data transformation**: The end goal of data engineering is to take historical data available on the data platform and transform it into integrated, meaningful, and easy-to-consume information for business users. This is the key stage of a data platform, where value is added by turning raw data into refined information for reports and for business users to understand.

4. **Consumption of refined information**: The most common interface for consuming refined information is business reports built with BI tools. They provide simple access to pre-built reports for general business users and may allow varying grades of self-service reporting for power users. Other options, like AI and data-driven apps, exist and are becoming increasingly common.

5. **Data writeback:** Business users can interact with data in reporting tools or data applications to generate new data. This user input, as well as the refined information or the machine learning insights derived from the aggregated information, is often fed back into the data platform and sent back to one or more source systems.

This is a very general flow that covers very different paradigms, but is useful for providing you with a general plan for what we are going to do with dbt and Snowflake. In this book, we will cover points 2, Data movement and storage, and 3, Data transformation, which is the maximal scope of dbt projects on Snowflake. If you want to know more, please refer to chapter four of my book, "Data Engineering with dbt," where I analyze the data lifecycle in detail.

In the next section, we will introduce the basic playbook that we use to develop our projects using the Pragmatic Data Platform tools and way of working.

Pragmatic Data Platform playbook

In this section, we will present you with the Pragmatic Data Platform playbook, which is our approach to starting the development of a data platform and establishing the way of working for its teams. It is a high-level, generic description of what we suggest you plan to do; you will find the details of the why and how in the chapters that follow.

High-level architecture

Let's start by recalling the Pragmatic Data Architecture from Chapter 1 and the role of each layer.

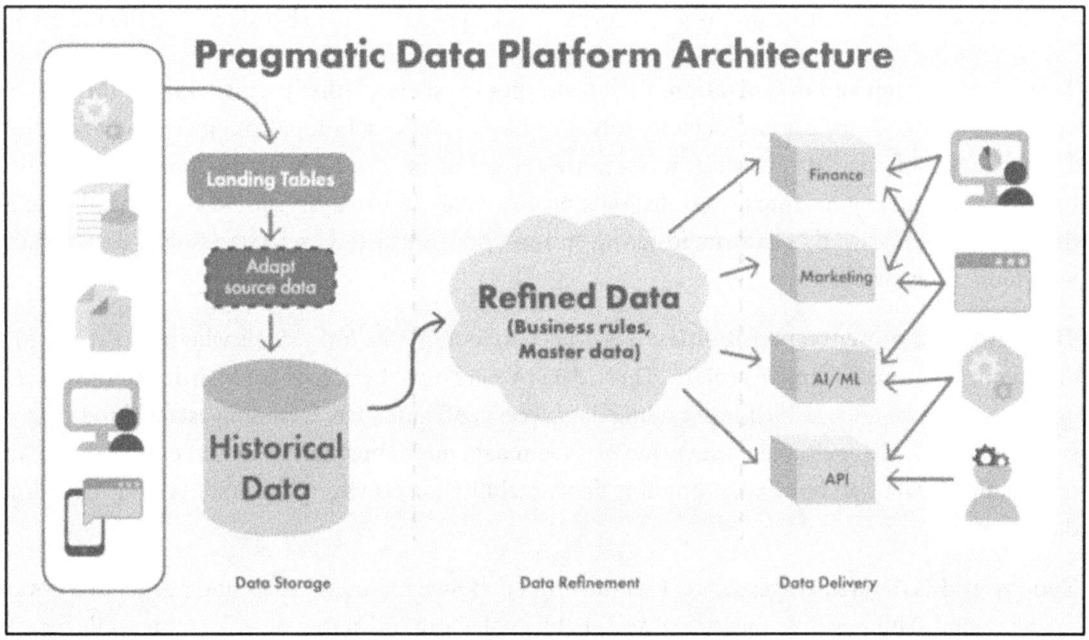

Figure 30: Pragmatic Data Architecture.

The layers in the picture are:

- **Data Sources**: It represents all types of input, structured and semi-structured, and the metadata from unstructured data. They may require data movement and ingestion from files, or be provided via Snowflake shares for greater convenience and less effort.
- **Data Storage**: The layer that makes sure we store permanently all the changes that we receive from the sources. It includes:
  - **Ingestion**: The part that loads data from Files into Landing Tables. The Landing Tables (LT) contain the same exact data as the files. NO CHANGES.
  - **Storage**: The part that makes the data usable without changing the meaning of the data and stores in an immutable way all the changes received. JUST RECORD HISTORY.

- **Data Refinement**: The layer that builds the Business Concepts, integrating the data from the available sources. It is logically stateless as any stateful model should be introduced only for performance and not for correctness. MAKE SENSE OF HISTORY.
- **Data Delivery**: The layer consists of data marts that deliver datasets for downstream consumption. The most common type is the reporting data mart, usually built according to Kimball architecture with Facts and Dimensions. LOOK AT A SPECIFIC PART OF HISTORY.

Portfolio level playbook

A data platform project can range from a single team's effort to a complex initiative involving many teams, depending on the organization's size and the data's scope. If you are in a smaller situation, you can focus on the Project-level playbook. For a multi-team/project scenario, it is beneficial to begin by addressing the following topics:

- **Team composition and organization:** Each team should possess, either permanently or through easy access, all the necessary competencies to fully own its part of the solution, from inception to delivery. This includes skills in data architecture, software development, and Agile methodologies. The shift towards analytics engineering means that data professionals and analysts should work together to build the core of a modern data platform, fostering end-to-end control and understanding of data semantics within their business units.
- **Team and data owner responsibilities:** It is crucial to identify the individuals who hold the key to the data required by each team or project. These data owners must be actively onboarded to the project and explicitly become responsible for providing data access and guidance, including establishing clear communication channels. Adopting principles from data mesh, business units can extend their data ownership to data warehousing, promoting accountability for providing and maintaining agreed-upon data products.
- **Tooling and Federated Governance:** Establishing a cohesive tooling strategy and a federated governance model is vital. This ensures consistency and enables collaboration across diverse teams while maintaining autonomy where appropriate. While you don't want to control how teams work, you want to make sure that different technologies, ways of working, assumptions, and the semantics of the delivered data products don't hinder collaboration and access to the data. A common agreement on selected technologies, such as Snowflake shares or Iceberg tables, and the requirement to provide strong contracts at boundaries, such as those provided by dbt Mesh, can significantly reduce these risks.
- **Portfolio level planning and Cross-project alignment:** Effective planning at the portfolio level is essential to developing the data platform in a sustainable, value-driven way. The organization of projects, their order, and their priorities are crucial. Cross-collaboration is a must. With a careful plan, you can prevent bottlenecks caused by dependencies on other teams and ensure everything aligns with your strategic goals.

You can refer to chapter 3, Pragmatic Governance, for a selection of good practices and principles you can adopt, with a special focus on decentralized data architectures and managing data as a product. Once these general, portfolio-level topics are covered, you can then proceed to consider project-level topics for each individual project.

Project-level playbook

Once the overarching portfolio-level considerations are in place, each project within the data platform initiative requires its own focused approach. The project-level playbook details the specific steps and best practices for teams to deliver high-quality, maintainable data solutions using dbt and Snowflake.

We will divide the playbook into three major phases:

- Project Inception and Definition.
- Solution Design and Development.
- Deployment, Operations, and Continuous Improvement.

The next sections detail these three points.

While there is a logical progression in these three phases, it is important to remember that we want an iterative, Agile development process. This means that it is possible to move to the activities of the next phase even if not all activities of the previous phase are completed. For example, it is possible to deliver the first few development iterations without all extraction tools in place, or to deploy to production even if monitoring and alerting are not yet complete.

***Adopt an Agile mindset. Delivering value is the primary measure of success**, but automation and quality controls must be in place to enable the project to scale without losing the ability to deliver.*
Don't let technical debt grow unchecked.

To immediately put these principles into practice, the following "Sample model organization" section introduces our standard file and folder structure, while the "Project QuickStart" section provides a concise, step-by-step guide to initiating a new data project with dbt and Snowflake.

Phase 1: Project inception and definition

This initial phase focuses on establishing the project's foundation, aligning it with business needs, and setting up the core collaborative environment and technical infrastructure:

- **Define project objectives and scope**: Clearly articulate the project's purpose, key business problems it addresses, and desired outcomes.

- **Define the data products or analytical insights to be delivered**: Scope the project into manageable, iterative increments to enable Agile delivery of value. Identify key business stakeholders and their requirements.

- **Establish communication channels**: Set up regular meeting cadences (e.g., stand-ups, sprint reviews) for internal project team communication. Define channels and cadences for communication with business stakeholders and dependent teams.

- **Set up infrastructure, tools, and project repository**: Define how data is extracted from sources and delivered to Snowflake or to files that dbt and Snowflake can access. Provision access to a Snowflake account and provide the ability to set up databases and roles as shown in Chapter 2. Create a dedicated

Git repository for the dbt project and set up the dbt Cloud project. This is also explained in Chapter 2. Set up and manage distinct dbt environments (e.g., DEV, QA, PROD) for isolated development and testing. Ensure Snowflake connections and credentials are properly configured for each environment. Use README files to document the project overview, setup instructions, key contacts, frequently used commands, contribution guidelines, and pull request templates.

Once the tooling is in place and it's clear what needs to be built, it's time to start iterating the core activities to build the data platform.

Phase 2: Solution design and development

This phase involves the core technical work of designing the data models and implementing transformations using dbt and Snowflake. It also includes all the activities to ensure the accuracy, reliability, and usability of the data products through rigorous testing and comprehensive documentation.

Design a layered solution, focusing on the specific goals of each layer:

- **Storage Layer:** Plan for the ingestion of raw source data and its storage, ensuring immutability and reproducibility. Define naming conventions and initial schema for landing and history tables.
- **Refined Layer:** Design transformations for cleaning, integrating, and applying business logic to the data from the storage layer. Identify common joins, aggregations, and data harmonizations.
- **Delivery/Mart Layer:** Structure aggregated, business-friendly data marts optimized for analytical consumption. Define the granularity and dimensions for key analytical use cases.

Implement Modular dbt Models: Develop dbt models by breaking complex transformations into smaller, reusable, and testable components for enhanced readability and maintainability. Ensure consistent data types and granularities across all models to maintain data integrity.

Implement comprehensive testing, but don't make it intrusive:

- **Data and Unit Tests:** Apply built-in tests and develop your own to validate data quality and model integrity. Use unit tests to ensure the correctness of complex business rules.
- **Data Freshness Tests:** Configure freshness checks on critical source data to ensure data timeliness. Give your business user access to the freshness report.
- **Acceptance Testing:** Collaborate closely with business stakeholders to define and execute user acceptance tests (UAT) that validate data accuracy and completeness against business expectations.
- **Regression Testing:** Design and execute tests to ensure that new changes do not negatively impact existing data pipelines or models. Add a test for each bug you discover, to prevent it from returning.

Leverage automated documentation: Utilize AI-driven dbt documentation generation capabilities to create a searchable data catalog, improved by human curation during UAT. Provide clear descriptions for relevant dbt models, columns, sources, and metrics. This is especially important for sources and models in the delivery data marts. Link technical documentation to the organizational business glossary to ensure a shared understanding of key terms and metrics across the business and technical teams. Create or generate exposures to document downstream dependencies on the project's models.

Once the project has reached a critical mass or if performance starts to decline, it is possible to adopt incremental build strategies that trade simplicity for performance. Pick the top three to five longest-running models and try to build them with an incremental logic to optimize query performance and reduce processing times by only processing new or changed data.

This next phase outlines the steps to bring the data solution to production and ensure its ongoing reliability.

Phase 3: Deployment, operations, and continuous improvement

This final phase encompasses deploying the data solution to production, managing its ongoing operations, and fostering continuous learning and refinement.

- **Establish CI/CD functionality with GIT integration**: Automate the build, test, and deployment of dbt code through Continuous Integration/Continuous Delivery (CI/CD) pipelines. Decide how you release to intermediate and production environments.
- **Automate orchestration and scheduling**: Schedule dbt jobs to run at appropriate intervals to ensure timely data freshness and availability, or trigger them on relevant events.
- **Implement monitoring and alerting**: Set up monitoring for dbt job failures, data quality anomalies, and performance issues within Snowflake. Configure alerts for critical events to ensure prompt notification and resolution by the team.
- **Foster continuous improvement**: Regularly review project performance, identify areas for optimization, and refactor code as needed. Encourage ongoing knowledge sharing within the project team and with the broader data community. Gather feedback from business users to iterate on and enhance data products.

By diligently applying the principles and practices outlined in this playbook, project teams can consistently deliver high-quality, trustworthy data products that meet business needs and contribute effectively to the overall data platform.

Organization of raw data, macros, and models

In this section, we provide a visual guide to the recommended organization of both your raw data files, exported from your sources and ingested into your project, and your dbt project's models and macros. This structured approach is essential for maintaining clarity, ensuring consistency, and effectively implementing the Pragmatic Data Platform architecture.

Raw data and storage accounts organization

The following textual representation illustrates a recommended approach for organizing raw exported source data files within a storage account. You don't see this in dbt, but you use it.

.

```
├── Your_Storage_Account/
│   ├── group_marketing_data/              # Marketing domain
│   │   ├── source_system_a/               # Source system A
│   │   │   ├── table_x/                   # Table X's exported data files
│   │   │   │   ├── data_file_1.csv        # Exported as CSV
│   │   │   │   └──...
│   │   │   ├── table_y/                   # Table Y's exported data files
│   │   │   │   ├── data_file_2.parquet    # Exported as Parquet
│   │   │   │   └──...
│   │   │   └──...
│   │   ├── source_system_b/               # Source system B
│   │   │   └──...
│   │   └──...
│   ├── group_crm_data/                    # CRM-related domain
│   │   ├── crm_system_p/                  # CRM system P
│   │   │   ├── customer_data/
│   │   │   │   └──...
│   │   │   └── sales_leads/
│   │   │       └──...
│   │   └──...
│   └──...
```

This structure groups related source systems and organizes data by individual tables. If the data volume is high, you can further split each table by year, month, date, or hour to speed up ingestion.

In this example, we used a single storage account, but in reality, you will eventually have data that requires stricter access controls. By putting the data in different storage accounts and folders, using different storage integrations as needed, and eventually ingesting it using separate dbt projects, you can easily match the required level of security and provide granular access to ingested data.

Ingestion macros and model organization

The following textual representation illustrates the recommended folder structure for your dbt project, organizing models and macros according to the Pragmatic Data Platform (PDP) architecture layers. This is what you will see every day in your dbt project, so make it comfortable for you!

```
.
├── ingestion/                      # Ingestion Layer (macros)
│   └── source_system_a/            # Ingestion for System A
│       ├── setup_sys_a.sql         # Ingestion setup—System A
│       ├── table_x.sql             # Landing Table for table_X
│       ├── table_y.sql             # Landing Table for table_Y
│       └──...
├── models/
│   ├── 01_storage/                 # Storage Layer
│   │   ├── source_system_a/        # Storage for System A
│   │   │   ├── stg_table_x.sql     # Staging model for table X
│   │   │   ├── hist_table_x.sql    # History model for table X
│   │   │   ├── ver_table_x.sql     # Version model for table X
│   │   ├── source_system_b/        # Storage for System B
│   │   │   ├──...
│   │   └──...
│   ├── 02_refined/                 # Refined Layer: Business concepts
│   │   ├── ref_orders_base.sql     # Refined model for orders
│   │   ├── refh_customer.sql       # Refined model for customers (w/history)
│   │   ├── refh_product.sql        # Refined model for products (w/history)
│   │   ├── agg_daily_sales.sql     # Aggregated—daily sales
│   │   └──...
│   └── 03_marts/                   # Delivery Layer: Curated marts
│       ├── sales_mart/             # Data mart for Sales
│       │   ├── fct_sales_transactions.sql  # Sales TX fact table
│       │   ├── dim_customer.sql            # Customer dimension (current)
│       │   ├── scd2_customer.sql           # Customer dimension (SCD2)
│       │   └──...
│       ├── marketing_mart/           # Data mart for Marketing
│       │   ├── fct_campaign_perf.sql # Campaign performance fact
│       │   ├── dim_channel.sql       # Marketing channel dim
│       │   └──...
│       └──...
│
└── dbt_project.yml      # dbt project configuration file
```

This structure promotes modularity, clarity, and maintainability.

Now that you've seen the recommended structure for your exported data and the dbt project folders, the "Project QuickStart" section will walk you through the immediate, actionable steps to get your first project initialized and developed in the first iterations.

Project QuickStart

The goal of this QuickStart is to cover the first few iterations of your projects, pointing you to the important actions and their general order.

This section provides a streamlined set of steps to get your new dbt project up and running quickly with Snowflake, allowing you to immediately start building and iterating on your data transformations.

Start by performing the initial setup for Snowflake, dbt Cloud, and GitHub. Follow the instructions **from Chapter 2** to set up the project repository in GitHub, the project databases, roles, and service users in Snowflake and the project, environments, and jobs in dbt Cloud.

Identify Your First Use Case. Select a first, simple, yet useful report or analytical output as your initial target. This use case requires you to implement an **end-to-end slice** of the data platform, from sources to delivery, ensuring you engage with all the necessary layers from the outset. It's better if the business rules are not overly complex.

Keep it small and not overly complex, but not entirely trivial. Three to five tables from a single source are ideal. Business rules should be straightforward, without many exceptions. Have a clear understanding of what you want to deliver. That is best expressed as a data model of the target data mart. Have a clear understanding of your starting point. This is best expressed by a data model of the source system(s).

Have a decent understanding of how you will bridge the gap between the source and target, including the business rules that need to be applied. A data model of the refined layer, coupled with a description of the business rules, is a good starting point. This provides flexibility to adjust initial expectations based on the data realities that emerge.

Export and Ingest Data into Landing Tables. This step is important to help you start making key decisions about your ingestion process. Validate your export tool and its intended use to either write directly to the Landing Tables or to export files. If exporting to files, pick a storage location and design a file organization strategy. One storage account with folders for related source systems (those in the same domain or with similar security requirements) and subfolders for tables is a good starting point.

Start designing the authorization to access the exported source files. One storage integration per storage account is a good initial approach. Defer adding complexity until stronger access differentiation is required.

Create the setup for the PDP ingestion of each source system. In dbt, use one folder and one setup file for each source system. Ingest the needed tables leveraging the PDP macros. Use a single file with metadata-driven macro calls for each table.

Add the Storage Layer for Ingested Tables. Configure dbt to build models in the `01_storage` folder within a storage layer-specific schema. If source systems have many tables, consider creating subfolders by source system and deploying each subfolder to its own schema. For each landing table, you will create its own storage pipeline, typically composed of:

- **Staging Model (STG)** to make the data usable. This model performs initial cleanup, standardization, type conversions, and other operations that make the data usable without altering its meaning. It also adds metadata to track when and from where the data was loaded into the data platform.
- **Historization Model (HIST)** to store all changes. Pick the right historization pattern for your use case to capture the full history of data changes.
- **Versioning Model (VER)** to make instance versions easy to use.
This model provides a simplified use of the historized data. It provides a stable historical key, the validity period for each version, and makes it easier for downstream models to access just the latest state.
- **Apply proper tests** on the sources, STG, HIST, and VER models to guarantee that incoming source data is as expected and that the historized data conforms to your data model.

- **Document the incoming tables**, focusing especially on keys (Primary Keys, Foreign Keys, Business Keys) and columns that will be important in business rules.
- **Ensure source freshness** is tracked for critical tables, typically facts and key dimensions.

Implement the Refined Layer. Build the business concepts that you need to complete your use case under the `02_refined` folder. Read data from the VER model in the storage layer, selecting either full historical data or the current version, as appropriate. Filter out deleted instances if necessary.

Remember to build modular models, breaking down complexity to maximize reuse and testability. Try to build models that have a well-defined meaning, ideally with only a single reason to change. If sensible, avoid applying many unrelated business rules simultaneously.

As you've tested the sources and will test the final outputs, here you primarily need to test only complex business rules or joins. This helps pinpoint where a problem is or might arise in the future. Document what would be difficult to infer from the code. This typically includes the *why* behind specific design choices, especially if they deviate from the most common approaches.

Create and Populate the First Data Mart. This involves setting up the delivery layer to hold the facts and dimensions (or wide tables) you planned for the use case. Create a subfolder under the `03_marts` folder for the data mart and configure dbt to deploy it to its own schema. Build the facts and dimensions in the data mart subfolder, using only models from the refined layer and explicitly selecting only the needed columns for each model.

Provide strict guarantees for your end users by applying data contracts and data tests to your facts and dimensions. Data contracts provide guarantees about names and data types, while data tests ensure the models' content meets expectations.

Initially, you can access these models from your BI tool using the default read-only role for the production or test environment created during the initial setup. In a future iteration, create a data mart-specific reader role and assign it to the service user impersonated by your BI tool. Add exposures to document the data mart and how downstream applications use the models. Provide clear documentation for all facts, dimensions, and their columns that you expose to end users.

Build First Reports/Dashboards and Conduct User Acceptance Tests (UAT). Develop initial reports or dashboards based on your data mart. Validate them through User Acceptance Tests (UAT) with business users and collect their feedback. This closes the loop on your end-to-end slice.

At the time you start writing the code of the first models, you should have already created a CI/CD job following the setup instructions from Chapter 2. If you have not done so yet, early in the process is a good time to do it.

Each individual step of the previous QuickStart is also a great candidate for exercising the CI/CD pipeline and your release process, and for fostering team collaboration and coaching less senior members by opening and discussing relevant Pull Requests, or through code walkthroughs if you want a more interactive discussion. Depending on the complexity of the chosen use case, you might implement everything in a single iteration or spread it across multiple iterations.

A good pattern is to start with a report built on a single data source and then, in subsequent iterations, extend it to integrate data from multiple sources, increasing the complexity of the required business rules and perhaps adding elements of a Master Data Management process. Once your team is familiar with the key steps presented here, it is time to introduce all the other activities highlighted in the project playbook, with special attention to those of Phase 3: Deployment, Operations, and Continuous Improvement.

Chapter review

In this chapter, you've gained a comprehensive understanding of how to build and scale your data platform using a pragmatic approach. You started by grounding yourself in the data life cycle and understanding the data flow within a data platform. You then explored the Pragmatic Data Platform playbook, including its high-level architecture. We delved into the specifics of both the portfolio-level and project-level playbooks, breaking down the latter into three distinct phases: Project Inception and Definition, Solution Design and Development, and Deployment, Operations, and Continuous Improvement. Finally, you saw how to apply these concepts, along with our suggested file, model, and macro organization, using the project QuickStart.

This chapter provides you with a detailed overview of the process to build a data platform without entering into all the details that we will cover in more detail for each layer in the next chapters, starting with the Ingestion layer. Once you complete the book, it will be a great reference to use during projects.

Recommended resources

- For a deeper understanding of the Pragmatic Data Platform's architecture and its comparison to other styles, refer to **Chapter 1, "A Pragmatic Data Platform."**
- For detailed guidance on setting up your project, including the default technology stack, security configurations, and automated setup processes, refer to **Chapter 2, "Pragmatic Project Setup."**
- For a more in-depth discussion on the data life cycle, refer to Chapter 4 of "Data Engineering with dbt" by Roberto Zagni (Packt Publishing, 2023).

CHAPTER 8

The Ingestion Layer

This chapter lays the groundwork for how data enters your Pragmatic Data Platform, marking the start of our deep dive into the practical implementation of the Pragmatic Data Platform (PDP) layers with Snowflake and dbt.

We begin with the Ingestion Layer, a critical first step in any data platform. While data movement is often seen as external to the core data platform development, understanding it is crucial. Coding and running it with the same tools used for your data platforms simplifies the pipelines, the data stack, and the knowledge your people need. This chapter explains how data arrives in your platform and, more importantly, how dbt and Snowflake, combined with the PDP macros, enable highly automated, robust data ingestion processes.

We will cover the following key topics:

- **Data Movement and Ingestion in customer cases**: How different companies have handled their data ingestion challenges and the insights gained from those experiences.
- **Data ingestion QuickStart**: A guide for data engineers who want to quickly set up data ingestion using the provided PDP tools and macros.
- **Data extraction and movement**: This section focuses on the high-level principles and methods for moving data from various sources into Snowflake.
- **Data Ingestion with dbt and Snowflake**: A practical, hands-on guide on how to implement the ingestion layer using dbt, Snowflake, and the PDP package.
- **Using and testing the ingested data**: A practical section showing how you validate the ingested data, its freshness, and make it available to dbt models.
- **Data Export to Files**: This topic covers the process of exporting data from Snowflake to external files, which is essentially the reverse of data ingestion.

Sample project and code

The sample dbt project is available at: **https://github.com/pragmatic-data/stonks**. The code samples for this chapter are in the sub-folder `chapter_08`, under the `code_samples_by_chapter` folder.

The samples for this chapter come from the integration tests of the Pragmatic Data Platform dbt package and demonstrate alternative ways to achieve the same outcome. For ingestion, you have both a base example and an advanced one that places the YAML configuration in a separate file, so it can be reused when ingesting multiple similar tables, or when you really want to factor out everything that is common. For the export, besides the base example using the easy-to-use high-level export macro, you also have a scripted version that uses the low-level PDP macros. You can use this as inspiration if you want to code your own export procedure.

Please note that, to better fit the limited space on the printed page, we omit most comments and might change names and formatting compared to the files.

Data movement and ingestion in customer cases

The Ingestion Layer is where raw data first enters the platform, and it often exposes the tension between speed and control. Fast-growing companies like Voi face the challenge of onboarding new sources at high velocity without breaking pipelines, while organizations like Rebtel must balance automation with the careful handling of small but business-critical datasets. The complete case studies for Voi and Rebtel can be found in Chapter 6.

Voi Technology

At Voi, rapid growth created constant schema evolution. As a fast-scaling startup, they needed highly automated ingestion to add new data sources from their scooters and app telemetry. Their team used automated dbt ingestion macros to quickly onboard new data sources and manage schema evolution.

Rebtel

Rebtel worked with small but business-critical datasets, including lists of countries, routing codes, and pricing rules that needed to be both trusted and traceable. Rather than building heavy ingestion pipelines for these, the team stored the data directly in their dbt project as small CSV files under version control, letting dbt load them into Snowflake. This approach made the datasets part of the codebase: every change went through Git review, could be tested, and was automatically deployed along with the rest of the models. It gave Rebtel precision and governance without extra tooling—perfect for small data that rarely changes but must always be correct.

Data ingestion QuickStart

This chapter covers the process in more detail, but if you already understand the ingestion or export process and want to get your hands dirty, this section is for you.

Ingestion playbook

The simplest way to extract and ingest the data you need is to use one of the off-the-shelf tools, like Fivetran, to extract the data from your source and load it directly to Snowflake tables that will act as your Landing Table. If you can't use such a tool, it's still quite easy: you "just" need to extract data to a file, make it reachable by Snowflake, and add a little of config to load it with our PDP package. These are the steps to ingest data in Snowflake with SQL only:

- **Export the data from your source into a format Snowflake can read**, such as CSV, Parquet, Avro, JSON, or a few others. Get the files to a location Snowflake can read.
  This can be a container in the AWS, Google, or Azure cloud (that you authorize Snowflake to access) or a Snowflake internal stage where you can easily load your files (using the PUT command in the SnowSQL command-line tool or Snowflake DB drivers).
- **Set up the ingestion in dbt with our PDP package**. This is a two-step process. First, perform a one-time setup of the schema, file format, and stage to reach your files. This is typically done once for each source system. Then, configure the table name, file pattern, and fields for each Landing Table that you want to ingest. This is done for each source table.

Data ingestion, when understood and properly planned, is a straightforward process that should not become complex. Complexity can come from scheduling, networking, security, and, in general, error handling, but the process itself is simple. After all, we know how to upload and download files since forever, and both traditional and modern data platforms implement bulk load/extraction commands like COPY INTO. Snowflake implementation makes our job even easier by automatically recognizing which files have already been loaded into a table, avoiding reloads with no extra code.

Ingestion how-to

Getting down to hands-on practicalities, here is how you can work the playbook:

1. **Extract data from your source**. Use a source-appropriate method to get data into files. You can use a shell script to run a COPY INTO command to extract data to a file, a legacy ETL tool like Talend or Azure Data Factory, a CDC connector, or a loader tool. This will depend a lot on your source and technical landscape.
2. **Move the file with the extracted data within reach of Snowflake**. Here are two major alternatives: if you already have a data lake or an established infrastructure for storing files in the cloud (or accessible from the cloud), a good bet is to extract or move the files there. If you don't have a ready place, loading the files directly into a Snowflake-managed container (an internal stage) is a good, easy option, either from the command line or using a Snowflake database driver in a programming language. The "Upload files to SF internal stage" sub-section gives an example. Organization-wise, a folder for each source system, with a

subfolder for each table, is a good starting point. Further partitioning by categories and/or dates should be considered based on the amount of data, retention, and other governance-related factors.

3. **Install the PDP package in your dbt project.** Add the PDP package in the `packages.yml` file (or `dependencies.yml` file for enterprise accounts) of your project:

   ```
   # Pragmatic Data Platform package
   - git: https://github.com/pragmatic-data/pragmatic-data-platform.git
     revision: 0.4.18
   ```

   You can check for the latest version and up-to-date instructions in the README of the repo at **https://github.com/pragmatic-data/pragmatic-data-platform**.
4. Create an `ingestion` or `in_out` folder to hold the ingestion/export code and add it to your list of macro paths in your `dbt_project.yml` file:

   ```
   macro-paths: ["macros", "ingestion"]
   ```

5. Create a subfolder with the name of the first source system you want to ingest. This folder will hold the ingestion setup and the files for each Landing Table.
6. **Create the source system's ingestion setup file** (`setup_systemX.sql`) that will contain the YAML configuration at system level. This file will also contain a few getter macros to easily access the names of the database, schema, file format, and stage configured for the ingestion. See the "Ingestion setup file" sub-section below.
7. **Create one file with the ingestion macro for each Landing Table** you need to ingest your data into. It will be executed with a `dbt run-operation` whenever you want to ingest new data, usually at each pipeline run. See the "Landing Table ingestion macro" sub-section below.
8. To simplify your life, create a utility macro named `load_all_system_A` that first calls the setup macro and then all the ingestion macros for the LTs. Then you can run the setup and ingestion for all tables with a single command, `dbt run-operation load_all_system_A`, at the start of pipeline runs.

Once you are done with these steps, which follow a repeatable pattern and can be highly automated for the variable parts, or even fully generated, you have an automated and reliable ingestion system that relies only on dbt and Snowflake, and some basic macros from our PDP package.

Upload files to SF internal stage

Uploading files to a Snowflake internal stage is very simple, secure, highly efficient, and does not require any tools beyond what Snowflake provides for free. Once you have locally installed **SnowSQL** or the more modern **Snowflake CLI** tool and configured the connection to the Snowflake account where you want to load the data, you just need to create a stage in Snowflake and then use the command line to load the data in your desired destination. The process for creating an internal Snowflake stage is even simpler than creating an external stage. The difference is that for an internal stage, you don't need to provide a target URL or authentication, so it can be done using the ingestion setup shown later. Once you have created the stage and installed the command line tool, you can log into the tool, connecting to a Snowflake account, and issue commands like the following to load as many files as you want from the local system to the stage:

```
PUT 'file:///<path>/<file_name>.*.csv'
    @<stage_name>/<folder>/
```

```
    AUTO_COMPRESS = TRUE
    OVERWRITE = FALSE
;
```

Instead of doing that manually, you can easily automate the process by creating a `.sql` file with multiple such commands and executing them with the following command line:

```
snowsql -c <connection_name> -f <path&file>.sql
```

And of course, you can schedule that command too with whatever comes to hand.

Ingestion setup file

For each source system to be loaded, we encapsulate the Snowflake setup process in a single `.sql` file in dbt, named `setup_<system_name>.sql`. This is for simplicity of organization, as it is common for each system to be stored in a different location, to require slightly different file format settings, and to usually want to keep the Landing Tables with their data in different database schemas. This file will contain four pieces of metadata as configuration: the name of the database and schema where you want the Landing Tables to go, the definition of the file format to be used to read/write the files, and the stage pointing to the files. Besides the YAML block defining the setup metadata, the file contains a macro calling the PDP library to generate the SQL code for the setup, one macro to execute that SQL, and a few getter macros that use the configuration content to expose the names of the configured objects for later use in the individual Landing Table configuration. The configuration in the setup file is as simple as this:

```
{% macro get_SYSTEM_A_inout_cfg() %}
{% set inout_cfg %}

inout:      # or landing: or export:
    database:    "{{ target.database }}"
    schema:      LAND_SYSTEM_A

file_format:
    name: SYSTEM_A_CSV__FF
    definition:
        TYPE: "'CSV'" # or 'Parquet' or …

stage:
    name: SYSTEM_A__STAGE
    definition:
        DIRECTORY: ( ENABLE = true )
        STORAGE_INTEGRATION: <storage integration name>
        URL: "'<url to your data>'"

{% endset %}
{{ return(fromyaml(inout_cfg)) }}
{% endmacro %}
```

Then you have a macro that uses the PDP package to generate the SQL code for the setup based on the YAML you put in the configuration:

```
{% macro get_SYSTEM_A_inout_setup_sql() %}
  {% do return(pragmatic_data.inout_setup_sql(
                   cfg = get_SYSTEM_A_inout_cfg() ) ) %}
{%- endmacro %}
```

and one that executes the SQL generated by the previous macro:

```
{%  macro run_SYSTEM_A_inout_setup() %}
    {% do run_query(get_SYSTEM_A_inout_setup_sql()) %}
{%- endmacro %}
```

Note that by having one macro generate the SQL and another one execute it, we allow you to easily inspect the generated SQL by simply calling the first macro.

Last, but not least, you have a few getter macros that just provide the names of the configured objects: database, schema, file format, and stage:

```
/* DEFINE Names   */

{% macro get_SYSTEM_A_inout_db_name(
     cfg = get_SYSTEM_A_inout_cfg() ) %}
  {% do return( cfg.inout.database  or target.database ) %}
{%- endmacro %}

{% macro get_SYSTEM_A_inout_schema_name(
     cfg = get_SYSTEM_A_inout_cfg() ) %}
  {% do return( cfg.inout.schema or target.schema) %}
{%- endmacro %}

{% macro get_SYSTEM_A_inout_csv_ff_name(
     cfg = get_SYSTEM_A_inout_cfg() ) %}
  {% do return(
      get_SYSTEM_A_inout_db_name() ~ '.' ~
      get_SYSTEM_A_inout_schema_name() ~  '.' ~
      cfg.file_format.name ) %}
{%- endmacro %}

{% macro get_SYSTEM_A_inout_stage_name(
     cfg = get_SYSTEM_A_inout_cfg() ) %}
  {% do return(
      get_SYSTEM_A_inout_db_name() ~ '.' ~
      get_SYSTEM_A_inout_schema_name() ~  '.' ~
      cfg.stage.name ) %}
{%- endmacro %}
```

These four macros allow us to easily reuse everywhere the definitions done here once.

Ingestion setup settings

The section defining the database and schema can be equally named in three different ways: `inout:` when you want to be generic or share the setup between both ingestion and export; `landing:` is more common if you are doing a setup for Landing Tables or `export:` if you are doing a setup for exporting data to files. The effect is the same. There are meaningful defaults behind the scenes, so if you do not define a database, the one for the environment executing will be used: `target.database`. Similarly, if you don't define the file format for the stage, the file format that you define under `file_format:` is used by default. You can specify more options than in this example, and for CSV files, you would usually do so, but for the vast majority of cases, that's about all that you need to configure. As shown in the stage configuration, if you use an external stage, we suggest using a storage integration to abstract Snowflake authorization for accessing your files. Look at the Snowflake docs on how to set up a storage integration. Please note that all macro names include the source system name (or acronym) to clearly identify to which system they refer, and also because macro names must be globally unique in a dbt project. You can find more examples in the sample project in the next chapter, and more information in the package's README files.

Landing table ingestion macro

After you have done the source system level setup, you just need to write a few lines of YAML in a `.sql` file to define the ingestion macro for each Landing Table. The file collects the required configuration using YAML definitions, then calls the appropriate PDP reusable macro to perform the actual ingestion based on the provided configuration. Here is an example:

```
{% macro load_table_AAA(recreate_table = false) %}
{%- set yaml_str -%}

ingestion:
    pattern: 'SYSTEM_A/table_AAA/.*/TABLE_AAA.*.csv.gz'
    stage_name: "{{ get_SYSTEM_A_inout_stage_name() }}"

landing_table:
    db_name:      "{{ get_SYSTEM_A_inout_db_name() }}"
    schema_name: "{{ get_SYSTEM_A_inout_schema_name() }}"
    table_name:   TABLE_AAA

    columns:
      - COLUMN1                        # NO data type => TEXT
      - COLUMN2: NUMBER NOT NULL   # full definition

{%- endset -%}

{%- set metadata_dict = fromyaml(yaml_str) -%}

{% do pragmatic_data.run_file_ingestion(
    landing_table_dict = metadata_dict['landing_table'],
    ingestion_dict   = metadata_dict['ingestion'],
    recreate_table = recreate_table
) %}
{% endmacro %}
```

You have real-life examples in the sample code under the `ingestion/` folder. As you can see in the YAML snippet, you need to configure two sets of values:

- **the files to read**: What stage to use and what files to read from that stage, configured under the `ingestion` attribute.

- **the Landing Table:** Where to put it, its name, and its columns (data types are optional), configured under the `landing_table` attribute.

The PDP package simplifies the ingestion to the point that -once you have set the right getters- often all you need to do is to clone the above file and edit only three fields in the YAML block: `pattern`, `stage_name`, and the list of `columns` to ingest.

You can generate the list of columns by either copying the CSV header and asking dbt Copilot or any AI to convert it to a YAML list, or by writing a query on the COLUMNS view of the INFORMATION_SCHEMA, which lists the columns for the table.

To identify the correct PATTERN to pass,
you can use the Snowflake LIST command to list the files visible on a stage.

The YAML config is parsed into a Python dictionary, and the two parts above are passed to the relevant macro that performs the ingestion, eventually creating the Landing Table if it does not exist. With version 0.4.16, both the ingestion of CSVs and of semi-structured files can be done with the `run_file_extraction` macro.

Again, while this is just an example setup, and you can pass more options, most of the time, that is all you need to define to ingest files from cloud storage or a Snowflake internal stage.

Ingestion of semi-structured data

Ingesting semi-structured data is similar to ingesting CSV data. Still, you need to also pass the information to extract the columns you want in your landing table from the variant that Snowflake will build from the semi-structured data, and you call the `run_file_ingestion` macro passing the Snowflake SQL expressions for the columns in the `field_expressions` attribute, which is a list of mappings, one for each column you want to have, like in the following example:

```
ingestion:
    field_expressions: #-- Map variant to desired columns
      #- src_data: $1       # full payload as variant
      - COLUMN1: $1:COLUMN1:TEXT
      - COLUMN2: $1:COLUMN2:NUMBER(38,5)
      - COLUMN3: $1:COLUMN3:INTEGER
       ...
```

The presence of the `field_expressions` attribute is what distinguishes a CSV ingestion from a semi-structured one. It can be easily generated with the following SQL:

```
select '- ' || column_name || ': ' || expression AS sql_txt
from table( INFER_SCHEMA(
  LOCATION => '@database.schema.stage_name/'
 , FILE_FORMAT => 'database.schema.file_format_name'
 , FILES => 'file_name.parquet'
 , IGNORE_CASE => FALSE
) );
```

This query leverages Snowflake's ability to parse the semi-structured files of your choice, and the `INFER_SCHEMA()` function's ability to provide a structured output detailing the contents of the file you point it towards, including the `expression` column, providing us with the SQL expression to read the column.

Snowflake ingests semi-structured data into a variant object.
This means that each row contains only one "object," and all the data for the object is in the only variant column returned, accessible via the $1 name, the same as used for the first column in CSV files.
The difference with CSV is that now $1 is a composite object, and to get individual columns, you need to specify what you want to extract and its data type by providing the correct Snowflake SQL expression in the form `$1:path_to_the_data::data_type`.

For the semi-structured ingestion case, you can generate the list of columns for the Landing Table configuration using the same piece of SQL as above, but omitting the part about the `expression` in the `SELECT` statement. Now that we have given you a quick start to ingestion with Snowflake and dbt, it's time to step back and cover the steps we have discussed in a little more detail.

Running the ingestion macros

The ingestion macros we write collect the configuration and defer execution to reusable macros from the Pragmatic Data Platform package, but if we do not execute them, nothing will happen, and your data will not be loaded. Luckily for us, dbt provides a very easy way to execute macros. The `run-operation` command exists exactly to execute macros that perform all the maintenance and the specialized logic that can be coded with SQL and Jinja, but does not belong in models, because it is not about transforming data using SQL statements. You run an individual ingestion macro, like the `load_table_AAA`, with the command:

```
dbt run-operation load_table_AAA
```

While you can run it at any time from the command line, the standard setup is to run all the ingestion macros just before running the transformation pipelines, so that you ingest and work on all available data. Similarly, with a partial ingestion for partial pipeline runs. As we suggested earlier, you can create a `load_all_SYSTEM_A` macro that just calls the setup macro for one system and then all the ingestion macros for that system, like in the following example, even if we have only one ingestion macro for now:

```
{%  macro load_all_SYSTEM_A() %}
{% do run_SYSTEM_A_inout_setup() %}
{% do ingest__generic_two_column_table() %}
{%- endmacro %}
```

If you have multiple systems to ingest data from, you can create a general `load_all` macro that runs all the system-specific `load_all` macros, so that when you start your pipeline, you just need one line for the ingestion and one for the pipeline. This is the simplest and straightforward way to run the ingestion macros, but it has one limitation: ingestion is done sequentially, one table at a time, as macros execute in a single thread.

The optimal, even for an XS Snowflake warehouse, is to run four to six ingestion threads in parallel. This is done automatically by Snowflake when you have many files to ingest into a single Landing Table, but if you have just a single file per table, there is no parallelism. If you want to improve parallelism, you can run the individual loads for each system or for groups of tables using a scheduler, and then start the pipeline when all the ingestion is complete.

A simpler alternative is to exploit the parallelism in dbt model execution to run the ingestion for a single Landing Table, a set of LTs, or the full system **as a side effect**, and use the model SQL code only to log some info from the ingestion results. In such cases, you execute the ingestion macros with a direct JINJA call placed inside the dbt model, even if the result of that call is not used in the model, and then use the model's SQL to read the Landing Tables and log any useful info. An example is found in the integration tests of the Pragmatic Data Platform package, in the model `integration_tests/models/in_out/system_A/ingest/ TEST_INGEST_GENERIC.sql`

Eventually, you might move the call to ingest every Landing Table in the STG model that reads from it, while adding a dependency on a model running the setup macro for the correct system. This last organization ties the ingestion to the execution of the STG model, so it is re-run every time you run the STG model. This can be both an advantage and a disadvantage, so it's up to you to decide.

Permanent storage of extracted data

Deep Dive: For a deeper discussion of the Data Extraction and Movement topic, please refer to the **Data Extraction and Movement Appendix** available for download at https://technicspub.com/Pragmatic-Data-Platform.

When extracted data is saved to files in a storage account, ensuring its long-term availability and manageability becomes crucial. The most straightforward approach is to land these files directly in a designated cloud storage location, such as an S3 bucket, an Azure Blob Storage container, or a Google Cloud Storage bucket. Together with the Pragmatic Data Platform macros, this ensures you can always re-create your data from these files.

Snowflake can easily access these files directly through external stages, allowing you to ingest the data using our Pragmatic Data Platform ingestion macros. This method is simple to set up and manage. However, if your data landscape is varied and you have other data platforms that need access to this raw data beyond just Snowflake, Iceberg tables can be a possible alternative.

Iceberg tables

Iceberg is an open-source table format for large analytical datasets that provides SQL-like table capabilities over files stored in object storage. By using Iceberg tables on top of your extracted files, you add a layer of management and structure to what would otherwise be a collection of static files. When adopted, Iceberg can offer benefits such as:

- **Schema Evolution:** Iceberg supports schema evolution, allowing you to add, drop, or reorder columns without rewriting the underlying data files. This can be valuable when source systems change their data structures over time.
- **Hidden Partitioning:** It automatically manages partitions, helping efficiently organize data for querying without users needing to manually manage the partitioning scheme.

- **Time Travel and Rollback**: Iceberg maintains a history of table changes, enabling "time travel" to query previous versions of your data and simplifying rollback to a previous state if errors occur. While this does not replace proper historization, it is a nice-to-have to recover from issues.
- **Concurrent Writes**: It helps reliably manage concurrent writes, which can be useful in environments where multiple processes extract and land data simultaneously.
- **Open Standard**: As an open standard, Iceberg offers flexibility and interoperability with various query engines and processing frameworks.

While Snowflake can directly access files in a stage, leveraging Iceberg tables provides a structured and managed layer over these raw files. This approach can be considered when a real use case for multiple data consumers or more advanced data governance features beyond simple file storage becomes a requirement for your ingested data.

Data ingestion with dbt and Snowflake

Data ingestion is the crucial first step in any data platform, bringing raw data from its sources into a form that can be processed and transformed. While traditional data ingestion often involves dedicated ETL tools, the Pragmatic Data Platform (PDP) champions a more streamlined approach that leverages dbt and Snowflake. Our focus here is on efficiently landing data "as is" and then using dbt to drive the subsequent transformations using Snowflake, aligning with the ELT paradigm.

Core concept: Landing tables

At the heart of modern ingestion strategies are **Landing Tables (LTs)**. Landing Tables are the raw, unmodeled representation of external data, ingested as-is. They provide an immutable record of what was received, when, and from where. Their goal is to isolate the problem of properly loading data from how to use it.

Landing Tables serve as the initial landing ground to load data from files or APIs, mirroring the structure of the incoming data as closely as possible. Generally, each LT loads only data coming from a specific source table or API endpoint. This might not always be strictly true; in IOT or other settings where you receive many similar semi-structured inputs, it can be useful to ingest all similar inputs into a single Landing Table and then separate the different inputs for historization, or even later, depending on the level of similarity. For structured data, you seldom, if ever, deviate from the "one-source-one-landing-table" pattern.

Landing Tables are naturally source-oriented, so they are grouped in dbt folders and Snowflake schemas based on the source system. This helps both in managing the code and in securing the data, as it is common for data from a source system to have homogeneous security and access requirements. The major benefits of Landing tables are:

- **Simplification**: decouple source volatility from models.
- **Auditability**: proof of what and when it was ingested.
- **Security**: ability to restrict raw data access with common DB roles.
- **Flexibility**: support reprocessing, historization, and debugging.
- **Performance**: great improvement as each file is read and parsed only once.

As we will see in the next sub-section, for each source system, we set up the schema that contains the Landing Tables and the other required Snowflake objects, namely stages and file formats. We also set up common names and helpers for reuse. Once these components are in place, individual LT ingestion involves using Snowflake's `COPY INTO` command. This command efficiently loads data from the specified files in a stage into your Landing Table, adhering to the rules defined by the file format. This process is encapsulated in an ingestion macro for each Landing Table. It collects a few lines of YAML to configure the ingestion and forwards them to the reusable macro in the PDP package that implements the ingestion process.

The macros to ingest all the Landing Tables from a source system are then chained into a utility macro that kicks off the setup and ingestion of the system. One key property of Landing Tables is that each file is automatically loaded into a LT only once, thanks to the built-in automation in Snowflake's COPY INTO command. This provides a significant performance boost over external tables and a major simplification, as the "find the new files" logic is fully handled by Snowflake.

The PDP package at **https://github.com/pragmatic-data/pragmatic-data-platform** contains the macros that perform ingestion and sample configurations that simplify the ingestion macro for each LT, along with other dbt objects to manage ingestion. This reduces effort, promotes reusability, and ensures consistency, as the SQL code for ingestion is generated from a few lines of parameters expressed in YAML.

Landing table and ingestion macro setup

The setup to create Landing Tables involves the identification and creation of a few Snowflake objects:

- **Database and Schema**: Each LT resides in a Snowflake database and schema. Organizing LTs by specific source system is useful for effective data governance and access control. The setup step ensures you pick the two parameters or defaults, making them reusable across all the LTs of that specific source system.
- **Stage**: for data that originates as files (e.g., CSV, JSON, Parquet), a stage is essential. This Snowflake object points to a specific location in the cloud storage, allowing Snowflake to read data directly from the files. Use an external stage, configured with a storage integration for external cloud storage (S3, Azure Storage, or GCS), or an internal stage if you load the files directly into a Snowflake-managed filesystem.
- **File Format**: To correctly interpret incoming files, a Snowflake file format object defines properties such as file type (CSV, JSON, PARQUET), compression, field delimiters, and error handling. This ensures that data is parsed accurately upon ingestion into the LT.

For each source system, we encapsulate the process to name and create these components in a single.sql file in dbt, named `setup_<system_name>.sql`. The configuration in the setup file is shown in the "ingestion setup file" section in the QuickStart at the beginning of the chapter. More info can be found in the sample project and the package itself.

Individual landing table ingestion

After you have done the setup, you just need to write a few lines of YAML in a separate macro file for each Landing Table that you want to start loading. The PDP package simplifies the ingestion to the point that all you need to do is provide the configuration in the next block of YAML:

```
{%- set yaml_str -%}

landing_table:
    db_name:      "{{ get_SYSTEM_A_inout_db_name() }}"
    schema_name: "{{ get_SYSTEM_A_inout_schema_name() }}"
    table_name:   TABLE_AAA

    columns:
      - COLUMN1                         # NO data type => TEXT
      - COLUMN2: NUMBER NOT NULL   # full definition

ingestion:
    pattern: 'SYSTEM_A/table_AAA/.*/TABLE_AAA.*.csv.gz'
    stage_name: "{{ get_SYSTEM_A_inout_stage_name() }}"

{%- endset -%}
```

As you can see in the above YAML snippet, you need to define two sets of values:

- **the Landing Table**: Where to put it, its name and its columns, types optional.
- **the files to read**: What stage to use and what files from that stage.

Again, while this is just an example and you can pass more options, most of the time, this is all you need to ingest files from cloud storage into a Landing Table. To get there, you have defined the stage and file format in the setup file, and you have used a storage integration to abstract away the authorization (suggested). Still, you could pass the URL and authentication (not a bright idea). Look at the Snowflake docs on how to set up a storage integration.

To identify the correct PATTERN to pass,
you can use the Snowflake LIST command to list the files visible on a stage.

Ingestion organization

We suggest organizing your ingestion code under a root folder named ingestion, which you add to the macro paths. Ingestion is handled through macros that leverage the YAML format to describe the configuration parameters for the macros. Inside that, we suggest organizing ingestion and export by source system, with one base folder for each system containing the system setup, and one subfolder each for ingestion and export containing the macros to ingest/export the individual tables. The suggested layout for each source system is:

```
system_X/
    ├── setup_system_X.sql
    ├── load_all_system_X.sql
    ├── TABLE_X1.sql              # macro name: ingest_TABLE_X1
    └── TABLE_X2.sql              # macro name: ingest_TABLE_X2
```

Start simple: create a folder per system that contains the setup and all other files. Then, if at some point you'll have both import and export that use the same stage and file format, you can create two folders and drag each file into the correct one.

```
system_X/
    ├── setup_system_X.sql
    ├── load_all_system_X.sql
    ├── export_all_system_X.sql
    ├── export/
    │    └── TABLE_X1.sql  # macro name: export_TABLE_X1
    └── ingest/
         └── TABLE_X1.sql  # macro name: ingest_TABLE_X1
```

This flexibility is a by-product of dbt, as macros are defined solely by their names, not the file or path where they are defined, so you can freely move their files around (as long as you keep them inside a folder marked for macros).

Dedicated ingestion database

An important architectural decision is whether to place the Landing Tables in the same database as your dbt models or to use a dedicated database solely for ingestion. While placing LTs in the same database might seem simpler initially, the Pragmatic Data Platform recommends a dedicated ingestion database. This separation offers significant advantages:

- **Clear Segregation of Concerns**: The ingestion database acts as a clear boundary for raw, untransformed data. This makes it easier to understand the data's origin and state.
- **Granular Permissions**: You can apply stricter security controls to the ingestion database with more ease. Limiting access to raw data only to specific roles or processes enhances your overall data governance posture.
- **Self-Contained Data for Easy Sharing**: Placing raw data in its own database, with a schema for each source system, creates self-contained units. This simplifies loading once and securely shares with many consumers. Iceberg tables can extend this reach to a diverse array of consumers, even outside Snowflake.
- **Isolation of Performance**: Ingestion processes, especially large initial loads, can be resource-intensive. Separating LTs into their own database and the code into its own dbt project can help isolate performance impacts and ownership.
- **Simplified Recovery and Audit**: In case of data corruption or issues with ingested data, a dedicated ingestion database simplifies recovery operations and provides a clear audit trail of raw data landed from sources.
- **Environment Management**: As discussed below, a dedicated ingestion database per environment enables the management of environment-specific LTs.

This dedicated database, often named something like `RAW_DB_<env>` or `INGESTION_DB_<env>`, completed by an environment identifier, reinforces the PDP's layered architecture, ensuring that each layer has a distinct purpose and controlled access.

Soft data mesh

The next logical step, after placing the Landing Tables in their own database, would be to move the storage layer, discussed later and created 1:1 with the Landing Tables, to sit alongside the Landing Tables in that database. With simple steps, we can start building a "soft data Mesh" that simplifies load and governance, historize data once, and securely share -only what is needed- with many downstream projects that can use -if allowed- the raw data, the current data, or the fully historized data, depending on the use case.

When you manage this ingestion and historization part with its own dbt project and hand it to the owners of the source system, you have created your first block of a "soft data Mesh" that improves flexibility with little to no extra cost or complexity. We will get back to this in Chapters 12 and 14.

Environment independence for landing tables

Following the principles of good software engineering, it is important to ensure that Landing Tables and downstream transformations are environment-independent. Having distinct instances of your Landing Tables for each environment is the only way to preserve the independence of the environments where you develop your models. With a single set of LTs, you would be forced to update all layers whenever one LT changes, or always use a pattern that freezes a LT upon changes to the source and creates a new LT version to be merged/reconciled with the old one, with no changes allowed.

Preserving environment independence means:

- **One Set of LTs per Environment**: Each dbt environment (development, QA, production) should connect to its own distinct set of Landing Tables. For example, your DEV dbt environment would write to INGESTION_DB_DEV, while PROD writes to INGESTION_DB_PROD.
- **Isolated Data Evolution**: This separation allows for independent evolution of ingestion processes. You can test changes to your ingestion pipelines (e.g., new file formats, different COPY INTO options) in a development environment without impacting production data.
- **Reduced Risk**: It minimizes the risk of accidental data corruption or overwrites in production environments during development or testing cycles.
- **Different data for PROD and staging:** Each dbt environment can receive different data, which is a crucial need in some industries, while it does not prevent loading all LTs from the same files when you can work with production data.

This approach is inherently supported by dbt's environment configuration and Snowflake's database and schema structure. By configuring your dbt profiles to point to environment-specific database names (e.g., using `target.name` in your database macros), you ensure that your ingestion macros, their LT definitions, and the downstream models are correctly connected in each environment.

While this works in most cases and for almost all tables, sometimes we indeed get huge tables for which the cost of loading multiple times makes no sense, despite the benefits. In such cases, it is enough to pin a single database to load data there from any environment, and thanks to Snowflake automation, each file will be loaded only once.

Sometimes we mix approaches, as you might want to load only a fraction of the big tables in the DEV environment and the full data in TEST/QA and PROD in a single LT.

```
landing_table:
  db_name:"{{ 'DB_DEV' if target.name == 'dev' else 'DB_PROD' }}"
```

With a simple Jinja expression like the one above on `target.name` or `target.database`, you can decide which database to use for the landing table in each environment. Then you need to use the same expression in your sources feeding the STG models to fetch the data from the right Landing Table.

Changes in upstream data

Time to address a common question: "If data changes in the source, the Landing Table for such a source will break and need a fix?"

Yes, that is in the nature of things: you either get to know about the change before it happens and prepare (this should be the norm), or you get surprised and need to react, fixing the ingestion to fit the new source layout (this is what often happens). A follow-up question is often: "If I have a LT for each environment, then I need to fix all of them?" That is true, but the fixing work is done once and then applied by releases. Furthermore, we hope that the following reasoning will allow you to appreciate that environment independence brings us choices, with little to no extra effort.

Stopping production due to an error when there is an unexpected upstream change is a useful precaution. It gives us the option to analyze the change and decide how it should be managed. That is why errors must be raised, not swept under the carpet until they are so severe that it's impossible to ignore them.

If we decide we can keep loading everything else while we code the change in DEV, we can simply comment out the line that loads such LT in PROD (and TEST/QA) and restart the load in PROD (and TEST/QA). All keeps working only with this LT, not getting new data. Easy and quick action, also clearly visible in the code and approved by peers. We can then focus on coding the right actions in DEV, and when it is released to TEST/QA and to PROD, the load on the changed table will resume. With independent LTs, the PROD STG models will not be affected by changes made to the DEV LT until the fix is complete and released to PROD, along with the code that uses the new version.

Given that we usually release multiple times a day, if the fix is simple and quick, the next day's load will resume as normal. Of course, we can always run the fixed ingestion and the models for the affected Landing Table right after merging the fix. If we had a single LT for all environments, when we work to fix the load and change the LT, it would apply to all environments, not just DEV. This will break downstream dependencies on the LT in the STG models, breaking all environments until the fix is released. This, in turn, often forces us to use the general pattern of freezing the old LT and creating a new one, rather than other approaches that require manipulating the LT.

These steps show how environment independence offers optionality at little to no additional cost. In the end, both ways are possible, and you must choose which one works for your case.

Reacting to source changes

In the previous section, we touched on how to fix a Landing Table when the upstream source changes abstractly. Here, let's discuss common patterns:

- **Freeze and add a new landing table**: The general and most transparent pattern to react to a change is to freeze the current LT, meaning to stop loading any new data, and create a new one following the new layout of the upstream source. This provides the best visibility into changes and the ability to reload past data, but can be seen as a bit excessive in some cases.
- **Update the existing landing table**: When changes are forward-compatible, like adding a nullable column, we can decide to change the existing LT if we can live with nulls for past data.
- **Backfilling a new LT with old data**: In other cases, like column renames or other easy-to-adapt changes, we can opt for an intermediate solution, freezing the old LT, but starting the new LT on top of the old data, initially loaded in the new LT with the minimal transformation to make it work. This enables us to read from a single LT, while also preserving the original data "as it was" in the old LT.

Remember that, downstream, you will need to account for the evolution of a single source table over time. Its data can be split into multiple Landing Tables. How you manage the LT evolution in each case will affect how you manage the unavoidable changes downstream in the STG and HIST models to historize the data.

The most general pattern for handling the change downstream is, again, to freeze the STG and HIST tables connected to the frozen LT, and create a new pair of STG and HIST tables to historicize the new layout. Watch out: if you have delta exports or are tracking deletions in your historization, you might also need the input from the last frozen history table to load data into the new one. This can be a complex operation that can be simplified by loading the initial data from the old frozen history table into the new history table.

An alternative (especially if there is no semantic change and you do not need perfect auditability) is to place a simple view before the STG model to implement data selection or blending across multiple LTs, and keep a pipeline with a single STG and HIST, eventually evolving them to accommodate the new data. This, of course, can reduce the auditability of the pipeline.

As always, we have choices, and the best way forward depends on your priorities: the general patterns provide a reliable solution that fulfils auditing and disaster management constraints, at the cost of a few more models around. Other solutions might be simpler and more intuitive, but may not be suitable in heavily regulated environments. To you, the choice.

Ingestion in case of full exports versus delta exports

The strategy for ingesting data into Landing Tables does not depend on whether your source provides full exports or delta (incremental) exports. After all, you just read the data and load it into the Landing Table. What changes a lot in these two cases is the proper maintenance of the Landing Tables and the downstream use of the data. As a rule, you want to maintain in the Landing Table all the data you need to quickly recreate the history tables or double-check input values, but not too many copies of the same old data, and in general, not huge amounts of data.

- **Full exports**: When a source provides a complete snapshot of the data with each export, you technically only need the latest export. In this case, if the export is reliable, you can also detect deletions by comparing the history table content with the new data in the landing table. What is missing in the last load? It means it has been deleted. We could empty the landing table before each load. Still, it makes sense to keep a few days of data, especially in the first stages of development, and if you are using the historization pattern that can load all the changes in a single run. By keeping a few loads in the LT, you do not risk losing changes if your historization stops for a few days (e.g., a weekend or holiday). In any case, the historization process can be configured to read only what's new, or even just the last batch of data ingested, so it's not really adding costs but rather adding flexibility. For big tables, it makes sense to configure cleanup to keep only a few days' worth of data, while for smaller tables, you can keep more if you ever take the time to configure the cleanup.
- **Delta exports (incremental loads)**: For sources that provide only changes since the last export, ingestion is even simpler: you just load the data into the LT and, unless the table is really big (toward the billions of rows), you can leave it there. In any case, even for very large tables, it is necessary to avoid deleting data from the Landing Table before you process it for historization.

Suppose you have the ability to choose what export to have for each table. In that case, our suggestion is to have a full export for most tables, using the delta export only for the biggest tables, and, if you can, tag the deletions (or the operation type) directly from the change data capture and ingest it as a normal column, instead of calculating it as the rows missing in the next full export. The reason for this is that a full export, while maybe less elegant and modern, is simple to use and quite self-contained, very resilient to errors and lost files. Even for tables of a few million rows, the extra cost to ingest and process a full export is very limited (a few seconds, often in parallel with bigger fish to fry), while the simplification is substantial.

When dealing with delta exports, it is necessary to have a very robust and well-monitored export system that never misses a beat, and to put in place ways to ensure that any export that is lost at some point is recovered before a certain time. This can be done by scheduling a full or extended export at regular intervals to catch anything that was missed beforehand. The Pragmatic Data Platform macros can ingest and historize it naturally. The only change will be the configuration needed for one advanced cross-test between the Landing and History Tables to verify that all keys are loaded, as the Landing Table will now contain extra data beyond what is expected for delta exports.

Data ingestion in special cases

Until now, we have seen "normal" data ingestion, but sometimes we get asked about ingesting other file types or data that are not readily readable by Snowflake or that do not really fit into the table layout. Common examples include Excel files, textual documents in text, docx, PDF, or other formats, and other non-structured data like images, audio, and video. In these cases, we have two orders of problems:

- Understand what we really want to do with the data in the files. Do we care about the content, like in an Excel file, or do we care more about metadata or calculations about it, like with an image or audio file?
- Once the first question is clearly answered, we can try to determine the best way to achieve it using what Snowflake provides and what dbt can use in our ELT process. This ranges from data libraries in multiple programming languages that enable access to all kinds of files to advanced ML/AI tools that summarize, perform sentiment analysis, extract features, perform image recognition, and much more.

Snowpark is the Snowflake service that supports running code in Java, Scala, or Python close to your database, making it simple to include in your ELT process operations that are difficult to perform in SQL. Python support is especially powerful thanks to built-in packages from the Anaconda distribution. You can code your solution directly, as most packages for data, ML, and AI are already available.

Here is a short discussion about some common cases:

- **Excel files.** In such cases, we usually want to load the data from one or more sheets in the Excel file. This can be done using Python-based libraries from Snowpark, or by running an external program over the Excel files to generate a CSV that is easy to import. Both works; do whatever's easier for you to set up.

- **Textual documents.** In this case, if what we want is the textual content, either load it "as is" or parse it. The approach is like Excel files: you can use Snowpark to read and parse the content of the files and store it as you wish. Anyway, nowadays we can do much more with textual data, and it's common to perform sentiment analysis, summarization, or even use these documents as a knowledge base for an AI large language model (LLM) to base its answers (this process is called RAG – Retrieval Augmented Generation). This is also available with a combination of Snowpark and Cortex AI tools available in Snowflake. In less than one hour, I have set up a Snowflake Cortex service to answer questions using the contents of my previous book, fed into the AI as a PDF.

- **Non-structured data.** Dealing with unstructured data is much like working with the content of textual documents; you just need the right libraries to read their formats and represent their contents. They are usually available in Snowpark. Then you need to decide what you want to extract from such files and save in your database. For images and audio, it could be some metadata like date, size/duration, or more advanced processing to generate AI captions, AI object recognition/tag list, and of course, much more specialized data if you are processing specialized files like satellite images or engine noise files.

The new capabilities of modern data platforms like Snowflake blur the boundary between loading data directly, such as making the content of a file available inside the database, and processing the data of a file to generate the data that you want to load, even using modern AI-based tools.

Geospatial data

Building on the previous section, a special mention is deserved for Geospatial data, as Snowflake is very well suited to ingest, manage, and operate on it. We can see three broad categories of use of geospatial data in Snowflake:

- **Loading geospatial data, performing little to no geospatial operations on it.** Snowflake is very well suited for this case, as it can effectively load and manage geospatial data as Geography (spheric) and Geometry (plane) data types.

- **Loading geospatial data, performing serious geospatial operations on it.** Snowflake is a great solution for this case, offering a wide array of geospatial operators that are very well optimized when using the Geography data type, which models Earth as a perfect sphere.

- **Loading geospatial-related data,** like satellite images, **to process them** and extract features according to some algorithm or ML/AI process. This is also a common Snowflake use case powered by Snowpark.

I have personally experienced the power of Snowflake doing joins of million x billions of rows on geospatial operators at amazing speed (20 min for a 6M x 1.5B geospatial join on a L warehouse), transformed data across geospatial reference systems, done calculations based on the contents of plots of land and serving data for both visualization and downstream ML/AI processing and I can tell Snowflake worked great, completely replacing Postgress for our use cases.

You can use the power of the Pragmatic Data Platform to ingest and store your geospatial data in Snowflake with dbt, then transform it using both Snowflake's native geospatial operators and advanced Python libraries via Snowpark.

In this section, we have covered all the major topics about ingestion, but of course, there is more to it, even just when looking at our own Pragmatic Data Platform dbt package. You can find more detailed technical information on using the package in the next chapter and in the package's GitHub repository.

Using and testing the ingested data

Once you have ingested your data into a Landing Table, how do you use it?

Well, like any time that you want to read a table that is not a dbt model, in dbt you do it by defining a **source** with a name and a position (database and schema) and then declaring the tables you want to read under it. This is the entry point for data in the dbt process and enables powerful features, such as data freshness checks and testing. See the dbt docs linked at the end of the chapter.

Defining a dbt source

In dbt, you define sources and the tables under them in YAML files. We define sources for Landing Tables in files that clearly identify the system the data is coming from, like `source_SYSTEM_A.yml`. The content is like the one below:

```
version: 2

sources:
 - name: SYSTEM_A
   database: "{{ get_SYSTEM_A_inout_db_name() }}"
   schema: "{{ get_SYSTEM_A_inout_schema_name() }}"
   tables:
     - name: TABLE_AAA
     - name: TABLE_BBB
```

Once you have defined the source for a Landing Table, you can refer to it with the `source()` function, with the syntax `source('SYSTEM_A', 'TABLE_AAA')`.

Checking source data freshness

With a couple of extra configs, dbt can optionally capture the "freshness" of the data in your source tables. This is useful for understanding if your data pipelines are working with the latest content and is a critical component of defining SLAs for your warehouse.

To configure source freshness information, add a `freshness` block and `loaded_at_field` to your source declaration and eventually redefine them for each table that deviates from this default configuration, like in the following example:

```
sources:
 - name: SYSTEM_A
   freshness:
     warn_after: {count: 3, period: day}
     error_after: {count: 5, period: day}
   loaded_at_field: TRY_TO_TIMESTAMP(SOME_DATE/TS)
```

You can redefine both the `freshness` and `loaded_at_field` for each table, especially setting `freshness: null` to disable the freshness check for a table.

Testing source data and the ingestion process

The other major benefit of defining a source is the ability to run dbt tests on it. This enables us to test both the content of the data ingested in the Landing Tables and the ingestion process itself for each table, like the following snippet exemplifies:

```
    - name: TABLE_AAA
      description: Landing Table for AAAs
      columns:
        - name: AAA_ID
          description: The unique ID.
          data_tests:
            - not_null
        - name: FROM_FILE
          data_tests:
            - not_null
            - file_order_is_correct
            - all_files_from_stage:
              pattern: 'SYSTEM_A/table_AAA/.*/TABLE_AAA.*.csv.gz'
              stage_name: "{{ get_IB_ingestion_stage_name() }}"
```

In the above block, we have shown a few tests for `TABLE_AAA`.

The first test checks that the `AAA_ID` column is not null. We cannot verify that it is unique because the Landing Table is designed to contain, over time, multiple versions of each record instance, so it is normal for the ID to appear multiple times.

The second set of tests is on the metadata column `FROM_FILE` that is added by the ingestion process. First, we test that the column is not null, as ingested data always comes from a file. Then, check that the order in which we ingested the files is correct. This is important, as by default and unless you have reliable, effective date/timestamp information, the most recently ingested data is considered the current data. We need the file names to be sortable to use this test, so design your names accordingly if you want to test it.

Lastly, we verify that we have ingested all the files in the Landing Table that match the specified pattern from the stage. It is obviously very important to verify that we have loaded all the data we have. Beware that if you happen to have empty files, totally empty or only the header without any actual data to load, you need to set an extra parameter to exclude from the check the files smaller than a certain size (the header size).

We will see more practical examples of ingestion in the next chapter, but you already have all the elements to configure, run, and validate the ingestion of your data.

In the next section, we will look at the symmetric operation of ingestion: data exports to files. That is also done with the COPY INTO command, so it should not come as a surprise that the process is very similar to ingestion and falls under the same section of the Pragmatic Data Platform package.

Data export to files

Ingestion and Export are symmetric operations on files: one loads data from files into tables, and the other writes data from tables into files.

Working on files, they both need to set up the DB objects for File Formats and Stages in a DB and Schema. Also, the operations for reading or writing data are similar, both using the `COPY INTO` command. For this reason, the library macros are bundled together under a common `in_out` folder in the Pragmatic Data Platform package, and as we have shown for ingestion, we suggest keeping together the ingestion/export macros in your projects, grouped by source system, under a common folder named `ingestion`, `export` or `in_out`, depending if you have only ingestion, export, or both.

The Pragmatic Data Platform macros, thanks to the power of Snowflake and the flexibility of dbt, can easily ingest from and export to CSV and SEMI-STRUCTURED files in internal or external stages, allowing you to ingest and export files from anywhere your Snowflake account is authorized to read and write.

The most common use case for exporting data is to produce refined information by blending data from multiple sources, making it available for downstream use or feeding it back into some sources. This is quite common: if you build valuable information into your data platform, it is often desirable to have it in other systems as well. Anyway, another use case is to make data available in different formats with or without transformation in between. Simple examples include format conversion (from CSV to Parquet or the other way around), while in more advanced cases, we can extract and flatten part or all of semi-structured, nested data. This can be handy when a legacy system cannot handle JSON or Parquet and needs the data flattened into a simple CSV.

An alternative to exporting data to files is to store the data you want to share in Iceberg tables, because they are an open format that most modern data tools and platforms can access, as we saw in the Iceberg tables section earlier in this chapter.

If your downstream dependency does not support Iceberg tables, or you want to keep an easy-to-access, file-based version of how a table was at the time of export, then you do need to export to files. They are also the quickest way to move large amounts of data between different platforms on the same cloud provider.

Data export playbook

These are the steps to export data from Snowflake with the Pragmatic Data Platform package:

1. **Create a dbt model (table or view) with the data that you want to export.**
2. **Set up the export in dbt using our PDP package**. This is the same one-time setup for ingestion: configuring a file format and a stage to hold your exported files, and a database and schema to hold these two Snowflake objects.
3. **Create a dbt macro to export the model's content to your desired location** and name in the stage you configured, using your file format of choice. This macro generally contains a YAML block to configure the source, the stage and format to use, the path and file names in the stage, and a few flags to configure the export behavior, passing them to the `run_table_export()` PDP macro.

Data export itself is a simple process, even easier than ingestion because it all is already in Snowflake. All you need to do is configure a stage to allow Snowflake to write files to the location you want, and then point our macro to the dbt model you want to download data from.

Data export how-to

We have already said that export is symmetric and very similar to ingestion, and you can see this in the fact that everything you need to do for export, you have already done for ingestion. If you look at the **ingest how-to** section earlier in this chapter, you will see that points one and two do not apply to preparing the export, but are replaced by the need to create or identify a model that provides the exact data to export. Steps three to six are identical, but you might want to configure a different stage for your export than for your ingestion. Last, but not least, you create the macro to perform the export.

The steps, therefore, are these: prepare a model that provides the data you want to export. Follow steps three to six of the ingest how-to section so that you have the PDP package installed and have set up a stage and file format for your export. Create the export macro, in its own file, to hold the configuration and pass it to the reusable `run_table_export()` PDP macro.

Given that the steps are the same, we will describe here only the last step: creating the export macro, which, unsurprisingly, will be very similar to the ingestion one.

Data export macro

After you have done the setup, for each data export, you just need to write a few lines of YAML in a .sql file like the one shown below, and then call the PDP macro, which will run the export based on the YAML metadata. The typical export macro file looks like this:

```
{% macro export__generic_two_column_table() %}

{% set table_ref = ref('GENERIC_TWO_COLUMN_TABLE') %}

{% set yaml_config %}
stage_cfg:
    format_name: "{{ get_SYSTEM_A_inout_csv_ff_name() }}"
    stage_name:  "{{ get_SYSTEM_A_inout_stage_name() }}"

export_path_cfg:
    export_path_base:             SYSTEM_A/generic/
    export_path_date_part:
    export_file_name_prefix:

flags:
    only_one_export:                true
    remove_folder_before_export:    true
    create_dummy_file:              true

{% endset %}

{%- set cfg_dict = fromyaml(yaml_config) -%}

{% do pragmatic_data.run_table_export(
    table_ref               = table_ref,
    export_path_cfg         = cfg_dict.export_path_cfg,
    stage_cfg               = cfg_dict.stage_cfg,
    flags                   = cfg_dict.flags
) %}

{% endmacro %}
```

As you can see in the YAML snippet, you need to define three sets of values:

- **Stage and file format**: Which stage and file format to use when writing the files.
- **Export path for your files**: Where to place the generated files within the stage.
- **Export control flags:** Three flags to control the behavior of the export.

The exported data will end up in files stored in the selected stage, located under a path composed of the base path you pass, plus a date part, the file prefix, and a sequence number, if there is enough data to export to fill more than one file (by default, 16MB of data per file).

Please note that Snowflake will work on the export in parallel, allocating sets of rows to each thread. Snowflake will try to get close to the required file size and keep it as the maximum size for generated files. For now, these options are not configurable in the Pragmatic Data Platform export macros, but they might be in the future.

Let's explore a bit more about the meaning of the YAML parameters:

- **format_name**: The format of the files to write, usually defined in the setup macro file.
- **stage_name**: The stage that gives access to the location where to write the files, from the setup.
- **export_path_base**: The slash-terminated path where to store the files, relative to the stage root path.
- **export_path_date_part**: A bespoken definition of the data part of the path, used to keep exports from different dates (and potentially times) in separate folders. By default, if nothing is passed, the export date is used in the Y-M-D format. You can pass any string, with more or less detail, or not even connected to dates, considering that any minus (-) character will be converted to an underscore (_) character to maintain path integrity.
- **export_file_name_prefix**: The initial, non-numeric part of the file name. By default, if nothing is passed, the table name is used as retrieved from the table reference used to read the data from, followed by two underscores (__).
- **create_dummy_file**: If we want the export process to create a dummy file at the end of the export, to signal that the export is complete. The dummy file is created with the name `dummy` and an extension depending on the file format associated with the stage you are writing to.
- **only_one_export**: If we want to limit the process to run only one export, for the current date (or other element defined in `export_path_date_part`). The effect, if `true`, is that if a dummy file from a completed export is found in the target folder, then the export is not run at all. If `false` (as set by default), the export is always run, even if a dummy file exists.
- **remove_folder_before_export**: If we want to remove the target folder and recreate it before running the export. This can help avoid getting files from a previous export, especially if the current one contains fewer files. The export overwrites existing files with new ones, using the same name. Still, if you generate 20 files and a previous run generated 25, the last five files will not be overwritten and will remain, unless you remove the folder before writing to it again. The folder is removed only if the export is to be run. If the `only_one_export` flag is true and an export already exists, nothing will be done, and the previous export will remain intact.

While ingestion occurs to some extent in almost all projects, Snowflake data export to files is less common, even when some form of data export is in place. We don't know whether it is because it is not widely known how to do it, because it's considered complicated, or for some other reason, but now you have this option too.

Chapter review

In this chapter, we began our deep dive into the practical implementation of the Pragmatic Data Platform (PDP) layers by focusing on the Ingestion Layer. We discussed how data arrives in your platform and, more importantly, how dbt and Snowflake, combined with the PDP macros, can automate and strengthen your data ingestion processes. We explored the ingestion playbook, which provided simple ways to ingest data using either off-the-shelf tools like Fivetran or Snowflake's own COPY INTO command. We outlined a two-step process for setting up ingestion in dbt with the PDP package: a one-time setup of schemas, file formats, and stages, followed by configuring the table name, file pattern, and fields for each Landing Table. The principles we've discussed apply equally to the Data Export process, which is essentially the reverse of ingestion. Ingestion and export are straightforward processes. While complexity can arise from scheduling, networking, security, and error handling, the process is simple.

We're now ready to look at ingestion at work and then move to the next layer of the PDP and continue building a modern, high-performance data platform. In the next chapter, **SAMPLE PROJECT—coding the Ingestion layer**, we will look at some real cases of data ingestion and the code to make it happen.

Recommended resources

Snowflake documentation

- Overview of data loading and unloading. https://docs.snowflake.com/user-guide/data-load-overview.
- Stages and File Formats
  https://docs.snowflake.com/en/sql-reference/sql/create-stage.
  https://docs.snowflake.com/en/sql-reference/sql/create-file-format.
- How to set up a storage integration. https://docs.snowflake.com/en/sql-reference/sql/create-storage-integration.
- List command to show and filter files in a stage. https://docs.snowflake.com/en/sql-reference/sql/list.
- Geospatial data types. https://docs.snowflake.com/en/sql-reference/data-types-geospatial.

Dbt documentation

- Dbt Sources. https://docs.getdbt.com/docs/build/sources.

Pragmatic Data Platform dbt package

- Ingestion and Export layer of the Pragmatic Data Platform (PDP) package:
  https://github.com/pragmatic-data/pragmatic-data-platform/blob/main/macros/in_out/README.md.

CHAPTER 9

Coding the Ingestion Layer

This chapter serves as a practical, hands-on guide to implementing the ingestion layer of the Pragmatic Data Platform (PDP) using dbt and Snowflake. Building upon the foundational concepts laid out in **Chapter 8**, we will take the **Stonks** sample project introduced in **Part 1, Chapter 5,** and bring its ingestion layer to life.

You will learn to set up the necessary Snowflake infrastructure, physically load raw data into a staging area, and, most importantly, build a highly automated ingestion process using custom dbt macros with little editing and a straightforward coding pattern. This process, powered by the PDP's reusable macros, will efficiently load data from your files into dedicated landing tables.

We will use real Interactive Brokers export files to make the task real, but you can use the files from your use case or broker. We will also address the practical need for ingesting small, manually managed datasets using dbt seeds, ensuring our entire ingestion layer is robust, auditable, and aligned with the PDP's core principles.

By the end of this chapter, you will have a fully functional, scalable ingestion layer ready for the next step in the data lifecycle.

The topics that we are going to cover in this chapter are:

- Introduction to the "Stonks" Ingestion Layer
- Setting up the Snowflake objects for ingestion
- Loading the Interactive Brokers files
- Building the Ingestion Processes with PDP Macros
- Using a Seed for Manual Data

Sample project and code

The sample dbt project is available at: **https://github.com/pragmatic-data/stonks.** **All the code** we will write in this chapter **is in the dbt project folders**, mostly in the `seed` and `ingestion` folders. The materials that do not belong in the project code will be in the sub-folder for this chapter, `chapter_09`, under the `code_samples_by_chapter` folder.

Please note that, to better fit the limited space on the printed page, we omit most comments and change the formatting of code blocks compared to the files.

Introduction to the Stonks ingestion layer

Welcome back to the Stonks project! In this chapter, we're going to get our hands dirty and start building the data platform for our mock investment portfolio. We've talked a lot about the Pragmatic Data Platform (PDP) architecture in theory, and now it's time to put those principles into practice. We will begin with the very first step in any data project: data ingestion.

As you recall from Chapter 8, the PDP's ingestion layer has one and only one job: to get raw data from its source into a dedicated landing table in Snowflake with zero transformations.

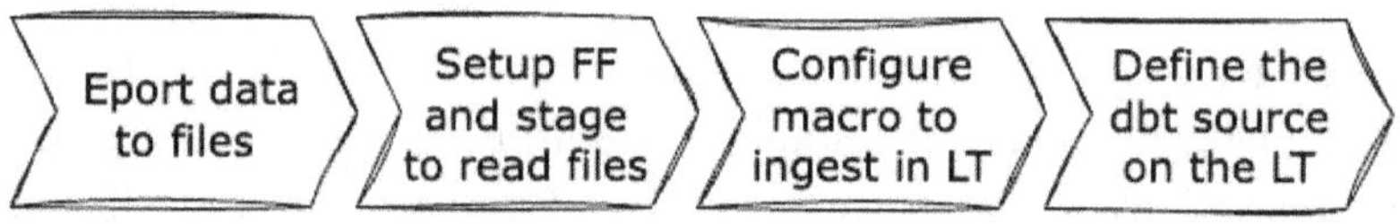

Figure 31: Workflow for extracting and ingesting data into Snowflake using the PDP macros.

Figure 31 shows the general workflow for extracting and ingesting data into Snowflake using the PDP macros. If you use an internal Snowflake stage, as we will do, you will also have a step to load the data into the stage, but that is less common in bigger projects, where organizations already have cloud storage and governance rules.

The ingestion layer isn't where we clean, join, or enrich our data. That work comes later, in the storage and refined layers. Here, our goal is simply to capture a faithful, immutable copy of the raw source data, give it an ingestion timestamp and other metadata for auditability and lineage. We're starting to build a foundation we can trust, which will culminate in our HIST tables in the storage layer serving as a single source of truth for all our upstream data.

For our "Stonks" project, we'll focus on the three primary data sources from a real broker (Interactive Brokers) that were introduced in Chapter 5: Trades, OpenPositions, and CashTransactions. You can adapt the code to use your broker's exports. Additionally, we will introduce a fourth, small, and manually maintained data source for Corporate Actions. We'll use these four sources to demonstrate how to build an ingestion layer that is not only functional but also automated, scalable, and easy to maintain, all thanks to the power of dbt and the PDP's custom macros.

To keep our project organized and maintain a clear separation of concerns, we'll place all our ingestion-related code under a dedicated ingestion folder within our dbt project. We will write ingestion macros, not yet dbt SQL models, so the separation is important, as we need to tell dbt to treat those files as macros and not SQL models.

The raw CSV files that we'll be maintaining by hand will be placed in the seeds folder, a standard dbt location for small, static, or manual datasets. We will also update our `dbt_project.yml` and `packages.yml` files to ensure our project is properly configured to use the necessary PDP macros, run our ingestion macros, and place the seed from the CSV file where we want it, how we want it.

The ingestion playbook

This chapter will follow a pragmatic playbook to build our ingestion layer step by step. By the end of this journey, you will have a clear, repeatable process for ingesting new data sources into your own PDP. Our plan is as follows:

- **Set up the Snowflake Infrastructure**: We'll begin by configuring and, eventually, creating the necessary database, schema, stage, and file format in Snowflake.
- **Load the Raw Data**: Next, we will use the `PUT` command to physically move the Interactive Brokers CSV files from our local system to the Snowflake stage. We take this step because we do not assume you have ready-to-use cloud storage. If you have one, just point and authorize the stage to use it in step 1 and skip this step.
- **Build the Ingestion Macros**: This is the core of our automated process. By providing minimal metadata, we will create a custom dbt macro for each data source.
- **Ingest Manual Data**: Finally, we will load the Corporate Actions data using a dbt seed, demonstrating how to handle small, manually managed datasets.

Once we are done with proper ingestion and loading data into the Landing Tables, to make the data usable in dbt, we must define these landing tables as dbt sources. This allows us to validate the data and perform thorough tests to ensure our ingestion process is working correctly. We will do this in Chapter 11, as validating the input belongs to the storage layer, where we use the Landing Tables to historicize and permanently store the data from our sample project.

Setting up the Snowflake objects for ingestion

The first step in building any data platform layer is to set up the necessary infrastructure.

In a traditional environment, this might involve manually running SQL scripts or using an infrastructure-as-code tool. However, in the PDP, we leverage the power of dbt to manage our database objects as code. This allows us to define and version our infrastructure directly within our project, treating it like any other piece of code. As discussed in Chapter 8, we achieve this by using setup macros that define and create the required Snowflake objects.

Project structure and configuration

To keep our project organized, we will create a dedicated folder for our ingestion-related macros. Inside the root directory of our dbt project, let's create a new folder named `ingestion`. Within this, a new subdirectory, `land_interactive_brokers`, provides a clear, descriptive namespace for our Interactive Brokers-related ingestion code. The name is self-explanatory: this code is for the "landing" of data from the specific source, Interactive Brokers, as we will not use it for export. A good alternative, especially in the case of mixed use, would have been to use only the source name.

Inside this folder, we will start by adding the setup file we discussed in Chapter 8. Then we will add ingestion macros for each source file to be ingested.

```
/<project root>
└─── ingestion/
     └─── land_interactive_brokers/
          └─── setup_interactive_brokers.sql
```

We need to tell dbt that the `ingestion` folder will contain macros by adding a macro-paths entry to dbt_project.yml. Let's do it.

```
# dbt_project.yml

macro-paths: ["macros", "project_setup", "migrations", "ingestion"]
```

The code snippet shows the `dbt_project.yml` file after adding the `ingestion` folder to the macro-paths. This is crucial for dbt to discover and compile our macros.

We also need to add the Pragmatic Data Platform package to the `packages.yml` configuration file, if it isn't there yet, so we can use the PDP macros.

```
# Pragmatic Data Platform package
- git: https://github.com/pragmatic-data/pragmatic-data-platform.git
  revision: 0.4.18    # Check the latest version in GitHub!
```

After saving the file, you need to update the packages by running the command `dbt deps` on the command line. We now also have the macros from the Pragmatic Data Platform package available, and we can get started using them for the Snowflake ingestion infrastructure setup.

The ingestion setup file

As seen in chapter eight, we create the Snowflake infrastructure using a setup file that contains a few macros: one for the configuration, one for generating the SQL, and one for executing the SQL. The file is completed with a few getter macros that make key configuration elements easily available throughout the dbt project. We will mostly use them in the custom ingestion macros and their tests, but you can use them wherever it suits you.

Ingestion configuration macro

The Ingestion Configuration Macro, `get_IB_ingestion_cfg`, is at the core of our infrastructure setup, collecting the configuration and returning it as a YAML object, which you can also consider a Python dictionary. This macro centralizes all the parameters needed to create our Snowflake objects. It is a best practice to define these configurations in a single place to ensure consistency and simplify maintenance. Let's look at the macro `get_IB_ingestion_cfg` for the Interactive Brokers source:

```
# setup_interactive_brokers.sql

{% macro get_IB_ingestion_cfg() %}
{% set ingestion_cfg %}

landing:
    database:    "{{ target.database }}"
    schema:      LAND_IB
    comment:     "'Landing table schema for IB.'"

file_format:
    name: IB_CSV__FF
    definition:
        TYPE: "'CSV'"
        FIELD_DELIMITER: "','"
        FIELD_OPTIONALLY_ENCLOSED_BY: "'\\042'"
        COMPRESSION: "'AUTO'"
        ERROR_ON_COLUMN_COUNT_MISMATCH: TRUE
        EMPTY_FIELD_AS_NULL: TRUE
        NULL_IF: ('', '\\N')

stage:
    name: IB_CSV__STAGE
    definition:
        FILE_FORMAT:
        DIRECTORY: ( ENABLE = true )
        COMMENT: "'Stage for CSV files from IB.'"
{% endset %}

{{ return(fromyaml(ingestion_cfg)) }}

{% endmacro %}
```

The `landing` block defines where (database and schema) you want the landing Tables to be located. The database must exist; the schema will be created if it does not. This, from a governance perspective, ensures that the role impersonated by the dbt service is allowed to write and create a schema in the designated database. Recalling the setup and governance chapters, it is important for the normal operation of the platform that the dbt user owns the schemas where it creates database objects, so it can change and, if needed, eventually delete them.

The `file_format` and `stage` blocks define the names and parameters for creating these two objects if they do not exist yet. This is important to remember because a change in the configuration will not take effect unless you drop the old objects. Use a migration to drop them so that the ingestion will re-create them.

This is the minimum configuration required to use the YAML configuration as the input of the `pragmatic_data.inout_setup_sql(...)` macro. Still, you can look at the Pragmatic Data Platform package documentation and code to find out more options, including the ability to create multiple file formats and/or stages in a single file. This might be useful when you have different types of input files or different locations or levels of security in accessing the source files. In a corporate setting, use a URL to your storage with a storage integration.

To find all possible configuration options for file formats and stages, look in the respective Snowflake documentation. Then you can pass them as YAML attributes in the configuration file with the format <parameter>: <value>.

The naming conventions used in the configuration improve readability and automate our operations. We use a short code for the source being set up to make macro names unique. In our case, we use IB for Interactive Brokers, whereas we used SYSTEM_A in the chapter eight samples. We also use a double underscore __ to separate the object's purpose (IB_CSV) from its type (FF for file format, STAGE for stage). This makes the configuration easy to understand at a glance and to automatically create a new copy when we want to set up another source system.

Ingestion setup, generation, and execution

The configuration macro returns the configuration as a YAML object parsed into a Pythoon dictionary.

To complete the setup, we need to pass the configuration to a macro that uses these values to generate the setup commands, and then pass the generated SQL to another macro that executes it. We keep the SQL generation in one macro and its execution in another to facilitate inspection and troubleshooting. This is a useful pattern to improve maintainability. The following macros, placed in the same `setup_interactive_brokers.sql` file as the configuration, will allow us to do just that.

First, the macro to generate the SQL by calling the PDP package passing the configuration:

```
{%  macro get_IB_ingestion_setup_sql() %}

{% do return(
      pragmatic_data.inout_setup_sql(
            cfg = get_IB_ingestion_cfg())) %}

{%- endmacro %}
```

and then the one executing the generated SQL commands:

```
{%  macro run_IB_ingestion_setup() %}

  {% do run_query(get_IB_ingestion_setup_sql()) %}

{%- endmacro %}
```

They are both very simple macros. The `get_IB_ingestion_setup_sql` macro passes the YAML configuration to the `input_setup_sql` macro of the Pragmatic Data Platform package to generate the SQL to create the required Snowflake objects: schema, file format, and stage. The `run_IB_ingestion_setup` macro takes the output of the previous macro (the generated SQL) and executes it, creating the Snowflake objects.

Note that the schema will be generated in the database specified in the configuration, or in the current environment's database (`target.database`) if no database is specified. Remember that this database must already exist, and usually, the dbt executor role cannot and should not even create it.

Configuration getter macros

To complete the setup and make the configuration easy to use without having to know its inner workings, we will create the following getter helper macros.

```
{% macro get_IB_ingestion_db_name(cfg = get_IB_ingestion_cfg()) %}
  {% do return( cfg.landing.database or target.database) %}
{%- endmacro %}

{% macro get_IB_ingestion_schema_name(cfg = get_IB_ingestion_cfg()) %}
  {% do return( cfg.landing.schema or target.schema) %}
{%- endmacro %}

{% macro get_IB_ingestion_csv_ff_name(cfg = get_IB_ingestion_cfg())%}
  {% do return( get_IB_ingestion_db_name() ~ '.'
             ~ get_IB_ingestion_schema_name() ~  '.'
             ~ cfg.file_format.name
  ) %}
{%- endmacro %}

{%  macro get_IB_ingestion_stage_name(cfg = get_IB_ingestion_cfg()) %}
  {% do return(get_IB_ingestion_db_name() ~ '.'
              ~ get_IB_ingestion_schema_name() ~  '.'
              ~ cfg.stage.name
  ) %}
{%- endmacro %}
```

The names of these macros should be self-explanatory, but note that the getters for the file format and stage return the fully qualified name (db.schema.object), while the getters for the database and schema just return the object name.

The difference is that both the database and the schema have meaningful defaults, and the getter is where you finally resolve whether you will use the default or a config value. At the same time, for the file format and stage, there is no default; you must always specify them in the configuration so that you can use `cfg.file_format.name` or `cfg.stage.name`. If you need it, you can get the non-qualified name everywhere in dbt with `get_IB_ingestion_cfg().stage.name`.

Note that the getter macros in the setup files always have the same code across all setup files; the only changes are their names and the getter name for the `cfg` value. Since macro names must be globally unique in the dbt project, we include the system name to distinguish between setup macros for different systems.

In practice, you do not write them every time; you create them by duplicating from another system or from the Pragmatic Data Platform package integration tests, and then automatically replace the name of the other system with the name of the system you are setting up. In this way, the setup of a system is reduced to copying a file, running a replacement of the system name, and then updating the configuration YAML block in the configuration macro to match what is needed for the new system.

Executing the setup macro

Now that you have completed the setup macro, you can inspect the generated SQL with this code in a dbt model: `{{ get_IB_ingestion_setup_sql() }}`. Compile the model to see the result of executing the macro; that is, your generated SQL. We suggest you inspect the generated SQL before executing the setup code by running the `run_IB_ingestion_setup()` macro.

Now, if you are happy with the SQL, you can finally run the macro and apply the setup with the following command line in your system or in dbt Cloud:

```
dbt run-operation run_IB_ingestion_setup
```

This command will execute the `run_IB_ingestion_setup()` macro manually, but, as we saw in chapter eight, it will usually be the first step in the `load_all` macro, which is called to perform the ingestion before starting the pipeline run.

Now that we have the infrastructure set up, let's get the files in and then ingest them.

Loading the interactive brokers files in a Snowflake stage

Now that our Snowflake infrastructure is in place, the next step in our ingestion playbook is to load the raw data files into the stage we created. The physical movement of data within our data platform's boundary is a critical step in many data platforms and is the precursor to the ingestion layer, as mentioned.

It's important to note that if your source files are already in a cloud storage location like Amazon S3, Google Cloud Storage, or Azure Blob Storage, as is common in most enterprise-level projects, you should just ingest them from where they are. In that case, you configure the Snowflake stage we created to point directly to that location, and you simply skip the data movement step entirely.

No code is the best code and is bug-free!

For the other scenarios where you need to move data and you don't have a ready-made or company-dictated destination, this section will walk you through the process of getting the files into Snowflake's reach with high reliability and minimal effort. For the sample project, we'll use files on your machine; of course, you can use the same logic and code from any server where you will have the data exports.

Organizing the sample files for upload

The sample Interactive Brokers files for this project are available in the book's GitHub repository.

You can download the sample files from the project repository at `https://github.com/pragmatic-data/stonks`, under the "code samples" section. In the `code_samples_by_chapter/chapter_09/source_data` directory, you will find the `sample_IB_files.zip` file.

We recommend that you download it and put it into a convenient location on your local machine. Once you unzip it, you will find the following subfolders: `open_positions`, `cash_transactions`, and `trades`, with each containing a few files, plus the same with `_future` in the name and many more files. You will also find a folder called `Transfers`. We will ingest immediately the files in the folders without `_future` in their names, leaving the other files for you to move there and load one or a few dates at a time and simulate time passing. See chapter five for more info on the sample project data.

We suggest creating a directory structure that mirrors the intended ingestion process. A good approach is to create a folder for each data source and a sub-folder for each table, as we did.

The SnowSQL and Snowflake CLI tools

To upload the local files to our Snowflake stage, we will use the SnowSQL tool, which is freely available with Snowflake. The Snowflake CLI (Command Line Interface) is a newer tool that does the same and much more, so it is the tool of the future. We have been using SnowSQL for a long time, so we will stick with it for the sample project.

These tools allow you to connect to Snowflake and execute commands directly from your terminal or create command files and run them through the tool.

You can find the official download links and detailed installation instructions on the Snowflake documentation website (see the links at the end of the chapter).

We are using SnowSQL for simplicity, but the PUT command can be executed programmatically from any Snowflake driver or connector. This is a common and effective approach if your data export process is already automated, allowing you to seamlessly integrate the data movement step into your existing code.

If you do not plan to move any data and want to load only the data to test the code in the sample project, you can also do so using the Snowflake UI for the stage.

Download one of the Snowflake tools and configure it to connect to your Snowflake account. If you pick `snowsql`, we suggest creating a named connection by editing the `config` file in the `.snowsql` subdirectory of your root directory. Add a connection for the Stonks project for each environment where you want to connect, adapting the following template for the dev environment:

```
[connections.stonks_dev]

accountname = <account-id>.<region>.<provider>
# e.g., accountname = ab1234.north-europe.azure

private_key_path = /Users/<youruser>/.ssh/<key_name>.p8
username = STONKS_DBT_EXECUTOR
rolename = STONKS_DEV_RW
dbname = STONKS_DEV
schemaname = LAND_IB
warehousename = COMPUTE_WH
```

Please consider that the eventual password is stored in plain text in the config file, so it's much better to use a key-pair as shown, or a programmatic access token (PAT) that you can create in the Snowflake UI under Admin > Users & Roles, and enter your user. For service users, the key-pair is the preferred method. Once you have set up the named connection stonks as shown above, you can run snowsql to start with the stonk connection using the command:

```
SNOWSQL_PRIVATE_KEY_PASSPHRASE="..." snowsql -c stonks_dev
```

replacing the "..." with the key passphrase. You can also set the environment variable in your environment, or you can leave it unset and SnowSQL will prompt you for the passphrase on startup.

Uploading the files

With the files organized and SnowSQL installed and able to connect to your account with your dbt executor user, we can now upload our sample data. Although you can upload each file individually, a better approach is to use a script to automate loading all the files in a folder and all the folders you need. This is a more pragmatic and scalable method.

In the previous section, we created a named connection that abstracts away where you want to connect and the authentication and authorization details. Now we will create a small script for the SnowSQL tool that includes the commands to execute. We will use the PUT command to load each source's files into the correct stage.

Since this is neither a dbt model nor a macro, we will place the file in a separate folder for utility scripts. Create a folder named `util_scripts` at the root of your project, and inside it, create a file named `put_ALL_files_to_stages.sql`. The command files for SnowSQL contain one command per row, so we will put here three commands for each environment, one for each source folder:

```
PUT 'file:///<path>/open_positions/*OpenPositions*.csv'
    @STONKS_DEV.LAND_IB.IB_CSV__STAGE/open_positions/
    AUTO_COMPRESS = TRUE
    OVERWRITE = FALSE
;

PUT 'file:///<path>/cash_transactions/*CashTransactions*.csv'
    @STONKS_DEV.LAND_IB.IB_CSV__STAGE/cash_transactions/
    AUTO_COMPRESS = TRUE
    OVERWRITE = FALSE
;

PUT 'file:///<path>/Trades/*Trades*.csv'
    @STONKS_DEV.LAND_IB.IB_CSV__STAGE/trades/
    AUTO_COMPRESS = TRUE
    OVERWRITE = FALSE
;
```

This sample shows only the commands for the DEV stage, but if your service user has access to all environments, you can add a command to copy the correct files to QA and PROD as well.

The PUT command copies the files selected by the pattern to the specified path inside the Snowflake stage. We use a subfolder structure (stage/<folder>) within the stage to keep our files organized, which is a key PDP best practice. Edit the path to the files and the folder name inside the stage to suit your preferences.

The `auto_compress` flag is a useful feature that automatically compresses the file if it's not already compressed. The `overwrite` flag set to false allows us to re-run the `snowsql` command as often as we like, but only move new files that are not already in the stage.

Now you can load all your files with a single command:

```
snowsql -c stonks -f <path-to-the-
repo>/stonks/util_scripts/put_ALL_files_to_stages.sql
```

For conciseness, we have not included the environment variable on the command line, as it is common to either set it in your environment or not pass it and provide the passphrase each time you run the `snowsql` tool when it asks for it to connect.

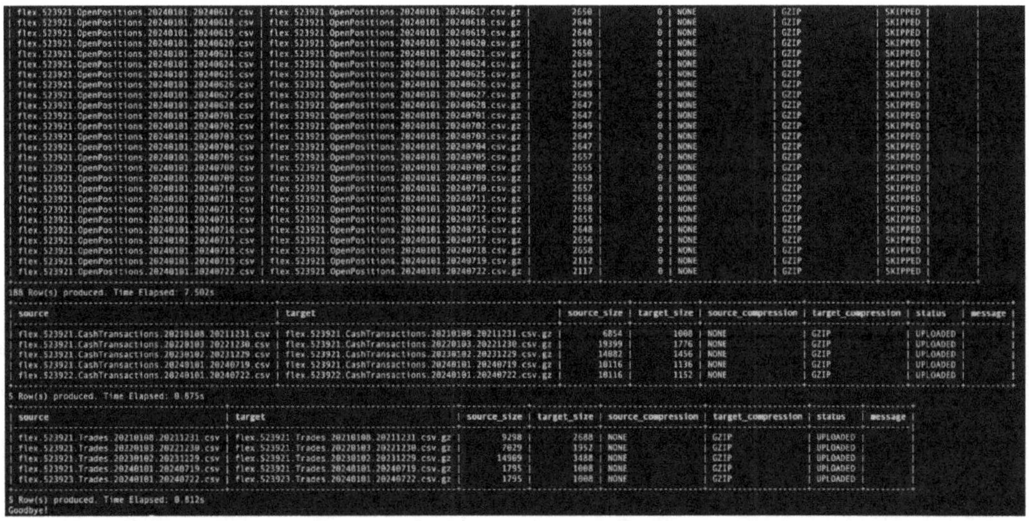

Figure 32: Snowsql output for the initial load of the sample project's files.

Figure 32 shows the result you should see. In the picture, the load of the OpenPosition files had already been done once, so the script processes the files but correctly skips uploading them again.

Verifying the upload

After the script runs, you get a visual report from the `SnowSQL` tool that summarizes which files were uploaded, their sizes, and whether they were compressed. You can also view which files are in the stage at any time to verify that they have been successfully uploaded using the Snowflake `LIST` command. You can use it through SnowSQL from the command line, in interactive mode, or in Snowflake Worksheets. This command line lists the files in a stage using snowsql:

```
snowsql -c stonks -q "LIST @STONKS_DEV.LAND_IB.IB_CSV__STAGE/;"
```

In the Snowflake Worksheets, or in an interactive session in SnowSQL, you need only the command inside double quotes. You can add a <path> after the stage name to limit the list to files within that path. Alternatively, you can use the Snowflake UI to explore the stage contents and even upload and delete files, but for automation, it's better to use the commands. In the UI, navigate to the database and schema for the stage in the Data > Databases menu; you will find the stage under the Stages element. Click it to see and interact with the stage content from the UI.

If you look up the stage in the Database view of a Worksheet, you don't see the stage contents. To see them, click the "Open Stage details in new tab" button in the top right of the stage details pop-up, then you will be in the Data menu view.

Use one method to check the files in the stage you created, and confirm that we are ready to ingest them into our landing tables.

Building the ingestion processes with PDP macros

Despite the high variability of the task and the variety of file formats and cases, you will see that the ingestion process, thanks to Snowflake, dbt, and the reusable macros from the PDP package, is surprisingly simple. I love that!

With our files accessible in Snowflake via a stage, we are now at the core of the ingestion layer: building automated processes to load them into our landing tables. In the Pragmatic Data Platform, we accomplish this with a specific, macro-driven pattern that makes the process highly reusable, testable, and maintainable. This approach moves the focus from manual data loading to a repeatable, code-based solution.

The PDP's ingestion pattern is simple yet powerful: each source table corresponds to a dbt macro that handles the ingestion of its files. This macro encapsulates all the necessary logic and configuration, separating it from the generic, reusable code that actually performs the load and comes with the PDP package.

The PDP library provides one core macro that takes a set of configuration parameters and execute the `COPY INTO` command to load the staged data into a designated landing table. Invoke the `run_file_ingestion` macro to ingest CSV files and semi-structured data, like Parquet, Avro, or JSON files.

This macro handles several key tasks for us:

- **Table Creation**: Automatically create the landing table, based on the column names and eventual data types that we provide, if it doesn't exist.
- **Data Load**: Execute the `COPY INTO` command to load the new files in the stage into the Landing Table (LT), with the highest possible efficiency.
- **Metadata**: For each row of data in the LT, capture the source file name, its modification timestamp, and the row in the file, and add an `ingestion_ts_utc` column to the table with the UTC timestamp of when the ingestion process starts. This is a crucial PDP principle for lineage and auditing, allowing us to know exactly from where and when a batch of data was loaded.

*The `ingestion_ts_utc` column records when the data enters our platform and has the same value for all data ingested in the same dbt run, regardless of whether it comes from multiple files or is split across different landing tables. Besides its temporal information, it also serves as a very useful shared **batch ID** across different tables.*

Our job in the rest of this section is to create a custom wrapper macro for each Interactive Brokers file type that we want to ingest. This custom macro serves as the configuration layer. It will define all the parameters required by the reusable macro `run_file_ingestion` in a clear, easy-to-read YAML object, making our ingestion process explicit and declarative.

We will strictly follow the no-transformation principle in this layer. The only acceptable "transformation" is column renaming, if needed. This is sometimes necessary if a source column name is not a valid SQL identifier (e.g., contains spaces or special characters). We will not change data types, filter rows, or add any business logic. This ensures our landing tables are a true, raw replica of the source data.

Please note that CSV files lack information about data types, treating everything as text. This is why, by default, when you provide only column names, our CSV ingestion treats everything as text. You can provide data type information in the configuration along with the column names, using the same format as the CREATE TABLE SQL command, and Snowflake will automatically convert the data to the data type you select. Beware that any implicit conversion error will stop the ingestion process.

That is why we prefer to ingest data as text and apply explicit data type conversion in the STG models that read from the Landing Tables, so you can handle bad data and errors. It is a best practice to keep the LT input flexible and convert to the correct data types in the STG models for long-term storage in the historized data. The base principle of doing one thing at a time and doing it well is valid.

Ingesting the trades data

Our first task is to create the ingestion macro for the Trades data.

We will define a `load_IB_Trades` macro that holds all the necessary configuration and then calls the `pragmatic_data.run_file_ingestion` macro to do the load.

- **Goal**: Create a custom dbt macro, `load_IB_Trades`, to automate the ingestion of the Trades data. This process will create a Landing Table (`TRADES`) and load the files from the `Trades` folder in the stage.
- **Code**: Create a new file named load_IB_Trades.sql in the ingestion/land_interactive_brokers folder.

This file will contain the following code:

```
{% macro load_IB_Trades(recreate_table = false) %}

{%- set ingestion_cfg -%}
ingestion:
    pattern: 'trades/.*Trades.*[.]csv.gz'
    stage_name: "{{ get_IB_ingestion_stage_name() }}"
    format_name:

landing_table:
    db_name:      "{{ get_IB_ingestion_db_name() }}"
    schema_name: "{{ get_IB_ingestion_schema_name() }}"
    table_name:  Trades
    columns:
      - ClientAccountID  #-- No type means TEXT
      - AccountAlias
      ... <more column names, see the online file>
      - Put_Call # was Put/Call, not valid, renamed
      ...
      - AccruedInterest

{%- endset -%}

{%- set cfg = fromyaml(ingestion_cfg) -%}

{% do pragmatic_data.run_file_ingestion(
        landing_table_dict = cfg['landing_table'],
        ingestion_dict  = cfg['ingestion'],
        recreate_table = recreate_table
) %}

{% endmacro %}
```

The `ingestion_cfg` YAML block defines the specific parameters for the Trades source, with the `ingestion` object used to identify the files and their format, and the `landing_table` object used to describe the Landing Table, its location, and its columns.

In the `ingestion` object:

- `stage_name` is the fully qualified name of the stage to use to read the files.
- `pattern` is a regular expression to identify the files to load inside the stage. Please pay attention, as the file and folder names are case-sensitive.
- `format_name` is the fully qualified name of the file format to read the files. It is optional; if empty or omitted, the file format defined for the stage is used.

In the `landing_table` object:

- `db_name` is the database where to create the Landing Table.
- `schema_name` is the schema where to create the Landing Table.
- `table_name` is the name of the landing table created by the macro.

- `columns` is the list of column names or column definitions of the Landing Table. Same syntax of the CREATE TABLE command (e.g., `quantity: int not null`). If only the name is provided, the column will be of type text and nullable.

The `columns` property must list all columns in the CSV file, in the same order they appear, as they are created and loaded in the LT in that order. We use the same column names from the files, replacing only the special characters to make them valid identifiers (e.g., "put_call" instead of "Put/Call"), which is the only transformation allowed in this layer. This is a best practice for auditability and ease of understanding of the ingestion process with respect to the exported data.

The place to make the data easy to use and provide good column names is the STG model in the storage layer, coming up next. The core of the ingestion macro, in the end, is the `ingestion_cfg` YAML block that is then converted into a usable Python dictionary and passed to the PDP macro. This single call performs the entire ingestion process. Quite simple, isn't it?

The `recreate_table` argument of the ingestion macro is a useful feature, especially during initial development, for recreating the Landing Table without changing the code. Just call the macro in a run-operation, passing true as the argument value (or by changing the macro signature before the call).

To try how this works, just use this command line:

```
dbt run-operation load_IB_Trades
```

In a few seconds, the Landing Table will be created, and your files will be ingested. If you get any error, double-check the names and case of your stage, folder, and files.

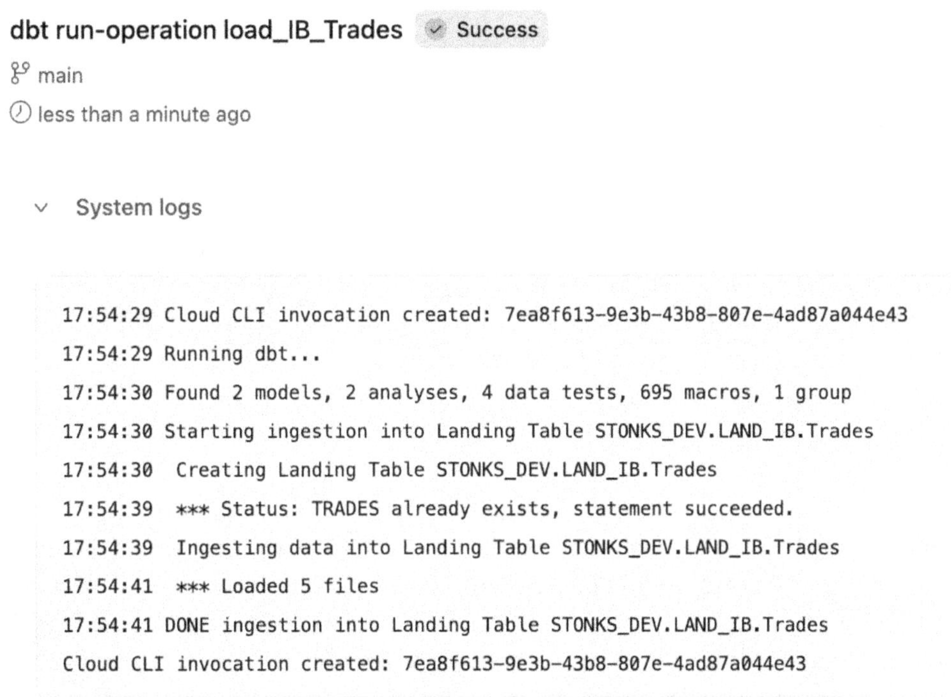

Figure 33: Result of a successful run of an ingestion macro.

The image shows what the result should be when running the ingestion in dbt Cloud.

Ingesting the open positions data

Next, we follow the same pattern for the `OpenPositions` data.

Goal: Create a custom dbt macro, `load_IB_OpenPositions`, to automate the ingestion of the OpenPositions data and create its landing table.

Code: Create a new file named load_IB_OpenPositions.sql in the ingestion/land_interactive_brokers folder.

This file will contain the following code:

```
{% macro load_IB_OpenPositions(recreate_table = false) %}

{%- set ingestion_cfg -%}

ingestion:
    pattern: 'open_positions/.*OpenPositions.*[.]csv.gz'
    stage_name: "{{ get_IB_ingestion_stage_name() }}"
    format_name:

landing_table:
    db_name:      "{{ get_IB_ingestion_db_name() }}"
    schema_name: "{{ get_IB_ingestion_schema_name() }}"
    table_name:   Open_Positions
    columns:
      - ClientAccountID  #-- No type means TEXT
      - AccountAlias
      ...
      - Put_Call
      ...
      - AccruedInterest

{%- endset -%}

{%- set cfg = fromyaml(ingestion_cfg) -%}

{% do pragmatic_data.run_file_ingestion(
        landing_table_dict = cfg['landing_table'],
        ingestion_dict  = cfg['ingestion'],
        recreate_table = recreate_table
) %}

{% endmacro %}
```

This macro works in exactly the same way as the `load_IB_Trades` macro, but with a different configuration specific to the `OpenPositions` data. Compared to the previous macro, we only had to change three configuration parameters (`pattern`, `table_name`, and `columns`). If you consider the ingestion of multiple tables from a system, like we are doing now, it is really that simple, because out of the seven configuration parameters in the configuration, we generally need to change only those three; the others are usually the same for all the Landing Tables for the same source system. In this very common situation, you can duplicate the first ingestion macro, change the macro and file name, and these three parameters, and you are ready to go. So simple!

To see how this macro works, execute the following command line:

```
dbt run-operation load_IB_OpenPositions
```

Again, the Landing Table will be created, and your files will be ingested in seconds, even when ingesting 188 files with 1654 rows and about 40 columns. It is amazing how quickly Snowflake can ingest small and large files.

Ingesting the cash transactions data

Finally, we'll create the ingestion macro for the `CashTransactions` data.

- **Goal**: Create a custom dbt macro, `load_IB_CashTransactions`, to automate the ingestion of the `CashTransactions` data and create its landing table.
- **Code**: Create a new file named load_IB_CashTransactions.sql in the ingestion/land_interactive_brokers folder.

This file will contain the following code:

```
{% macro load_IB_CashTransactions(recreate_table = false)%}

{%- set ingestion_cfg -%}

ingestion:
    pattern: 'cash_transactions/.*CashTransactions.*csv.gz'
    stage_name: "{{ get_IB_ingestion_stage_name() }}"
    format_name:

landing_table:
    db_name:      "{{ get_IB_ingestion_db_name() }}"
    schema_name: "{{ get_IB_ingestion_schema_name() }}"
    table_name:  Cash_Transactions
    columns:
      - ClientAccountID          #-- No type means TEXT
      - AccountAlias
      ...
      - ClientReference

{%- endset -%}

{%- set cfg = fromyaml(ingestion_cfg) -%}

{% do pragmatic_data.run_file_ingestion(
        landing_table_dict = cfg['landing_table'],
        ingestion_dict  = cfg['ingestion'],
        recreate_table = recreate_table
) %}

{% endmacro %}
```

Again, this macro works exactly the same way as the previous two, just with changes to three configuration parameters specific to the `CashTransactions` data. To see how this macro works, execute the following command line:

```
dbt run-operation load_IB_CashTransactions
```

See that the landing table is created and the data loaded. With these three macros in place, you now have a fully automated, declarative, and repeatable ingestion layer for your primary data sources. This powerful pattern is a cornerstone of building a pragmatic, low-maintenance data platform.

Creating an all-in-one ingestion macro

As a final step to improve our workflow and demonstrate the power of macro composition, we will create a single "master" macro to run our entire Interactive Brokers ingestion process. This macro, which we will call `load_all_interactive_brokers`, will orchestrate the execution of all the individual macros we've just created.

The logic is simple: the master macro will first call the setup macro to ensure all Snowflake infrastructure is in place. It will then call each of the three individual ingestion macros in sequence. This approach is highly pragmatic because it bundles a complex series of steps into a single, easy-to-use command. This reduces the risk of human error and allows anyone on the team to run the full ingestion with one simple action.

Place the following code in a new file, `load_all_interactive_brokers.sql`, within the `land_interactive_brokers` directory.

```
{% macro load_all_interactive_brokers() %}

   -- 1. Setup the Snowflake infrastructure
    {% do run_IB_ingestion_setup() %}

   -- 2. Run the individual ingestion macros
    {% do load_IB_Trades() %}
    {% do load_IB_OpenPositions() %}
    {% do load_IB_Transfers() %}

   {{ log("Successfully ran all Interactive Brokers ingestion macros.",
info=True) }}

{% endmacro %}
```

To run this entire sequence from your command line, you will use the dbt run-operation command, which is designed to execute dbt macros outside of a model run:

```
dbt run-operation load_all_interactive_brokers
```

This single command will now perform everything needed for the ingestion: setting up the database and schema, creating the stage and file format, and loading all the raw data into the appropriate landing tables. This is a powerful and very pragmatic way to manage complex data pipelines.

Using a seed for manual data

Our macro-driven approach is perfect for ingesting machine-generated, recurring files of any size and frequency, from a few minutes to days or more. Data platforms often need to handle small, static datasets that are manually maintained. These could be lookup tables, business configuration data, or, in our case, manual adjustments for corporate actions. This data changes rarely, is small in size, and it is often good to version-control its evolution and include a PR explaining the change. The PDP addresses these use cases with dbt's seeds.

Seeds explained

A **dbt seed** is a CSV file in your dbt project that will be loaded into your data warehouse as a table. Think of it as a way to manage static data in a version-controlled environment, just like you would with your SQL models. They are ideal for:

- **Small, Static Datasets**: Data that changes infrequently and is small enough to be manually maintained in a CSV file.
- **Lookup Tables**: Mapping IDs to names, currency codes, or product categories.
- **Configuration Data**: Business rules values or settings that influence your code.

Seeds are loaded as a single batch with line insert (quite slow by design) and don't support incremental updates. They are best suited for data that is part of the codebase itself, not for a data source with its own lifecycle. You should not use seeds for large datasets, transactional data, or anything that requires a scheduled, automated ingestion.

The corporate_actions seed

For the Stonks project, we'll use a seed to manage corporate actions, such as stock splits or other corporate actions, that change our positions but are not captured in our regular data feeds. We'll create a simple CSV file, adding records as needed.

First, create a new file named `ib_corp_act_manual.csv` inside your dbt project's `seeds` folder. To ensure the file's content is accurate and reflects real-world data, we'll use the Interactive Brokers file with a few actions applied to the stocks we are following. Here are the first few columns of the corporate actions seed file for the stocks we are tracking. The full file, including all columns, is in the sample project.

```
BROKER_CODE,CLIENT_ACCOUNT_CODE,LISTING_EXCHANGE,SECURITY_CODE,SECURITY_S
YMBOL,SECURITY_NAME,...

IB,U***1429,NYSE,CA1363851017,CNQ,CANADIAN NATURAL RESOURCES,...

IB,U***8402,NYSE,CA1363851017,CNQ,CANADIAN NATURAL RESOURCES,...

IB,U***8402,NASDAQ,US88160R1014,TSLA,TESLA INC,...
```

Next, to tell dbt how to handle this seed, we need to add a configuration to `dbt_project.yml`. This is where we specify the schema for our seeds and we define the data types for each column to ensure Snowflake creates the table correctly. Defining the data types is optional, and you can let dbt infer all columns from the first few rows, but watch out for errors or imprecisions, like using integer in place of float, or using double instead of fixed-precision numbers for financial values. This is a crucial step for data integrity and the precision of your calculations.

To configure seeds in the `dbt_project.yml` file, we add a seed section and specify the configuration we need, such as the schema where to create the seed tables. The seed configuration is hierarchical: we can apply configuration and properties to all seeds, to the ones in our project, or to a specific seed, depending on where you put the code. Let's see how we configure seeds:

```
seeds:     # applies to all seeds, including packages
  stonks:  # applies to seeds in our project
    +schema: seeds
    ib_corp_act_manual:  # applies to the named seed
      +column_types:
        broker_code: varchar
        client_account_code: varchar
        ...
        corp_act_order: integer
```

In the snippet above, we have configured all the seeds from our stonks project to be created in a `seeds` schema, and we have also specified the column data types for one specific seed. As always, the full code is in the sample project in the GitHub repo. If you have previously created a seed table and you want to change data types or column names, you'll need to run `dbt seed --full-refresh` for changes to the column types to take effect. Also, note that you will need to explicitly name all folders on a seed path in the `dbt_project.yml` file when configuring `column_types`.

Please note that column data types can also be configured in any YAML file that references the seed, not just in the `dbt_project.yml` file. We prefer this second setup because it avoids bloating the `dbt_project.yml` file with overly specific configurations scattered across the project and keeps the configuration closer to the seed. In the repo, you will find the configuration in the YAML file we introduce next. Now, you can load the seed from the command line using the dbt seed command:

```
dbt seed -s ib_corp_act_manual
```

This command will create a new table in your data warehouse, in the schema you configured, and populate it with data from the CSV file. You can now reference this table by name in your dbt models using the `ref()` function just as you would any other dbt model: `ref('ib_corp_act_manual')`.

Automatically adding ingestion_ts_utc to a seed

A core principle of the PDP is to track the ingestion time for all data, regardless of its source. This provides essential lineage and auditability. While dbt doesn't automatically add an `ingestion_ts_utc` column to seeds, we can achieve this with a post-hook.

A **post-hook** is a SQL statement that runs after a model or seed has been built.

We will use a post-hook to add an `ingestion_ts_utc` column to all our seeds and fill it with the dbt run startup timestamp. We do this by adding the following post-hook and its queries to the seed configuration we already have in `dbt_project.yml`.

```
seeds:     # applies to all seeds, including packages
  stonks:  # applies to seeds in our project
    +schema: seeds
    +post-hook:
      - "ALTER TABLE {{ this }} ADD COLUMN IF NOT EXISTS ingestion_ts_utc
timestamp"
      - "UPDATE {{ this }} SET ingestion_ts_utc = '{{ run_started_at }}'
WHERE ingestion_ts_utc is null"
      ...
```

In the snippet above, we added a post-hook with two queries to run after any seed is loaded in our stonks project. The first query adds the `ingestion_ts_utc` column, the second fills it with the dbt run startup timestamp. The `{{ this }}` variable is a Jinja reference to the current table, which ensures the hook operates on the correct object, the seed being loaded in our case. Note that the timestamp in the seed will match the `ingestion_ts_utc` column in our Landing Tables and models executed in the same dbt run. This simple addition ensures that even our static, manually loaded data adheres to the PDP's auditability standards.

Data testing and documentation for seeds

A fundamental principle of the Pragmatic Data Platform is that all data is treated with the same level of care, regardless of its source. This means even our small, manually loaded seed data must be documented and tested to ensure its quality. Just because we created the file ourselves doesn't mean it's free of errors. Manually created data is more prone to errors than machine-generated data. This is especially true if a different team member or business user updates the file.

The Seed YAML companion file

For each seed, we will create a companion YAML file to add documentation and data tests. A good practice is to place the file in the same folder as the seed itself, with the same name as the seed but with the `.yml` extension. Let's do it for our corporate actions seed.

The `description` property is where we explain the purpose of the table and the meaning of its columns. This information is a crucial component of our data documentation and will be rendered on the dbt documentation catalog. The `config` property allows us to move some configurations, not all, from the `dbt_project` file. For example, the column data types. The `tests` section is where we define the data quality checks for the wider seed, while column-specific tests are specified under each column definition.

Testing data as it enters the data platform is a cornerstone of a reliable data platform. It helps us catch issues early, before they can propagate through downstream models and impact business decisions. For our corporate actions seed, we should enforce some basic rules. For example, in the snippet, we show some invariants we want to validate, as it's easy to get them wrong when entering data manually. We use the `expression_is_true` generic test from the `dbt_utils` package.

We also exploit the ability to declare columns with SQL expressions to add a unicity test on a list of columns using the `concat_ws()` SQL function. We could have used instead the `dbt_utils.unique_combination_of_columns` test. Given the table's tiny size, it makes no difference and allows us to add a description to the test.

```
version: 2
seeds:
 - name: ib_corp_act_manual
     description: Manually entered TX for Corporate Actions
     config:
       column_types:  # only the ones we want to change/be sure
         CORP_ACT_DATE: TIMESTAMP_NTZ
         QUANTITY: NUMBER(38,9)
         FX_RATE_TO_BASE: NUMBER(38,9)
         TX_MONEY_FX: NUMBER(38,9)
         TX_MONEY_BASE: NUMBER(38,9)
         COST_BASIS_FX: NUMBER(38,9)
         NOTES_CODES: TEXT
         TRANSACTION_ID: TEXT
     tests:
       - dbt_utils.expression_is_true:
           expression: QUANTITY * COST_BASIS_FX >= 0

       - dbt_utils.expression_is_true:
           expression: TX_MONEY_FX * TX_MONEY_BASE >= 0

     columns:
       - name: concat_ws('|',BROKER_CODE,CLIENT_ACCOUNT_CODE,
                         SECURITY_CODE,LISTING_EXCHANGE,CORP_ACT_DATE)

         description: TX for Corporate Actions are unique
         data_tests:
           - unique
           - not_null
```

As always, the snippet is shortened compared to the full file you find in the repo. With this YAML file, the next time you run dbt test or dbt build, dbt will automatically check these quality rules. This simple step transforms a manual data file into a trusted and auditable asset.

Of course, be pragmatic: if you have multiple closely knit seeds in a sub-folder with similar needs, or if using YAML anchors makes sense, it might make sense to just make a single file with the test and documentation for all these seeds!

Final exercise

Now that you have seen both how to ingest files into a landing table and how to load manually maintained CSV files with dbt seeds, we give you a simple exercise. In the zip file with the sample data, there is a folder, Transfers, with a single CSV file, since it is not common to transfer files between accounts. Logically, this is not a manually maintained file you want to source-control. It is a set of machine-generated files that very seldom have new files, every few years or once a year, even in years when you have no stock transfers.

We leave you the task of ingesting this file as well, evaluating the pros and cons of the two methods. In my own portfolio project, I ingest it using the ingestion macro, but the macro for this file is not in the load-all-master macro. I just call it when I know there are new transfers to lead every few years.

Chapter review

In this chapter, you've successfully built a robust and automated ingestion layer for the "Stonks" project, putting the theoretical principles of the Pragmatic Data Platform (PDP) into practice. You started by setting up the necessary Snowflake infrastructure using a simple, repeatable dbt macro powered by the PDP package macros, demonstrating how to treat your data infrastructure as code. You then physically loaded the raw CSV files into Snowflake's internal stage, a critical first step in the data ingestion process. The core of our work focused on building a series of custom dbt macros that, in turn, leverage the reusable PDP macros to perform the actual ingestion. This pattern is a cornerstone of the PDP, enabling you to automate data loading from multiple sources with minimal, declarative code. We also addressed the pragmatic need to ingest small, manually maintained datasets using dbt seeds, complete with data type definitions, documentation, and data tests.

You now have a fully functional and scalable ingestion layer that is:

- **Automated**: The entire process, from infrastructure setup to data loading, can be executed with a single dbt command that is easily scheduled or triggered by events.
- **Auditable**: Every landing table and seed strictly adheres to the original source and includes an ingestion TS column, providing clear timing, lineage, and audit trail.
- **Tested**: You've applied data tests directly to the seed data, catching potential issues at the earliest possible stage. We will do the same on the ingested data as the first step in the storage layer, when we define it as a source.

In the next chapter, we will move to the **Storage layer**, the heart of the PDP. This is where we will begin applying our first transformations to the raw data, creating clean, persistent models that will form the foundation for all subsequent data products. We'll learn how to organize and store our data in a way that is both easy to maintain and quick to access, setting the stage for more complex analysis and reporting.

Recommended resources

Snowflake documentation

- **CREATE SATAGE** command: Creates a new named internal or external stage to use for loading data from files into Snowflake tables and unloading data from tables into files. https://docs.snowflake.com/en/sql-reference/sql/create-stage.
- **CREATE FILE FORMAT** command: Creates a named file format that describes a set of staged data to access or load into Snowflake tables. https://docs.snowflake.com/en/sql-reference/sql/create-file-format.

- **Snowflake CLI** tool. https://docs.snowflake.com/en/developer-guide/snowflake-cli/index.
- **SnowSQL tool**, configuration and using a named connection:
    - https://docs.snowflake.com/en/user-guide/snowsql.
    - https://docs.snowflake.com/en/user-guide/snowsql-config.
    - https://docs.snowflake.com/en/user-guide/snowsql-start#connecting-to-snowflake-using-a-named-connection.
- **PUT command.** https://docs.snowflake.com/en/sql-reference/sql/put.
- **COPY INTO Command**: The central command for ingesting data from a stage into a table. Understanding its various options is crucial for building flexible ingestion processes. https://docs.snowflake.com/en/sql-reference/sql/copy-into-table.

dbt documentation

- run-operation command documentation and a discussion about operations, with multiple useful use cases, like cloning a DB or creating a Snowflake share:
    - https://docs.getdbt.com/reference/commands/run-operation.
    - https://docs.getdbt.com/docs/build/hooks-operations#about-operations.
- **dbt Seeds**: Dive deeper into using dbt seeds, including best practices for configuration, data types, and use cases. https://docs.getdbt.com/docs/build/seeds.
- **dbt Packages**: Explore the wider dbt ecosystem. The pragmatic-data package is one of many that can accelerate your development. https://docs.getdbt.com/docs/build/packages.
- **dbt_utils Package**: A popular dbt package containing a wide range of macros and data tests, including some used in this chapter.https://hub.getdbt.com/dbt-labs/dbt_utils/latest/.

CHAPTER 10

The Storage Layer

This chapter marks the next step in building our Pragmatic Data Platform (PDP), moving from raw data ingestion to proper storage and organization. This is a critical phase in which we **transform source data into reliable, auditable historical records**. We will delve into the core of the PDP's architecture, exploring how we make data usable, without altering its semantics, recognize and store its changes over time, and prepare it for the refined layer, where we will implement the real business logic.

In this chapter, you will understand the principles behind a robust storage layer and have a clear pattern for implementing it using dbt, Snowflake, and the PDP macros.

The key topics we will cover in this chapter are:

- **The Storage Layer, A Foundation for Your Data Platform**: The architecture of this layer, its core benefits, and the key concepts of identity and data semantics.
- **The Role of dbt Sources**: Connect to LTs and ensure input data quality with testing.
- **The Staging Model (STG)**: The logical core, where we apply make data usable.
- **The Historization Model (HIST)**: The technical core, where we do historization.
- **The Versioning Model (VER)**: The user-friendly interface to our historical data.
- **A Pattern for Adding New Entities**: A repeatable process for building the entire storage pipeline for any new entity in minutes using templates and simple SQL.
- **Advanced Concepts in the Storage Layer**: A look at more advanced topics, including bi-temporality, data restatement, and the evolution of history tables.

Sample project and code

The sample dbt project is available at: **https://github.com/pragmatic-data/stonks**. The code samples for this chapter are in the sub-folder `chapter_10`, under the `code_samples_by_chapter` folder.

You will also find the code for the storage layer in the executable part of the sample dbt project itself, which is discussed in detail in the next chapter. Please note that, to better fit the limited space on the printed page, we omit most comments and change the formatting of code blocks compared to the files.

The storage layer in customer cases

The Storage Layer is the unshakeable foundation of the Pragmatic Data Platform, designed for two primary purposes: to hold a **complete, immutable history** of source system data and to act as the **single, reliable source** for subsequent transformations. The need for a rock-solid Storage Layer is driven by two critical enterprise requirements: **regulatory compliance and auditability**. The proper design of the Storage Layer transforms data handling from a technical pipeline problem into a **core asset for meeting legal and financial requirements**. Two examples illustrate this well: Stena Fastigheter, where GDPR compliance shaped how personal data was separated and historized, and Scania's financial services unit, where strict audit requirements drove the adoption of full historization and snapshots.

The complete case studies for Stena Fastigheter and Scania are in Chapter 6.

- **Stena Fastigheter**: GDPR compliance drove the need for historized and immutable storage (separating PII). Stena Fastigheter's data team needed to comply with GDPR's "right to be forgotten." They built dedicated PII models in their storage layer, isolating personal data from core histories, so that PII could be deleted while preserving relational integrity of the data.
- **Scania** (TFS): Regulatory and audit requirements in finance demanded full historization and dbt snapshots for traceability. Scania's financial services unit driver was regulatory audits. They used HIST and VER models with dbt snapshots to provide auditors with a complete trace of data changes over time.

The Storage layer: A foundation for your data platform

The storage layer is the bedrock of a robust and maintainable data platform. Its primary goal is to act as the single source of truth for all business entities, ensuring that the platform's state is auditable and reliable. By centralizing the technicalities for handling upstream data changes, this layer absorbs complexity and reduces the need for constant rework in downstream models.

A strong Storage layer is key to a simple to build, easy to fix, and straightforward to evolve data platform.

The Pragmatic Data Platform (PDP) separates the storage of raw, unprocessed data (in the ingestion layer) from structured, historically aware, ready-to-use source entities. This separation ensures that the downstream layers (the Refined and Delivery layers) can focus on building business concepts, analysis, and reports without needing to understand the intricacies of the source systems.

Motivation and benefits

A dedicated storage layer is crucial for several reasons:

- **Change absorption**: Source systems are notoriously volatile. Changes in their schemas or data quality can break downstream pipelines. The storage layer acts as a buffer, allowing you to manage these changes in one place without affecting the rest of the data platform.
- **Centralized knowledge**: This layer distills the knowledge about upstream systems and source system rules into a set of well-defined, documented models. This institutionalizes knowledge and makes it accessible to the entire team.
- **Reduced rework**: By handling the complexities of historization and data preparation here, you simplify the refined and delivery layers. You avoid duplicating complex source-specific logic, which makes the entire platform more resilient and easier to maintain.
- **Better ownership**: By focusing this layer on storing source-aligned data without changing semantics, you can hand over ownership of ingestion and storage code to the source system's owners. They know their data and the automation does the rest.

Identity and semantics: Sources versus business concepts

A core task of the storage layer is to bridge the gap between source data and business concepts. Raw data from source systems, like the `TRADES` report we ingested, is just a collection of records. The storage layer transforms these records into meaningful business entities and manages their identity and mutability.

There are four important concepts that you need to master to understand and manage data: **Entities, Instances, Identity, and Versions.** A business **entity** represents a real-world object, such as a customer, a product, or, in our case, a financial trade. An **instance** is a specific occurrence of that entity (e.g., `trade #1234`). The **identity** of an instance is defined by a unique business key, and different values of the key distinguish between different instances of one entity. One instance can go through different **versions** over the course of time. The key stays the same, while other attributes change.

Source systems generally do not provide ready-to-use business concepts, as source data often lacks a clean business key or contains inconsistent values. Sometimes, in a single source file, we have multiple business entities, as we saw with Securities. The staging (STG) model is where we apply our expertise to start correcting this. For example, a `TransactionID` might need to be combined with other fields to form a truly unique business key. The storage layer's mission is to resolve these ambiguities and create a stable, reliable representation of the source entity, and putting in place the correct business keys to identify the business concepts that will be developed in the refined layer.

We will primarily use two types of keys:

- **Business Keys**: Natural keys from the source system that uniquely identify a business instance (e.g., `TransactionID`).
- **Surrogate Keys**: Technical, system-generated keys (like a `TRADE_HKEY` in the sample code) used to ensure uniqueness and simplify relationships, especially when business keys are complex.

The last key aspect of managing data is that **data changes over time**. An entity might have multiple versions, and it's essential to track these changes to understand its history. The storage layer handles this by creating a complete, auditable record of every change, which we will see in the HIST models.

Data enters the storage layer as raw sources, is ingested by us into Landing Tables, or delivered there by data movement tools. At the end of the storage layer, the raw data is still source-oriented, but it has clear identities and versioning, and can be split along the business concepts of our domain. To fully build the Business Concepts in the refined layer, we might need to implement business rules and merge data from multiple source systems. In the storage layer, we prepare as much as possible by identifying the business keys and eventually splitting the source data according to these identities.

The data storage pipeline (STG + HIST + VER models)

The PDP's storage layer operates as a pipeline, with each step having a clear, distinct purpose. This pipeline, powered by dbt and the PDP macros, takes raw data and produces a set of highly usable, historical tables with clearly identified keys and metadata.

The process begins by declaring the landing table as a **dbt source**, making the raw data available to the pipeline. From there, the data flows through three models:

- **Staging (STG) Model**: The first step and logical core of the pipeline. It cleans and standardizes the raw data, applying basic conversion and usability logic (like date parsing), and generating the keys for historization. This is the only part of the storage pipeline where a developer's specific knowledge of the source system and strong SQL skills are required.
- **Historization (HIST) Model**: The technical core of the pipeline. It is an insert-only table that stores every change to an entity's instances, evolving as its source changes. It uses the keys and other fields generated in the STG model to identify new versions and save them, creating a full historical record. It is the key table that permanently stores the historical data of our platform, enabling auditability and the ability to recreate downstream layers at any time. It is paramount to keep it safe.
- **Versioning (VER) Model**: The final step, key to simple downstream use. It provides an augmented, yet simplified view of the HIST model, facilitating access to the data. It makes it easy to get the full history or just the latest version of each entity instance, to filter out deleted instances, and to access the validity interval for each version, easing time-based operations. It is the primary table that downstream users will query to access the base data.

The three steps for each entity have no joins or external dependencies. This makes them perfect for leveraging the massive parallel processing of dbt and modern cloud platforms, like Snowflake. This, combined with the insert-only pattern, ensures fast and cost-effective execution.

Gaining access to data: The role of dbt sources

Data can only be transformed and historized once it is accessible to dbt. As we saw in Chapters 8 and 9, the ingestion layer or an external data movement tool is responsible for loading data into Snowflake's landing tables. Now, the storage layer needs a way to reference those tables. This is where dbt sources come in.

dbt sources are a powerful feature that allows us to define, document, and validate the raw, external data that our dbt project relies on. The most visible benefit of sources is that, instead of hardcoding table names like `LAND_IB.TRADES` in our models, we can use a deployment-independent logical reference like `{{ source('IB', 'TRADES') }}`.

This approach provides several other key benefits:

- **Centralized Metadata**: All our sources are documented in one or a few YAML files. This centralizes knowledge about the raw data, including its description, columns, and data tests.
- **Dependency Tracking**: dbt's lineage graph automatically tracks dependencies between our models and their source tables. If a source is updated or removed, dbt knows exactly which models will be affected.
- **Adaptability**: It allows for easy adaptation to different environments. We can set up a different schema for our landing tables in a development or QA environment, and our dbt source will automatically point to the correct location without any code changes.

Connecting to landing tables with dbt sources

The first step in building our storage layer is to define our dbt sources in a YAML file, typically located in the same folder as the storage layer models for the system. The sample project uses the `source_Interactive_Brokers.yml` file to define sources for raw data from Interactive Brokers. In this file, we declare our source system with a name (`IB`) and list the tables that we will use under that name. The sample code shows that, along with the source and table declarations, we can also add configuration, documentation, and tests for the entire source and for individual tables. Here's an excerpt from the `source_Interactive_Brokers.yml` file used in the sample project, showing the definition of the TRADES source and a few extra things:

```yaml
version: 2
sources:

  - name: IB
    loader: Pragmatic Data Platform Ingestion
    schema: LAND_IB
    freshness:
      warn_after: {count: 30, period: day}
      error_after: {count: 90, period: day}
    loaded_at_field: TRY_TO_TIMESTAMP(REPORTDATE)

    tables:
      - name: TRADES
        description: Trades on Interactive Brokers accounts
```

```
        columns:
          - name: CLIENTACCOUNTID
            description: The unique ID of a client account.
            data_tests:
              - not_null
          - name: FROM_FILE
            data_tests:
              - not_null
              - pragmatic_data.all_files_from_stage:
                  pattern: 'Trades/.*Trades.*[.]csv.gz'
                  stage_name: "{{ get_IB_..._name() }}"
              - pragmatic_data.file_order_is_correct
```

Defining the source database and schema

The source block must define the source name but can also specify the database and schema where the raw data resides, along with a few other configuration options. While the example above uses only the schema, it is useful to include both if the landing tables are not in the environment database (`target.database`), which is the default value for the database. You can use Jinja to make these values dynamic, even using dbt and environment variables, a pattern useful if you have shared landing tables or if you are keeping them in separate databases or schemas with environment-specific naming. We could rewrite our config with these Jinja expressions:

```
sources:
  - name: IB
    database: "{{ target.database }}"
    schema: "{{ var('IB_ingestion_schema', 'LAND_IB') }}"
```

Following the Least Surprise Principle (LSP), we decided to keep the configuration shorter and simpler by not specifying the database, because it is the same as the environment where we are executing, that is, both the default setting for the sources and the default location where we put all data in our sample project.

This flexibility ensures that, with a little Jinja expression, your dbt project can connect to the correct data for each source from any environment, no matter what setup you use.

Data freshness

A key aspect of a reliable data platform is knowing if your data is up to date. dbt sources offer a built-in freshness check that allows you to define thresholds for how old your data is allowed to be:

- **warn_after**: Triggers a warning if the data is older than the specified time. This is useful for monitoring potential delays.
- **error_after**: Triggers an error if the data exceeds a critical age, signaling a serious issue with the ingestion pipeline. This can be used to send notifications or even fail the pipeline load.
- **loaded_at_field**: The column in your source table that dbt uses to measure freshness. This is typically a timestamp that indicates when the data was created or loaded.

In our `source_Interactive_Brokers.yml` file, the freshness block checks the `REPORTDATE` field and raises a warning if the data is older than 30 days and an error after 90 days. This is ok for a sample project, but you will set a lower SLA for real projects. The freshness declaration, which you can set at the source level and fine-tune for each source table, provides a simple yet effective way to automatically monitor the health of our ingestion processes directly within our dbt project and present it to your business users.

Describing the incoming data and running source tests

Good documentation is a core tenet of data engineering and the Pragmatic Data Platform. It's not enough to simply declare a source; we must also describe it so that other developers can understand its contents and limitations without needing to query the raw data directly or go through a new phase of data exploration.

In the YAML files, we use the description field at both the table and column levels. This metadata is then rendered in the dbt documentation website, making it easy for the entire team to understand the raw data. This is also the simplest step toward formalizing our knowledge and expectations about the data before we even begin writing transformation logic.

The `data_tests` specified in the source definition are a crucial component of data quality in the PDP. We must test the raw data from our ingestion pipelines to ensure our expectations for its shape and content are met. The provided YAML sample already includes a few examples of tests, some ubiquitous and some specific to our ingestion process:

- **not_null**: Probably the most common tests. Used to ensure that a critical column, such as `CLIENTACCOUNTID` or an expression, is never `null`.
- **all_files_from_stage**: A custom dbt test from the PDP package that confirms all expected files have been ingested, an important validation of our ingestion.
- **file_order_is_correct**: Another custom test that checks if files were processed in the correct order, which is essential in most ingestion cases.

These tests, along with the freshness block, give us confidence that the data we are about to process is complete and correct before any transformation begins, and that we can stop the ELT process before any bad data gets into our history tables.

Do not undervalue the power of simple `not_null` and `unique` tests on the sources. They can be used to provide an initial assessment of what you are getting and its data quality. You can quickly generate or add `not_null` tests on all columns of a source, and try out the uniqueness of multiple potential business keys.

In my experience, a 5- to 10-minute exercise for each new (meaningful) source table gives you a better insight into the real data than most people working on them for years have. This saved me countless headaches and earned a quasi-mystical aura for finding issues the tech teams were oblivious to. For sure, it is a great way to get started with practical knowledge of the data and ask useful questions to both tech and business people. Leaving unexpected results as comments, like 3 rows of a BK column failing a `not_null` test, is a pragmatic way to keep them visible and avoid sweeping problems under the carpet, even if they cannot be tackled immediately.

The Staging Model (STG)

The staging model is the logical core of the storage layer. This is the one place where a developer's expertise is most crucial, as they must apply their knowledge of the source system's idiosyncrasies to prepare the data for the historization process and downstream use in business rules and analytics. The staging model takes the raw, possibly messy data from the landing tables and transforms it into a clean, standardized, and coherent format, adapting it without changing its fundamental meaning. E.g., parse a date or convert a timestamp to UTC time zone.

The staging model, with its transformations, prepares each row of data for historization by the HIST and VER models, giving it the form that will be historized and used by everyone in the future. That is why it is paramount to maximize the usability of the data and the clarity of the column semantics. While some columns may not require any treatment, others might need multiple operations. These operations should only make the data as usable as possible, not altering its meaning.

When more extensive operations are performed, it is advisable for auditing and troubleshooting purposes to retain the original field alongside the improved one. Preserving and storing the original value in the HIST table costs little (just a bit of storage) but allows us to audit the pipeline and eventually re-calculate the extracted data.

The primary goals of a staging model are:

- **Generate Keys**: A critical function of the STG model is to explicitly define the unique identifier for our entities. Defining the HKEY is an important best practice, as it clarifies the entity's identity and granularity. The STG model must define the primary key (HKEY) and the hash difference (HDIFF) that are essential for the downstream historization process. It should also define the HKEYs corresponding to foreign keys to other business entities. Possibly, define the HKEY as the key of the Business Concept that this entity will contribute to.

- **Standardize and Cleanse**: This involves normalizing naming conventions, cleansing data of undesirable characters, recasting data to the appropriate data type based on its content, handling null values, and the like. The goal is to ensure a consistent and predictable dataset for downstream models. Apply only semantic neutral technical rules, not business rules.

- **Make Semantics Explicit**: The staging model, together with its documentation and metadata, should clarify the meaning of the data. It means adding useful context, with names, types, or extra data, and deriving new fields that make the data easier to understand without altering its meaning. A single source column could be broken into two or more, or new columns could be derived from existing ones. These are the only acceptable "clarifications", more than "transformations" in the storage layer.

Typical transformations in an STG model

The minimal transformations performed in a staging model are not meant to apply business logic or join data. Instead, they are about making the raw data more usable and its semantics explicit. Here are some common examples:

- **Renaming columns**: We rename columns to provide clear names and follow a consistent standard, improving readability and helping developers and business users understand each column's purpose. Proper names are single-handedly the greatest contributors to clear code.
- **Applying the correct data type and units**: Data must be converted to the correct data type and representation (unit, decimals) according to the semantics of the column. Common examples include: parsing dates and timestamps from strings, converting non-UTC timestamps to UTC, converting binary markers like 0/1 or true/false text to proper Boolean data type, and applying precise numerical types like `Number(38, 9)` instead of imprecise floating-point types (Float/Real) for monetary amounts.
- **Flattening semi-structured data**: If we receive semi-structured data with nested objects (e.g., `JSON`), we may want to extract important fields so we can refer to them directly in standard SQL, while leaving less important and optional fields in semi-structured format in a `VARIANT` column.
- **Conforming to conventions**: It's common for some source systems to have hard rules or limitations. The STG should adapt data to follow conventions, such as converting values to uppercase or lowercase, or adding/removing padding.
- **Adding process metadata**: When we ingest data, we add metadata such as the ingestion timestamp (INGESTION_TS) and information about the source file (FROM_FILE and ROW_NUMBER). These values are used for monitoring and are crucial to version models properly.
- **Adding default values**: For entities representing dimensional data, it is important to have standard values that represent common error states like "not available", "missing", "late", and others that are traditionally represented with negative ID values like -1, -2, and so on. We can add them to the STG model if the raw source data does not provide them.
- **Extracting encapsulated data**: To make data easier to use, we might split fields (e.g., a URL into its components: protocol, server, path) or extract a specific part of a field (e.g., the email provider from an email address) into a new column.
- **Extraction of embedded entities**: When a raw source includes data from multiple entities, we will split those entities. That is not achieved with a single STG model, but rather by using multiple models on the same source, as we are going to do with the Security entity in our sample project in the next chapter.
- **Making status or deletion explicit**: When a source provides information on the status or deletion of a record we must make it available in a standardized way across all systems. Setting correctly a Boolean column like "deleted" or "active" is a good way to make the information actionable without knowing the system's inner details. Try to be consistent with names.

When we change source information in a way that isn't immediately apparent, it's best practice to retain the original field for auditing and troubleshooting. Preserving the original value costs little (some storage that is generally inexpensive), but allows us to audit the pipeline and eventually re-calculate the extracted data if needed.

The "stage" macro in action

The Pragmatic Data Platform simplifies the process of applying typical STG model operations by providing the **stage macro**, `pragmatic_data.stage`, which is part of the PDP package identified by the `pragmatic_data` prefix. This macro generates the boilerplate SQL for you, allowing you to focus on key identification, column operations, and optional activities such as providing default values. Let's look at a simplified version of our `STG_IB_TRADES.sql` model to see its use.

```
{%- set source_model = source('IB', 'TRADES') %}

{%- set stage_cfg -%}

source:
    columns:
        include_all: false
    where: STARTSWITH(CLIENTACCOUNTID, 'U')

calculated_columns:
  - Transaction_ID: TransactionID
  - Transaction_Type: TransactionType

  #-- Core FKs => Account, Security and Position
  - BROKER_CODE: '!IB'
  - CLIENT_ACCOUNT_CODE: "'U***'||RIGHT(CLIENT…ID, 4)"
  - SECURITY_CODE: coalesce(SECURITYID, CONID)
  - LISTING_EXCHANGE: LISTINGEXCHANGE

  #-- many more column definitions
  ...

hashed_columns:
    TRADE_HKEY:
      - Transaction_ID

   SECURITY_HKEY:
     - SECURITY_CODE
     - LISTING_EXCHANGE

   TRADE_HDIFF:
     - Transaction_Type
     - Transaction_ID
     ...

{%- endset -%}

{%- set cfg = fromyaml(stage_cfg) -%}

{{ pragmatic_data.stage(
    source_model = source_model,
    source = cfg['source'],
    calculated_columns = cfg['calculated_columns'],
    hashed_columns = cfg['hashed_columns'],
    default_records = cfg['default_records '],
    remove_duplicates = cfg['remove_duplicates']

) }}
```

This code snippet showcases the typical contents of an STG model, and you'll find the same logic of operation again: a block of YAML configuration followed by a call to a macro that generates the needed SQL for us. The `source_model` variable stores a Jinja relation object pointing to the table we want to read from, usually a Landing Table defined through a dbt source. We use a Jinja variable instead of a parameter inside the configuration to keep the relation object intact. As a parameter, it would be converted to the string representing the relation.

The `stage_cfg` variable collects the configuration information we need to provide to the stage macro to generate code for the dbt model, much as we saw previously in the ingestion macros. The `pragmatic_data.stage` macro abstracts away the code generation, which is entirely guided by the configuration objects passed. Here, we have already broken down the macro's parameters to represent its major operations.

Within the YAML block, we define:

- **source_model**: The source table to query (e.g., `TRADES` in the `IB` source).
- **source**: Here, we can use the `*` SQL operator (STAR) to read the source columns, and a SQL predicate in the `WHERE` clause to filter the inputs. If we use the `*` operator, by setting `include_all: true`, we can use its extended syntax with the exclude, replace, and rename extensions, allowing us to easily manipulate only selected source columns.
- **calculated_columns**: This is the key place in the STG model where we can create new columns and perform all necessary transformations on the source columns using any valid SQL expression in a SELECT statement. Here, we rename columns, cast data types (FX_RATE_TO_BASE), create new fields, and perform all transformations for the STG model using SQL code. Each entry in the `calculated_columns` list pairs a column name with an optional SQL expression. The following snippet exemplifies the common cases.

  ```
  # Column selected and left unchanged (no expression)
  - COLUMN_A

  # A new COLUMN_1 defined by renaming another column
  - COLUMN_1: ColumnX

  # A new COLUMN_2 defined by an SQL expression
  - COLUMN_2: UPPER(ColumnY)
  ```

- **hashed_columns**: Here we define all the hashed keys, including HKEYs that represent primary and foreign keys, and HDIFFs that hash the payload columns to allow easy checks for changes in entity data. For example, here we define `TRADE_HKEY` and `TRADE_HDIFF` for the historization of the model.
- **default_records**: We can create one or more default records providing data for the desired columns. The value of all other columns will be null.
- **remove_duplicates**: The parameters to add a `QUALIFY` clause to remove duplicates or undesired rows when reading from the source model. Remember that the SQL predicate for the WHERE clause goes in the source definition and that filtering with WHERE is more efficient than QUALIFY.

By using this macro, we avoid writing repetitive SQL statements and boilerplate code, allowing us to focus on the essential tasks of data preparation and key generation without altering the data's inherent meaning. You might have noticed that we can apply transformations in both the `source` and the `calculated_columns` sections. The first one is a bit less flexible and is intended for the case where most columns are fine unchanged, while the second gives you the total freedom to define or redefine any column, as you would do in a `SELECT` clause. You can use both at the same time. Our suggestion is to use them in a complementary role to make it as easy as possible to understand what you are doing. For example, if you have ten columns and you redefine (some more, some less) six of them, maybe it's better not to use the * operator and define all columns in the `calculated_columns` section. If instead you had 50 columns, it's more readable to let the 45 unchanged columns pass through the * operator and explicitly show the changes to the six you are redefining.

You can find more examples in the code in the next chapter, where we will implement the storage layer for the sample project, discussing in detail the full contents of this file and the storage layer code in general. Detailed information is also available in the macro's documentation in the Pragmatic Data Platform package.

The historization model (HIST)

The Historization model is the technical core of the storage layer.

Here, the raw, processed data from the staging model is used to identify and store new versions of the current entity's instances. Unlike the STG model, which requires developers to understand the source and have SQL expertise, the HIST model is designed for high automation. Its purpose is to create a complete, auditable, and append-only record of every change an entity undergoes over its lifecycle.

The concept is simple: by comparing a new incoming record from the STG model with the last known version in the history table, we can determine if a change has occurred. If a change is detected, a new row is added to the history table, preserving a snapshot of the instance at that point in time. This approach ensures that we never lose data and can always trace an entity's instance evolution.

The STG model provides the two key columns that make this magic happen:

- **HKEY**: A hash key that uniquely identifies each instance of an entity. It is stable and does not change over the lifetime of an instance, allowing us to group all versions of a single entity instance.
- **HDIFF**: A hash difference that represents the state of the instance. By comparing the HDIFF of a new record with the last stored version for the same instance, we can efficiently detect a change in the instance's data.

Historization patterns

The pragmatic-data-platform dbt package provides several macros for historization, each implementing a specific pattern tailored to different use cases. It is the developer's responsibility to choose the most suitable one for the entity being modeled.

The current historization patterns are:

- `save_history_with_multiple_versions`: This macro is the default and most robust pattern. It is designed to handle multiple changes for the same entity instance within a single data load. This is crucial for sources that might contain multiple updates for an instance since the last ingestion. This macro requires that we provide a sorting expression to order the versions. This ensures that no changes are lost, creating a complete audit history and making it highly reliable and secure. This macro, depending on the configuration of its parameters, can capture even versions that arrive out of order, with some limitations, and serve them correctly when coupled with the right settings in the VER macro.

- `save_history`: This is the simplest and quickest pattern. It assumes, and it is your responsibility to guarantee, that only the latest version of an entity instance will be present in the incoming data. It does not use a sorting expression, as it expects and can store only one version at a time. If multiple versions arrive for one historization round, you must leave out the intermediate changes from the input. This pattern is suitable for the frequent load of append-only sources or for cases where only the most recent state is relevant for historization. This is often the macro of choice for very big sources, where speed of execution is vital, and storing only the latest change in the input is acceptable.
- `save_history_with_deletions`: This macro detects and marks records as deleted if an entity that was previously in the data is no longer present. This requires a stable source and can be used only with full data exports. Similar to the previous pattern, this macro also assumes that only the latest version of an entity instance is present in the input.
- `save_history_with_deletion_from_list`: This macro detects and marks records as deleted based on a list of deleted keys provided as input, in parallel to the new data from the data source. It is more general and offers an alternative to the previous one when there is no full data export, when the size makes a full comparison expensive, or in any other case where we have a reliable source for the deleted entities. Having two sources of input (the source data and the deletion list) can lead to inconsistencies if the two sources are not consistent. It is up to the user to ensure the two sources are consistent so that the same key is not in both.

The `save_history_with_multiple_versions` macro is our default choice for the PDP. Its ability to handle multiple versions in a single ingestion makes it the most resilient and reliable option for most data sources, ensuring the integrity and auditability of our historical record. You only need to put in the extra effort to provide a sorting expression to put the multiple versions in the right order.

Even if your export and ingestion patterns would generate only one new version for each export, ingestion, and historization cycle in ideal conditions, errors and pipeline stops still happen. They can create a situation in which multiple new versions are in the Landing Table, awaiting historicization. The most common case is when you have an error before the historization model, and you don't fix it immediately, like on the weekend.

In our opinion, the extra complexity of providing a sorting expression and the small performance cost of sorting the inputs are well worth the benefit of a historization pattern that can automatically ingest multiple exports or versions storing all changes, making our pipeline resilient to unexpected stops or inputs and saving valuable time for the data team without leaving out any data.

For macros that expect only the latest version to be present in the input, you can use the `remove_duplicates` configuration in the STG model to easily filter out older versions and keep only the ones that need to be passed to the historization macro. Doing this can be as expensive as sorting the versions, but it's the only option when you want to recognize deletions.

The save_history_with_multiple_versions macro in action

The `HIST_IB_TRADES.sql` model -that we will discuss in detail in the next chapter- is a straightforward example of a HIST model. Its configuration is minimal because all the logic is encapsulated within the macro. Only the first three parameters (`input_rel`, `key_column`, and `diff_column`) are mandatory; all others are optional with sensible defaults. That said, it is quite common to also explicitly provide the `sort_expr`, given its importance.

```
{{ config( materialized='incremental') }}

{{ pragmatic_data.save_history_with_multiple_versions(

   input_rel                   = ref('STG_IB_TRADES'),
   key_column                  = 'TRADE_HKEY',
   diff_column                 = 'TRADE_HDIFF',

   sort_expr                   = 'EFFECTIVITY_DATE, Transaction_ID,
RECORD_SOURCE, FILE_ROW_NUMBER',

   load_ts_column              = 'INGESTION_TS_UTC',
   high_watermark_column       = 'INGESTION_TS_UTC',
    high_watermark_test         = '>',
    input_filter_expr           = 'true',
    history_filter_expr         = 'true',

) }}
```

In the HIST models, the macro does the heavy lifting, based on the configuration:

- **input_rel**: This parameter specifies the upstream STG model that provides the data. It is almost always a `ref()` relation, such as `ref('STG_IB_TRADES')`.
- **key_column**: The column that defines the identity of the entity being historicized. It's usually an HKEY column, even if any single column, working as a key, is fine.
- **diff_column**: The column to compare between rows to identify the changes of an entity. It usually is an HDIFF column, but any single column is fine. The HDIFF must contain the key columns and all columns from the entity payload that grant a new version to be stored. In this way, we can check both the identity and the version with a single-column comparison. We can set it equal to the key column to make the rows immutable. In such cases, only the first occurrence of an instance is stored, with all subsequent changes ignored, since the key is immutable for an instance.
- **sort_expr**: This expression tells the macro how to order the incoming data to correctly identify the latest version of an instance. Although optional, defaulting to the ingestion TS, it is a critical parameter for handling multiple versions within a single load. It is a best practice to always provide it explicitly.
- **high_watermark_column**: This parameter is optional and, in conjunction with **high_watermark_test**, allows the macro to process data incrementally, considering only new records since the last successful run.
- **input_filter_expr** and **history_filter_expr**: These parameters are optional, and they are seldom used. They exist for the few special cases when you want to filter the history table or the input source before the historization process. For example, one use case is filtering large fact tables we receive as delta exports,

where changes are concentrated in the recent period, such as invoices or accounting records. The process is much more efficient if we check the input only against a small period of history. The price to pay is that we might insert again unchanged data that is older than the period we check. That would just use a bit of storage, but we'd still get the correct data from our history table.

This minimal configuration ensures that the historization process is simple, repeatable, and highly automated. In most cases, the only parts that change for a new entity of a source system are the input relation, the key and diff columns, and maybe the sort expression, making the HIST model a predictable and easy-to-manage component of the pipeline.

The versioning model (VER)

The Versioning model (VER) is the final stop in the storage layer pipeline. Its purpose is to present the dense, append-only history table in a clean, user-friendly format. The VER model simplifies the use of historical data, making it easy for downstream layers (the Refined and Delivery layers) to query the most recent version of an entity or analyze how an instance has changed over time without writing complex window functions. The VER model is a view on top of the HIST table, meaning it doesn't store duplicate data, saving on storage costs and improving pipeline efficiency.

Key columns added by the VER model

The core value of the VER model lies in the additional metadata it provides for historical data. These columns make the contents of the HIST table much easier to consume:

- `IS_CURRENT`: A simple boolean flag that identifies the latest, most up-to-date version of each instance. This is incredibly useful for analysts who just want the current state.
- `DIM_SCD_HKEY`: A unique hash key for each version of an instance. This is an important concept from Slowly Changing Dimensions (SCD) and allows you to uniquely identify each row in the VER model. This key is used in downstream joins, so you can join to a specific version of a dimension at a point in time.
- `VALID_FROM` and `VALID_TO`: These columns define the time interval for which each version of the entity was valid. `VALID_FROM` indicates when the version was first detected, and `VALID_TO` marks when a newer version superseded it.

The VER model adds a few additional columns, explicitly recording the number of versions per instance and the version number for each instance. It also provides the ingestion and load batch numbers, based on the ingestion and historization metadata.

The versioning macro in action

The VER model is created using the `versions_from_history_with_multiple_versions` macro. This macro takes the HIST model as input, along with the usual key and diff columns, and automatically generates a view with all the columns discussed above. Here's the code from `VER_IB_TRADES.sql`:

```
{{ pragmatic_data.
     versions_from_history_with_multiple_version(

   history_rel                = ref('HIST_IB_TRADES'),
   key_column                 = 'TRADE_HKEY',
   diff_column                = 'TRADE_HDIFF',

   version_sort_column        = 'EFFECTIVITY_DATE'
) }}
```

In this model, like in the HIST macro, the macro does all the work. You simply specify:

- `history_rel`: The HIST model to read from.
- `key_column`: The KEY used in the HIST model.
- `diff_column`: The version comparison column used in the HIST model.
- `version_sort_column`: The column identifying the timeline on which to sort the versions for each instance of the entity. This is explained in detail in the next section.

As you can see, the VER model is very close to the HIST model, which enhances, with the main choice being the timeline for reading versions from the history table.

Ingestion versus business timelines

A critical parameter in the versioning macro is the `version_sort_column`. This column tells the macro how to order the versions when determining which one is the "current" or "latest." This is where the distinction between the ingestion timeline and the business timeline becomes crucial.

- **Ingestion Timeline**: This is the order in which data physically arrived in your data platform, typically represented by a system timestamp like `INGESTION_TS`. If you use the ingestion timestamp as the sorting column, the latest and current versions will be the last records loaded.

- **Business Timeline**: The order of events as they happened in the real world, typically represented by a business-related timestamp such as `EFFECTIVITY_DATE`. Using the business timeline for sorting ensures that your data reflects the true sequence and validity times of events, even if records arrived or were produced out of order with respect to the business timeline.

For example, for the `TRADES` entity, `EFFECTIVITY_DATE` is the correct choice because the business cares about when a trade was executed, not when the data about it was loaded into the system. The macro uses this column to correctly determine which version is the most up-to-date from a business perspective.

A pattern for adding new entities

The Pragmatic Data Platform is built on the principle of repeatable, pattern-based development. The storage layer is where this approach shines the most. When adding a new entity to the storage layer, we can follow a simple four-step playbook that ensures consistency and automation. This pattern is designed to be quick and efficient, leveraging the templates, SQL snippets, and macros we've discussed to minimize manual work. The goal is to enable developers to create the storage layer for an entity in minutes when the entity key is known, and the other major choices are either done or straightforward.

The PDP storage layer playbook

These are the steps to create the storage layer pipeline for a new entity:

- **Define the Source**: Declare the landing table in your dbt sources YAML file. This makes the raw data accessible to your project. Add descriptions and tests for the important columns, and tests to validate the ingestion process.
- **Create the STG Model**: This is the core logical step. You create a new `.sql` file that uses the `pragmatic_data.stage` macro to clean, standardize, and prepare the raw data for historization.
- **Build the HIST Model**: Create a history table to store every version of the entity. This model uses the appropriate historization macro to automate change detection and the insertion of new versions, depending on your use case.
- **Build the VER Model**: Create the final versioning model, a view on top of the HIST table, providing a simple, user-friendly interface to your historical data.

To perform these steps, you do not need to start from an empty model every time, but you should leverage the PDP templates and supporting SQL queries that allow you to make the least effort, entering only the needed configuration and generating it for the parts that require a lot of text, like the columns for a STG model.

You can find the complete templates and supporting SQL queries in the sample project repository, in the `analyses/TEMPLATES` folder. We encourage you to create your own queries and templates. In the next sections, we discuss the key PDP templates, possibly edited for readability.

Step 1: Define the source

Start by adding a new entry to your dbt sources YAML file. This is your contract with the data ingestion layer. The template looks like this:

```
version: 2

sources:

  - name: your_source_system_name
    schema: your_landing_schema
    tables:

      - name: your_source_table_name
        description: A description of your landing table.

        columns:
          - name: your_key_column
            data_tests:
              - not_null
              - unique

          - name: FROM_FILE # src file name from ingestion
            data_tests:
              - not_null
              - pragmatic_data.all_files_from_stage:
                  pattern: '…/.*TABLE_ONE.*.csv.gz'
                  stage_name: "{{ get_..._stage_name() }}"
              - pragmatic_data.file_order_is_correct
```

You can find the complete template in the `10_SOURCE_template.yml.txt` file in the sample project, under the `analyses/TEMPLATES/storage` folder. Remove the .txt extension we had to add to avoid running tests on non-existent sources. Regarding the source file, there is a general part that you need to set up only once: when you define the first source table inside a source system. Later, you just add new source tables with their definitions and tests.

To configure the general part, use a consistent naming convention to name the source systems. Decide between uppercase or lowercase, full or short names, and so on. For example, `IB` for Interactive Brokers or `SAP` for SAP. Enter the database name (if not using the same DB as the environment) and the schema for the landing tables. Document the source with a clear description. Make explicit the generalities about how exports are done, including whether you use full or incremental exports and the like. This is a quick and valuable help for anyone who follows you. Enter some general freshness settings that should be fine for most tables.

Once you have defined the source, add the first landing table and the important columns. To configure individual tables, add the table definition with its description. Make the description useful, and explicitly note any deviations from the system settings for the export. Name the important columns, providing a description and basic data tests like `not_null` and `unique` to define expectations and catch issues early. Err on the side of testing more columns, and comment out, but keep in the file the tests that fail unexpectedly, along with the result of failed test, like `# [FAIL 6 in 0.24s]`. Whether you comment these tests out or turn them into warnings, they deliver useful information for the team.

Complete the tests that validate the ingestion under the `FROM_FILE` column. The `all_files_ from_stage` test verifies that all files in the stage appear in the landing table. Handle eventual empty files with the `min_file_size` parameter. The `file_order_is_correct` test verifies that the order of the files is correct. This test assumes that filenames are sortable. If they are not, you cannot use this test; you should build one appropriate for your files. The quickest way to configure the ingestion tests under the `FROM_FILE` column is to copy the relevant values from the ingestion macro for the landing table.

When you need to add more tables, the quickest way is often to duplicate the definition of one existing table and adapt/edit the relevant fields, maybe with the help of a query on the information schema. After the first table, you should be able to add the others in a handful of minutes. Max.

Step 2: Create the STG model

The staging model is where you prepare the data for the source entity. The heavy lifting is done by the `pragmatic_data.stage` macro and its YAML-based configuration that you provide. The great news is that most of the configuration content can be generated with simple SQL queries, as shown in the following section. The template (`stg_your_entity_name.sql`) looks like this:

```
{%- set source_model = source('SYSTEM_ABC', 'TABLE_ONE') %}
```

The `source_model` variable identifies the source model to read from.

```
{%- set configuration -%}

source:
    columns:
        include_all: true             #-- True enables '*'
        exclude_columns:              #-- columns to exclude
          - e1
          - e2
        replace_columns:              #-- columns to replace
          - col1: exp1
          - col2: exp2

        rename_columns:               #-- columns to rename
          - new1: old1
          - new2: old2
    where: "SOME_COL != 'SomeValue'"  #-- Any SQL predicate
```

The `source` block allows you to concisely handle columns from the source using the `*` operator and its clauses. The `where` attribute defines a predicate to filter the input data read from the source model.

```
calculated_columns:
  - OLD_COL123    #-- old column used without changes
  - NEW_COL1: OLD_COL1:date      #-- casting and renaming
  - NEW_COL2: LEFT(OLD_COL1, 4)  #-- general SQL expr
  - NEW_COL3: NEW_COL2:integer   #-- general SQL expr

  #-- metadata from ingestion macro (makes it explicit)
  - RECORD_SOURCE: FROM_FILE         #-- renamed
  - FILE_ROW_NUMBER: FILE_ROW_NUMBER
  - FILE_LAST_MODIFIED_TS_UTC: FILE_LAST_MODIFIED_TS_UTC
  - INGESTION_TS_UTC: INGESTION_TS_UTC
```

The calculated_columns block allows you to handle both the columns coming from the source, if you did not use the source block for that, and add new columns.

```
default_records:
  - not_provided:     #-- default record 1
      - COLUMN_1: "'-1'"   #-- Str literal as "'string'"
      - COLUMN_2: '!NOT Provided'       #-- as '!string'
      - RECORD_SOURCE: '!System.DefaultRecord'
      - INGEST…: "'{{ run_started_at }}':TIMESTAMP_NTZ"

  - missing:            #-- default record 2
      ...
```

The default_records block, which is optional, allows you to define multiple default records that are added to the source model's input.

```
hashed_columns:

   ENTITY_1_HK:
      - ENTITY_1_CODE

   ENTITY_X_HK:
      - ENTITY_1_CODE
      - ENTITY_2_CODE
      - WEAK_KEY_COL

   ENTITY_1_HD:
      - ENTITY_1_CODE
      - OLD_COL1
      ...
      - NEW_COL2
```

The hashed_columns block allows you to easily and quickly define multiple columns, each being the binary hash of the provided list of columns. This is used to build HKEY and HDIFF columns.

```
remove_duplicates:
   partition_by:
      - ENTITY_1_HK
      - INGESTION_TS_UTC
   order_by:
      - RECORD_SOURCE desc  #-- file path/name has date
      - FILE_LAST_MODIFIED_TS_UTC desc  #-- When written
      - FILE_ROW_NUMBER asc      #-- Position in the file
```

The remove_duplicates block, which is optional, allows you to configure a QUALIFY clause to filter out duplicates or to limit the data read from the source model. The where attribute in the source block is more efficient, but it operates only on the columns defined in the source. The QUALIFY clause defined here can use window functions and operates on the newly defined columns.

```
{%- endset -%}

{%- set cfg = fromyaml(configuration) -%}

{{- stage(
    source                    = cfg['source'],
    calculated_columns        = cfg['calculated_columns'],
    hashed_columns            = cfg['hashed_columns'],
    remove_duplicates         = cfg['remove_duplicates'],
) }}
```

Finally, the YAML configuration is parsed, converted to a Python dictionary, and passed to the stage macro that produces the SQL for your model that dbt will run.

Tips for Quick Development

The key to a quick development of the STG models is the use of the provided template together with the SQL queries to produce the lists of columns to handle, coupled with the following general best practices.

Maintaining consistent naming conventions will pay huge dividends.

Naming is very important for model names, such as STG_YOUR_ENTITY_NAME; for hashed columns, like YOUR_ENTITY_HKEY and YOUR_ENTITY_HDIFF; for metadata and effectivity columns; and, in general, for business keys and all other columns that repeat often across models.

Use the source system or tap any support, even before ingestion, to identify the business key columns in the landing table to create the HKEY. Ideally, you should ask the business requesting ingestion of a source to provide you with the source's primary key. Then use dbt tests to verify. Similarly, ask them which columns define a "change" for your entity, and use those columns to create the HDIFF. It usually contains all source payload that is not clearly metadata, but some columns like `updated_at` might raise doubts. Generate the list of columns using the SQL queries provided below.

Make effective use of the `source` and `calculated_columns` configs to minimize the code you need to write and make changes stand out. Learn to use the exclude, replace, and rename clauses of the * operator to handle a few changes to the original columns, if most are ok. Use the `calculated_ columns` configs for the new columns that you create, including metadata like `effectivity_date`, and for the ones you cannot handle with `*`.

If you need to work on many or all columns in the `calculated_columns` config, take advantage of the SQL queries and AI tools in the dbt Cloud editor or elsewhere to generate and transform column names in bulk. Add the default records if you already know you need them; otherwise, you can add them at any time when you realize you need them. If you pick a historization macro that expects a single version in the input, use the `remove_ duplicates` config to pick the latest version for each instance. If you are historizing a very big source table or one with a lot of data in the Landing Table, you can use the `source.where` config to filter out older data. You can use the `ingestion_ts` column to either keep the most recently ingested data or keep only the last N batches of ingested data in the STG model.

While this seems like a long and time-consuming list of things to do, you will see in the next chapter that by following such suggestions, you can often duplicate a previous model and use search and replace to change the entity-dependent names, while generating most of the rest with the following SQL queries.

When we write an STG model, it means we already have data in Snowflake that we are passing through the STG model to be adapted and prepared for historization. Luckily for us, Snowflake, like most modern databases, has the `INFORMATION_SCHEMA` Schema in every database. This is a virtual schema made of views powered by the database engine, which we can query with normal SQL to learn almost everything we want about the database's contents.

SQL queries to generate the STG code

The following query, expressed as plain SQL for the `Trades` Landing Table, provides the foundation to generate whatever code you need based on the contents of the Landing Tables or any other database object.

```
SELECT
  '    -' || COLUMN_NAME || ': '|| COLUMN_NAME ||
  ' -- ' || DATA_TYPE as calculated_columns_text_with_types

FROM STONKS_DEV.INFORMATION_SCHEMA.COLUMNS
WHERE TABLE_SCHEMA = 'LAND_IB'
 and TABLE_NAME = 'TRADES'
ORDER BY ORDINAL_POSITION
```

The query points to the database and schema where your LT are, and uses the `COLUMNS` table to generate our code base in the column names and their data type. The output is something like the following

```
  — COLUMN1: COLUMN1       -- TEXT
  — COLUMN2: COLUMN2       -- TEXT
  — COLUMN3: COLUMN3       -- TIMESTAMP_NTZ
  — COLUMN4: COLUMN4       -- TEXT
```

For each column in our landing table, we have a row that serves as a good starting point for transforming the column in the `calculated_columns` section. The following code would require very little editing and offers good documentation:

```
  — COLUMN_1: COLUMN1                -- TEXT
  — COLUMN_2: COLUMN2:integer        -- was TEXT
  — COLUMN_3_DATE: COLUMN3:date      -- was TIMESTAMP_NTZ
  #— COLUMN4: COLUMN4                -- TEXT
```

Here, we renamed COLUMN1 by adding an _ where we wanted it, casted `COLUMN2` to an integer, and renamed it with minimal effort, and the same for `COLUMN3`. We have instead commented out (and therefore excluded from the STG model) the `COLUMN4` column, but leaving it there commented out is more explicit about our choice than just leaving it out.

Another advantage of generating the list of columns to transform with this SQL code is that we are sure we have all columns from the source, and, as we did for `COLUMN4`, we can explicitly show which ones we did not want to propagate.

In the sample project, you will find the same query as a dbt model (with Jinja variables) in the `21_STG_generate_columns.sql` file in the template folder. This provides even greater ease of use in dbt, as you can just change the LT name, and it will automatically handle database and schema changes. Once you complete the `source_model`, `source`, and `calculated_columns` configurations, you are ready to deploy the first version of your STG model to your DEV environment. This is done with one button in dbt Cloud. We do this to use the initial STG model as the target of the query above to generate the list of columns, with the new names set in the STG model, to complete the `hashed_columns` configuration and, primarily, the `HDIFF` column. The following query generates a list of all columns in the STG model in a suitable format, with one or two tabs removed, for use with the HDIFF column.

```
SELECT
    '- ' || COLUMN_NAME  as hdiff_text

FROM STONKS_DEV.INFORMATION_SCHEMA.COLUMNS
WHERE TABLE_SCHEMA = 'MY_SCHEMA'
 and TABLE_NAME = 'STG_TRADES'
ORDER BY ORDINAL_POSITION
```

You can easily take the result of this query and use it to complete the HDIFF definition, eventually re-ordering the columns and excluding the ones you don't want in the HDIFF. You can use the same column names to define the HKEYs (PKs and FKs) and, eventually, to compile the `default_records` and `remove_duplicates` sections of the STG model configuration.

Thanks to these simple helper SQL queries, we can avoid a lot of time-consuming typing. If you couple that with the AI abilities of the dbt Cloud editor or of other AI coding helpers that understand the dbt syntax and way of working (spoiler: most do), you can do even quite advanced transformations with the minimum effort, but retaining full control of the process, which for us is essential.

This process is so repeatable that, in some cases, the entire configuration or STG model can be pre-generated, with the developer mostly performing validation. This is especially true if you have many sources to load and you have good metadata about them. In one case, a customer we've been working with generated the ingestion and storage for about 450 tables and needed only minor adjustments, saving considerable time in building these layers.

Step 3: Build the HIST model

The history model is almost fully automated thanks to the PDP macros. We must write little, and more often than not, we can change the three values that change in any HIST model with a search-and-replace, as the `XXXXXX` placeholder suggests. This is another reason for the best practice to name your objects well. The template (`hist_your_entity_name.sql`) looks like this:

```
{{ config( materialized='incremental') }}

{{ pragmatic_data.save_history_with_multiple_versions(
    input_rel                 = ref('STG_XXXXXX'),
    key_column                = 'XXXXXX_HKEY',
    diff_column               = 'XXXXXX_HDIFF',

    sort_expr                 = 'EFFECTIVITY_DATE,...
) }}

{# Optional params for perf, with their default settings
    load_ts_column            = 'INGESTION_TS_UTC',

    high_watermark_column     = 'INGESTION_TS_UTC',
    high_watermark_test       = '>',

    input_filter_expr         = 'true',
    history_filter_expr       = 'true',

#}
```

In general, for the quickest development, you can duplicate another HIST model from the same system or this template. Most of the time, you only need to change three parameters in the template: `input_rel`, `key_column`, and `diff_column`, and you can do it automatically. The value for the `sort_expr` is, in fact, often the same for all models of the same system. There is close to nothing to do here, just create the model and edit a few names.

Step 4: Build the VER model

The versioning model is a simple view that makes the HIST table easy to consume. Like the HIST model, there is little to edit here. The template (`ver_your_entity_name.sql`) looks like this:

```
{{ pragmatic_data.versions_from_history_with_multiple_versions(
    history_rel               = ref('HIST_XXXXXX'),
    key_column                = 'XXXXXX_HKEY',
    diff_column               = 'XXXXXX_HDIFF',

  version_sort_column         = 'EFFECTIVITY_DATE'
) }}
```

In general, for the quickest development, you can duplicate another VER model from the same system or this template. This model is the simplest of all four. You just need to specify the usual three parameters, `history_rel`, `key_column`, `diff_column`, that describe the historization, and the `version_sort_column` that allows you to choose the timeline to order the versions. The macro handles the rest.

By following the four steps of this pattern, you can quickly and confidently add new entities to your data platform with minimal effort, knowing each one is consistently structured, well-documented, and ready for use in downstream models.

Advanced concepts in the storage layer

The storage layer we've built so far is robust and handles a wide range of common scenarios. However, data platforms often encounter more advanced challenges. In this section, we'll discuss five concepts that extend the functionality of the PDP's storage layer: embedded entities, historization across different business-concept grains, bi-temporality, data restatement, and the evolution of history tables.

Embedded entities

Sometimes, a source export contains multiple entities, with one entity playing a principal role and one or more nested or embedded entities to complete the data set. This is often the case for exports in the form of reports, which aim to provide usable data that is self-standing and does not require other datasets. Another common case is with semi-structured data, where related objects can be included instead of just being referenced by their Key.

A good example is the Security entity we've discussed in Chapter 9. A Trade is a financial transaction, but it is always tied to a Security, which is an entity in its own right. The TRADES data we receive, besides trade-specific information, also contains all Security information rather than a foreign key to a Security object.

The designer role is to decide whether to treat these embedded entities as separate, independent concepts or just as part of the containing entity. If the embedded entity is in the project's domain, it should be extracted. We recommend this separation for several reasons:

- **Auditability**: When you treat the embedded entity as a separate concept with its own history table, you can audit its changes independently of the parent entity. A change in a Security's name, for example, is captured as a new version in the HIST_SECURITY table, regardless of whether a new trade has occurred or in what portfolio it happened.
- **Reusability**: By creating a standalone HIST and VER model for the embedded entity (e.g., HIST_IB_SECURITIES and VER_IB_SECURITIES), we make this data available to all downstream models that need information about Securities, not just the Trades model. This prevents redundant logic and ensures a single source of truth for the entity's data.
- **Centralization**: The Security entity is embedded in multiple sources. By extracting it and centralizing its historization, we can collect all the changes and use them independently of the individual source.

When we extract the Security entity, the STG model of the parent entity (e.g., STG_IB_TRADES) will still contain some information from the embedded entity (e.g., SECURITY_CODE, SECURITY_NAME), including the key, as with any other relation. We will also feed the full embedded entity data (Security) into a separate pipeline that builds the HIST and VER models for the embedded entity. This requires careful consideration of the HKEY and HDIFF of the embedded entity to ensure that its changes are tracked correctly.

Historization and business concept grain

When we historize a business concept, we create a history table with an **HKey** that defines the identity of the entity and an **HDiff** that defines its versions. The relationship between the grain of the business concept and the grain of the source table/report from which its data is coming is a very important consideration.

- **Same Grain**: When the business concept has the same grain as the source, the historization is straightforward. The HIST table for the concept can directly use the HKey and HDiff from the source's STG model and sort the inputs on the technical timeline. Luckily, this is the case for the vast majority of cases.
- **Different Grain**: When the business concept has a different grain than the source table, we must handle this explicitly. For example, if a POSITION entity includes an embedded SECURITY entity that can change independently, the SECURITY concept has a different grain than the POSITION, as the changes will happen on different, independent columns for each entity.

In this case, the HIST table for the Security must use its own HKey and HDiff, which are independent of the position's keys. To recognize and track changes in the embedded concept separately from changes in the source table, it is convenient to create a **DELTA model**. This ensures that a change to the security's data can be recorded as a new version of the security, even if there is no new version of the position.

Example for a POSITION with embedded SECURITY:

Let's imagine a source provides account POSITION data (Pos-HK is the POSITION HKey, Pos-HD its Hdiff that tracks the changes only in position data), and Security data is also embedded in the position (with Sec-HKey and Sec-Hdiff tracking the Security data).

We can easily get a situation like the following, where positions and securities change:

```
TS    Pos-HK    Pos-HD    Sec-HKey   Sec-HDiff

T1    P1        v10       S100       v100
T2    P1        v11       S100       v100
T3    P1        v11       S100       v101
T1    P2        v20       S100       v100
T2'   P2        v21       S100       v100
T3    P2        v21       S100       v101
```

In this example, at T3, a change to Security S100 occurs, with no changes to the positions P1 and P2, which are for the same Security in different accounts. If we were to naively historize the POSITION data alongside the Security data, we would get new POSITION versions at T3 for both P1 and P2, but the change would be limited to the underlying SECURITY entity.

By creating a dedicated DELTA model, we can detect this change in the Sec-Hdiff independently from the position and trigger a new version only in the HIST_SECURITY table, not in the HIST_POSITION table. The POSITION table would only get a new version if its own data changed, as it happened at T2 with v11 and T2' with v21.

In the next chapter, when developing the sample project, we will see multiple examples of this when dealing with Security across multiple entities.

Bi-temporality

Bi-temporality is a crucial concept for a truly auditable and modern data platform. It means that we track not just one, but two different timelines for our data:

- **Validity Time** (**Business Time**): When an event or a change actually occurred in the real world. This is the timeline that matters most for business analysis. We've already captured this in our VALID_FROM and VALID_TO columns, derived from a business timestamp that we associated with the EFFECTIVITY_DATE column.
- **Ingestion Time** (**Technical Time**): When a record was physically recorded in our data platform. In the Pragmatic Data Platform, we often have two such timelines: when we ingested data into a Landing Table (INGESTION_TS_UTC), and when we added an instance to the HIST table (HIST_LOAD_TS).

These connected timelines are essential for data governance and debugging, as they tell us exactly when a version of the data was made available in our system. By maintaining these timelines in our HIST and VER models, we can answer two very different but equally important questions:

- "What was the state of a customer's account on December 31st, 2023?" To answer this, we must look at the Validity Time.
- "What was the state of our data about that customer on January 5th, 2024?" To answer this, we must look at the Ingestion or Hist load Time.

The case of INGESTION_TS_UTC and HIST_LOAD_TS shows that it is easy to add data points along the technical timeline when we have permanent storage. The Pragmatic Data Platform macros automatically add these two data points. You are welcome to add your own, but to have any temporal depth, you need to add them to an incremental table.

Data restatement

Data restatement is the process of updating or correcting historical data. In an ideal world, source data would be perfect and never change. In reality, sources often provide corrections or a full historical snapshot of the data, which can invalidate previously ingested records.

The PDP's approach to restatement is pragmatic. Instead of relying on complex UPDATE or MERGE statements on our history tables, which would break auditability by making the previous data disappear, we simply treat the new, restated data as a new version and add it to the HIST table. All the historization macros are designed to handle this seamlessly. When a restated record arrives, its HKEY will match an existing one, but its HDIFF will be new, causing the macro to insert it as a new version. This append-only approach is simpler, more performant, and more auditable than a full rewrite of history. It maintains the integrity of the transaction time, as we can see exactly when the restated record was loaded without losing the original record that was loaded beforehand.

If the source does not provide a business timeline, the restatement can only happen at the current time; that is not really a restatement, but it is the best we can have without business temporal information. If the source has a business timeline, the restatement arrives in the technical timeline now and takes effect at a prior (or even future) time in the business timeline.

A Business timeline exists only if there is temporal information about the business's validity in the payload received for an entity (fields like `last_updated`, `report_date`, or `transaction_ts`). These temporal columns belong in the HDiff of the entity, since different updates result in different versions. This also ensures that we cannot have the same HDiff for two different validity times/dates, even if all other columns are equal. Therefore, we will always store all updates/versions received at different business times.

When we read data from the storage layer on the Business timeline, we should sort it by Business timeline first, then by the technical timeline to pick the latest added (the restatement) when multiple versions have the same validity in the Business timeline.

The evolution of history tables

While the HIST models are designed to be stable, the schemas of the upstream source data and the STG models they produce can and will change. A well-designed data platform must be able to evolve gracefully, continue storing new historical data, and serve the old data without breaking downstream dependencies.

In the PDP, we handle these changes in one of two ways. The default approach to handling schema changes, always valid and safe, is to freeze the old HIST model and create a new one. The new HIST model (e.g., HIST_IB_TRADES_V2) exists in parallel to the old one, to be renamed as V1. Downstream models keep reading from the old base name without version, which is now a view with the task of merging the data from the two history tables to present a uniform history. Sometimes, for simplicity and performance, the new history table (V2) is initialized with the data of the old table (V1) migrated to the new format. The use of a new history table provides a clear breakpoint for the change, and retaining the previous history tables unchanged ensures that historical data remains fully auditable. The view with the base name ensures downstream continuity.

However, for minor, non-breaking changes such as adding new columns, an efficient and acceptable approach is to evolve (alter) the existing history table. This involves automatically altering the HIST table during a database migration, as presented in Chapter 3: Deployment and Security, to add the new column or make the necessary changes. This can also be used to re-hash a table following a change in the Hdiff.

Sometimes, no matter how much effort is put into it, it is impossible to create a uniform history that covers the entire timespan of all existing history tables for an entity. In such cases, we suggest approaching it with a similar pattern to API evolution: you keep the old history available, adding new data if possible or freezing it otherwise, and you also make a new version available at the same time, so that downstream dependencies can be updated. The new version should try to use as many of the older history tables as possible, so that migrating to the new history would not mean losing time depth. In dbt, you can explicitly manage multiple table versions and deprecate older versions. This feature is very useful if you are implementing a data mesh that shares the storage layer (VER models).

History table evolution is a powerful feature that allows your data platform to grow with your business needs without requiring a full rebuild. By replacing the original table with an evolution view, we often make the change transparent for downstream users. When that is not possible, you can still offer business continuity and a path to evolution with model versioning. This approach ensures that your storage layer remains resilient and adaptable, allowing you to handle the complexities of a real-world data platform while maintaining a clean, auditable, and reliable foundation.

Quick history evolution during the initial development phases

When a history table is not yet well established, preserving the history it stores might not be as important as it would be if it contained years of data. If we can afford to lose that little bit of data, or we can easily re-generate it, we have a simpler way out of a change that would otherwise require an evolution of the history table. This is common in the early phases of development, when we can often change our minds about column names, and new data can push us to change entity keys as well.

A full refresh is the dbt way to drop and recreate an incremental table, like history tables are. By doing a full refresh, we lose the data in the history table, but it is recreated according to the current schema, addressing the need for evolution. The choice between a full refresh (re-creation) and the evolution of the history table, as discussed earlier, involves trade-offs:

- **Full-Refresh**: This is the quickest method, especially for major changes (including changes to the HKEY or HDIFF logic). It provides a clean slate and ensures that all data is in a single format. With the multiple version macro, you reload all the versions from the Landig Table.
- **Evolution**: This is the safe method, but it usually requires more effort.
  It can be quite efficient if we alter the history table to handle minor, non-breaking changes, whereas freezing the old history, creating a new one, and creating an evolution view is definitely more effort.

During development, we can often go with a full refresh approach. Still, once a history table is established, we should forbid full refreshes on it, eventually overriding the behavior of the full-refresh command by adding `full_refresh = false` to the history table, so that it cannot be full-refreshed even by error.

Chapter review

In this chapter, you have completed the most critical part of the Pragmatic Data Platform's implementation: the storage layer. We began by understanding the principles behind this layer—how it serves as the definitive, auditable foundation for all your data, capturing every change without altering the data's core semantics. You learned the purpose of each of the three key components:

- **The Staging Model (STG)**: The logical core where you apply your data knowledge and SQL expertise to standardize and clean raw data, explicitly define its identity with HKEY, and prepare it for historization.
- **The Historization Model (HIST)**: The technical core where automation takes over. You explored the different flavors of the historization macros. You saw how HKEY and HDIFF efficiently track and store every version of an entity in a simple, append-only table.
- **The Versioning Model (VER)**: The final layer that makes the history table easy to consume. The versioning macro automatically adds crucial metadata like IS_CURRENT, VALID_FROM, and VALID_TO, along with a stable SCD_Key, making it easy to query any entity at any point in time.

We also discussed the simple, repeatable four-step pattern for adding new entities, allowing you to quickly and consistently expand your data platform. You add a source table, then implement the three core models to prepare, save, and serve its data. Finally, we covered advanced topics such as bi-temporality, handling embedded entities, and the trade-offs of evolving your history tables.

In the next chapter, we will bring these concepts to life by coding the storage layer for our sample project, solidifying your understanding with practical examples.

Recommended resources

dbt documentation

- dbt sources. https://docs.getdbt.com/docs/build/sources.
- dbt incremental models. https://docs.getdbt.com/docs/build/incremental-models.
- dbt Data Tests. https://docs.getdbt.com/docs/build/data-tests.
- dbt Full Refresh. https://docs.getdbt.com/reference/resource-configs/full_refresh.

dbt Packages

- Pragmatic Data Platform dbt package. https://github.com/pragmatic-data/pragmatic-data-platform.
- dbt_utils Package. https://hub.getdbt.com/dbt-labs/dbt_utils/latest/.

Snowflake documentation

- Snowflake Data Types. https://docs.snowflake.com/en/sql-reference/data-types.
- Snowflake Table Types (Permanent & Transient). https://docs.snowflake.com/en/user-guide/tables-temp-transient.
- MD5 Hash Function. https://docs.snowflake.com/en/sql-reference/functions/md5.

CHAPTER 11

Coding the Storage Layer

This chapter serves as a practical, **hands-on guide to implementing the storage layer** of the Pragmatic Data Platform (PDP) using dbt and Snowflake. We will bring the Stonks sample project to life by building a robust, auditable data storage layer that stores all historical data. Following a simple, repeatable playbook, we will create the models needed to handle a range of entities, from simple financial transactions to more complex embedded data. You will learn to apply the STG, HIST, and VER models, ensuring your data platform is ready for the next layers of refinement and delivery.

The topics that we are going to cover in this chapter are:

- **The Storage Layer Playbook**: The `STG`, `HIST`, and `VER` models pipeline playbook.
- **The Structure for the Storage Layer**: Naming convention to organize our storage layer.
- **Building the Storage Layer for the Trade Entity**: Our primary, step-by-step coding example by applying the STG, HIST, and VER models to the Trade entity.
- **Handling Other Simple Entities**: Feel the reusability of the PDP patterns.
- **The Security Embedded Entity**: How to extract and historicize a complex entity.
- **The Open Position and Position History Entities**: Building the history for positions, including closed ones that you don't find in your input.
- **The Security Merged History**: How to merge data from multiple Security histories.

Sample project and code

The sample dbt project is available at: **https://github.com/pragmatic-data/stonks**. **All the code** we will write in this chapter **is in the dbt project folders**, mostly in the `storage` folder. The materials that do not belong in the project code will be in the sub-folder for this chapter, `chapter_11`, under the `code_samples_by_chapter` folder.

Please note that, to better fit the limited space on the printed page, we omit most comments and change the formatting of code blocks compared to the files.

The storage layer playbook

This chapter transitions from the theoretical concepts of the storage layer to a hands-on implementation using the Stonks sample project. Our objective for this project is to construct a robust, auditable data storage layer for all our Interactive Brokers (IB) data. We'll bring the core **STG**, **HIST**, and **VER** models to life by applying our templates to a variety of entities, including a complex, embedded one. The playbook for building the storage layer for each entity is straightforward and repeatable. It consists of four main steps:

- **Define the input as a dbt source**: We begin by locating the raw data for our entity, whether it's in a landing table, a seed file, or another source, and defining it as a dbt source, making it accessible and testable by dbt.
- **Code the Staging Model (STG)**: This is where we prepare the raw data, standardize its format and naming conventions, explicitly define the HKEY and HDIFF that will be used for historization, and make the data as usable as possible.
- **Code the Historization Model (HIST)**: Using one historization macro, we build an append-only table that captures every version of the entity.
- **Code the Versioning Model (VER)**: The versioning macro creates a user-friendly view on top of the HIST table, making historical data easier to query.

Figure 34: Create the storage layer for one entity.

Figure 34 illustrates the steps to create the storage layer for one entity. This process usually happens inside a GIT branch opened before adding the source definition, and is closed with a Pull Request after the VER model. You can code a few related entities in the same branch, but we suggest making a commit for each step, and a PR once a few related entities are ready. We will apply this playbook to the following entities from our sample project:

- **TRADES**: A straightforward entity we use to show the code in detail.
- **CASH_TRANSACTIONS**: Another simple entity, to show the reusability of PDP code.
- **TRANSFERS** (from a landing table): Another simple table, code only in the repo.
- **CORPORATE_ACTIONS** (from a seed file): Same as above, code only in the repo.
- **SECURITY**: An entity extracted from four sources, with advanced use of configuration.
- **OPEN_POSITIONS**: Interesting case as we need to create and store the closed positions, which are implied by not being present in the source data.

The structure for the storage layer

A well-organized project structure is crucial for a scalable and maintainable data platform. The Pragmatic Data Platform (PDP) uses a logical, layered folder structure that aligns with its architectural principles. This approach ensures that as your project grows, models remain easy to locate, understand, and manage. We place all models for the storage layer in a dedicated sub-folder within the dbt project. Here we describe how to organize the files for the Stonks project.

Folder structure

All models for the storage layer reside under the `models/01_storage/` directory. The `01_` prefix serves to enforce a clear, layered hierarchy that matches the data flow in the PDP from ingestion (in its own folder) to storage(01), refined (02), and delivery (03). Within this folder, we will create a folder specific to the data source, such as `interactive_brokers/`, to contain all the related models. The full path is `<dbt_project>/models/01_storage/interactive_brokers`. We try to keep the code organized by layer and aligned with our architecture and best practices: by source in storage and by domain in refined and delivery. Anyway, if you have different teams working on different sources or domains and you want to keep everything in a single dbt project, you might opt to reverse this part of the folder structure and use <source or domain>/<layer> instead to provide clear areas of competence for your teams. This is especially useful if you are building both source-specific operational reporting (which will be inside a source folder, managed by the source team) and integrated reporting across sources (managed by the domain team).

Source definitions

To maintain logical cohesion, the YAML file containing the source declarations for a specific data source should be placed close to the models that use them. For our project, the `source_interactive_brokers.yml` file will be located directly within the `interactive_brokers/` folder, which will contain all the code for IB data. This co-location makes it easy to find and manage the source definitions.

Entity specific code and YAML file

To avoid a flat, unmanageable list of models, we will create a dedicated sub-folder for each entity. This modular approach groups the STG, HIST, and VER models for a single entity together, along with the YAML file containing their documentation and tests. For instance, all models related to the Trade entity will be stored in `trades/` creating a structure that will generally look like this:

```
dbt_project/models/01_storage/interactive_brokers/
      trades/
            STG_IB_TRADES.sql
            HIST_IB_TRADES.sql
            VER_IB_TRADES.sql
            trades.yml

      positions/
            ...                 # position .sql and .yml files

      cash_transactions/
            ...                 # cash TX. sql and .yml files
...
```

This organized structure simplifies navigation and makes it easy for new team members to understand the project's layout and find the models they need to work on.

Naming conventions

Consistent naming conventions are paramount for readability and maintainability. We follow a clear pattern for all models and columns across all layers. Let's have a look at the core conventions for the storage layer.

Role and Source Prefix

All model names begin with a **role-specific prefix**, followed by a short abbreviation for the source system. This allows for quick identification of a model's purpose and origin. Examples are:

- **STG_IB_**: Staging model for Interactive Brokers data.
- **HIST_IB_**: Historization model for Interactive Brokers data.
- **VER_IB_**: Versioning model for Interactive Brokers data.

Entity name and hashed key columns

The model's name is completed with the name of the entity it represents (e.g., TRADES, OPEN_POSITIONS) after the role and source prefix.

The columns used to uniquely identify an entity and its version, follow a standard pattern:

- **ENTITY_HKEY**: The Hash Key uniquely identifies a business entity. For the Trade entity, this is TRADE_HKEY.
- **ENTITY_HDIFF**: The Hash Diff identifies a specific version of an entity, representing a hash of all the attributes that matter for historization. For the Trade entity, this is TRADE_HDIFF.

Metadata Columns

The metadata columns added by the PDP macros to support historization and versioning have clear, descriptive names:

- **INGESTION_TS_UTC** and **HIST_LOAD_TS_UTC**: The timestamp of when the record was ingested into the platform (LT) and in the HIST table.
- **EFFECTIVITY_DATE**: The business date or timestamp that defines the validity of a record. You can use EFFECTIVITY_TS too, but a consistent name is better for humans than two type consistent names.
- **IS_CURRENT**: A Boolean flag indicating whether the record is the most recent version of an instance or if it is a past version, if false.
- **VALID_FROM** and **VALID_TO**: The validity time range for a specific version.

This systematic approach to naming ensures consistency across all models and makes it simple to understand the role of each table and column at a glance. Remember that the **Least Surprise Principle** (**LSP**) is a core tenet of good software design. A system's naming and behavior should be predictable and consistent, matching the expectations.

In other words, a system should not do anything that would surprise or confuse its users. The LSP enables developers to work more efficiently and with greater confidence, reducing the need for constant code review and validation.

Building the storage layer for the trade entity

Now that we have a solid understanding of the storage layer's principles and a clear project structure, let's bring it all to life by coding the storage layer for the Trade entity.

This will serve as a detailed, step-by-step example of how to apply the PDP playbook to a straightforward financial entity. We will build the data's journey from its raw landing table to a fully versioned and auditable history. It is a good practice to isolate the work to add a storage layer for a new entity or a set of related entities in its own Git branch, and complete the development with a Pull Request to merge the code into your DEV environment. To start, create a new branch named `storage-trades` or follow your team's branch naming convention.

Step 1: Source declaration and validation

The first step to use the raw data is to declare our TRADES landing table as a dbt source. This not only makes our code more readable by abstracting the table location but also allows us to set up crucial data tests to validate the data at the point of ingestion. You can get a quick start using the template `10_SOURCE_template.yml` found in the `analyses/TEMPLATES/storage` folder of the sample project. We define the "IB" source, its schema, and add the TRADES entry to our new YAML file, `source_Interactive_Brokers.yml`, located in the .../`interactive_brokers/` folder.

```
# models/01_storage/interactive_brokers/source_Interactive_Brokers.yml
version: 2
sources:
  - name: IB
    schema: LAND_IB

    tables:
      - name: TRADES
        description: Trades on Interactive Brokers accounts

        columns:
          - name: Transaction_ID
            description: The unique ID of a Trade.
            data_tests:
             - not_null

          - name: FROM_FILE
            data_tests:
             - not_null
             - pragmatic_data.all_files_from_stage:
                 pattern: 'Trades/flex.*[.]Trades.*[.]csv[.]gz'
```

```
                stage_name: "{{ get_IB_..._name() }}"
            - pragmatic_data.file_order_is_correct
```

Please note that the full and correctly spaced file is in the sample project. This is a compacted version to make the code easy to read, even if not good to execute. We define the TRADES landing table and data tests on two key columns. The `not_null` test ensures our `Transaction_ID` and `FROM_FILE` columns are never empty, which is critical for downstream models.

Even though `Transaction_ID` is the PK of the Trades entity, the column is not unique in the landing table because it contains data from multiple files. To validate that all expected files have been loaded and are processed in the correct order, we use custom ingestion tests: `all_files_from_stage` and `file_order_is_correct`. This provides an early warning system for any ingestion issues.

To confirm that the source is defined correctly and passes these tests, run the following command in your terminal:

```
dbt test -s source:IB.TRADES
```

Fix the tests as needed and once it works as expected, you can commit the code to your branch.

Step 2: The staging model (STG_IB_TRADES)

The staging model is the logical core of the storage layer. Its primary role is to prepare the raw data for historization by cleaning it, casting data types, and, most importantly, calculating the HKEY and HDIFF that define the entity's identity and version.

Configuring the deployment of the storage layer

It is time to start coding our storage layer, so we must configure where we want to create our tables and views. If we do nothing, dbt will create them in the target database and schema configured in our connection. If you remember, during setup, I configured my target schema to `RZ` because we planned to deploy using custom schemas defined in the `dbt_project.yml` file, as explained in the **Organizing deployment with custom schemas** section in Chapter 4. To add the configuration for the storage layer, replace the configuration for the example code we did in chapter four in the `dbt_project.yml` file with the following:

```
models:
  stonks:
    01_storage:
      interactive_brokers:
        +materialized: view
        +schema: ib_storage
```

In the above example, I decided to store each source system in its own schema, so I placed my configuration under the `interactive_brokers` folder within the `01_storage` folder and named the schema accordingly (`ib_storage`). Since STG and VER models are intended to be views, and HIST models are intended to be incremental models, we configure the default materialization for the folder as `view`. We will override it to be incremental in the HIST file.

Another option is to put all storage models from all source systems into a single schema, but you might end up with hundreds of database objects, making it difficult to find what you want. Our suggestion is to deploy the staging layer for each source in its own schema. You can use `01_<source>` as schema name, if you want to make the layering obvious.

Before starting to code the models for our sample projects, it is a good time to also clean up the models folder by deleting the example code we got when we initialized the repository. Delete the `example/` folder inside the `models/` folder. If you also want to clean up your database, run the following command in Snowflake after adapting it with the name of the schema of your example models:

```
DROP SCHEMA STONKS_DEV.RZ_EXAMPLE;
```

YAML Definitions and Data Tests

Before we build the model, let's define its properties and tests in the `ib_trades.yml` file. We will place this file in the same `trades/` sub-folder. This practice ensures that our documentation and tests are co-located with the model code.

```
version: 2
models:
  - name: STG_IB_TRADES
    description: Trades in all asset classes...

    data_tests:
      - pragmatic_data.has_sortable_versions:
          key_column: TRADE_HKEY
          diff_column: TRADE_HDIFF
          sort_columns: EFFECTIVITY_DATE, RECORD_SOURCE

      - dbt_utils.unique_combination_of_columns:
          combination_of_columns:
            - Transaction_ID
            - RECORD_SOURCE
```

The full code is in the sample project. Here, we start looking at the table-level tests.

The `has_sortable_versions` test from the PDP package is important as it validates that the versions in the staging model can be correctly sorted for the historization process by ensuring a unique version for each business key within a given effective date and file (RECORD_SOURCE contains the file name). This test should always be used when the `save_history_with_multiple_versions` historization macro is used. The `unique_combination_of_columns` test from the `dbt_utils` package is used here to verify that the `Transaction_ID` is unique across files, since the landing table contains the same transaction from multiple files, as explained before. And here are some interesting column-level tests, with reduced indenting:

```
columns:

  - name: concat(BROKER_CODE, LISTING_EXCHANGE,
                 SECURITY_SYMBOL, SECURITY_CODE)
    description: Position BK is not null for position TX
    data_tests:
      - not_null:
          where: ASSET_CLASS not in ('CASH', 'FOP')

  - name: SECURITY_CODE
    data_tests:
      - relationships:
          to: ref('STG_IB_TRADES_SECURITY')
          field: SECURITY_CODE
          where: |
            ASSET_CLASS not in ('CASH', 'FOP')
            and trade_date_time >= '2024-01-01'
            # Before 2024 some short-lived positions
            # where opened and closed between exports
```

The first column does not test an existing column, but instead uses a SQL expression built with the `concat()` function. This is a common way to test whether a list of columns is unique - use `concat_ws(...)` - or whether all columns are not null (one null would make the `concat` result null) on small tables. On bigger tables, it's better to use `unique_combination_of_columns`, which is much more performant. The second column is a real column, a foreign key (FK) to the Security entity, and performs a relationship test. It is interesting to note the use of the `|` (pipe symbol) to allow the use of multiple lines of text as the value of the `where` parameter. The use of the `where` parameter in both tests is a key element that enables testing even when a test does not apply to all the data, but only to an important subset.

Writing tests before writing the code

Working with models in a test-driven development (TDD) style can be highly effective. By writing our data tests in the YAML file before we write the SQL code, we're defining the model's expected behavior first. This not only forces us to think about data quality upfront but also provides a clear "definition of done" for our development work. When the tests pass, we know the model is working as intended. We will use the `stage` macro to efficiently code the STG models. This macro hides the technicalities for generating SQL code for our STG model, allowing us to focus on its block-by-block configuration. We are going to build the STG model using the template available in the `20_STG_template.sql` file in the `analyses/TEMPLATES/storage` folder. As you can see in the full code of the sample project, the STG model is primarily a set of configurations passed to `pragmatic_data.stage` macro.

This is our general **STG model editing playbook**:

1. Clone the STG template or an STG model from the same system, whatever gives you a better start, or make your own template for a specific system

2. Define the **source model** and decide if you are going to use the `*` operator (setting `columns.include_all: true` in the `source` block) or not. Aim for the least editing, as it

usually provides the best readability. If you decided to use the * operator, add the code for the exclude, replace, and rename parameters in the `source` block to handle all the incoming columns.

3. Code the **`calculated_columns`** block. You have two options here:

   A. When using the * operator. Just add the new calculated columns that you want.

   B. When **not using** the * operator. Use the helper SQL in the TEMPLATE folder to generate a good starting point (in the form `col: col`), as you might need to edit all the columns. Re-order the columns and edit them manually or with the help of dbt Copilot or other tools to enforce your naming convention and the changes you need.

4. Build the STG model in dbt with the new column names you have decided on, then use the helper SQL query to generate the list of columns for the HDIFF column. Use the "new" column names to populate the HKEY fields for the PK and all the FKs.

5. If you need them, complete the STG model with the `default_records` and `remove_duplicates` blocks, using the new column names.

Here is the resulting code for the `STG_IB_TRADES.sql` model, block by block:

```
{%- set source_model = source('IB', 'TRADES') %}

{%- set configuration -%}
source:
    columns:
        include_all: false          #-- True enables '*'
    where: STARTSWITH(CLIENTACCOUNTID, 'U')
```

In this first block, we see the definition of the `source_model`, which specifies the source data for the STG model. This is usually done by calling the `source()` dbt function. Then we have the `source` configuration, which allows us to work on the source columns using the * operator when `columns.include_all` is set to true, and we define a predicate for the `where` clause of our query on the source data. In this example, we set `include_all` to false, so the SELECT on the landing table will not have the * operator, but we have set a `where` clause, and that will be in the query against the LT. In this case, we use a quite strange predicate, but let me explain: the file we ingest, and therefore the Landing Tables, have multiple headers per file, so we must load them as "normal" rows in the LT. The `CLIENTACCOUNTID` column will contain "ClientAccountID" for header rows and "U***..." for data rows. Our predicate works well and picks exactly what we want, so we are happy with it. A riskier, but easier-to-read alternative could be `CLIENTACCOUNTID != 'ClientAccountID'`. The next block is `calculated_columns`, where we make the incoming data usable, especially if we do not use the `source` block to handle the original columns using *.

```
calculated_columns:
  - Transaction_ID: TransactionID
  - Transaction_Type: TransactionType

  #-- Core FKs => Account, Security and Position
  - BROKER_CODE: '!IB'
  - CLIENT_ACCOUNT_CODE: "'U***' || RIGHT(CLI…ID, 4)"
  - SECURITY_CODE: coalesce(SECURITYID, CONID)
  - LISTING_EXCHANGE: LISTINGEXCHANGE
... 45 more definitions...

  #-- core metadata
  - EFFECTIVITY_DATE: DateTime:TIMESTAMP_NTZ
  - RECORD_SOURCE: FROM_FILE
  - FILE_ROW_NUMBER
  - FILE_LAST_MODIFIED_TS_UTC
  - INGESTION_TS_UTC
```

The `calculated_columns` block defines all the extra columns we want in our staging model, in addition to the ones (eventually) handled by the `source` block. The pattern of use is `column_name: sql_expression`, and it generates the following SQL code: `sql_expression as column_name`. The `sql_expression` is optional; if absent, the named column is read unchanged. This is consistent across all Pragmatic Data Platform macro configurations. It enables us to define columns using everything we can code in SQL. Still, the most common operations are renaming columns, casting data types, and adding new calculated fields using very simple SQL expressions such as plain source column names, literal strings, and calls to SQL functions.

Please note that we do not expect you to manually write long lists of columns. In the next section, **Streamlining Column Generation**, we show how you can generate the list of columns you want to use and prepare for this section with little to no effort.

The code snippet for `calculated_columns` shows some interesting examples of column definitions:

- **Column renaming**: `Transaction_ID: TransactionID` generates `TransactionID as Transaction_ID`.
- **Column as a string value**: `BROKER_CODE: '!IB'`. The exclamation mark `!` as the first character of a string produces a quoted literal in the SELECT statement, generating `'IB' as BROKER_CODE` as the full column expression.
- **Function call**: `SECURITY_CODE: coalesce(SECURITYID, CONID)` generates `coalesce(SECURITYID, CONID) as SECURITY_CODE`.
- **Casting**: `EFFECTIVITY_DATE: DateTime:TIMESTAMP_NTZ` generates `DateTime:TIMESTAMP_NTZ as EFFECTIVITY_DATE`.

The pattern should be pretty clear, but you can always play a bit with the definitions and look at the dbt-generated code to gain a deeper understanding. Just click the compile button and inspect the generated code. The columns that you want to output without any change, like `INGESTION_TS_UTC` can be listed alone. The self-rename `INGESTION_TS_UTC: INGESTION_TS_UTC` works too, but it is less clear. The next block, `hashed_columns`, defines the hashed columns. We define HKEYs for primary keys and foreign keys, and HDIFF for the version identification.

```
hashed_columns:

  TRADE_HKEY:
      - Transaction_ID

  POSITION_HKEY:
      ...

  PORTFOLIO_HKEY:
      ...

  SECURITY_HKEY:
      - SECURITY_CODE
      - LISTING_EXCHANGE

  TRADE_HDIFF:
      - Transaction_Type
      - Transaction_ID
      ...
      - Orig_Order_ID
```

The stage macro takes the columns listed under a column name, such as `TRADE_HKEY` and `TRADE_HDIFF` and generates the corresponding hash values using the `pdp_hash` macro from the Pragmatic Data Platform package, which uses the `MD5_BINARY` Snowflake function to generate a binary hash. We use binary hashes because they use less storage, are quicker, and humans tend to leave them alone; that is good. Please note that in the `hashed_columns` block, we use the new names defined in the `source` and `calculated_columns` blocks.

The `TRADE_HKEY` is calculated from the business key: the `Transaction_ID`. When the HKEY is a single-column table, we can use the column directly, but for consistency, we prefer to always generate and use the HKEY in the storage layer. When the HKEY is multicolumn, as in position, portfolio, and security, the advantage of having a single column as a key is self-evident.

In an STG model, you can define the HKEYs for all foreign keys in the entity so they are ready to use in the refined layer. The TRADE_HDIFF is a hash of all columns we deem relevant for changes to the Trade entity. If any of these values change, the HDIFF will change, signaling a new version. This is often a long list of columns, but we expect you to generate it with simple SQL, as shown later. We eventually end the STG model by defining the default records and removing duplicates, then call the `stage` macro with the data from the configuration.

```
remove_duplicates:     # Empty (or left out) if we need no removal

{%- endset -%}

{%- set cfg = fromyaml(configuration) -%}

{{- pragmatic_data.stage(
    source_model                = source_model,
    source                      = cfg['source'],
    calculated_columns          = cfg['calculated_columns'],
    hashed_columns              = cfg['hashed_columns'],
```

```
    remove_duplicates          = cfg['remove_duplicates'],
) }}
```

The YAML configuration data is parsed and converted into a more usable Python dictionary, cfg, by the `fromyaml` function.

Building the Model

To build and test this model, run the following command:

```
dbt build -s STG_IB_TRADES
```

Now you can see your model in Snowflake. Fix any issues or failing tests, then you can commit the code for the STG model and its tests in the YAML file. Building and testing the model now should succeed, but once you also have the `STG_IB_TRADES_SECURITY` model, it might fail with a message saying "DateTime" is not a valid timestamp. What is happening is that Snowflake is pushing up the WHERE clause that we wrote for our STG model to the reading of the Landing Table.

In our STG model, we excluded the header rows, so the `trade_date_time >= '2024-01-01'` filter on the test works, when executed on the STG model, but not if pushed to the Landing Table. Snowflake is right to push the filter earlier to give us the best possible performance, since SQL does not guarantee the order of the filters, even if it is a bit counterintuitive. We have two ways to avoid that. The first is to materialize the model as a table. The second is to declare the view as secure using the following code in the STG model:

```
{{ config( secure = true ) }}
```

A secure view is a special type of view in Snowflake that sacrifices some optimizations in favor of a stricter security model to prevent data leakage. As an example, we now know that there is a row where the `trade_date_time` column has the value `DateTime`. With a secure view, our query is slightly slower but works fine and does not expose any info if you cannot query it.

Streamlining Column handling

The list of columns for the `calculated_columns` block can be very long, as it often is the definition of the HDIFF column. Instead of manually typing them out, you can use your database to generate the list quickly. You query the `INFORMATION_SCHEMA.COLUMNS` view to get the complete list of columns for your source table.

The `COLUMN_NAME`, `DATA_TYPE`, and `ORDINAL_POSITION` columns are your best friends for generating code that is (almost) ready to use and well-documented. We recall the sample SQL code introduced in the section "**SQL queries to generate STG code**" in Chapter 10.

```
SELECT
  '    -' || COLUMN_NAME || ': '|| COLUMN_NAME ||
  ' -- ' || DATA_TYPE as calculated_columns_text_with_types

FROM STONKS_DEV.INFORMATION_SCHEMA.COLUMNS
WHERE TABLE_SCHEMA = 'LAND_IB'
 and TABLE_NAME = 'TRADES'
ORDER BY ORDINAL_POSITION
```

You can find an extended version in the `21_STG_generate_columns.sql` file under the `analyses/TEMPLATES/storage/` folder of the sample project. The output of this query will give you all the column names your model can use from the Landing Table it will be reading. You can then copy and paste this list into your YAML configuration and manually rename the columns, or code the other casts and adaptations you need.

Even better, tools like dbt Copilot and other AI-powered assistants can help you quickly apply general transformations, from simple underscore additions to finding good column names, saving you time and effort.

Step 3: The historization model (HIST_IB_TRADES)

The HIST model is where the magic of historization happens with full automation and minimal coding on our part, thanks to the historization macros of the PDP package.

> *This is the technical core of our storage layer, responsible for storing every version of an entity we receive from the source. The HIST table is append-only, meaning we only ever insert new records, never update or delete old ones. This is the foundation of our auditable data platform.*

Continuing with our TDD-inspired way of working, we add the `HIST_IB_TRADES` model and its corresponding data tests to the `ib_trades.yml` file. This is key to ensuring the data integrity of our history table at all times. Let's start with table-level data tests:

```
- name: HIST_IB_TRADES
  description: History table for the trades entity.

  data_tests:

    - pragmatic_data.keys_from_landing:
        landing_rel: "{{ source('IB', 'TRADES') }}"
        landing_rel_filter: STARTSWITH(CLIENTACCOUNTID, 'U')
        key_fields_landing: TransactionID
        key_fields_hist: Transaction_ID
    - dbt_utils.unique_combination_of_columns:
        combination_of_columns:
          - TRADE_HKEY
          - RECORD_SOURCE
```

As usual, please note that the code is compressed to fit; the code with correct indentation is in the sample project. First, the `keys_from_landing` test ensures that the history table contains all the business keys from the landing table. This is a cross-check to validate our load process and the health of our history table. The PDP package also provides the test `keys_and_ts_from_landing`, which is even stronger, as it verifies that we have the latest version from the LT in the history table. However, it is unsuitable when you have exports with overlapping content, as in our case.

Then, the `unique_combination_of_columns` test ensures that the HKEY is unique in each file. While TXs are immutable, their exports sometimes differ in column values across export files. These values are related to the

Security columns we have kept for a Trade, such as the security symbol and name. And then the column-level data tests:

```
columns:

  - name: Transaction_ID
    description: >
      BK is not null, BUT NOT unique (despite immutable TX)
      as Security info can change
    data_tests:
      - not_null

# SECURITY_CODE test on the HIST table
...
```

As usual, please note that the code is partial and compressed to read well. Here, we expose only the `not_null` test on the `Transaction_ID` column, mostly to introduce the use of the > symbol in YAML to define a value as a multiline string. The peculiarity of > is that the string will not retain newlines, as it does with the | symbol.

In the complete code in the sample project, you will also find, again, a relationship test on the `SECURITY_CODE` column, but here testing the relation between the hist tables. Having both, and maybe a third one on the VER views, might be overkill, but it helps pinpoint whether a problem is a process or a data issue more quickly.

Consider that tests are code. They use resources to create, run, and maintain. Useless or redundant tests are just a drag on your project and should be eliminated. It is up to you to evaluate when a test is no longer useful, too expensive to run or maintain, and better removed or run sparingly or upon manual invocation.

Coding the HIST Model

We will build our history with the `save_history_with_multiple_versions` macro, so that we can ingest and retain multiple versions of the same instance in a single run. This is going to be handy, as we will ingest four years of data in one go!

Like all history tables, this must be an incremental model, as we definitely want the table's contents carried over between model executions. The macro handles the logic of comparing new input data from the STG model against the existing HIST table and inserting only the records that represent a new version. This is our general HIST model editing playbook:

1. Clone the HIST template or a HIST model from the same system, whatever gives you a better start, or make your own template for a specific system.
2. Replace the entity name in the three mandatory arguments (`input_rel`, `key_column`, and `diff_column`) to match the names in the STG model.
3. Pick the right columns for the `sort_expr` parameter to order the versions.
4. Eventually, consider if you need to change the default settings for the optional parameters that control the high-water mark and filtering.

Here is the code for `HIST_IB_TRADES.sql` model:

```
{{ config( materialized='incremental') }}

{{ pragmatic_data.save_history_with_multiple_versions(
    input_rel                 = ref('STG_IB_TRADES'),
    key_column                = 'TRADE_HKEY',
    diff_column               = 'TRADE_HDIFF',

   sort_expr = 'EFFECTIVITY_DATE, Transaction_ID
             , RECORD_SOURCE, FILE_ROW_NUMBER',
) }}

/** Default values, mostly to manage load performace
    load_ts_column            = 'INGESTION_TS_UTC',
    high_watermark_column     = 'INGESTION_TS_UTC',
    high_watermark_test       = '>',
    input_filter_expr         = 'true',
    history_filter_expr       = 'true',
*/
```

The macro's parameters are quite simple to explain:

- **input_rel**: The staging model (`STG_IB_TRADES`) that provides the new data.
- **key_column**: The HKEY column (`TRADE_HKEY`) that identifies a unique entity.
- **diff_column**: The HDIFF column (`TRADE_HDIFF`) that defines versions.
- **sort_expr**: The expression used to order versions and determine which record is the newest. This is used to determine the order in which to compare the versions, and which are new versions to be stored and which are copies (not stored).

The other optional parameters control the high-water mark filtering, the technical timeline column, and other performance-related columns. The goal of the historization models is to store a new version the first time it appears. After that, we do not need to store it again, but if we do, the history table will continue to work well, just taking up a bit more storage.

Correctly setting the sorting expression is important to capture only the minimum amount of data, minimize the size of the history table, and avoid duplicates there. Most of the time, a wrong sorting expression is more of a nuisance than a problem.

Now that we have the model ready, build it by running the following command:

```
dbt build -s HIST_IB_TRADES
```

You now look at the table in your Snowflake database. Fix any issues or failing tests, then you can commit the code for the HIST model and its tests in the YAML file.

Step 4: The Versioning model (VER_IB_TRADES)

The final step in completing the pipeline for an entity is to make the data in our HIST table easier to use for downstream consumers by adding the VER model. The HIST table, in general, contains multiple records, one for each version, for a single instance of the entity, which is not ideal for reporting based on the current data, as requested in 99% of the cases. The VER model solves this by providing a simpler, easier-to-query view of the data by adding a few columns, based on metadata, that make the HIST model very easy to use.

The HIST table stores every version of a record whenever they arrive, making it difficult to find the "current" or "active" version at a specific point in time without advanced SQL skills. The VER macro addresses this by adding three key columns:

- **IS_CURRENT**: This is a Boolean flag that is set to TRUE for the latest, most up-to-date version of a record and FALSE for all previous versions. It simplifies queries by allowing you to filter only for active records.
- **VALID_FROM**: This timestamp indicates when a specific version of a record became effective. It is set by the content of the `version_sort_column`, in our case, and often, the EFFECTIVITY_DATE of the record itself.
- **VALID_TO**: This timestamp indicates when a record ceased to be the latest version, either because a newer version arrived or because the record was effectively "deleted" from the source. For the `IS_CURRENT = TRUE` record, this value is set to a far-future date (`9999-09-09`), indicating that it is currently active.

These columns transform the HIST table from a raw, append-only ledger into a **Type 2 Slowly Changing Dimension** (**SCD**), a standard data warehousing technique for tracking changes over time. They allow for easy "point-in-time" analysis, enabling you to ask questions like "What was the Trade entity like on March 1st, 2024?" by simply filtering the VALID_FROM and VALID_TO dates.

The VER model also introduces **SCD_Key**, a unique hash generated from the TRADE_HDIFF and VALID_FROM columns **that uniquely identifies each version**, even when two rows have the same content but are valid at different times. This key is useful for dimension-like entities when doing dimensional modeling with full history, where fact tables need to relate to a specific version of a dimension. By adding a foreign key to a certain entity, both the HKEY and the SCD_Key, you can reference both the current version of the dimension (SCD1 = DIM) and the historical one (SCD2), ensuring data integrity and correct historical reporting.

In our case, the Trades entity is not a dimensional one, so we will make good use of the IS_CURRENT, VALID_FROM, and VALID_TO columns, while the SCD_Key is not interesting for this entity.

YAML Definitions and Data Tests

Let's complete our entity by adding the YAML definitions for the VER model. Thanks to the IS_CURRENT column, this is also the best place to validate expectations that are valid or can be checked only on current data, as they might not be true for older versions. One key example is the unicity of PKs and BKs. As an example, add the following definition to our `ib_trades.yml` file:

```
- name: VER_IB_TRADES
  description: All versions of the trades entity.
  data_tests:

    - dbt_utils.expression_is_true:
        expression: >
          IS_CURRENT and VALID_TO = '9999-09-09':date

    - dbt_utils.mutually_exclusive_ranges:
        lower_bound_column: VALID_FROM
        upper_bound_column: VALID_TO
        partition_by: TRADE_HKEY
        gaps: not_allowed
        zero_length_range_allowed: true

  columns:
    - name: Transaction_ID
      description: BK not null, unique on current version
      data_tests:
        - not_null
        - unique:
            where: IS_CURRENT
```

We leverage two tests from the **dbt_utils package** to verify that our pipeline works well.

The `expression_is_true` test verifies that the current record (`IS_CURRENT = true`) always has the VALID_TO column set to the "end of time" defined in our project. The date '9999-09-09' is the default value from the PDP package, but you can change its value and type by defining two variables in `dbt_project.yml`:

```
pdp.end_of_time: 9999-12-31  # PDP default 9999-09-09

pdp.end_of_time_type: DATE    # could be timestamp
```

This would set VALID_TO to 31st December 9999 for all VER views.

The `mutually_exclusive_ranges` test verifies that the validity intervals defined by the VALID_FROM and VALID_TO columns for each record do not overlap, have no gaps, and may eventually have zero validity time. This is not so important for the Trades entity, which is an immutable transaction, and for facts in general, as you normally work only with the current version. It is, instead, very important for dimensional entities where changes occur, and it is important that we track them correctly.

We then have an example of a column test using the where attribute to filter the current records and verify that the Business Key (Transaction_ID) is unique.

Coding the VER Model

We will use the `versions_from_history_with_multiple_versions` macro. This macro takes the HIST table as input and automatically adds crucial metadata, including IS_CURRENT, VALID_FROM and VALID_TO dates, the SCD_KEY column, and a few other utility columns. This is our general VER model editing playbook:

1. Clone the VER template or a VER model from the same system, whatever gives you a better start, or make your own template for a specific system.
2. Replace the entity name in the three mandatory arguments (`input_rel`, `key_column`, and `diff_column`) to match the names in the HIST model.
3. Pick the column for the `version_sort_column` parameter. This is often the `EFFECTIVITY_DATE`, as you want to read the data by the business timeline.

This is the simplest and quickest model to code in the pipeline, usually done in a minute. Here is the code for the `VER_IB_TRADES.sql` model:

```
{{pragmatic_data.versions_from_history_with_multiple_versions(

    history_rel                 = ref('HIST_IB_TRADES'),
    key_column                  = 'TRADE_HKEY',
    diff_column                 = 'TRADE_HDIFF',

   version_sort_column         = 'EFFECTIVITY_DATE'
) }}
```

The macro's parameters are straightforward and similar to the HIST model:

- **history_rel**: The history model (HIST_IB_TRADES) to be enhanced.
- **key_column**: The HKEY column (TRADE_HKEY) that identifies a unique entity.
- **diff_column**: The HDIFF column (TRADE_HDIFF) that defines versions.
- **version_sort_column**: The column used to order versions, define the timeline for the VALID_TO and _FROM columns and calculate the SCD_KEY. It is a key decision when coding the model.

The other optional parameters define the technical timeline and which columns and rows you read from the HIST model (by default, all columns and rows). The role of the VER model is to be a helper, making historical data easier to use. It is not necessary to have it, and a common case to avoid it is with immutable transactions: each row is always active, the validity is from its creation onwards, and they are facts, so you will not use its SCD_Key column. Anyway, it costs so little to code and build them that, in most cases, you could just have them for completeness.

Now that we have the model ready, build it by running the following command:

```
dbt build -s VER_IB_TRADES
```

The view is now in your Snowflake database. Fix any issues or failing tests, then you can commit the code for the HIST model and its tests in the YAML file.

Validating the Entire Entity Pipeline

Once you have created the source definition and all three models, you can run and test the entire dependency chain with a single command. The + symbol tells dbt to run the specified model and all its parents. Leave no spaces between it and the model name!

```
dbt build -s +VER_IB_TRADES
```

This command will first build STG_IB_TRADES, then HIST_IB_TRADES, and finally VER_IB_TRADES, while running all the associated tests defined in the YAML files. If you have built every model after coding it, you should have no surprises, and all will be green. Note that you can build this pipeline as many times as you want, and the final result will always be the same. This is a key benefit of our models being idempotent.

Now that you have coded and run the test for all the models, you might wonder if we have too many tests. YES, we do have too many, and that is normal when you are starting to code, as you use tests to validate both your assumptions and your code. We have already said that tests, even if defined only in YAML, are code and add complexity and maintenance costs, in addition to slowing down builds. The very last thing to do is a final review of your tests to see if you can remove any (logical) duplicates or identify any important ones you may be missing.

Our general rule of thumb for tests is as follows:

- Test on the source definition the ingestion process using the FROM_FILE column and the expectations for source data (PK, FK, important columns), whenever possible.
- Test on the STG model the expectations that cannot be easily tested on the source before the data is "adapted", what is added in the STG model, and the version sorting.
- Test on the HIST model the integrity of the table and that you have the keys from the LT.
- Test on the VER model the validity ranges and anything else that is valid for the current data.
- Test relationships where you think better, with a preference for VER models.

This is our opinionated suggestion, which has to be adapted to the reality on the ground, especially regarding the size of the tables, as tests on large tables might become very resource-intensive. Review the tests and remove and add as you see fit, then confirm everything works with another build of the pipeline:

```
dbt build -s +VER_IB_TRADES
```

In a few seconds, you have rebuilt all models and run all tests while keeping the history safe. You can now write a SQL query in Snowflake to inspect the results of the pipeline by querying the VER_IB_TRADES view. A query like the following shows how the raw data has been transformed into a clean, well-structured, and auditable history.

```
SELECT * FROM VER_IB_TRADES
ORDER BY ACCOUNT_ALIAS, SECURITY_SYMBOL, EFFECTIVITY_DATE
```

This simple query provides an overview of the trades on the two accounts and the four stocks for which we have data in the sample project. There are many columns, so you might want to pick a few to make more sense of the data. Besides the data about the transactions, you will see many columns created in the pipeline, like the HKEY and HDIFF values, as well as the added VALID_FROM and VALID_TO columns that define the life cycle of each record.

Releasing the code

We are now done with the pipeline for this entity, and you can open a Pull Request (PR) to have your colleagues review the code. If you followed our setup from the early chapters, you will notice that a Continuous Integration (CI) build is automagically started a few seconds after opening the PR.

That will be your first line of defense against trouble as your code runs. The second line of defense is your colleagues' eyes. Review their feedback and adapt the code accordingly. Once you complete the PR, the code will be in your QA environment, available for eventual user acceptance testing and ready to be released to production.

Storage layer for the other simple entities

The core advantage of the Pragmatic Data Platform's architecture becomes evident when you apply its patterns repeatedly. The process of building the storage layer for new entities is streamlined and predictable. Once the initial infrastructure is in place, creating the models for other simple entities is a matter of applying the same, repeatable playbook from STG to HIST to VER.

The efficiency of this process is a direct result of the modular design and the automation provided by the PDP macros and helper SQL queries, which avoid unnecessary typing. You have completed the implementation of the storage layer for our first entity. The pattern is now set, and you are ready to apply this same, repeatable process to the other entities in our project.

Cash transactions

Modeling the CASH_TRANSACTIONS entity follows the same pattern as the TRADES entity. It begins with the declaration of the source and its data tests. In this case, we check for null values and validate that the ingested files are present and in the correct order.

```
  - name: CASH_TRANSACTIONS
    description: Cash Transactions on IB accounts

    columns:
      - name: CLIENTACCOUNTID
        description: The unique ID of a client account.
        data_tests:
          - not_null
      - name: FROM_FILE
        data_tests:
          - not_null
          - pragmatic_data.all_files_from_stage:
              ...
          - pragmatic_data.file_order_is_correct
```

As you can see, the definition is almost the same as the one we used for the Trades entity.

From this point, the process is a simple loop: a STG model is created using the `stage` macro to select, rename, cast columns, and calculate the HKEY and HDIFF. An incremental HIST model is built using a historization macro to store all new, unique versions of a cash transaction. A VER view is created using the versioning macro to provide a clean, user-friendly view with VALID_FROM, VALID_TO, and IS_CURRENT flag.

This showcases the power of the pattern. You don't need to reinvent the wheel for each new dataset; you simply apply the same tested and proven methodology. We suggest that you either duplicate the models from the Trades entity or start from the generic templates and code your models, then compare them with our code in the sample project. You can make a branch with a PR and release for each entity, but, as you will see, the process is so swift that it also makes sense to have a branch running across multiple, if not all entities.

Corporate actions

The CORPORATE_ACTIONS entity presents a slight but pragmatic variation. Because this is a small, manually maintained dataset, we won't load it from an external source. Instead, we are managing it as a dbt seed. This is a perfect use case for seeds, which provide a simple, version-controlled way to manage lookup tables and other small, static datasets directly within your dbt project.

Despite the different ingestion method, the subsequent steps remain identical. The seed file, once loaded into Snowflake, acts as the raw data source. From there, we proceed with the standard STG, HIST, and VER pattern. You can reference the seed table with the `ref()` function, so you will define the source of your STG model using the `ref()` function in place of the `source()` function.

```
{%- set source_model = ref('ib_corp_act_manual') %}
```

While you could define a source on the seed, there is little benefit, unless you see the seed as a temporary source that will be replaced by some ingestion in the future. This demonstrates the flexibility of the PDP. Regardless of whether data enters the platform via automated ingestion pipelines or a simple dbt seed, the storage layer provides a consistent and robust framework for historizing and versioning it. It also provides a simple way to start with a seed and evolve into a landing table.

Transfers

In Chapter 9, the implementation of the ingestion layer for the TRANSFERS entity was assigned as an exercise. Now, you can complete the data journey for this entity by applying the same storage layer pattern we just saw. The process for TRANSFERS is identical to that for the TRADES and CASH_TRANSACTIONS entities.

Start with a source declaration, then create the STG, HIST, and VER models in sequence, using the PDP macros and SQL helpers to handle the heavy lifting of hashing, historization, and versioning. By now, this pattern should feel familiar and efficient. Once you are done with these three entities, create a PR, check that the CI passes, handle the review, and finally, you have completed another release to your QA environment.

Let's move to the pipeline for the Security entity, where we will start using new tools to handle differences in granularity and to factor common metadata into YAML files.

The security embedded entity

Not all entities reside cleanly in a single source and it is common for end-user exports to be wide reports with multiple entities. Our Security entity, as an example, is embedded within multiple exports (TRADES, OPEN_POSITIONS, TRANSFERS, and CORPORATE_ACTIONS).

Each of these sources may contain slightly different information about the same security, as they provide snapshots of the Security data at the time the export was produced, and they follow different timelines and granularities: a new trade or position doesn't necessarily mean the security's attributes have changed, and even if a trade did not change a new export will use the latest security data, that might be different from when the trade was done.

To ensure the accuracy and auditability of our data, the Pragmatic Data Platform handles this complexity with a straightforward, source-agnostic approach. Instead of a single messy pipeline, we create independent, parallel pipelines, one for each source, to extract and historize the Security information. You have already seen how quick is to create a pipeline in the PDP. Factoring the definitions into a YAML file will make creating these four pipelines very efficient. This guarantees that we capture every piece of information about a security as it arrives, without mixing data from different origins. The decision on how to reconcile these separate historical records is a business rule, and we will handle it later in the Refined layer.

If you don't need a precise history for an embedded entity, you can historicize them inside the main entity they come along with, and extract them -usually only the current version- in the refined layer. This is what we will do with the Portfolios.

Factoring definitions with shared YAML

To avoid code duplication and maintain consistency across the four pipelines, we define all shared definitions in a central YAML file, `ib_security.yml`, under the fictional entity `ABSTRACT_IB_SECURITY`. This file uses YAML anchors and aliases to create reusable blocks of code for column definitions, data tests, hashed columns, and any other definition you need.

The following sample shows how we can define YAML anchors with the `&` symbol and reuse them later with the `*` symbol to partially or totally define model attributes. The STG model for the TRADES source simply references the shared YAML blocks using `*`, with the same-named definitions defined with `&`. This approach ensures that any change to the Security entity's definition (e.g., adding a new column to the hash) is applied consistently across all four pipelines by updating a single file.

The `<<:` symbol is used inside the STG models to blend a code `&` definition with some locally defined extra columns or overrides of columns from the YAML anchor. You can look at the full YAML file and its use in the sample project. Blending and overriding work only for objects (dictionaries), not lists.

```
version: 2
models:

  - name: ABSTRACT_IB_SECURITY
    config:

      source_columns: &security_source_columns
        #... list of all relevant security columns...
        - Conid
        - SecurityID
        - ListingExchange
        - Symbol

      calculated_columns: &security_calculated_columns
        - BROKER_CODE: '!IB'
        - SECURITY_CODE: coalesce(SECURITYID, CONID)
        - LISTING_EXCHANGE: LISTINGEXCHANGE
        #... other calculated security columns...

      hashed_columns: &security_hashed_columns
        SECURITY_HKEY:
          - BROKER_CODE
          - SECURITY_CODE
          - LISTING_EXCHANGE

        SECURITY_HDIFF:
          - CURRENCY_PRIMARY
          - SECURITY_SYMBOL
          - SECURITY_NAME
          - ASSET_CLASS
          #... all other relevant columns...

  - name: STG_IB_TRADES_SECURITY
    config:
      calculated_columns: *security_calculated_columns
      hashed_columns:     *security_hashed_columns
      default_records:    *security_default_records

    columns: *security_stg_column_tests     # tests
```

The security pipeline from the TRADES source

This is the most complex of the four Security pipelines because a TRADES file can contain multiple, redundant entries for the same security. Even a single order may execute as several trades on the same stock throughout the same day, and the security's attributes (like its name or ticker) are captured at every execution, potentially with some differences. This effect is increased by multiple orders executed and reported across multiple portfolios.

Furthermore, when we export the Trades, the IB system exports historical trades from some arbitrary time with the new version of a Security, changing the overall export record relative to what we have in the LT, even if the Trade itself is not changed. This is a classic example of different timelines across the different granularities in the source data and the entity we want to historize, complicated by an unfavorable decision about how the data is exported. To address this mismatch between the source files and the historization, we introduce a new model, the DELTA model, into our pipeline between the STG and HIST models. Its role is to capture only the changes in the secondary entity.

Step 1: Staging the embedded entity

The first step is to create an STG model that extracts the Security attributes from the TRADES source and prepares them, as we did for the Trade entity. We are reading from the same source, the Trades Landing Table. What is different in this STG model is that we define the keys and we keep only the columns we need for the Security entity.

```
{%- set source_model = source('IB', 'TRADES') %}

{%- set configuration -%}

source:
  columns:
    include_all: false
  where: STARTSWITH(CLIENTACCOUNTID, 'U')

calculated_columns:
  <<: {{ config.get('calculated_columns') }}
  EFFECTIVITY_DATE: DateTime:TIMESTAMP_NTZ
  Transaction_ID: TransactionID

hashed_columns:
  <<: {{ config.get('hashed_columns') }}
  TRADE_HKEY:
    - Transaction_ID

default_records: {{ config.get('default_records') }}

remove_duplicates:

{%- endset -%}

{%- set cfg = fromyaml(configuration) -%}

{{ pragmatic_data.stage(
    source_model               = source_model,
    source                     = cfg['source'],
    calculated_columns         = cfg['calculated_columns'],
    hashed_columns             = cfg['hashed_columns'],
    default_records            = cfg['default_records'],
    remove_duplicates          = cfg['remove_duplicates']
) }}
```

This STG model, STG_IB_TRADES_SECURITY, is similar to the STG_IB_TRADES model, but serves a different purpose. Instead of preparing the Trade entity, it extracts and prepares the SECURITY entity embedded inside the TRADES. In this model, you can also see some advanced use of the dbt `config()` function that allows you to add metadata in a YAML file under the `config` attribute and use it inside your dbt model. Config will provide the data as a Python dictionary.

This, combined with YAML's own support for anchors and redefining attributes, allows us to define the `calculated_columns` and `hashed_columns` blocks using most of the data from the config, while locally redefining or adding only the attributes we need. Besides the advanced use of the `config()` function and YAML anchors to import shared definitions, the STG model is just a perfectly normal STG model. We must admit that, with the added indirection, the model is less readable than usual, requiring us to look up definitions in the YAML file, but it saves us a lot of effort and improves the project's maintainability by managing related information only once, in a shared location.

Step 2: Creating a DELTA model

The DELTA model is a crucial step in extracting Security info from the TRADES and OPEN_POSITIONS sources, as they have a different granularity and hence a different timeline than Securities.

Historization is about sorting versions on a timeline and recognizing changes. If we had only a single-grain difference, we might be able to use the rows of the Trades source and apply some sort of method to recognize changes in the Security versions. With two grain differences, it is impossible to put versions in the right order just by sorting. That is why we need **the DELTA model: it will provide only the real changes for the entity we are interested in**. This, in turn, allows us to align Security changes with our desired timeline, despite the grain difference.

We continue using the usual STG model features to prepare the data for the Security entity. We use the DELTA model as a filter, placed downstream of the STG model, to let only true changes in SECURITY_HDIFF to pass through. The DELTA model compares the SECURITY_HDIFF of one Trade with the previous HDIFF for the same TRADE_HKEY, sorted by source file (following our technical timeline), and retains only the actual changes in the Security entity. This ensures we don't create unnecessary historical versions for security that haven't actually changed.

```
WITH
tx_changes as (

   SELECT *

       , LAG(SECURITY_HDIFF)
           OVER(PARTITION BY TRADE_HKEY ORDER BY RECORD_SOURCE)
         as PREV_HDIFF__TX

       , CASE
             WHEN PREV_HDIFF__TX is null THEN true    -- first record
             ELSE (SECURITY_HDIFF != PREV_HDIFF__TX)
         END as CHANGE_IN_TX

   FROM {{ ref('STG_IB_TRADES_SECURITY') }}
   QUALIFY CHANGE_IN_TX
)

SELECT * EXCLUDE(PREV_HDIFF__TX, CHANGE_IN_TX)
FROM tx_changes
ORDER BY RECORD_SOURCE, TRANSACTION_ID
```

The SQL of the DELTA model uses a Window Function (LAG) to look at the previous record's hash and a QUALIFY clause to keep only the rows where the hash has changed. The output of this model is the same as the STG model, reduced to security versions with actual changes, ready for historization.

Steps three and 4: Historization and versioning

The final two steps, historization and versioning, are now identical to those for our simple entities. The only difference is that we pass the DELTA model name to the historization model rather than the STG model name. This is the HIST_IB_TRADES_SECURITY.sql model:

```
{{ config( materialized='incremental') }}

{{ pragmatic_data.save_history_with_multiple_versions(
    input_rel    = ref('DELTA_IB_TRADES_SECURITY'),
    key_column   = 'SECURITY_HKEY',
    diff_column = 'SECURITY_HDIFF',

    sort_expr    = 'RECORD_SOURCE, TRANSACTION_ID',
) }}
```

You can see that our sorting expression uses the `RECORD_SOURCE` column, which contains the source file names, and is equivalent to sorting entries by export date, which is the timeline over which the Security changes, even though the Trade and its columns do not. That is why the Trade `EFFECTIVITY_DATE`, aka execution time, is not a good sort for historization of Securities.

This is the VER_IB_TRADES_SECURITY.sql model:

```
{{ pragmatic_data.versions_from_history_with_multiple_versions(

    history_rel = ref('HIST_IB_TRADES_SECURITY'),
    key_column  = 'SECURITY_HKEY',
    diff_column = 'SECURITY_HDIFF',

    version_sort_column      = 'EFFECTIVITY_DATE'
) }}
```

Once we have correctly historicized the Security versions, we can use the Trade `EFFECTIVITY_DATE`, even if not perfect, to sort the changes we have historicized. The ideal situation would be to have a proper `EFFECTIVITY_DATE` for the Security itself. Still, in our export files, there is no better date between the extracted payload and the metadata the pipeline builds.

When we do not control the export logic, we often find ourselves in situations where we do not have a perfect value that represents what we want. It is not perfect, but we can often find a solution that is "good enough" to provide usable data for our analyses.

With some care, we have built the HIST model that incrementally stores unique changes, and the VER view that adds extra metadata, including the **SCD_Key**, which is important for the security dimension, creating a usable **Type 2** Slowly Changing Dimension.

The other security pipelines

The process for the Security entity from the **OPEN_POSITIONS** source is identical to the one described above, as it also requires a DELTA model. For the **TRANSFERS** and **CORPORATE_ACTIONS** sources, the data is small and simple enough that a DELTA model is not necessary, as we can find a good sort for our Security changes, allowing us to feed the STG model directly into the HIST model.

If you are wondering "how can I figure out when I need a DELTA model"... the answer is: "you generally don't". It is the pipeline itself, through failing tests, that will tell you that the historization has duplicates, and by analyzing why you get them, you will notice that you cannot find a good sort of the full STG model and you need to put in place a DELTA model to keep only the real changes.

The full code for all four pipelines can be found in the sample project, in the `01_storage/interactive_brokers/security` folder.

The open position source and position entities

The OPEN_POSITIONS source presents two key challenges that require us to complement our standard STG model with an ad hoc model to build a unified STG for the entity we want to store, before applying our three-step STG-HIST-VER pattern. First, the source data only contains positions that are currently open, leaving a critical gap in our portfolio history. Second, a single record in the OPEN_POSITIONS file contains both the position itself (e.g., 500 shares of APPL) and its daily valuation (e.g., last close price), which changes daily and would create an artificial stream of historical versions.

We will address these complexities with our usual approach of historizing each entity independently, preserving the integrity of its historical records while maintaining a modular and auditable process. First we will discuss how to correctly historize all positions, opened and closed ones, and then how we store as a separate entity the daily position values.

Modeling open and closed positions

The OPEN_POSITIONS source, as its name suggests, does not contain positions that have been closed. If we only historicize open positions, a sold position will appear to remain open forever in our data platform, making all our calculations wrong. To create a complete and accurate representation of our portfolio, we must recognize and correctly account for these closed positions.

We start by creating the `STG_IB_OPEN_POSITIONS` model using our standard approach, defining the HKEY and HDIFF and passing them to the `stage` macro. This handles the initial cleaning and preparation of the raw data for all **open positions**.

To handle closed positions whose records are not explicitly present in the source, we could use a historization macro-deletion detection pattern. However, this pattern is less suitable here because it relies on storing a single version for each historization round. In this project, we want to retain the ability to ingest long historical periods with multiple changes in a single step. We will model closed positions as a separate entity derived from the same source. We will then union open and closed positions and continue as usual with HIST and VER.

We create a custom `STG_IB_CLOSED_POSITIONS` model that identifies positions that appear in one daily file but are absent in the next. This model uses a SQL query to find the last record for a given position and infers its closing based on its absence in the subsequent day's report. This provides a clear, auditable trail of how we determine a position's closure and fits neatly into our existing modular framework. The `STG_IB_CLOSED_POSITIONS` model's logic leverages the existing STG model for the open positions to handle data preparation, so we don't need to rebuild the core staging logic. It is a prime example of reusing and extending existing code.

Let's look at this manual STG model. Before we start with the SQL, we define two Jina variables: one with the columns for the HDIFF, and one with the source of our data, that is, the STG model for the open positions.

```
{% set position_hdiff_columns %}
... list of columns in the HDIFF
{% endset %}

{% set stg_open_positions = ref('STG_IB_OPEN_POSITIONS') %}
```

The first thing we do in SQL is to generate the list of dates for which we have reports.

```
WITH
report_dates as (
    SELECT distinct REPORT_DATE
    FROM {{ stg_open_positions }}
)
```

The core of the model joins the open position records with this list of report dates using the `ASOF JOIN` Snowflake construct to find the next export in the future (a report with a date greater than the one of the record being considered). If we have an export in the future providing a potential closing date and the next report date for the position is null, it means that the position does not exist in the next export, so it has been closed between its report date and the future report's date.

```
, positions_to_close as (
    SELECT p.*
        , LEAD(p.REPORT_DATE) OVER(PARTITION BY POSITION_HKEY ORDER BY
p.REPORT_DATE) as NEXT_REPORT_DATE
        , r.REPORT_DATE as CLOSING_DATE
    FROM {{ stg_open_positions }} p
    ASOF JOIN report_dates r
    MATCH_CONDITION( p.REPORT_DATE < r.REPORT_DATE)
    QUALIFY NEXT_REPORT_DATE is null
            and CLOSING_DATE is not null
)
```

Next, we set the correct column values for the closed positions identified in the previous CTE.

```
, src_data as (
    SELECT *
        EXCLUDE(NEXT_REPORT_DATE, CLOSING_DATE)
        REPLACE(
            CLOSING_DATE as REPORT_DATE,
            CLOSING_DATE as EFFECTIVITY_DATE,
            0 as QUANTITY,
            0 as OPEN_PRICE,
            0 as COST_BASIS_PRICE,
            0 as COST_BASIS_MONEY,
            'Closed' as SIDE,
            'System.Calculation' as RECORD_SOURCE,
            null as FILE_ROW_NUMBER,
            null as FILE_LAST_MODIFIED_TS_UTC,
            '{{ run_started_at }}':timestamp as INGESTION_TS_UTC
        )
    FROM positions_to_close
)
```

Lastly, we calculate the HDIFF using the updated values for the new closed position.

```
, hashed as (
    SELECT * REPLACE(
      {{ pragmatic_data.pdp_hash(
            fromyaml( position_hdiff_columns )) }}
      as POSITION_HDIFF
    )
    FROM src_data
)

SELECT * FROM hashed
```

You will find the full code, which includes the list of columns in the HDIFF, in the sample project.

For ease of reading, we define it at the top of the model, but we could have defined it as a config in the YAML file for the STG model for the open positions and then reused it here as a config for this model, as we did for many configs in the Security models.

This example shows how you can combine the ease of use of our automated STG model with the flexibility of manually coding a STG model to surface data that is only implied in the actual data that you receive from your sources. We are comfortable with having a model with some (heavy) logic in the storage layer, as this is not business logic but export technicalities, and it is not something that our business decisions can even change. The same goes for the values we set for the closed position.

Building a unified history for all positions

Now that we have separate STG models for both open and closed positions, we can unify them into a single `STG_IB_ALL_POSITIONS` model. This model will simply `UNION ALL` the two sources, ensuring we have a complete and comprehensive dataset before starting the historization process.

The SQL for this is straightforward:

```
SELECT * FROM {{ ref('STG_IB_OPEN_POSITIONS') }}
UNION ALL
SELECT * FROM {{ ref('STG_IB_CLOSED_POSITIONS') }}
```

From this unified STG model, we can apply our standard, repeatable pattern to create the final `HIST_IB_ALL_POSITIONS` and `VER_IB_ALL_POSITIONS` models. These will provide a complete history of our entire portfolio's positions. A separate, parallel flow will be created for the `POSITION_ DAILY_VALUES` entity, following the same methodology of unifying the open and closed values into a single `STG_IB_ALL_POSITIONS_DAILY_VALUES` model before historicizing and versioning. You can find the full code for both pipelines in the sample project.

Separating position and valuation

A single OPEN_POSITIONS record contains two distinct entities: the position (the number of shares, the security, and the account) and the daily valuation of the position (the market value, the FX rate, etc.). These two components have different update cadences. The position changes only when a trade occurs, but we receive valuation changes every day (with every export).

We could historicize the entire record on a daily basis, then create a filtered HIST view that shows only the true position changes, with a VER model on top. While this approach would require fewer models, it would also result in a much larger history table with substantial redundancy. More importantly, it would break our established pattern of separating concerns and historicizing entities at their most appropriate grain, a practice we have already seen with the Security entity. Instead, we prefer creating two independent pipelines from the same source:

- **Position Entity**: This pipeline historicizes only the position-related information. The HKEY is based on the account and security, and the HDIFF is a hash of the position-specific columns (e.g., QUANTITY).
- **Position Daily Value Entity**: This pipeline historicizes only the valuation-related information. It uses the same HKEY but a different HDIFF that includes the daily valuation columns (e.g., MARKET_VALUE_FX, LAST_CLOSE_PRICE).

This modular approach keeps our data clean, our history tables compact, and our process consistent.

Building the position daily value pipeline

In the previous sections, we have established the pipeline for the core Position entity. Now we can apply the same modular approach to its related data: the daily valuation. As we discussed, this information changes daily. It should be historized separately to avoid redundant storage and, most importantly, so that the versions in the position history actually reflect a fundamental change in the position.

The Position Daily Value pipeline will use the same position HKEY, but a different HDIFF definition, focusing on the valuation-specific fields. We will create a `STG_IB_ALL_POSITIONS_DAILY_VALUES` model by combining the daily values from the open and closed positions. The model will `UNION ALL` two sources:

- **The daily values for the open positions**: This is the straightforward part, as this is just another normal STG model on the OPEN_POSITIONS source. Here, we select the valuation-related columns, create a valuation-specific HDIFF, and pair them with the position's HKEY.
- **The daily values for closed positions:** The valuation data is not in the source, but it is straightforward since it is zero. So we can just identify closed positions using the `STG_IB_CLOSED_POSITIONS` model we discussed earlier and set their values to zero.

After this STG model with all the position values is created, the rest of the process is business as usual. We will build a `HIST_IB_ALL_POSITIONS_DAILY_VALUES` model using the `save_history_with_multiple_versions` macro to capture every daily change in the valuation of each position when open, and zeroing it out once closed. Finally, a `VER_IB_ALL_POSITIONS_DAILY_VALUES` view will provide current and historical snapshots, enabling precise point-in-time analysis of our portfolio's value over time. By keeping these two entities separate, Position and Position Daily Value, we ensure that our HIST tables remain clean and focused on their specific business concept.

This modularity not only simplifies the code but also makes the entire data platform easier to maintain and troubleshoot. As usual, you can find the full code for both pipelines in the sample project. As an exercise, you can try ingesting the full positions with the daily values, then extract the actual position changes from the daily valuation changes.

The final step: Pull request and release

You have now completed coding all Storage layer models for our sample project. The final step is to share your work with the rest of the team and prepare it for deployment to the QA and PROD environments. As discussed in Part 1, the Pragmatic Data Platform follows a structured, collaborative workflow. You should commit your changes, including all the new `STG`, `DELTA`, `HIST`, and `VER` models, as well as the updated YAML files.

Once committed, open a Pull Request (PR) in your version control system. This PR serves as a formal review, allowing other team members to check your code for consistency, quality, and adherence to the project's standards. You can also activate automated linting and code quality checks.

The first and any subsequent commit to the branch of the PR will automatically trigger your Continuous Integration (CI) pipeline, which will build and test the branch code. If all tests pass, you just need to wait for your colleague's reviews. If not, fix the failing tests and commit the fixes.

When the PR is approved, you should complete the PR, which will merge your changes into the main branch, and trigger the QA job that will release the new code to the QA environment, if you don't have a merge job that will do that automatically. With this process, you ensure that every change to the data platform is peer-reviewed, thoroughly tested, and deployed in a controlled, automated manner. This is the essence of a pragmatic, reliable data platform.

A quick recap of the steps:

- **Code Complete:** All models for the Storage layer are complete and have been tested locally.
- **Commit and Push:** Commit your final changes and push them to your branch.
- **Create PR:** Open a Pull Request for peer review of the code in your branch. This will trigger the CI pipeline to validate your code and confirm to you and your colleagues that it works.
- **Merge and Release:** Once approved, merge the PR, and trigger the QA build to release to QA.

After the QA environment has validated the new models and UAT is performed, it is a great time to perform a final production release. That is too a simple PR (to the PROD branch) followed by running a job, as explained in **Chapter 4, Agile Development**, under the "**Release management and branching strategy**" section.

This is the moment to celebrate your work! 🎉

Chapter review

In this chapter, we brought the Storage layer to life by implementing it for our sample project using dbt and Snowflake. We transformed raw data, ingested straight from the source files, into a clean, auditable, and usable historical record, following the principles of the Pragmatic Data Platform. We began with the straightforward, **four-step storage pattern** for simple entities like Trades, defining the source table and building a pipeline from `STG` to `HIST` to `VER` models. You learned how the STG model cleans and prepares data, the HIST model captures every change, and the VER view turns that history into a user-friendly resource with IS_CURRENT, VALID_FROM, and VALID_TO flags. We also saw how the SCD_Key can be used to link facts to a specific version of a dimension.

Next, we tackled more complex scenarios:

- **Embedded Entities:** We learned how to handle entities such as Security, which appear inside other sources. We created independent pipelines for each source providing Security data and used a DELTA model to correctly handle the change in data granularity.

- **Derived Entities:** For the Open Position source, we saw how to handle data that is implied, and not explicitly available in the source, the closed positions. We built separate STG models that were unified and fed a single pipeline to historicize both open and closed positions, creating a complete history for the Position entity.

- **Separating Entities:** We learned the importance of separating different concepts within a single source, such as the Position entity and its Position Daily Value, when they have different update speeds. We built two distinct pipelines, each with its own HDIFF definition, to keep our history tables focused and efficient.

By the end of this chapter, you should feel confident in your ability to apply these powerful and repeatable patterns to any data source, no matter how complex. This hands-on experience has prepared you for the next stage of our journey: the Refined layer, where we will start applying business logic.

Recommended resources

The major source of information for this chapter is the sample project, as explained at the start of the chapter, where all the source code for all the models is available. The following materials offer more information on the topics of this chapter.

dbt Packages

- Pragmatic Data Platform dbt package: https://github.com/pragmatic-data/pragmatic-data-platform.
- dbt_utils Package: https://hub.getdbt.com/dbt-labs/dbt_utils/latest/.

dbt documentation

- dbt Sources: https://docs.getdbt.com/docs/build/sources.
- dbt Data Tests: https://docs.getdbt.com/docs/build/data-tests.
- dbt incremental models: https://docs.getdbt.com/docs/build/incremental-models.

Snowflake documentation

- Snowflake Data Types: https://docs.snowflake.com/en/sql-reference/data-types.
- MD5 Hash Function: https://docs.snowflake.com/en/sql-reference/functions/md5.
- Window Functions: https://docs.snowflake.com/en/sql-reference/functions-analytic .

By the end of this chapter, you should feel confident in your ability to apply these powerful and repeatable patterns to any data source, no matter how complex. This hands-on experience has prepared you for the next stage of our journey: the Refined layer, where we will start applying business [illegible].

CHAPTER 12

The Refined Layer

Welcome to the business heart of the Pragmatic Data Platform: the **Refined Layer, where data turns into powerful information.** In the previous chapters, we focused on building a robust, auditable Storage Layer that serves as a faithful, immutable record of our source data. Now, we shift our focus from storing data to transforming it into valuable, reusable business information.

We cover the principles and patterns for building a clean, modular, and stateless Refined Layer. This is where we apply business logic, integrate data from multiple sources, and create the trusted business concepts that serve as the foundation for all downstream analytics. Unlike the highly structured, pattern-driven Storage Layer, the Refined Layer is where your organization's unique logic comes to life. Before diving into the data transformation, we will first establish a solid structure for our project folders and files, and detail how to configure dbt to manage schemas and materializations effectively, using principles from Domain-Driven Design (DDD). We will then explore how to handle the complexities of historical data, how to bridge different domains with Master Data Management (MDM), and use the powerful features of dbt Mesh, such as contracts and model versioning, that enable us to build a scalable and maintainable data platform that is ready to evolve into a Data Mesh. By the end of this chapter, you will have a clear framework for designing and implementing a Refined Layer that is both powerful and pragmatic, setting you up for success in the final Delivery Layer. The topics that we are going to cover in this chapter are:

- **Goals and contents of the refined layer**: The purpose of the Refined Layer, explaining its role as the stateless, business-oriented bridge between raw storage and final delivery.
- **Structuring and Configuring the Refined Layer**: structure, conventions and configs.
- **Handling Historical vs. Current Data**: historical versus current data and time-aware joins.
- **Domain-Driven Data Design and Master Data Management**.
- **Data Mesh with dbt Mesh**: dbt Mesh features, data contracts, model versioning and patterns to manage platform complexity and build reliable data products.
- **Testing business rules**: data quality by validation of business rules and transformations.

Sample project and code

The sample dbt project is available at: **https://github.com/pragmatic-data/stonks**. The code samples for this chapter are in the sub-folder `chapter_12`, under the `code_samples_by_chapter` folder. Please note that, to better fit the limited space on the printed page, we omit most comments and change the formatting of code blocks compared to the files.

The refined layer in customer cases

The Refined Layer is the data platform's intellectual core, where raw and cleaned data are transformed into coherent, reusable business concepts. The cases of Lindex, OutSystems, and Metso demonstrate that a well-architected Refined Layer is not just about transformation; it's about liberation, governance at scale, and massive cost savings. These real-world examples provide the practical grounding for the principles and patterns we will explore in detail in this chapter.

The complete case studies for Lindex, OutSystems, and Metso are in Chapter 6.

- **Lindex**: Moved from rigid Informatica/Oracle ETL to dbt models. The team replaced hand-built marts with reusable domain concepts, cutting time-to-change from weeks to hours and letting business teams drive refinements.
- **OutSystems**: Serves 700+ BI users who expect the same numbers everywhere. They defined canonical "gold" models and enforced them with tests and CI, which stopped report drift and made changes predictable.
- **Metso**: Consolidated fragmented Databricks logic into a governed, refined layer. Standard patterns removed duplicate pipelines across sites and saved roughly €200–300k per asset in maintenance while keeping analytics consistent.

Goals and contents of the refined layer

The Refined Layer is the business core of the data platform. It is where raw, source-aligned data from the Storage Layer is transformed into valuable, trusted, and reusable business information.

While the Storage Layer focuses on faithfully capturing and historizing what the source systems provide, the Refined Layer's purpose is to apply business logic, integrate disparate sources, and model data in a way that reflects how the business thinks about its own operations.

This is the primary transformation stage, where the heavy lifting of turning data into meaningful, query-ready business concepts occurs. The models built here serve as a stable foundation for all downstream use cases, whether for reporting, advanced analytics, or operational applications.

Architectural role

Architecturally, the Refined Layer acts as the stateless, logical bridge between the immutable Storage Layer and the use-case-specific Delivery Layer. Its position is strategic, designed to decouple the complexities of source systems from the specific needs of data consumers. As shown in the PDP architecture in Chapter 1, the platform's essential state—the complete and auditable history of source data—is confined to the Storage Layer. The Refined Layer reads from this stable foundation and produces its outputs. Because it is logically stateless, this entire layer can be rebuilt from scratch at any time by re-running the dbt models, with incremental models used only when needed to improve performance. This statelessness is a core tenet of the PDP, providing immense agility and resilience. It allows developers to modify business rules, fix bugs, or add new enrichments, and to apply these changes across the entire historical dataset without complex, slow, and risky backfilling operations.

Key characteristics

To fulfill its architectural role effectively, the models within the Refined Layer adhere to a set of key characteristics that ensure they are maintainable, understandable, and scalable.

Key principles

The refined layer is where business rules are applied and where data from different sources is integrated to build the business-centric concepts ready for consumption by downstream layers and applications. The refined layer is where most of the data platform's development effort is focused, making the application of software engineering principles crucial to success. Adhering to the following principles ensures that the code powering your business concepts remains clean, easy to understand, and resilient to the inevitable changes driven by evolving business needs or new data sources.

- The **Single-Responsibility Principle** (**SRP**) principle, in the context of building a data platform, means that each model or CTE should have a single, well-defined purpose, focusing on doing one thing well. For example, you follow this by avoiding complex queries that try to do everything at once. A model with a single responsibility is easier to understand, test, and maintain, and it's less likely to break when changes are made elsewhere in the project.
- **Least Surprise Principle** (**LSP**): It suggests that a model should behave as its name and position in the project would suggest. A user should be able to rely on a model's name to understand its function without being surprised by unexpected behavior. For example, a model named `REF_MONTHLY_SALES` should focus on sales aggregation rather than perform complex customer segmentation, which would be surprising to a user and also violate the single responsibility principle.
- **Modularity**: This is a fundamental principle of dbt and the PDP, particularly in the refined layer. It involves breaking down complex transformations into smaller, reusable, and testable components. This approach prevents loops in the data lineage, forbidden by dbt, and enables the creation of idempotent models that can be rebuilt at any time without issues. The use of clear naming conventions and the organization of models by business concepts further enhances modularity and readability.

This approach minimizes rework and helps keep the data platform manageable and accessible to all team members.

Stateless by Design

The models in the Refined Layer are designed to be idempotent, meaning their correctness does not depend on the state of the tables before a run. They are stateless by design. While incremental models may be used as performance optimization, they are a tactical choice for very large datasets, not a common necessity. The underlying logic must always support a full refresh from the Storage Layer, allowing the entire layer to be recreated at will. This design philosophy provides several benefits:

- **Agility**: Changes to business logic can be applied to all historical data simply by re-running the models. This also makes it very easy to apply historical rules to historical data and new rules to new data, as needed by your business.
- **Maintainability**: Debugging becomes simpler, as developers can isolate issues to a specific transformation without worrying about the accumulated historical state. It also makes it easy to apply unit tests to complex business rules, where needed.
- **Resilience**: In the event of data corruption or errors, the entire layer can be dropped and rebuilt from the trusted Storage Layer, ensuring a clean recovery.

Not having to manage the state in the Refined layer allows your team to concentrate on writing correct business rules and checking them thoroughly, providing trusted data to your business, reducing rework, and the maintenance baseline after every iteration, as discussed in the article "The economy of modern data warehousing" in the Pragmatic Data blog (see Recommended resources section).

Business-Oriented

The Refined Layer marks a key shift in perspective from source-oriented to business-oriented modeling. Models in the Storage Layer retain names and structures close to their origin; models in the Refined Layer must adopt the **ubiquitous language of the business**.

Column and model names should reflect established business terminology, not technical jargon from source systems. Care should be taken to build models that align with the domain's business concepts, so that both naming and business rules have a natural home and changes are applied only to the concepts involved. For example, in our sample project, data from multiple TX tables, including manual and rule-generated transactions, would be integrated into a single, consistently named `ref_position_transactions` model, with general business rules applied to it, while specific rules are applied to the models feeding into it. This Modular approach is a core tenet of dbt and the Pragmatic Data Platform. This practice is important for several reasons:

- **Consistency**: It ensures that a single concept, such as "customer" or "revenue," is consistently named and defined across the entire platform, reducing ambiguity and errors. Everybody can reuse these models, saving time and complexity.
- **Clarity**: Clear names, specific business rules, and precise documentation make the data understandable to a wider audience, including other developers, analysts, and stakeholders.
- **Collaboration**: It fosters better collaboration between technical and business teams, as everyone is speaking the same language.

The refined layer is where key software engineering principles, like the Single-Responsibility Principle (SRP) and the Least Surprise Principle (LSP), are used to keep complexity in check and achieve widespread code reuse, better code quality, and lower maintenance footprint.

Integrated and reusable

The Refined Layer is where the "single source of truth" for business entities is created. Data from various source systems, each with its own quirks and identifiers, is combined, cleansed, and conformed into a single, authoritative model for each business concept. For example, in the STONKS project, the `ref_securities_merged` model integrates security information from Trades, OpenPositions, and other sources. Each source might provide slightly different or updated information on the same security. The `ref_securities_merged` model resolves these differences to create one golden record for each security.

Once these integrated, reusable models are built, they become the definitive building blocks for the rest of the data platform. Any downstream model that needs information about customers, products, or securities should use the corresponding refined model, ensuring that all analytics are derived from a single, trusted, and consistent source. This modular approach prevents the proliferation of redundant transformation logic and is fundamental to building a scalable and maintainable platform.

Structuring and configuring the refined layer

A well-organized Refined Layer is the key to a scalable, maintainable, and collaborative data platform. While the Storage Layer is highly standardized, the Refined Layer requires a deliberate structure to manage complexity. A clear organization ensures that developers can easily find, understand, and reuse models, preventing the project from becoming an unmanageable "spaghetti code".

This section provides a pragmatic blueprint for organizing your dbt project's files and folders and configuring `dbt_project.yml` to enforce this structure. By following these conventions, you apply best practices and software engineering principles, making your platform more robust and easier for your team to work with.

Folder and model organization by domain

The most effective way to structure the Refined Layer is to organize it around business domains, a core concept of **Domain-Driven Design (DDD)**. Instead of a flat list of models, we group them into folders that represent distinct business areas.

Folder Structure

All models for this layer should reside under a main `02_refined` directory. The `02_` prefix reinforces the data flow of the PDP architecture, making the layered structure immediately obvious. Within this directory, we create subfolders for each business domain:

```
models/
└── 02_refined/
    ├── finance/
    ├── marketing/
    ├── operations/
    └── master_data/
```

This structure promotes modularity and clear ownership. The finance team can primarily work within their folder but can also easily discover and use models from the marketing domain, fostering cross-functional collaboration. This, together with the group feature in dbt Mesh that we will see later, can be very powerful for promoting model sharing in a safe, governed way. Of course, multiple layers of folders are possible, and general-purpose or common domains are also common and very useful, including a `master_data` one.

If your business rules are complex and even more so if you are also building operational reporting for your sources, it is common to also have source-oriented domains, where data is progressively refined in the scope of one or a few closely knitted sources, but is not yet converted to master data codes and therefore not yet globally usable. The same often happens with geographical domains: different countries use different tools, and to bring the business concepts to a comparable level, it is first required a local step of integration, followed by master data and global business rules. While we cannot offer a general organization that works for all cases, we encourage you to adopt the one that feels right for your case and make it as self-evident as possible, using longer, clear names and, eventually, domain prefixes.

Model Naming Conventions

To ensure models are self-documenting and predictable, we use a consistent naming convention that gives model names this format: `PREFIX_DOMAIN__ENTITY.sql`. This pattern immediately communicates a model's role, the business domain it belongs to, and the entity it represents. For example, a model named `ref_finance__monthly_revenue.sql` clearly indicates it's a refined, reusable model (`ref_`) in the finance domain (`finance__`) representing the monthly revenue business concept (`monthly_revenue`).

As we said, for folders, your mileage might vary, and we encourage you to find the best yet simplest structure that works for your case. Adding a geographical or organizational part, along with standard or shortened domain names, is a common variation on this structure.

Prefixes Defining Model Roles

The prefix is a critical part of the naming convention, as it defines the model's role.

The Pragmatic Data Platform uses a standardized set of prefixes, many of which were introduced in the previous book. You are welcome to pick the ones you want to use, add your own, or change our prefixes, as long as it's all clear to your teams. The following list describes the standardized prefixes used across the Pragmatic Data Platform. For completeness, we also include those for the Storage and Delivery layers. As you already know some names, you may appreciate how they make the code clear.

Storage Layer Prefixes

These models are source-oriented and form the foundation of the platform. They reside in the `01_storage` folder and its sub-folders:

- **`stg_` (Staging)**: The first transformation step after ingestion. Its role is to adapt source data by cleaning, renaming, casting data types, and calculating keys (HKEY, HDIFF) for historization. It makes data usable without altering its business meaning.

- **`hist_` (History)**: An incremental model that stores every version of an entity, creating a complete and auditable historical record. It is the core of the PDP.
- **`ver_` (Version)**: A view built on a `hist_` table that simplifies access to historical data by adding metadata columns like `IS_CURRENT`, `VALID_FROM`, `VALID_TO`, and the version-specific key `SCD_KEY`.
- **`delta_` (Delta)**: A specialized intermediate model used to isolate true changes (deltas) in an embedded entity, when the source changes do not align with the entity's change frequency, as seen with Security in our stonks project.
- **`pii_` model**: The role of this highly specialized model is to store the actual **P**ersonally Identifiable Information (PII) data apart from the normal history so that it can be used in the delivery layer where needed, only for authorized people and while still available (think of, for example, the GDPR right to be forgotten). See the section "A pragmatic PII framework" in Chapter 2.

Refined Layer Prefixes

These models are business-oriented and are where most business logic is implemented. They reside in the `02_refined` folder:

- **`ref_` (Refined)**: A core, reusable business concept that has been cleaned, integrated, and is ready for consumption. Represent the current state of an entity (e.g., `ref_customers`) with all its attributes.
- **`refh_` (Refined History)**: This prefix is used for models that expose the full, versioned history of a business concept. Used for SCD2 dimensions, point-in-time analysis, and auditing (`refh_customer_address`).
- **`ts_` (Time Series)**: A time series, typically a fact table where there is a single value for each time interval (e.g., `ts_daily_exchange_rates`). If the HKEY includes the time interval, it is equivalent to a REF model; otherwise, it is equivalent to a REFH model, with some work to pick one entry per interval.
- **`int_` (Intermediate)**: This prefix, short for "intermediate," designates a model that serves as a stepping-stone in a more complex transformation. It is not intended for direct consumption outside its specific data flow and can be considered a "private" building block. This convention is an alternative to other prefixes such as `tr_` (transformation), `tmp_` (temporary), `prv_` or `pvt_` (private) to provide a standard term used also by dbt Labs.
- **`agg_/aggh_` (Aggregated)**: An aggregated model that summarizes data from another model (usually `ref_` or `refh_`). Often created for performance reasons or to simplify analysis at a higher level (e.g., `agg_daily_sales`).
- **`map_` (Mapping)**: A model that serves as a mapping table, typically used in Master Data Management to bridge keys between different source systems (e.g., `map_crm_customer_to_erp_customer`).
- **`mdd_` (Master Data Dimension)**: A dimension that represents the "golden record" for a core business entity: Same as REF but sourced from an official MDM system. In the previous book, this was referred to as MDM, but has been updated to MDD to avoid ambiguity with the broader concept of MDM.

- **`pivot_` (Pivot)**: A specialized model where data has been pivoted from a row-based format to a column-based format for specific analytical needs. The opposite `unpivot_` is also possible, yet less frequent.
- **`brg_` (Bridge)**: A bridge table is used to resolve many-to-many relationships between two or more entities. A common pattern, but most of the time, we use a `REF` prefix with the name of the "bridging" concept (e.g., `REF_SHIFTS`).
- **`spine_` (Spine)**: A spine model is often used as a base scaffold to ensure all entities are represented in a dataset, even if they have no activity. A common example is a date spine that contains every single day, which can be joined against to fill gaps in time-series data.

Compared to the previous book we have dropped the use of the **`curr_` (Current)** prefix because now we have the VER models that make trivial to get only the current data, so we do not need an extra model for that operation, and because the introduction of the REF and REFH prefixes has given us a good way to label current versus historical models.

Delivery layer prefixes

These models are tailored for specific end-user consumption and reside in the `03_delivery/marts` folder:

- **`dim_` (Dimension)**: This prefix explicitly identifies a Kimball-style dimension table, which contains selected descriptive attributes of a business entity. By convention, `dim_` represents a Type 1 (SCD1) dimension that contains only the current version. Comes from a REF or MDD model in the Refined Layer, selecting the necessary columns, with possible filtering.
- **`scd_` (Dimension History)**: A Type 2 (SCD2) dimension table with selected attributes for all the versions of the entities. Includes a version-specific key (SCD_KEY) along with the entity primary key (HKEY). Sometimes `dimh_`, `dim2_` (dimension Type 2) or `scd2_` are also used as a prefix with the same meaning. Pick one and be consistent!
- **`fct_/fact_` (Fact)**: A Kimball-style fact table, which contains business events, measurements, and foreign keys to dimension tables (HKEY and eventually SCD_KEY to use SCD2 dimensions). Usually derived from a REF model, as you (almost) always want only the current version in the fact table.
- **`filter_` (Filter)**: A model used to define a business-specific cohort or filter that can be applied to other models within a data mart (e.g., a list of high-value customers or groupings of zip codes). A specialized model whose role is to make it extremely clear how one or more facts/dims are filtered based on requirements that exist only in the specific data mart where the filter model lives. If for general use, move it to the REF layer. The use of such a model serves two main purposes. The first is to modularize the code and improve the filtering's visibility, providing an independent DB object that can be used in reporting tools. The second purpose is to make the maintenance of the filtering logic simple and explicit. This is even more important when the filter is applied to more than just one object in the same data mart, as you want to keep them aligned.
- **`report_` (Report)**: A single model used to deliver wide tables that can power a report or an AI/ML use case (feature tables), or a good way to provide explicit and validated composite facts (when multiple facts are joined) for use in a single data mart. A wide table is a pre-joined subset of a data mart in which the (composite) fact is already joined to all required dimensions. This is less efficient for storage, but much more efficient for querying, so it can pay off when you build once and query many times. Generally, it is

not used in Kimball-style data marts unless you use it to highlight a local composite fact; it can live alongside facts and dimensions for use with other tools or just to exchange disk space for performance.

You can use the prefixes for models and CTEs in any layer, but most prefixes just make sense in their layer, with the refined layer offering the greatest variation in your code, and prefixes to label a wide range of roles. The roles and operations needed in the other layers are pretty much standardized.

Configurations in dbt_project.yml

The `dbt_project.yml` file is the main configuration file of our dbt project, where we enforce our structural decisions through code. By configuring models at the folder level, using the hierarchical folder structure, we can set consistent behaviors for each domain and layer with minimal effort.

Schema and Materialization Configuration

The Pragmatic Data Platform advocates for a "view by default, table for performance" strategy. We set this as the default for the entire Refined Layer, then override it for specific models that are either computationally expensive or frequently queried, such as those in the `master_data` folder.

To ensure logical separation and better governance, each domain in the Refined Layer should be deployed to its own schema in Snowflake. This is easily configured in `dbt_project.yml`:

```
models:
  stonks:
    02_refined:
      +materialized: view   # Default x entire refined layer
      +schema: refined      # Default x unconfigured folders

      master_data:
        +materialized: table      # Set once and for all
        +schema: md_refined

      finance:
        +schema: finance_refined
```

Here, we used schema names with the domain first (in shortened form), then the layer, so that all schemas for the same domain are close together in the UI. This is a good choice if you have domain teams. Another common pattern is layer first, keeping the layer number for better ordering.

The materialization of models should not affect their correctness and should be just a performance versus flexibility choice. For this reason, we usually place the materialization override as a configuration block at the top of the few individual models that need it. If you want them to apply to full folders or make them stand out, place them in the `dbt_project.yml` file.

In the sample project, we will see that materialization as a chain of views, in rare border cases, can affect the correctness of a model. Optimizations by the DB engine can result in applying filters in a different order than in our model sequence, therefore introducing errors. Reordering is allowed by SQL standards, as long as the final result is the same, but it does not account for errors. We will also see our options to deal with it.

Model access with groups and access control

To effectively manage a domain-driven architecture in which multiple teams collaborate and prepare for scalability, we need to define clear boundaries and public interfaces for our models. dbt introduced two key features for this with its dbt Mesh release: model groups and the access modifiers.

- **Groups** logically bundle models that belong to a specific business domain or data product. By defining a group, you establish a clear owner and a boundary for a set of related models.
- **Model access control** is a configuration applied to models that defines their visibility and reusability inside and outside of the group they belong to. It is a critical feature for logic encapsulation and to create stable interfaces between domains.

The access levels of a model define what other models can access it:

- **public**: any model can access this model. This also includes models from other projects in our dbt account (requires dbt Cloud Enterprise account). The model is a stable, well-tested "API" intended for consumption by other groups or dbt projects. Changes to public models should be managed carefully (ideally with model versions) to avoid breaking downstream dependencies. This is seldom applied to models in the Refined layer, as for cross-project collaboration, we prefer to create specialized data marts with an API role.
- **protected**: This is the default for all models in a dbt project. The model can be referenced by any other model within the same dbt project, independently of its group. Still, it is not visible for other dbt projects (dbt Cloud Enterprise account).
- **private**: This model is accessible only to other models in the same group. This is ideal for intermediate models that are part of a multi-step transformation and should not be used directly by others or contain sensitive info. Logic and data encapsulation is encouraged.

These concepts, along with model versioning, are key to building refined layers or related projects where multiple teams can thrive. We will explore these concepts in greater detail in the Data Mesh section. The following example shows how you configure access in the `dbt_project.yml` file.

```
models:
  stonks:
    02_refined:
      finance:
        +group: "finance" # All folder's models in the finance group

      int_finance__revenue_unioned:
        +access: private
        # This is an internal model of the finance group

      ref_finance__monthly_revenue:
        +access: public
         # This is a public API that other domains can use
```

The access configuration in the example shows how to define clear interfaces between domains in a fictional ref layer, even though we mostly use access in marts to define cross-project APIs.

We use the folder structure, clear prefixes and names, and open communication across teams to manage the responsibilities of models and developers within the same project, unless the project becomes so large as to become impractical. Then the choice is between keeping a single big project with model groups and managed access control or moving to a dbt Mesh of multiple, smaller projects.

Handling historical versus current data

The Storage Layer provides a powerful asset through its VER models: a complete, versioned history of every business entity. Each time an attribute of an entity changes in the source system, a new version is recorded in our HIST tables and made accessible through the VER models. This gives us a full audit trail and the ability to travel back in time.

However, this richness from the Storage layer presents a critical design decision in the Refined layer: for any given transformation, should we use the most up-to-date version of an entity, or should we know what that entity looked like at a specific point in the past? The answer to this question depends on the business needs and determines the pattern we use. The right choice is key to building correct and performant business logic.

The Default approach: Working with current data

For the vast majority of analytical use cases—aggregating monthly revenue, building a list of active customers, or summarizing current inventory—we are only interested in the current state of our data. We want the latest customer's name, the current product category, and the most recent account status.

The Pragmatic Data Platform is optimized for this common scenario. The VER models in the Storage Layer include an `IS_CURRENT` boolean flag, allowing easy selection of the latest version of each entity instance. The pattern for working with current data is simple and should be your default approach. For example, to get the current securities and use them in your other queries, you could create a very simple model, `ref_securities.sql`.

```
SELECT *
FROM {{ ref('ver_ib_securities') }}
WHERE IS_CURRENT
```

You could also put the same code into a CTE named `current_securities` in each model using the securities; the "extra" cost is the addition of the line with the `WHERE` predicate, rather than just reading from `ref_securities`. The choice is up to you. Using this pattern provides three key benefits:

- **Simplicity**: The logic is explicit and easy for any developer to understand. No complex window function is needed to find the latest record.
- **Performance**: Filtering on a pre-calculated boolean column is highly efficient, allowing Snowflake to process only the relevant slice of the historical data.
- **Correctness**: It ensures that aggregations and reports are not skewed by outdated attributes or duplicated records from historical versions.

Working with historical data is powerful but more complex than working with current data, so we advise doing the simplest thing that works for your use case.

Unless you have an explicit requirement for point-in-time analysis, you should always start by filtering for `IS_CURRENT = TRUE` *when reading from a versioned source.*

Working with historical data

While working with current data is the default, there are use cases where understanding the past is essential. This is where the true power of the versioned VER models shines. By leveraging the full history in our Storage layer, we keep the ability to answer crucial business questions that depend on historical context, and apply a business rule to all versions, while leaving the decision about using current or historical data to the models in the Refined layer.

Common use cases for historical data include:

- **Accurate Fact Enrichment**: When analyzing a historical transaction, such as a sale from last year, you need to join it with the product, customer, and salesperson attributes as they existed at the time of the sale. Joining to the current state in general produces incorrect reports (e.g. attributing a sale to a different sales region when the customer moved).
- **Trend Analysis**: Analyzing how entities change over time. For example, tracking how a customer's status has evolved or how a product's price has been modified.
- **Historical Reporting**: Understanding the reason or recreating the content of a report as it was on a specific date, such as for financial audits or regulatory compliance.

The mechanism enabling this is the `VALID_FROM` and `VALID_TO` timestamp columns in the `VER` models. These columns define the exact period during which a specific version of an entity was active. To find the correct versions for a specific point in time, you can use a simple `BETWEEN` clause, like in the following query:

```
-- Find the Security versions active on June 15, 2023
SELECT *
FROM {{ ref('ver_ib__securities') }}
WHERE '2023-06-15':date BETWEEN VALID_FROM AND VALID_TO
```

This works well for querying a single entity, enabling you to roll back time for one table at a time, but it creates a more complex problem: how do you correctly join a table of historical facts (such as transactions) to the appropriate version of a historical dimension? This is what we will see in the following section on Time-Aware Joins.

A special case: Working with time series

A time series sits halfway between current and historical data. It is a sequence of measurements recorded at regular time intervals, such as daily stock prices, monthly active users, or hourly sensor readings. We can use the `ts_` prefix for these models (e.g., `ts_daily_exchange_rates`) to highlight their time-series nature. Otherwise, we could treat them as normal models with the REF prefix, like with `ref_inventory`.

A **time series** tracks the evolution of one or more values over time, like exchange rates by date, hour, or minute. The historical depth and frequency of the changes are a feature of the time series itself. How a time series is modeled depends on the primary key we have picked for the entity:

- If the **date/time interval is part of the key**, like when the date is part of the daily exchange rate key (the HKEY includes the interval). In this case, the "current" version provides us with the latest entry for each interval, even if we store multiple price value snapshots per currency per interval. This is the most explicit definition of a time series, as we also define a target granularity.
- If the **time interval is not part of the key**, like when no date is in the rate key (the HKEY only covers the entity PK). In this case, we do not explicitly model a time series. We'll need logic in the refined layer to pick a single value for each interval (e.g., the day's last price).

In the end, we would store the same incoming data in an HIST table, but choosing a different identity definition for our entity (with or without time in the key) affects how we extract time-series data at our desired time granularity from our historical data. Time series models are primarily used for trend analysis, forecasting, and visualization. They are also frequently joined to fact tables to provide point-in-time context in a simpler way than a full historical join, such as converting sales transactions to a standard currency using one rate (latest, average, mid-day's rate) from the transaction date instead of the quote closest in time to the event.

In our sample project in the next chapter, we will see that we can build a time series of the value of our positions to analyze and visualize the trend of each position and the whole portfolio over time.

The Pragmatic solution: Time-aware joins

A standard `LEFT JOIN` between a fact table and a historical dimension (VER or REFH model) on the entity HKEY is incorrect. It would join each fact record to every historical version of the entity, creating a Cartesian product of versions and leading to massively duplicated and incorrect results.

The solution is a time-aware join (or temporal join). The goal is to join each record in one base table to the one and only one record that was valid in any other table at the time when the base table record is considered valid. While this can be achieved with complex SQL using date range comparisons, Snowflake provides a more powerful and performant feature called `ASOF JOIN` for the case when you want to join on a specific time from the base table record. To make this advanced functionality simple, safe, and repeatable, the Pragmatic Data Platform provides the **`time_join` macro**. This macro wraps the complexity of `ASOF JOIN` in a clear, declarative interface. The `time_join` macro takes the base table (`bt`), one or more joined tables (`t1`, `t2`, ...), the join keys, and the timestamps from all tables as YAML configurations, as we have already seen with the ingestion and stage macros. It generates the correct `ASOF JOIN` logic to ensure each record in the base table (usually a fact) is accurately enriched with its corresponding point-in-time attributes from other tables, typically historical dimensions.

The `TS_IB_REPORTED_POSITIONS_DAILY_VALUES` model is a complete example of using the `time_join` macro to join the daily position values, with the position fact and security dimension, enriching the daily valuation with their attributes. Here is how to use the macro, going through the simplified sections of that model:

```
{%- set configuration -%}
```

```
calculated_columns:
  - gain_fx: bt.position_value - t1.cost_basis_money
  - gain_pct_fx: DIV0(gain_fx,ABS(t1.cost_basis_money))*100
```

The `calculated_columns` section allows us to calculate new values based on the results of the join. The syntax is the same as we saw in the Storage layer `<new_column>: <SQL expression>`.

```
base_table:
    name: "{{ ref('VER_IB_ALL_POSITIONS_DAILY_VALUES') }}"
    include_all_columns: false
    columns:
      - position_value_date: REPORT_DATE
      - POSITION_VALUE
      ...
```

Next, we define the **base table** (**bt**) of our join. The `name` attribute has the fully qualified name of the model. The `include_all_columns` attribute works the same way as in the stage macro. The `columns` attribute works like the `calculated_columns` attribute in the stage macro, allowing you to name, rename, and calculate new columns from the base table columns, accessed via the **`bt`** **alias**.

```
joined_tables:
    {{ ref('VER_IB_ALL_POSITIONS') }}:
        time_column:
            EFFECTIVITY_DATE: EFFECTIVITY_DATE
        time_operator: '>='
        join_columns:
            POSITION_HKEY: POSITION_HKEY

        columns:
          - POSITION_VERSION_HKEY: DIM_SCD_HKEY
          - position_change_date: REPORT_DATE
          - quantity
          - SIDE
          - cost_basis_money
          ...
```

Next, we define the joined tables, one at a time. The fully qualified name of the first joined table (`t1`) is obtained with the Jinja reference `{{ ref('VER_IB_ALL_POSITIONS') }}` to the table. Under it, we define the `time_column` and `time_operator` to be used for the time part of the join. The `join_columns` attribute can contain one or more rows, each defining a pair of columns to compare and identifying the PK/FKs of the relation between the two tables for the non-time-bound part of the join. The implied syntax for the joined table configurations is:

```
BaseTable_column: JoinedTable_column

bt.BaseTable_column <operator> tN.JoinedTable_column
```

Each joined table is identified by an alias with the form `tN`, where N is the position of the table in the `joined_tables` configuration (starting at 1).

```
    {{ ref('REFH_IB_SECURITIES') }}:
        time_column:
            EFFECTIVITY_DATE: EFFECTIVITY_DATE
        join_columns:
            SECURITY_HKEY: SECURITY_HKEY
        columns:
            - SECURITY_NAME

{%- endset -%}

{%- set cfg = fromyaml(configuration) -%}
```

Then we add as many other joined tables as we like, close the YAML definition, and parse it to produce the `cfg` Python dictionary holding the parsed configuration.

```
{{- pragmatic_data.time_join(
    base_table_dict      = cfg['base_table'],
    joined_tables_dict   = cfg['joined_tables'],
    calculated_columns   = cfg['calculated_columns']
) }}
```

Finally, we call the `time_join` macro passing its parameters from the `cfg` sections. This macro generates an `ASOF JOIN` that correctly looks up the position and security version that was active at the time of the `EFFECTIVITY_DATE` for each position value.

This pragmatic pattern, coupled with consistent naming and an opinionated structure, makes complex historical analysis both manageable and reliable, turning a difficult SQL problem into a simple, reusable component.

Domain-driven data design and master data management

As a data platform grows, its complexity can quickly spiral out of control. Without a clear architectural strategy, the Refined Layer risks becoming a "big ball of mud"—a tangled web of interdependent models that is difficult to understand, maintain, and extend. This is what has doomed and will keep dooming many data platforms, forcing organizations to declare slow and expensive "evolution", "revolution", and "re-evolution" initiatives, sometimes along with a change of tools and directors.

To manage this complexity, we turn to two complementary principles from software engineering: Domain-Driven Design (DDD) and Master Data Management (MDM), which ideally complement what we have already introduced. DDD provides a "divide and conquer" strategy, breaking down the platform into logical, manageable pieces. MDM provides a "unify and govern" strategy, creating consistency for the business entities that are shared across domains. Together, they provide a robust framework for building a modular and scalable Refined Layer.

Structuring logic with domain-driven design

Domain-Driven Design (DDD) is an approach to software development that focuses on modeling a system around the business domains it serves.

When applied to data engineering, it means we structure our dbt project not around technical layers or data sources, but around distinct areas of business expertise, such as Marketing, Finance, or Operations.

The core idea is to treat each domain as a semi-independent unit with clear boundaries to be managed carefully. This approach has several profound benefits for a growing data platform:

- **Reduced Cognitive Load**: Developers can focus on the logic and entities within a single domain without needing to understand the entire platform at once.
- **Clear Ownership**: Each domain can be owned by the team with the best expertise in its data and rules, fostering accountability and higher quality.
- **Defined boundaries**: Each domain and the boundaries with its neighbors are well defined, together with clear naming and integrity rules for data moving across domains.
- **Modularity and Loose Coupling**: Changes within one domain are less likely to cause unintended side effects in another. This makes the platform safer and faster to evolve.
- **Data as a Product**: Each domain can be thought of as a "data product team" that produces a set of well-defined, trusted, and documented public models for the rest of the organization to consume.

In the previous section, we saw the practical implementation of this principle: organizing models into domain-specific folders and defining clear public interfaces using groups and access modifiers. DDD provides the strategic "why" behind this tactical structure.

Unifying entities with master data management

While DDD helps us divide our platform into logical domains, most businesses have core entities that are shared across these domains. A Customer, for example, exists in the Sales domain (orders), the Marketing domain (campaigns), and the Finance domain (invoices). If each domain creates its own version of the customer, the result is inconsistency and a lack of trust in the data.

Master Data Management (MDM) is the practice of creating an authoritative, trusted "golden record" for these critical, shared business entities. While some companies invest in expensive, dedicated MDM tools, the Pragmatic Data Platform can also be used as a lightweight, SQL-based approach using dbt to achieve the same core goals. This pragmatic MDM approach typically involves two patterns:

- **Mapping Source-Specific Keys**: Different source systems often have their own unique identifiers for the same entity. The CRM might have a `contact_id`, while the ERP has a `client_number`. To create a single view, we must first link these different keys to a single, master key. This is done using a mapping table, which we prefix with `map_`. This mapping table serves as the crucial bridge that connects data from different sources. If we have the correct business key columns to build a compatible `HKEY` across all sources, we can calculate it in their STG models, avoid building the mapping table (since all sources share a common key), and happily move to the next step to build the golden record. If one or more sources do not provide the information needed to directly build the HKEY, we can often use other information to build the mapping table by establishing a connection between the source key and the correct HKEY value in the other sources. In the worst case, someone has to manually create or at least confirm the mappings, hopefully created with the help of some tool and some heuristic rules.

- **Merging Attributes to Create a Golden Record**: Once the keys are mapped, half the work is done, but we can still easily find ourselves with multiple slightly different customer names, different addresses, and more. Our next goal is to reach agreement on business rules to create the "golden record" by merging attributes from the various sources into a single, authoritative model (often with an MDD or REF prefix). The logic for merging can range from simple COALESCE statements to complex business rules that prioritize one source over another. A perfect example is the `ref_securities_merged` model in our stonks project. It takes security information from multiple source files (trades, open positions, etc.), each of which might contain slightly different or more up-to-date attributes for the same security. The model then uses business logic to select the best available value for each attribute, creating a single, conformed, and trustworthy view of each security.

DDD and MDM: A symbiotic relationship

Domain-Driven Design and Master Data Management are not opposing forces; they are two sides of the same coin. They work together to create a platform that is both modular and consistent. You can think of it like this:

- **DDD defines the boundaries of the domains and their ubiquitous language**. It's like organizing a city into distinct neighborhoods. Each neighborhood has its own local government and can manage its own internal affairs and names.
- **MDM builds the bridges between the domains**. It's the city's shared infrastructure—the main roads, the power grid, the water supply—that every neighborhood uses. These are your master data entities (Customer, Product, Security).

This symbiotic relationship allows for both autonomy and interoperability. The finance team can evolve its internal models without breaking the marketing team's work. At the same time, both teams can join their domain-specific data to the same trusted `mdd_customers` model, ensuring their analyses are consistent and comparable. This combined approach is the key to building a dbt project (or a set of dbt projects connected in a dbt Mesh) that can scale with your organization.

Data mesh with dbt mesh

The principles we have established in the Refined Layer—modularity, statelessness, and Domain-Driven Design—are best practices for building a cleaner, more maintainable data platform. They work for any project dimension. They are also essential prerequisites for evolving your architecture toward a Data Mesh, which becomes increasingly attractive as the number of teams grows, especially when you can align them well with your domains. This modern, decentralized approach is designed to solve the scaling challenges that plague traditional, monolithic data platforms. Moving to a Data Mesh doesn't require throwing away your work; on the contrary, the Pragmatic Data Platform is a natural stepping-stone to a Data Mesh. The tools and features that enable this transition in dbt are collectively known as dbt Mesh.

This section will introduce the core concepts of Data Mesh and data products, explain the specific dbt Mesh features that serve as technical enablers, and outline pragmatic patterns for implementing a Data Mesh in the real world.

Why data mesh? The shift to data products

As an organization grows, a centralized data platform managed by a single team often becomes a bottleneck. The central team cannot be experts in every business domain and struggles to keep up with the ever-increasing demand for new data sources, models, and insights. The result is long delivery times, frustrated stakeholders, and a data team that is constantly fighting fires.

Data Mesh is a socio-technical paradigm, first articulated by Zhamak Dehghani, that addresses these scaling issues by decentralizing data ownership. Instead of a single pipeline, it envisions a network of independent, interoperable data products. The architecture is built on four core principles:

- **Domain-Oriented Ownership**: Data ownership is shifted from the central team to the business domains closest to the data and best positioned to understand it.
- **Data as a Product**: Data is not treated as a technical byproduct but as a first-class product, designed to be valuable, usable, and accessible for its consumers. A data product must be discoverable, trustworthy, and self-describing.
- **Self-Serve Data Platform**: The central platform team shifts its focus from building pipelines to providing the tools and infrastructure that enable domain teams to build, deploy, and manage their own data products.
- **Federated Governance**: A cross-functional group sets global standards for interoperability, quality, and security, which are then automated and enforced across the platform.

The fundamental unit of a Data Mesh is the data product. In dbt terms, a public and well-documented model with a data contract is a perfect implementation of a data product. A single model is a minimal data product, and a data mart is a more common data product.

In the Pragmatic Data Platform, we prefer to organize the models that have the roles of data products in data marts. These product marts define an API to facilitate management, discovery, and governance. We also advocate reducing technical friction between data products by using a single data platform or, if multiple platforms are needed, interconnecting them with open solutions like Apache Iceberg tables, thereby limiting the need for additional work to use the data from multiple products.

The dbt Mesh toolkit

dbt Mesh is not a separate product but a suite of features within dbt that provide the technical toolkit to implement a Data Mesh. These features allow teams to define clear boundaries, create stable interfaces, and collaborate across project lines.

Model Contracts

A model contract is a formal agreement that guarantees the "shape" of a model's results. By enabling a contract, you promise downstream consumers that the model will always return a specific set of columns with specific data types. You define and enforce a contract as a config in a .yml file:

```
models:
  - name: ref_finance__monthly_revenue
    config:
      contract: {enforced: true}        # Enforce the contract

    columns:                            # Define the contract
      - name: revenue_month
        data_type: date
      - name: total_revenue
        data_type: number(38,2)
```

A model's contract must list all columns with the correct names and data types, and if a code change causes the model's output to violate its contract (e.g., a column is renamed or its data type changes), dbt will fail the build. A failed build is a call for the developer to decide whether the change is non-breaking (a new column, a stricter subtype) and can be accommodated with a contract update, or a breaking change requiring a new model version. This prevents breaking changes from propagating through the platform, making your data products trustworthy and reliable. It also help to recognize and fix before a release unitended changes, that are quite common.

Please note that changes are most frequent when a model is "young", so it is common to have an initial "preview" period for a model where there are few well-known dependencies and changes to the contract are fine, followed by its "general availability" (GA) when the model contract becomes rigid and only non-breaking changes are allowed without a version bump.

The above tip also hints at why it's preferable to use views in an API data mart (in the delivery layer) to provide access to a data product. The reason is independent control over which columns are exposed, their names, and their data types. To expose a REF model, you would need to make a contract on all its columns and data types, making it rigid and brittle to even minimal changes, hindering its ability to serve multiple use cases. If you expose a view with only the required columns, you limit what becomes rigid, and the view still gives you some degree of freedom to absorb (small) changes in the underlying model.

Model versioning

Sometimes, a breaking change is unavoidable to improve a data product. Model versioning lets you introduce a new version of a model without breaking downstream dependencies by making both the new and old versions available, giving consumers time to migrate. To implement this, dbt requires that the physical SQL files for each version follow a specific naming convention. If your model is named `ref_customers`, the corresponding SQL files for versions must be named `ref_customers_v1.sql`, `ref_customers_v2.sql`, and so on. This file-naming pattern allows dbt to associate multiple physical files with versions of a single logical model name. You can define a new version in the model's YAML configuration along with the old one:

```
models:
  - name: ref_customers
    latest_version: 1           # Defines the "current", default version

    versions:
      - v: 1  # Original model definition, still the default

      - v: 2  # New model definition with breaking changes
```

Downstream consumers can continue to reference the old, stable version using `ref('ref_ customers', version=1)` while new development can adopt the new one with `ref('ref_ customers', version=2)`. Using simply `ref('ref_customers')` will resolve to the `latest _version` as defined in the config; initially it will be v1, but after a while you can move it to v2. This allows domain teams to evolve their data products while providing a graceful migration path for their consumers. You can also formally deprecate older versions, which will cause dbt to show warnings during runs using the deprecated models.

Model access and visibility

As we introduced in the previous section, "Model Access with Groups and Access Control", groups and access modifiers, and dbt projects, are the primary tools for defining the boundaries of your domains/data products.

Groups assign a set of models to a specific domain owner. **Access controls** define the visibility of those models. In a Data Mesh context, this relationship is simple and powerful. A model with `access: public` is the stable, contracted API of your data product. It is the only thing consumers outside your domain should depend on. Models with `access: protected` or `access: private` are the internal implementation details of your domain/product. They can be refactored or changed at will without impacting external consumers, providing true domain autonomy. The existing data contracts will check you do not break external commitments. Of course, when you have a contract to fulfill, the freedom to change your private details is somewhat limited, but as long as you can keep your final external interface stable, you are free to change your details. API data marts simplify this.

Real-world data mesh implementation patterns

The ultimate goal of a dbt-powered Data Mesh is multi-project collaboration.

The Enterprise Edition of dbt Cloud allows one project to `ref()` public models from another project, automatically stitching together a unified lineage graph and documentation across the entire organization, as shown in the following image showing models from two distinct dbt projects.

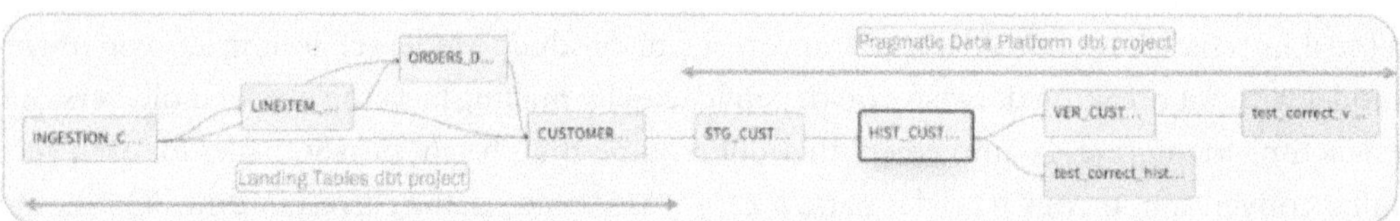

Figure 35: Lineage for a sample two-project dbt mesh.

If you are not on the Enterprise Edition of dbt Cloud, you can get the same functionality by defining the public models of your upstream model as sources in your downstream project, but you will not have a unified lineage and documentation experience. This capability opens the door to pragmatic, incremental adoption of a Data Mesh by extracting parts of a larger project into their own sub-projects. We once evolved from a single dbt project with over 1200 models into a dozen projects with way less than a week of work, mostly spent on initial coordination between a few teams taking ownership of the new individual projects.

The next sections present two common patterns for structuring a multi-project Data Mesh.

The soft mesh

This pattern is an excellent first step toward a Data Mesh.

Source-oriented teams own one or more dbt projects responsible for the Ingestion and Storage layers of their data sources. These teams are preferably co-located with the data source owners or, even better, comprise the same people maintaining the data sources.

- **Data Products**: The data products published by this core project are the clean, historized, and source-oriented VER models from the Storage Layer. These are exposed as public models with enforced contracts using API views. This setup allows for distinguishing between current data and full history data products, and produces personalized data products that fulfill quite different downstream needs (PIIs, data depth, available details, ...).
- **Domain Projects**: Each business domain (Finance, Marketing, etc.) has its own separate dbt projects. They install the needed source projects as dependencies. From there, they are free to build their own Refined and Delivery layers to meet their needs, eventually integrating with their project-specific sources, such as seeds or full-fledged sources, with project-local ingestion and storage.

This "soft" mesh decentralizes the creation of business logic while pushing the work of ingestion and historization where the source data knowledge is greater. It also provides high leverage for source teams and data owners, providing a consistent way to deliver domain-specific data products that are maintained with low effort in a single, well-governed dbt project.

The domain-oriented product mesh

This is a more mature Data Mesh implementation that grants greater autonomy to the individual domains and is closer to the original vision:

- **Domain Projects**: Each domain owns one or more full, end-to-end dbt projects for the data sources under its responsibility. This includes ingestion, storage, refinement, and delivery.
- **Data Products**: A domain can publish multiple data products. These typically contain high-value, business-oriented models built in their Refined layer (e.g., `finance__customer_ltv` or `mkt__campaign_perf`). Each data product, along with its related models such as dimensions and filters, is deployed to its own data mart for clear separation.
- **Consumption**: Other domains consume these business-level data products directly, getting access through established roles, and combine them to create new insights.

This pattern enables domain autonomy and keeps more data private, making it ideal for sensitive data domains where you might not want to distribute source data, but only aggregated or refined data in the agreed forms. It requires a higher level of maturity within domain teams and a strong federated governance body to ensure standards are met across the organization.

These two implementation patterns are not rigid at all, and you can draw a continuum from a soft mesh that provides only source data to a highly encapsulated domain-mesh that provides only high-value data products and zero source data. A common solution is to start with a soft data mesh and, over time, add on top of the source data some widely adopted refined data products that offer an efficient and authoritative use of the source data. At the same time, adopting a model closer to domain-oriented projects is a good way to start projects in sensitive domains like HR.

Testing business logic

In the Storage Layer, our testing strategy was focused on validating the integrity and structure of the incoming source data. We checked for unique keys, non-null values, and referential integrity to ensure we were faithfully capturing the data from our upstream systems. As we move into the Refined Layer, our testing philosophy shifts. We now assume that the data from the Storage Layer provides a correct and complete historical record. Our focus is no longer on the integrity of the source data, but on the correctness of our business logic and transformations.

We are no longer asking, "Is the data valid?" but rather, "Have we transformed the data correctly according to our business rules?"

The Storage Layer tests are like a chef checking if the raw ingredients are fresh and of high quality.
The Refined Layer tests the final dish to ensure it was cooked according to the recipe and tastes, as expected.

To do this, we employ two complementary testing strategies: data tests and unit tests.

Validating outcomes with data tests

Data tests, also known as generic tests in dbt, are the most common way to validate business rules. These tests run SQL queries against the models that have been built in your data warehouse. A test passes if the query returns zero (uncompliant) rows. While the built-in tests (`unique`, `not_null`, `relationships`, `accepted_ values`), that we have been using extensively, are still useful, the real power for testing business logic comes from packages like `dbt-utils` and `dbt_expectations`, which offer many useful tests.

The most versatile test in this package is `expression_is_true`, which allows you to assert that a given SQL expression is true for every row in a model. This is perfect for validating business invariants. For example, in a financial model, we can assert that the `revenue` column is always equal to the `quantity` multiplied by the `unit_price`, accounting for any discounts.

Here is how you would define this test in your model's .yml file:

```
models:
  - name: ref_finance__line_items
```

```
    data_tests:
      - dbt_utils.expression_is_true:
          expression: >
            revenue = (quantity * unit_price) * (1 - discount_pct)

    columns:
      - name: line_item_hkey
        tests:
          - not_null
          - unique
```

We will do something similar in our sample project when working with dividends. The two named packages provide many useful tests that let you validate even complex requirements, such as the overlap of validity periods that we did for the VER models, using just a few lines of YAML.

When you run `dbt test`, dbt will execute a query that looks for any rows where this expression is false. If it finds any, the test fails, immediately alerting you to a bug in your transformation logic or an unexpected edge case in your data. Data tests are excellent for validating the final outcome of your logic on the real dataset.

Leveraging the `where` property, which you can add to any generic test, you can apply any test only to a subset of the complete dataset, allowing you to perform tests that only apply to part of the rows in your models. This is useful for applying different tests to different categories or for limiting tests to recent data when older data is not in good enough shape.

Storing test failures for easier debugging

When a data test fails, dbt simply reports the failure. For complex issues, it's incredibly helpful to see the exact rows that caused the failure. You can instruct dbt to save these failing records to a table in your database using the `--store-failures` flag in a command like the following one:

```
dbt test --store-failures
```

This creates a new table in your schema for each failed test, containing the records that violated the test's condition. You can then query this table directly to efficiently debug the problem. You can also make this the default behavior for your project by setting it in `dbt_project.yml`, but this is not something you want always on.

```
tests:
  +store_failures: true
```

Creating custom generic tests

Sometimes you'll find yourself writing the same kind of `expression_is_true` test repeatedly or writing similar singular tests (see next). dbt lets you create reusable, generic tests to encapsulate this logic. A generic test is simply a macro that takes `model` and `column_name` as arguments (plus any other parameters you need) and returns a SQL query. A test is defined in a special `test` block instead of a `macro` block. For example, if you frequently test that a column's values are positive, you can create a `test_is_positive.sql` file in your `macros/` or `tests/generic/` folders.

```
{% test is_positive(model, column_name) %}
SELECT *
FROM {{ model }}
WHERE {{ column_name }} <= 0
{% endtest %}
```

You can now use this new test in any .yml file, just like a built-in test:

```
models:
  - name: ref_finance__line_items
    columns:
      - name: quantity
        data_tests:
          - is_positive
```

This makes your testing logic more declarative, reusable, and easier to read.

Note that while you can put a test anywhere under a macro path, they must be in the `generic/` subfolder of a test path, with the other test folders dedicated to singular tests.

With the first option, you can also keep a test close to the eventual support macros you create for its development, making it much more versatile.

Singular tests for complex validations

Generic tests are great for validating conditions on a single column or within a single row. However, some business rules are more complex and may involve multiple columns or even multiple tables. For these scenarios, we use singular tests.

A **singular test** is a standalone SQL query saved in a .sql file within a sub-folder in the test path, like the default `tests/` folder. Just like any other dbt test, it must be a SELECT statement that returns zero rows for the test to pass, but you can use any SQL you like. For example, a critical business rule might state that a product's `ship_date` must always be on or after its `order_date`. This is a perfect use case for a singular test:

```
-- tests/assert_ship_date_after_order_date.sql
SELECT o.order_hkey, o.order_date, s.ship_date
FROM {{ ref('ref_orders') }} AS o
JOIN {{ ref('ref_shipments') }} AS s
   ON o.order_hkey = s.order_hkey
WHERE s.ship_date < o.order_date
```

We suggest you organize and name your singular test in a similar way to how you do for your models, to make them easy to find and their ownership clear. dbt will automatically discover and run any `.sql` file in the `tests/` folder when running a dbt test command that references the tables in the test. Singular tests give you the full power of SQL to validate complex, multi-row, or multi-table business logic that cannot be easily expressed with a generic test.

Isolating logic with unit tests

Data tests are essential, but they have limitations, especially with complex logic:

- **Slow Feedback Loop**: They can only be run after a model has been built, which can be time-consuming for large, incremental models.
- **Dependency on Data**: A test might fail due to an issue in the underlying data rather than a bug, making it harder to debug the transformation itself.
- **Difficult to Test Edge Cases**: Your development data warehouse may not contain the specific edge cases (e.g., nulls, zeros, negative numbers) needed to fully validate your logic.

To address these challenges, we can adopt **unit testing**, a practice from traditional software engineering. A unit test isolates a piece of code—in our case, a dbt model—and tests it independently of its dependencies (models, macros, and data). The process follows the classic "Arrange, Act, Assert" pattern and is defined directly in normal `.yml` files:

- **Arrange**: You define mock inputs for your `ref()`, `source()`, and macro calls. These are small, in-line tables of data that simulate the model's dependencies and macro return values.
- **Act**: The `dbt test` command compiles your model's Jinja and SQL logic in memory using your mock data.
- **Assert**: The framework compares the compiled output against an `expect` block containing the exact output rows you expect the model to produce.

This entire process happens without ever touching your data warehouse, and you can limit it to only the columns you really need to test. This provides an incredibly fast feedback loop for developers.

One key strength of the unit tests is that you do not need to test all columns from all inputs, like you would do if you had to create fake source data.

Our suggestion is to create small, focused tests that use only the few columns needed to test a single business rule (or a single branch of it). This reduces the effort required to create the test, makes it well-focused, less prone to change, and gives you pinpoint accuracy. Here is an example of a unit test for a model that calculates a customer's status based on their order history. As you can see in this example, we provide only three input columns and check only two output columns, even though the model could have dozens. Unit tests are a perfect complement to data tests. You use unit tests to get fast, iterative feedback and validate the correctness of your code in isolation, especially for edge cases. You use data tests to validate the outcome of that code on your real, production-scale dataset.

```
# models/02_refined/customers/customers.yml

models:
  - name: ref_customers
    unit_tests:
      - name: test_ref_customers_status_logic
        description: "Tests the status calculation..."

        given:
          - input: ref('int_customers__orders_aggregated')
            rows:
 … - {customer_hkey: 'A', total_orders: 10, is_active: true}
 … - {customer_hkey: 'B', total_orders: 0, is_active: true}
 … - {customer_hkey: 'C', total_orders: 5, is_active: false}

        expect:
          rows:
            - {customer_hkey: 'A', status: 'VIP'}
            - {customer_hkey: 'B', status: 'New'}
            - {customer_hkey: 'C', status: 'Churned'}
```

Monitoring performance with dbt cloud run artifacts

While a dedicated performance testing framework can be complex to set up, you can gain significant insights into your project's performance by simply analyzing the artifacts generated by every dbt Cloud run.

These visual tools are invaluable for identifying bottlenecks and debugging failures. After every job run, dbt Cloud provides several tabs with detailed information. Two of the most useful for monitoring and debugging are Model timing and Lineage. The Model timing tab provides a Gantt chart that visualizes the execution of models across all available threads. Each colored block represents a step in your pipeline, corresponding to a model or test execution, and its length to its runtime.

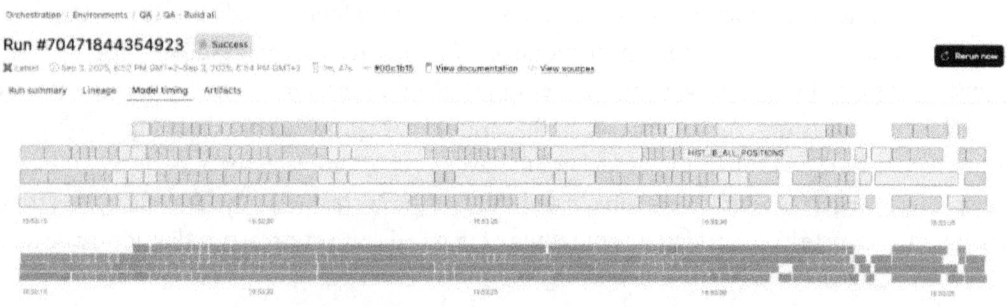

Figure 36: Model timing tab from a dbt job in the sample project.

This view is the quickest way to spot performance bottlenecks. A single, long block immediately draws your attention to a slow-running model.

A model like `HIST_IB_ALL_POSITIONS`, taking significantly longer than others, becomes a prime candidate for optimization, perhaps by refining its SQL or changing its materialization strategy. In the sample project's case, we are talking about a 20-second total run, so there is no need for optimizations yet, since any model runs in less than three seconds. But in a bigger project, you might find bigger surprises. The Lineage tab provides a complete Directed Acyclic Graph (DAG) of the run, with each model color-coded according to its execution status (e.g., Success, Error, Skipped).

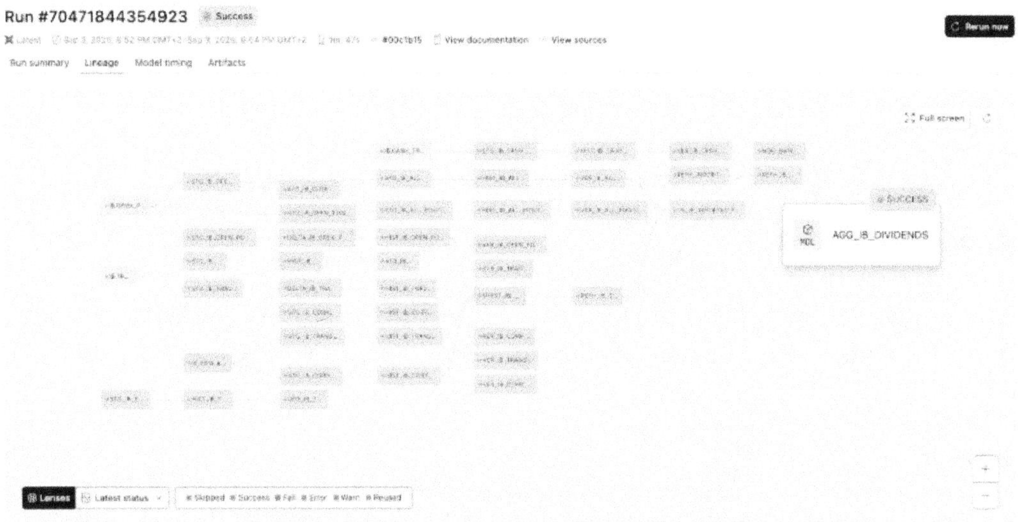

Figure 37: Lineage tab from a dbt job in the sample project. Hovering on AGG_IB_DIVIDENDS model.

This is a powerful debugging tool. Instead of scrolling through hundreds of lines of logs to find an error, you can instantly see the red node that failed and its dependencies upstream to understand the root cause. A similar view, showing individual test statuses, is available by switching the lens view from Latest status to Test status. This visual approach to monitoring and debugging allows your team to quickly identify and resolve issues, keeping your data platform healthy and reliable.

Chapter review

In this chapter, you have learned the core principles and patterns for building a robust, scalable, and maintainable Refined Layer. We have established its crucial role as the stateless, business heart of the Pragmatic Data Platform, where raw, historized data is transformed into trusted business concepts and actionable information ready for downstream consumption. You began by exploring the goals of this layer and key software engineering principles, such as SRP and LSP, that ensure your code remains clean and understandable. We then established a pragmatic blueprint for structuring and configuring the project, using domain-driven folders and consistent naming conventions with model prefixes.

You now have a clear framework for handling both current and historical data, understanding when to filter for the latest version and when to leverage the full history for point-in-time analysis using time-aware joins. We covered how Domain-Driven Design (DDD) helps manage complexity by dividing the platform into logical domains, and how Master Data Management (MDM) provides the patterns to unify core entities across those domains. Finally, we looked toward the future by exploring how a well-architected Refined Layer, supported by dbt Mesh features such as data contracts and model versioning, serves as a natural stepping stone to a decentralized Data Mesh. You also learned how to shift your testing strategy to focus on the correctness of business logic, using a combination of data tests and isolated unit tests.

In the next chapter, **SAMPLE PROJECT—coding the Refined Layer**, we will put these principles into practice. We will build out the Refined Layer for our "Stonks" project, implementing time-aware joins, and structuring our models into clear, reusable domains.

Recommended resources

The following materials offer more information on the topics of this Chapter. A good list of materials about Data Mesh and Domain Driven Design is in the Recommended Resources section of Chapter 2, so we will not repeat them here.

Pragmatic Data blog

The author's blog contains an article on the economy of modern data warehousing and a series of articles that dive deeper into the concepts of Data Mesh and Domain-Driven Design, which are central to this chapter.

- Article "**The economy of modern data warehousing** or why the Pragmatic Data Platform saves you time and money". https://pragmaticdataorg.wordpress.com/the-economy-of-modern-data-warehousing/.
- Article "**Why adopting a Data Mesh approach**" https://pragmaticdataorg.wordpress.com/2025/02/01/intro-to-data-mesh/.
- Article "**Building a Data Mesh with dbt and the PDP**" https://pragmaticdataorg.wordpress.com/2025/02/17/building-a-data-mesh-with-dbt-and-the-pragmatic-data-platform/.
- Article "**Domain Driven Design and Product thinking**" https://pragmaticdataorg.wordpress.com/2025/02/24/domain-driven-design-and-product-thinking/.

Dbt Documentation

The official dbt documentation is the best source for up-to-date information on the features discussed in this chapter.

- **Model access control and model grouping:** https://docs.getdbt.com/docs/mesh/govern/model-access.
- **Model Contracts:** https://docs.getdbt.com/docs/build/contracts.
- **Model Versions:** https://docs.getdbt.com/docs/build/model-versions.
- **Unit Tests:** https://docs.getdbt.com/docs/build/unit-tests.

Snowflake Documentation

- **ASOF JOIN**: For a deeper understanding of the underlying technology that powers the `time_join` macro, refer to Snowflake's official documentation. https://docs.snowflake.com/en/sql-reference/constructs/asof-join.

Data Engineering with dbt (Previous Book)

- For more foundational concepts on modularity and Master Data Management, refer to chapter 13 in the author's first book, "Data Engineering with dbt". The section "Modularity in the refined layer" provides background on structuring the Refined Layer for reusability. The section "Master Data Management" introduces the core concepts of MDM and presents a light, SQL-based approach.

CHAPTER 13

Coding the Refined Layer

In the previous chapter, we established the principles and patterns for building the Refined Layer. Now, it's time to put that theory into practice. This chapter is a hands-on journey in which we will build the Refined Layer for our "Stonks" sample project, transforming historized source data from our Storage Layer into meaningful, integrated business concepts. We will start by configuring our project and then tackle one of the most common challenges in data warehousing: creating a unified, "golden record" for an entity that appears across multiple sources, in our case, the Security entity. Next, we'll dive into time-series analysis, using the PDP `time_join` macro to accurately calculate the daily value of our positions. We will then explore advanced, real-world scenarios, such as handling data quality issues in our dividend data by implementing both reversal and restatement patterns. We will conclude with a powerful event-sourcing pattern that builds a complete position history from a unified stream of transactions using a recursive model. Throughout the chapter, we will also demonstrate how to apply the appropriate tests to validate our business logic. By the end of this chapter, you will have translated the architectural theory of the Refined Layer into tangible, working dbt models that solve real-world data challenges.

The topics that we are going to cover in this chapter are:

- **Refined Layer Structure and Configuration**: Configuring schemas and folder structures.
- **Creating a Unified Security Dimension**: Build a single, authoritative "golden record".
- **Building a Time Series with Time-Aware Joins**: How to use the `time_join` macro.
- **Advanced Data Handling and Data Quality**: Address data quality issues in dividend data.
- **Calculating Positions from Transactions**: Implement an event-sourcing pattern.
- **Testing the Business Logic in Practice**: Apply testing strategies to validate our models.

Sample project and code

The sample dbt project is available at: **https://github.com/pragmatic-data/stonks**. **All the code** we will write in this chapter **is in the dbt project folders**, mostly in the `refined` folder. The materials that do not belong in the project code will be in the sub-folder for this chapter, `chapter_13`, under the `code_samples_by_chapter` folder.

Please note that, to better fit the limited space on the printed page, we omit most comments and change the formatting of code blocks compared to the files.

Refined layer structure and configuration

In Chapter 12, we discussed the principles for creating a scalable and maintainable Refined Layer. Now is the time to translate that theory into a practical project setup. A clean, well-organized foundation is not just a matter of aesthetics; it is crucial for long-term maintainability, team collaboration, and the application of software engineering best practices that are core to the Pragmatic Data Platform. This first section will walk you through the initial setup for our Refined Layer in the "Stonks" project. We will implement a domain-driven folder structure, configure our `dbt_project.yml` file to manage our database schemas, and set a sensible default materialization strategy.

Before we configure the Refined Layer, it is worth noting a small piece of project hygiene we performed. To improve clarity and consistency, we updated the schema configuration for the IB models in the Storage Layer in `dbt_project.yml`. We are renaming it from the initial `storage_ib` to `ib_storage`. This will allow us to visually keep all layers for each source/domain close together. If you prefer a layer-based sorting, keep the old name and maybe add the `01`, `02`, `03` prefixes too. Agreeing on naming conventions and being consistent with them is a simple practice that greatly improves readability. Consistency is more important than perfect names.

Folder structure by domain

As we established in Chapter 12, organizing our models around business domains is the most effective way to manage complexity. For the Stonks project, even though we have a single data source, we can still identify distinct logical domains. We will implement this structure within the `02_refined/` directory. The `02_` prefix reinforces the layered data flow of our platform, making it immediately clear where these models fit in the architecture.

Our project will have two primary domains in the Refined Layer:

- **`interactive_brokers/`**: This will contain all models specific to the business logic of our Interactive Brokers data, including calculating position values, enriching dividends, and processing transactions.
- **`master_data/`**: This domain is for canonical, shared data that provides business context across the project. Our first piece of master data will be a date calendar dimension.

This results in the following folder structure:

```
models/
├── 01_storage/
│   └── interactive_brokers/
│       └──...
└── 02_refined/
    ├── interactive_brokers/
    └── master_data/
```

This clean separation makes the project easier to navigate. It sets the stage for defining clear ownership and interfaces, which is essential as a project grows or evolves into multiple projects integrated in a Data Mesh.

Configuring schemas and materializations

Next, we translate this logical folder into a physical database structure using our `dbt_project.yml` file. This is where we tell dbt how to build and organize our models in Snowflake. Our configuration will achieve two goals:

- Deploy models into domain-specific schemas for better governance and isolation. For very interconnected domains, you might challenge the separation and opt for a shared schema. One goal should be to have mono-directional dependencies only.
- Set the default materialization for the Refined Layer to `view`, following the "view by default, table for performance" principle.

We add the following configuration to the `models:` section of `dbt_project.yml`:

```
models:
  stonks:
    #... other configurations for storage layer...

    02_refined:
      +materialized: view  # Default x entire refined layer

      interactive_brokers:
        +schema: ib_refined

      master_data:
        +schema: md_refined
```

Let's break down what this configuration does:

- `02_refined`: This block applies configurations to all models within the `models/02_refined/` directory.
- `+materialized: view`: This sets the default materialization for the entire Refined Layer to view. As discussed in Chapter 12, views are a cost-effective and Agile starting point, as they are fast to build and always reflect the latest transformation logic. We can override this for performance-intensive models.
- `interactive_brokers` and `master_data`: These blocks apply configurations to their respective sub-directories.
- `+schema: ib_refined` and `+schema: md_refined`: These rules instruct dbt to deploy models from the `interactive_brokers` folder into a schema named `<target_schema>_ib_refined` (e.g., PROD_IB_REFINED) and from the `master_data` folder into `<target_schema>_md_refined`.

With this simple configuration, we have a robust and scalable foundation. Let's now build our first refined models.

Creating a unified security dimension

Our first task in the Refined Layer is to build our first true business-oriented concept: a unified, authoritative dimension for all the securities in our portfolio. This is a perfect, real-world example of applying the Master Data Management (MDM) principles we discussed in Chapter 12. Consolidating multiple sources into a "golden record" is one of the most common actions in data warehousing. Even though our project uses a single-source system (Interactive Brokers), the information about our **Security business concept** is scattered across multiple data exports. By consolidating this fragmented information, we can create a single "golden record" that will serve as the trusted source of truth for all downstream models. This process demonstrates that MDM is not just for integrating different systems, but also for creating coherence within a single, complex source.

The challenge of embedded entities

The core of our challenge is that **Security** is not a standalone entity in our source files. Instead, it is an embedded entity, with its attributes (such as name, asset class, etc.) attached to other business objects, such as trades, dividends, and open positions. In **Chapter 11**, we built several `ver_ib_..._security` models, one for each source. This approach is great for faithfully capturing the source data, but leaves us with a few problems:

- **Fragmentation**: Information on securities is spread across multiple `ver_` tables.
- **Incompleteness**: One source might provide the security's name or most attributes, while another might provide only a few attributes.
- **Stale Data**: A security's name or symbol might be updated over time, and this update might only appear in one source. A common case is that we see changes in `OpenPositions` files, not in the original `Trades` file where we first saw the security.

Our goal is to solve these problems by combining all these fragmented, time-variant pieces of information into a single, coherent, and complete historical view for each security.

Merging histories for a single source of truth

To build our golden record, we will first create a merged history to gather, prioritize, and consolidate all the historical records from our various `ver_` models into a single, unified timeline. This model is `mhist_ib_securities.sql` (Merged History). This model is much more sophisticated than a simple union. It intelligently combines the sources by prioritizing them, then compresses the history to retain only records that reflect a true change. The logic involves three key steps:

- **Prioritize and Union Sources**: The model first reads from each source (trades, open positions, transfers, and corporate actions) and assigns a `PRIORITY` to each. Trades, positions, and transfers are given a higher priority (`1`), while corporate actions receive a lower priority (`2`) because their data is often sparse. These prioritized sources are combined with a `UNION`.
- **Select the Best Source**: Using a `QUALIFY rank()` clause, the model selects only the records from the highest-priority source for each security. This is a powerful pattern for ensuring that, when multiple sources describe an entity, you build your history from the most reliable ones, not considering information from lower-priority sources.
- **Identify True Changes**: In the final step, the model uses the `LAG()` window function on the `SECURITY_HDIFF` column. It compares the HDIFF of each row to that of the previous row for the same security, sorting on the business timeline. Only rows where the HDIFF has changed (or is the first) are kept. This intelligently "compresses" the history, filtering out redundant records without changes.

In this case, we are taking full records from each source by keeping only the records from the most reliable sources. This is a simple way to merge information; in other cases, you might need to explore the nuances of merging data field by field, as we'll show in the next section on filling sparse data.

Here is the code that performs the record-by-record merge operation:

```
WITH

trade_security as (
    SELECT *, 1 as PRIORITY
    FROM {{ ref('HIST_IB_TRADES_SECURITY') }}
),

--... other sources with their priority...
corp_act_security as (
    SELECT *, 2 as PRIORITY
    FROM {{ ref('HIST_IB_CORP_ACT_SECURITY') }}
),

all_versions as (
    SELECT * FROM trade_security
    UNION
    SELECT * FROM pos_security
    --... union other sources...
),

top_priority as (
    SELECT *
    FROM all_versions
    QUALIFY rank()
      OVER(PARTITION BY SECURITY_HKEY ORDER BY PRIORITY) = 1
),

composite_hist as (
    SELECT *
        , LAG(SECURITY_HDIFF) OVER(PARTITION BY SECURITY_HKEY ORDER BY
EFFECTIVITY_DATE, EXTRACTION_PERIOD_START) as PREV_HDIFF

       , CASE
            WHEN PREV_HDIFF is null THEN true
            ELSE (SECURITY_HDIFF != PREV_HDIFF)
          END as TO_BE_STORED

    FROM top_priority
    QUALIFY TO_BE_STORED
)

SELECT * EXCLUDE (PREV_HDIFF, TO_BE_STORED, PRIORITY)
FROM composite_hist
```

This model produces a clean, prioritized, and compressed stream of historical changes, which is the perfect input for our final versioning step.

Building the final historical dimension

The `mhist_ib_securities` model provides a clean history of changes, but it doesn't yet include the standard versioning columns that make historical analysis easier (`VALID_FROM, VALID_TO, IS_CURRENT`). The final step is to create our user-facing historical dimension, `refh_ib_ securities.sql`. This model performs two critical functions:

- **Create Versions**: It takes the merged history model as input and uses our usual versioning macro to calculate the versioning columns. This macro correctly handles the merged history because, technically, it's just a normal historical table.
- **Correct the Timeline**: This is the most important **business logic** in the model. It solves a subtle but critical real-world data problem. For older data, our position reports were generated at the end of a month or quarter. This means a position's `EFFECTIVITY_DATE` would be, for example, `2021-03-31`. However, events like dividends might have occurred on `2021-03-15`, making it appear the dividend occurred before the position existed. The code fixes this by checking if the first version of a security is coming from an `Open_Positions` record. If so, it backdates the `EFFECTIVITY_DATE` and `VALID_FROM` to the beginning of the reporting period (`EXTRACTION_PERIOD_START`) to provide a more usable, pragmatic validity for the position. Here is the code that implements this logic in the `refh_ib_securities.sql` model:

```
WITH

ver_security as (
    {{- pragmatic_data.versions_...(

        history_rel   = ref('MHIST_IB_SECURITIES'),
        key_column    = 'SECURITY_HKEY',
        diff_column   = 'SECURITY_HDIFF',
        version_sort_column   = 'EFFECTIVITY_DATE'
    ) }}
)

, fixed_start_dates as (
    SELECT * REPLACE (

           CASE WHEN VERSION_NUMBER = 1 AND
STARTSWITH(UPPER(RECORD_SOURCE), 'OPEN_POSITIONS/')
                 THEN coalesce(EXTRACTION_PERIOD_START, '2021-01-
01':date)
                 ELSE VALID_FROM END
        as VALID_FROM

   ) FROM ver_security
)

SELECT * FROM fixed_start_dates
```

This model produces a perfect SCD Type 2 dimension that is not only versioned correctly but has also been pragmatically adjusted to reflect the true business timeline. As before, we do not need a separate `ref_` model, as the current state can be queried directly from this model using `WHERE IS_CURRENT`.

Filling sparse data

The approach above is simple and robust. However, in scenarios where source data is particularly sparse and attributes are frequently `NULL`, it might be important to collect information from multiple sources, based on priorities or wherever it is available, rather than picking full records based on source priority. Another operation that you can perform when building a golden record is to pre-process the data to "fill in the blanks" before historization. We can use SQL window functions (LAG and LEAD) to look forward and backward in a security's timeline to find the last or next known value for an attribute.

The column_filled macro

To make this complex logic reusable, we can encapsulate it in a Jinja macro. Let's create a macro named column_filled that generates the necessary SQL.

```
{% macro column_filled(column_name, entity_keys, sort_columns) %}
   COALESCE(
        {{ column_name }},
       LAG({{ column_name }}) IGNORE NULLS
           OVER (PARTITION BY {{ entity_keys|join(', ') }}
                 ORDER BY {{ sort_columns|join(', ') }}),
       LEAD({{ column_name }}) IGNORE NULLS
           OVER (PARTITION BY {{ entity_keys|join(', ') }}
                 ORDER BY {{ sort_columns|join(', ') }})
   ) AS {{ column_name }}_filled
{% endmacro %}
```

Using the column_filled macro

With this macro, you could create a more sophisticated model that produces a richer dataset before compressing the history and sending it to the versioning macro. You use the above macro like in the following snippet:

```
WITH all_securities_history AS (
    -- The same UNION ALL logic as before
    ...
)

SELECT
    SECURITY_HKEY,
    EFFECTIVITY_DATE,

    {{ column_filled(
        column_name='SECURITY_NAME',  # The column to fill
        entity_keys=['SECURITY_HKEY'],
        sort_columns=['EFFECTIVITY_DATE'])
    }},

    --... other columns

FROM all_securities_history
```

This pattern adds complexity and blurs the lineage and timeline, but it is very powerful to handle sparse data. It can be used alongside the previous approach to add column-filling capability. For the stonks project, our approach is sufficient and more pragmatic as we keep data from a single source at a time.

Building a time series with time-aware joins

One of the most common and valuable outputs of a financial data platform is a time series of daily position values. The goal is to see not just what a position is worth today, but what it was worth on any given day in the past, complete with all the relevant context about the position and the security as they existed at that specific time. This is a non-trivial task. The attributes of a security can change due to corporate actions (such as a stock split or a merger), and the cost basis of a position can change with each trade. Furthermore, if the position is in a foreign currency, you need the correct historical foreign exchange rate to accurately value it in your base currency. A simple join to the current state of the position or security would yield anachronistic, incorrect historical reports. This is precisely the problem the time-aware join pattern from Chapter 12 is designed to solve.

Defining the time series identity

Before we build the model, it's important to understand how we define the identity of our time series, as this impacts how it's versioned and used. As discussed in the previous chapter and in the `position_values.md` document that you can find in the sample code repository, we have two main approaches for a time series based on an existing entity like a `Position`:

- **Use the base entity's key** (`POSITION_HKEY`) and add the time dimension (the `REPORT_DATE`) to the HDIFF. This means each daily value is treated as a new version of the underlying position.
- **Create a new key** by combining the base key with the time dimension (`POSITION_HKEY` + `REPORT_DATE`). This creates a brand new, distinct instance for each daily snapshot.

For the stonks project, we have chosen the first approach. This keeps the model directly linked to the position entity, and we avoid creating a separate HKEY that would be easy to confuse and would not provide any benefit, since our source data provides only one snapshot per position per day.

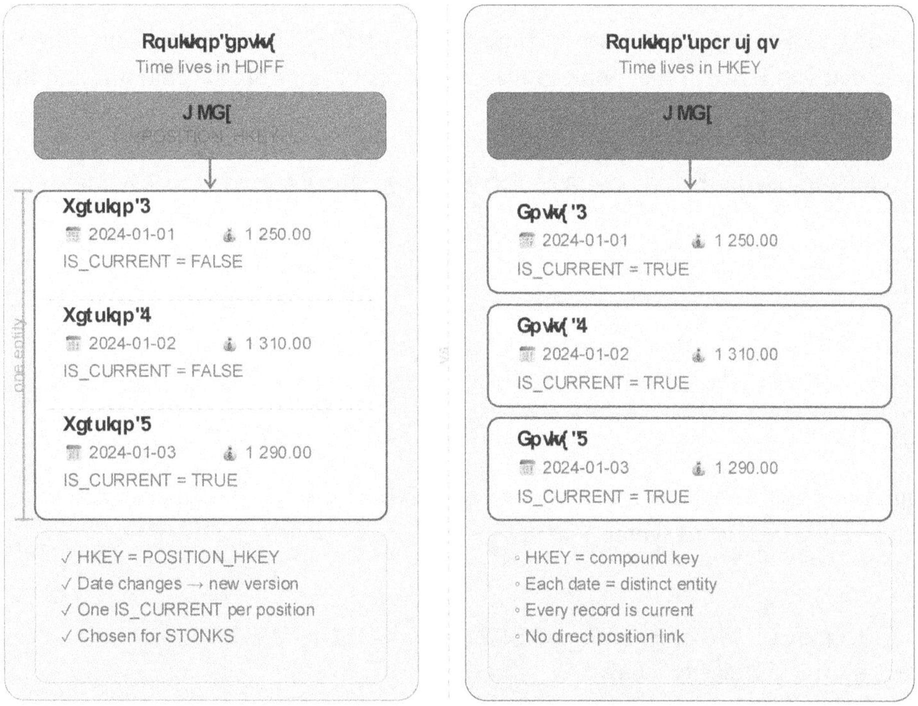

Figure 38: Alternative approaches to time-series identities.

We enforce the requirement for a unique record for each `POSITION_HKEY` and `position_value_ date` using a data test in the `position_values.yml` file, ensuring the integrity of our time series.

Using the time_join macro

The model that builds our time series is `ts_ib_reported_positions_daily_values.sql`. While the logic to perform multiple time-aware joins can be complex, the `pragmatic_data.time_join` macro simplifies it dramatically by allowing us to define the entire process in a declarative YAML configuration block at the top of the file. The macro takes a **base_table** (our daily position values, aliased to `bt`) **and joins it to a list of other tables** (aliased to `t1, t2,` and so on). The cardinality is the same as the base table, like for a left join.

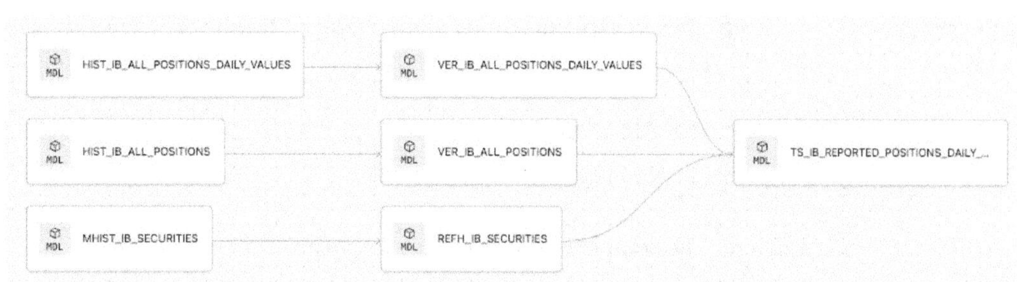

Figure 39: Lineage for the position value time series model.

The previous lineage graph shows the inputs to our model and the neat alignment of models produced by our design patterns.

The `time_join` macro handles the complexity of joining the position daily values from its `VER_` model (the base table, `bt`) with the correct historical versions of positions and securities (from the VER and REFH models, used as joined tables `t1` and `t2`). For each join, it uses the timestamp from the base table to look up the version of the record in the joined table that was active at that point in time. Your config controls the columns and the direction of the time comparison of each join.

Let's look at the configuration in the `TS_IB_REPORTED_POSITIONS_DAILY_ VALUES` model:

```
{%- set configuration -%}

calculated_columns:
  - gain_fx: bt.position_value-t1.cost_basis_money
  - gain_base: gain_fx * bt.fx_rate_to_base

  - UNDERLYING_SYMBOL: COALESCE(t2.UNDERLYING_SYMBOL, t2.SECURITY_SYMBOL)
```

The first configuration block lists the new columns we want to calculate based on the results of the time join. It uses the usual `calculated_columns` syntax.

```
base_table:
    name: "{{ ref('VER_IB_ALL_POSITIONS_DAILY_VALUES') }}"
    include_all_columns: false
    #... columns to include...
```

The `base_table` block lists the columns we want in the result from the base table.

```
joined_tables:
  - name: "{{ ref('REFH_IB_REPORTED_POSITIONS') }}"
      time_column:
          EFFECTIVITY_DATE: EFFECTIVITY_DATE
      time_operator: '>='
      join_columns:
          POSITION_HKEY: POSITION_HKEY
      columns:
          #... other columns...

{%- endset -%}
```

The `joined_tables` block provides, for each table to be joined with a temporal join, the join configuration and the columns to bring into the resulting table, as explained in detail in chapter 12, section "The Pragmatic Solution: Time-Aware Joins".

```
{%- set cfg = fromyaml(configuration) -%}

{{- pragmatic_data.time_join(...) -}}
```

Finally we call the `time_join` macro. The complete code is in the sample project's repo.

This declarative approach is powerful. We simply list the tables we want to join, specify the join keys, the timestamp columns and operator, and list the columns we want to bring into the final model. The macro generates the complex `ASOF JOIN` SQL code, making the model easier to read and maintain. This ability to encapsulate complex functionalities behind a simpler interface (the YAML config in our case) allows us to greatly leverage the competence of our most senior developers, who can create easy-to-use macros and patterns, to empower less senior developers to do very complex tasks safely and with ease, also learning from the generated code.

A practical walkthrough: The 'CNQ' option exercise

Sometimes, looking only at snapshot-based models, like the previous time series, can reveal changes that seem strange without understanding the underlying events. Let's look at our position in Canadian Natural Resources (CNQ) stock in August 2023. The snapshot from early August shows a position of +100 shares with a cost basis of $6,042.96. The next available snapshot on August 31, 2023, shows a position of +300 shares with a cost basis of $17,398.37. Looking at the snapshots alone, the change seems clear, but the cost basis might seem odd, especially if you know that the 200 shares were purchased as the exercise of two call options with a strike of 55$. You would expect the cost base to increase by $11.000, not $11,355.40.

However, the snapshot is the result of several complex transactions that occurred on August 18, 2023:

- **2 CNQ long Call Options were exercised**: This increased our cost basis by the amount we originally paid for the options ($355.40).
- **200 CNQ Shares were purchased at the strike price**: We exercised the options to buy 200 shares at $55 each, increasing our cost basis by $11,000.
- **2 CNQ short Call Options expired**: This simultaneously realized a gain from the premium received when we sold the options, with a booked profit of +$578.59.

These events perfectly explain the final cost basis: $6,042.96 + $355.40 + $11,000 = $17,398.36, but looking only at snapshots, you cannot understand all the details of what happens. This snapshot-based time series, anyway, provides a fantastic "low-hanging fruit": a high-value data product with relatively low complexity. It shows us the state of our portfolio on any export day without having to deal with individual transactions.

In Section 5: Calculating Positions from Transactions (An Event-Sourcing Approach), we will see how to build a model that reconstructs history from these events, providing even deeper detail. The cost will be dealing with much more complex code and building (manually or via rules) the transactions for Corporate Actions.

Performance considerations and incremental models

A model that performs multiple complex joins like this can be slow and expensive to run when the input contains tens or hundreds of millions of rows. This would make it a perfect candidate for an incremental model, while it's an overkill in our sample project.

By adding `{{config(materialized='incremental')}}` at the top of the file, we instruct dbt to build the model as an incremental model, that is, a table that is not recreated from scratch at every run.

Crucially, the `time_join` macro contains specialized, built-in logic to recognize when it's used in an incremental run and handle it correctly, processing only new data from the base table compared to previous runs. No need to add any extra configuration, but you can fine-tune the behavior by passing the parameters `high_watermark_column` and `high_watermark_test`. You can also change the project-wise defaults by redefining the variables `pdp.high_watermark_column` and `pdp.high_watermark_test`.

In an incremental run, only **new data from the base table** will be processed and applied to the **full joined tables**, as we cannot generally limit new base table rows to match only a subset of the join timeline. This ensures temporal accuracy even in incremental runs, a complexity that the macro handles automatically for us. If your special use case allows you to filter also some of the joined tables, you can add filters on the joined tables using the filters key. They can reference any column from the tables in the join and the model being built, and even the usual high watermark code like `(select max( {{high_watermark_column}} ) from {{ this }})`.

Filling the gaps in a time series

Our current model produces one record for each day we have a snapshot from our source system, which means there will be gaps for weekends, holidays, and any day when we do not have an export. For many analyses, you may want a continuous time series where the last known value is carried forward. You can achieve this as a subsequent enhancement.

Use the `mdd_date_calendar` dimension, introduced in the next section "Advanced Data Handling and Data Quality," to generate a complete series of dates for the positions. Join this complete date series (a spine) back to our time-series model so that each date joins with the latest record available before or at that date. For this task, you could even use the `time_join` macro again.

By using the calendar as the `base_table` and our time series as a `joined_table`, the `ASOF JOIN` logic will naturally find the last known position value for each date in the calendar, effectively carrying the values forward. When carrying data forward, it's a good practice to keep the original date as metadata, so you always know the record's original date, versus which date it was carried forward to.

Advanced data handling and data quality

So far, we have focused on creating clean, versioned dimensions and time series. Now, we will tackle a more complex business use case: analyzing dividend income. This scenario is a perfect illustration of the Refined Layer's purpose, as it requires us to handle data imperfections, enrich raw events with business context, and aggregate noisy source data into a clean, analysis-ready model.

The challenge with our dividend data is that a single, logical dividend event is often represented by multiple rows in our `CASH_TRANSACTIONS` source. A corresponding tax withholding transaction might accompany a dividend payment, and if corrections are required, multiple reversal rows may also be present. This multi-row format is difficult for analysts to work with.

Our goal is to build a clean, aggregated model, `agg_ib_dividends`, where each row represents a single dividend event with all its components (gross amount, tax, costs, net amount) clearly laid out and with the reversals correctly accounted for.

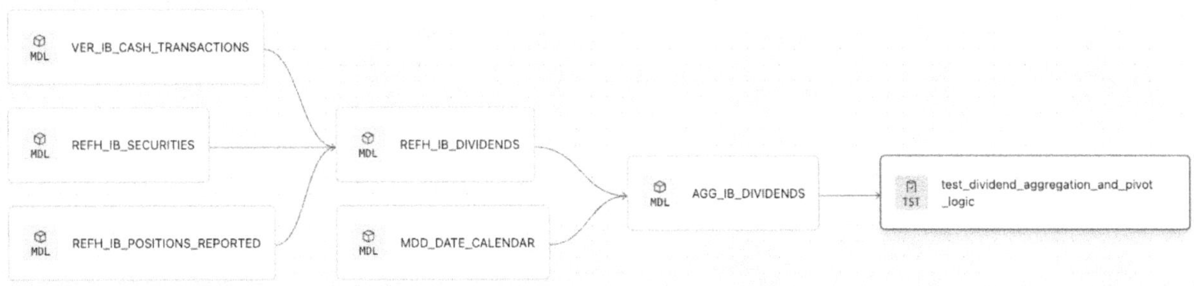

Figure 40: The lineage graph of the aggregated model for dividends.

As the lineage graph shows, this process is also a great example of modularity in action. We won't be starting from scratch; instead, we will reuse the REFH_IB_SECURITIES dimension we've already built, ensuring consistency and saving development time.

If you focus on building models that represent real business objects, you are likely to be able to reuse them frequently and naturally.

Preparing historical position snapshots

Before we can enrich our dividend data, we need a reliable, point-in-time view of our historical positions. While we have the `VER_IB_ALL_POSITIONS` model from the Storage Layer, we will create a new model, `refh_ib_positions_reported`, to address a subtle but critical issue with the snapshot-based data we get for positions. The problem is that our older position reports were generated at the end of a period (month or quarter). A position opened on March 15th with a dividend on the 20th might only appear in a report with an effective date of March 31st. This can make it seem like events like dividends occurred before the position existed. In the previous sections, we did not encounter this mismatch because both the position values and the reported positions came from the same file. The new REF model will be more usable than the source data.

To fix the issue, our `refh_ib_positions_reported` model intelligently backdates the `VALID_ FROM` and `EFFECTIVITY_DATE` for the very first version of any position, setting it to the beginning of the reporting (extraction) period when it appeared.

It is important to acknowledge the inherent limitations of this coarse, snapshot-based data: any positions opened and closed between two monthly exports would be completely missed by this model. This is a key reason why we will build an alternative, event-sourced position model, based on transactions, in the next section.

```
-- REFH_IB_POSITIONS_REPORTED.sql
--... CTEs to get versions and parse period dates...
, fix_first_effectivity_date as (
    SELECT
        p.* EXCLUDE (EFFECTIVITY_DATE, VALID_FROM),
        --... logic to extract EXTRACTION_PERIOD_START...
        CASE
           WHEN VERSION_NUMBER = one
           THEN coalesce(EXTRACTION_PERIOD_START, '2021-01-01':date)
           ELSE EFFECTIVITY_DATE
        END as EFFECTIVITY_DATE,

       CASE
           WHEN VERSION_NUMBER = one
           THEN coalesce(EXTRACTION_PERIOD_START, '2021-01-01':date)
           ELSE VALID_FROM
        END as VALID_FROM
    FROM ver_positions p
)
SELECT * FROM fix_first_effectivity_date
```

Enriching dividend transactions

With our positions prepared, the next step is to enrich our raw dividend transactions with point-in-time context from our historical position and security dimensions. For this, we build the `refh_ib_dividends` model, which once again uses the declarative `time_join` macro. The model uses `VER_IB_CASH_TRANSACTIONS` as its base table and joins it with `REFH_IB_SECURITIES` and our newly created `REFH_IB_REPORTED_POSITIONS` to enrich the results.

```
{%- set configuration -%}
base_table:
    name: "{{ ref('VER_IB_CASH_TRANSACTIONS') }}"
    filter: >
      TRANSACTION_CATEGORY = 'DIVIDENDS'    # only divs
      and bt.IS_CURRENT  # only the last (restated) version
    #... columns to include...

joined_tables:
    {{ ref('REFH_IB_SECURITIES') }}:
        #... join configuration...

   {{ ref('REFH_REPORTED_POSITIONS') }}:
        #... join configuration...

{%- endset -%}
{%- set cfg = fromyaml(configuration) -%}
{{- pragmatic_data.time_join(...) -}}
```

This enriches each raw transaction with valuable information, like the quantity of the position held and its cost basis at the time of the dividend. We deliberately keep calculated columns to a minimum here. Since we still have multiple rows per logical dividend event, complex row-level calculations would not be very meaningful until after we aggregate the data.

Introducing a Master Data Dimension (MDD)

To support more advanced financial analysis, we need a calendar dimension.

We create `mdd_date_calendar.sql` as a classic example of master data. It's a project-wide, canonical model that provides context for any date-related analysis. In its initial form, the model is simple. It generates a series of dates and extracts common attributes, such as day of the week, month, and year. The real power comes from its ability to be extended with business-specific logic.

```
WITH date_spine AS (
    -- Generates a nicely spaced range of dates
    -- using the dbt_utils.date_spine(…) macro
)

SELECT
    date_day,   -- The name of the date column in the spine
    EXTRACT(YEAR FROM date_day) AS year,
    --... calculate other date parts...
FROM date_spine
```

We could easily enhance this model to include corporate fiscal calendars, specific stock exchange holidays, or other business-relevant date information, making it an invaluable and reusable asset. A simple approach is to create a separate CSV file containing the holidays and the information you want to add to the base calendar. Then you left-join the base calendar with the CSV to create your "operational" calendar. In your "operational" calendar, you should calculate a Boolean column `is_holiday`. In the CSV, you can list the date, the holiday name, and other attributes such as work time, flag, or religious rules/info. You can also have multiple holiday files, like one for each exchange/country you care about.

Aggregating dividend events

Now we come to the final step: transforming the noisy, multi-row transaction data into a clean, analysis-ready format. The `agg_ib_dividends` model consolidates all transactions for a single dividend event into a single row.

The model groups enriched transactions by the keys that identify a unique dividend event (such as `POSITION_HKEY` and `DIVIDEND_SETTLEMENT_DATE`), then uses conditional aggregation to pivot the monetary amounts into distinct columns. While the core technique used here is pivoting data based on the `TRANSACTION_TYPE` column, we use the `AGG_` prefix. This is because the model's primary business purpose is to create a meaningful aggregation of a single business event, a broader, more descriptive role than a simple technical pivot.

```
SELECT
    POSITION_HKEY,
    DIVIDEND_SETTLEMENT_DATE,
    --... other grouping columns...

    SUM(CASE WHEN TRANSACTION_TYPE = 'DIVIDEND'
      THEN AMOUNT_IN_FX ELSE 0 END) as gross_dividend_fx,

    SUM(CASE WHEN TRANSACTION_TYPE = 'WITHHOLDING_TAX'
      THEN AMOUNT_IN_FX ELSE 0 END) as tax_withholding_fx,

    SUM(AMOUNT_IN_FX) as net_dividend_fx

   --... other calculations...

FROM {{ ref('refh_ib_dividends') }}
GROUP BY 1, 2,...
```

The complete model is in the sample project and includes a further CTE to join to the calendar and enrich the dividends with common temporal information, such as year, quarter, or month, based on the `DIVIDEND_SETTLEMENT_DATE`. To ensure this model is trustworthy, we add critical data tests in the `ib_dividends.yml` file. These tests validate our core business assumptions:

- A `unique_combination_of_columns` test ensures that we have successfully aggregated the data to one row per dividend event.
- An `expression_is_true` test provides a crucial financial sanity check, asserting that for every row, `NET_CASH_RECIVED` + `TAX_PAID` + `COSTS_PAID` is equal to the `GROSS_DIVIDEND_RECIVED`.

These tests build confidence that our final, aggregated data product is both structurally sound and mathematically correct. This aggregated view makes analysis dramatically simpler.

A good layout of data has the positive side effect of making data quality issues easier to spot. For example, when querying this model, we can clearly see a problem with a dividend for the AM stock on **2022-02-09**: the tax return transaction was incorrectly given the same effectivity of when it was recorded, on **2023-02-15**, a full year later. The following table clearly shows the problem.

DIVIDEND_SETTLEME	CURRENCY_PRIMARY	GROSS_DIVIDEND_RE	TAX_PAID_IN_FX	COSTS_PAID_IN_FX	NET_CASH_RECIVED_	AVG_FX_RATE_TO_BA	GROSS_DIVIDEND_
2021-11-10	USD	900.0	24.3	0.0	875.7	0.873585	784.134
2022-02-09	USD	787.5	118.13	0.0	669.37	0.8754	689.3775
2022-05-11	USD	787.5	11.81	0.0	775.69	0.94339	749.014875
2022-08-10	USD	787.5	11.81	0.0	775.69	0.95333	764.670375
2022-11-09	USD	787.5	11.81	0.0	775.69	0.96722	786.547125
2023-02-08	USD	787.5	21.26	0.0	766.24	0.92645	735.076125
2023-02-15	USD	0.0	-106.32	0.0	106.32	0.93565	0.0

Figure 41: Dividend events for AM stock.

This brings us to our final topic: how to fix bad data.

Correcting historical data: reversal versus restatement

Using this AM stock dividend tax date as an example, we can explore two approaches to correcting historical data in an immutable data platform:

- **Reversal:** This is a purely additive approach favored by accountants. We add new transactions that counteract the incorrect ones and then add another set of transactions with the correct information. For our example, this would mean adding up to four new rows to our source data: one to reverse the incorrect tax payment, one to reverse the original dividend, and two new rows with the correct values on the correct dates. This pattern is simple and maintains a perfect, immutable audit trail.
- **Restatement**: This pattern involves creating a new version of the incorrect transaction. We would add a new record to our source file for the tax transaction, using the same primary key but the correct date. Our Storage Layer would capture this as a new version in the `HIST` table. The `VER` model would then mark the old record as `IS_CURRENT = FALSE` and the new one as `IS_CURRENT = TRUE`. Our `refh_ib_dividends` model, which filters on `IS_CURRENT`, would then automatically pick up the corrected data on the next run.

Both methods are valid. Reversal is often simpler from a data-processing perspective, while Restatement can yield a cleaner final history for analysts. To apply either fix, you would upload manually created and aptly named CSV files with the new records and then run the ingestion and build process, running the following commands as discussed in Chapters 8 and 10, discussing the ingestion and storage layers:

```
# Ingest the updated source files into Snowflake
snowsql -c stonks -f.../put_ALL_files_to_stages.sql

# Load the staged data into the Ingestion Layer
dbt run-operation load_all_IB

# Re-run the entire pipeline to apply the correction
dbt build
```

You can find an example CSV in the samples folder for the chapter with the name `restatement.CashTransactions.20250901.20250901.csv`. Please note that while we changed the initial part of the name, we have followed the expected conventions to recognize the content as Cash Transactions and to provide the "extraction" period, which, for us, is the date we produced the fix.

Calculating positions from transactions

In the previous sections, we worked with position data derived from periodic export snapshots (the OpenPositions that ultimately produced `REFH_IB_POSITIONS_REPORTED`). As we saw in the CNQ option exercise example, this approach provides a valuable summary of our portfolio's state but obscures the multiple events that lead to those states.

Now, we will build a more powerful and granular view by reconstructing our entire position history from the ground up using an event-sourcing pattern. We will first prepare and unify our transactions, then walk through them recursively, and finally apply our trusted VER model to make the history easier to use. Instead of relying on state snapshots, we will treat each position-altering event—a trade, a transfer, or a corporate action—as a transaction. By replaying this transaction stream in chronological order, we can calculate the precise state of any position at any point in time. Our source data provides proper transactions for Trades and Transfers, but not for Corporate Actions. Therefore, our first task will be to construct these missing corporate action transactions ourselves. We will do this in two ways: with a simple rule for the most common scenario, and by using manually entered data for more complex cases.

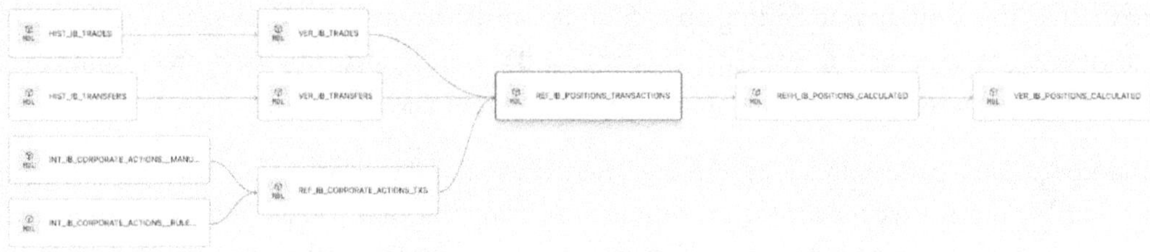

Figure 42: Lineage of the models that build the calculated positions.

The lineage graph above provides a clear roadmap for what we are about to build. It shows how we will gather data from multiple sources, combine them into a single stream of unified transactions, process that stream with a recursive model to generate our final, calculated position history, and finally build a VER model for better usability.

Preparing corporate action transactions

Corporate actions are critical events, such as stock splits or mergers, that change a position's quantity or the security itself. Since our source data doesn't explicitly include these transactions, we need to create them. We do this by combining two different sources:

- **Rule-Based Corporate Actions**: Many corporate actions, like a simple change in a stock's ISIN or ticker, follow a predictable pattern. The `int_ib_corporate_actions__rule _based.sql` model implements a clever heuristic to automatically detect these. As the comments in the code explain, it looks for a Closed position in our reported position history that is immediately followed by a new position with the same `SECURITY_ SYMBOL` but a different `SECURITY_CODE`. When this pattern is found, it generates two transactions: one to formally close the old position and one to open the new one. A key detail is that this process correctly creates a new `POSITION_HKEY`, acknowledging that a change in the security code results in a fundamentally new position.

- **Manual Corporate Actions**: For events we cannot catch with that rule, we use manually entered data. As discussed in Chapter 9, we created a dbt seed file (`corp_act_manual .csv`) to record these events. We can add and modify these records over time, and the history of changes will be correctly captured. The `int_ib_corporate_actions__manual.sql` model reads the current version of these records from `VER_IB_CORP_ ACT_MANUAL` and formats them into a standard transaction schema.

Finally, the simple `ref_ib_corporate_actions_txs.sql` model unions the two intermediate models, yielding a complete set of corporate action transactions.

You can find all the models in the sample project, in the `positions_calculated` folder in the refined layer for IB. If you prefer, you can isolate these three models in their own folder within the refined layer IB folder, or under the calculated position one.

Unifying position-changing transactions

With all our event sources ready, the next step is to combine them into a single, canonical stream of events that contains the current version of each transaction. This is the job of the `ref_ib_positions_transactions.sql` model. It pulls transactions from Trades, Transfers, and our newly created Corporate Actions, and unifies them into a single model with a consistent schema. This model showcases two important dbt development practices:

- **DRY Code with Jinja Variables**: The model defines the Jinja variable `common_columns` at the top of the file. This variable lists all the columns that are shared across the different transaction sources. Using the Jinja expression `{{common_columns}}` instead of copy-pasting the list of columns in each CTE's SELECT statement ensures consistency, reduces boilerplate, and makes the model much easier to read and maintain.
- **Handling Restatements with `IS_CURRENT`**: The model selects from the VER tables for Trades and Transfers and applies a `WHERE IS_CURRENT` filter. Taking only the current version of an event is common practice; coupled with our storage layer, it allows our models to seamlessly handle data corrections. If a transaction is ever corrected in our source data (a restatement), our Storage Layer will create a new version. This filter ensures that our event stream always uses the latest, most accurate version of every transaction.

Let's briefly analyze the `ref_ib_positions_transactions.sql` model.

```
{% set common_columns %}
    #-- the names of the common columns, in SQL syntax
{% endset %}

WITH
trades as (
    SELECT
        {{common_columns}},
        ... -- columns that need a local definition
    FROM {{ ref('VER_IB_TRADES') }}
    WHERE IS_CURRENT and ASSET_CLASS != 'CASH'
),

transfers as (
        ... same as trades, but for transfers
),

corp_actions as (
    SELECT * FROM {{ ref('REF_IB_CORPORATE_ACTIONS_TXS') }}
)

SELECT * FROM trades
UNION ALL
SELECT * FROM transfers
UNION ALL
SELECT * FROM corp_actions
```

We created a reusable list of columns in SQL syntax that we used in the `trades` and `transfers` CTE to define the common columns that did not need any action. Then, each of the two above CTEs defines the other columns with the correct SQL expression based on the content of the source, and retrieves the current version of the transactions that are not about currencies (`CASH`). Note that the `corp_actions` CTE just reads the transactions, as we already prepared them in the previous step.

Finally, we union the three streams of transactions. This model uses very basic SQL and basic Jinja to build an important business concept (the transactions that change our position), allowing us to validate its output and expose it for analysis and eventual reuse.

Building position history with a recursive CTE

This is the heart of our event-sourcing pattern. The `refh_ib_positions_calculated.sql` model takes the unified transaction stream and uses a recursive CTE to build the complete, running history of each position. The generated history is no longer limited to daily snapshots; it now reproduces the state of each position after every transaction. The logic works as follows:

- **Sort Transactions:** First, a CTE called `sorted_transactions` uses `row_number()` to assign a sequential order (`TX_ORDER_IN_POSITION`) to each transaction.
- **Base Case:** The recursion starts with the first transaction for each position (WHERE TX_ORDER_IN_POSITION = 1). This establishes the initial state of the position.
- **Recursive Step:** The UNION ALL then joins the CTE back to itself, taking the next transaction in the sequence. It then applies the quantity and cost basis changes from this new transaction to the previously calculated state, creating the new state of the position.

This process repeats until all transactions for every position have been applied, resulting in a complete, auditable history. Let's break down the `refh_ib_positions_calculated.sql` model step-by-step to understand how it works.

1. Sorting the transactions

The first step in any event-sourcing model is to ensure the events are in the correct chronological order. The `sorted_transactions` CTE uses the `row_number()` window function to assign a sequential number (`TX_ORDER_IN_POSITION`) to every transaction for a given position.

```
WITH RECURSIVE
sorted_transactions as (
    SELECT *,
    row_number() OVER(partition by POSITION_HKEY
        order by EFFECTIVITY_DATE, RECORD_SOURCE, FILE_ROW_NUMBER)
    as TX_ORDER_IN_POSITION
    FROM {{ ref('REF_IB_POSITIONS_TRANSACTIONS') }}
)
```

This ordered stream of transactions is the input for our recursion.

2. The Base case: initializing the position

A recursive CTE has two parts. The first is the "base case" or "anchor member," which is the starting point. Here, we select the very first transaction for each position (`WHERE TX_ORDER_IN_POSITION = 1`) and calculate its initial state.

```
, position_calculation as (
    SELECT
        t.* EXCLUDE(COST_BASIS_FX)
            RENAME(QUANTITY as POSITION_QUANTITY_CHANGE),
        t.QUANTITY as POSITION_QUANTITY,
        --... set initial SIDE, COST_BASIS_FX,...
    FROM sorted_transactions t
    WHERE TX_ORDER_IN_POSITION = 1
```

In this step, we push forward most columns unchanged (`t.*`), while handling the columns that require special treatment at the first position. The core logic here is to establish the initial `SIDE` of the position with a simple `CASE`.

3. The recursive step: Iterating through transactions

The second part is the "recursive member," which joins back to the CTE itself to build the history step by step. It takes the state calculated in the previous step (`c`) and applies the next transaction (`t`) to it.

```
   UNION ALL
    SELECT
        t.* EXCLUDE(COST_BASIS_FX)
            RENAME(QUANTITY as POSITION_QUANTITY_CHANGE),

   c.POSITION_QUANTITY + t.QUANTITY as NEW_POSITION_QUANTITY,

-- CASE statement to calculate NEW_SIDE
   based on the NEW_POSITION_QUANTITY just calculated

-- Logic to calculate the new cost basis
CASE
  WHEN NEW_SIDE = 'Closed'
  THEN 0    -- The cost basis for closed positions is zero
  WHEN (NEW_SIDE = 'Long' and t.QUANTITY > 0)
       OR (NEW_SIDE = 'Short' and t.QUANTITY < 0)
  THEN c.COST_BASIS_FX + t.COST_BASIS_FX    -- Add TX cost
  ELSE c.COST_BASIS_FX / c.POSITION_QUANTITY *
       NEW_POSITION_QUANTITY   --AVG cost * remaining stocks
END as NEW_COST_BASIS_FX

       --... other calculations...

   FROM position_calculation c
    JOIN sorted_transactions t
    ON (c.POSITION_HKEY = t.POSITION_HKEY AND
        c.TX_ORDER_IN_POSITION +1 = t.TX_ORDER_IN_POSITION)
)
```

The core business logic resides in the CASE statement for NEW_COST_BASIS_FX, which correctly applies the average cost method depending on whether we are adding to or reducing a position. The other key step in this part is fetching the next transaction, that is the one with the next order in the sorted TXs for the position with respect to where we are in the calculation (t.tx_order_in_position = c.tx_order_in_position + 1).

4. The final selection and HDIFF calculation

This REFH model is perfectly compatible with our PDP patterns, and to feed it to the versioning macro, we need a HDIFF column that uniquely identifies each version. The TX_ORDER_IN_POSITION column generated by the sorted_transactions CTE serves the purpose perfectly, as each new transaction creates a unique number for that position. For clarity and consistency, we create a formal POSITION_ CALCULATED_HDIFF that will satisfy the code readers of the VER model.

```
SELECT *,
    TX_ORDER_IN_POSITION || '-' || POSITION_HKEY:text
    as POSITION_CALCULATED_HDIFF
FROM position_calculation
```

The final SELECT statement gathers all the rows generated by the recursion and calculates POSITION_CALCULATED_HDIFF, providing a unique, changing value that remains consistent even if it is not strictly a hash. The comments in the code discuss other approaches to calculating the HDIFF.

Building a VER model on top of the position history

Our refh_ib_positions_calculated model is a complete history table that conforms to the HIST model pattern. To make it easy for end-users to query, we create a final ver_ib_positions_ calculated model on top of it. As with all other VER models in our platform, this is a simple, declarative call to a PDP macro. It adds the standard user-friendly versioning columns (VALID_FROM, VALID_TO, IS_CURRENT, and SCD_Key). For example, in our data for the AR stock in Portfolio2 on 2023-05-03 at 13:15:57, nine transactions are recorded simultaneously. The VER model correctly creates multiple distinct versions at this timestamp. The intermediate versions have a VALID_FROM and VALID_TO with the same timestamp. In contrast, the final version from that moment remains valid until the next event at a different time, perfectly modeling the intra-day state changes. Anyway, for events with the same exact values on the timeline (effectivity, ingestion, and load times), the relative ordering of their versions by the VER model, as we used it until now, is random and unstable, potentially resulting in a different order from the one in the position history.

```
{{ pragmatic_data.versions…(
    history_rel = ref('REFH_IB_POSITIONS_CALCULATED'),
    key_column  = 'POSITION_HKEY',
    diff_column = 'POSITION_CALCULATED_HDIFF',

    version_sort_column = 'EFFECTIVITY_DATE',
    extra_sort_columns   = 'TX_ORDER_IN_POSITION'
) }}
```

In the VER model, we can also handle events with the same exact timeline by adding the `extra_sort_columns` parameter, as shown in the code below. It allows us to add further sorting columns beyond the timeline columns (effectivity, ingestion, and load times) to make sorting stable and deterministic. We set the `extra_sort_columns` parameter to the version order in the history model, which provides us with the stable sort we were looking for. By the end of this process, we have demonstrated the power and consistency of the Pragmatic Data Platform's patterns. We created a REFH model (our calculated history) that behaves just like a standard HIST table, and we placed a standard VER model on top of it. This adherence to consistent patterns embodies the Least Surprise Principle (LSP); any developer familiar with our platform can immediately understand how to use this complex, calculated position history because it looks and feels just like every other versioned entity in all our projects.

Testing the business logic in practice

In Chapter 12, we discussed how to do tests in the Refined Layer. Now, it's time to translate that theory into practice. This section walks you through implementing a robust testing suite for the stonks project to ensure the accuracy of our business logic. Note that we kept testing as a separate argument to simplify its discussion, but in reality, testing must be done at the same time when you build your models; it is not something added later.

It is also important to reiterate the shift in testing focus for this layer. In the Storage Layer, our tests focused on the integrity of the source data—validating uniqueness, non-null constraints, and relationships to ensure we were faithfully capturing what the upstream systems provided. In the Refined Layer, our focus shifts to validating the correctness of transformations. We are going to test our code and the data it produces.

We will show three distinct types of tests, each suited for a different purpose:

- **Generic Data Tests**: For enforcing row-level business rules and invariants.
- **Singular Data Tests**: For complex, cross-model reconciliations.
- **Unit Tests**: For isolating and validating complex transformation logic.

Validating business rules with generic tests

Generic tests are the workhorse of our data validation strategy. They are ideal for defining business rules and invariants that must hold for every row in a model. We'll use the powerful tests available in the **dbt_utils** package to encode our business assumptions directly into our project. Remember that you can always target a subset of rows by using the `where` argument to run the test only on the rows that make sense.

Example 1: Validating dividend aggregation math

The `agg_ib_dividends` model consolidates multiple transactions into a single row. We must ensure this aggregation is mathematically sound. To do this, we use an `expression_is_true` test to confirm that for every row, the component parts (net cash, tax, costs) correctly sum up to the gross dividend amount.

```
# in ref_ib_dividends
- name: AGG_IB_DIVIDENDS
  data_tests:
    - dbt_utils.expression_is_true:
        expression: "abs(NET_CASH_RECIVED_IN_FX + TAX_PAID_IN_FX +
COSTS_PAID_IN_FX—GROSS_DIVIDEND_RECIVED_IN_FX) < 0.01"
```

This test builds trust in our data product. The small tolerance (< 0.01) is a best practice when comparing floating-point numbers to account for potential rounding differences. In the sample project, you will also find the same test in the precise version we can run when using decimal numbers for monetary amounts, as we suggest.

Example 2: Enforcing a simple business invariant

A simple, reasonable business assumption is that a gross dividend payment should not be negative. We can enforce this rule with another generic test on the `AGG_IB_DIVIDENDS` model.

```
# ref_ib_dividends.yml, under columns of AGG_IB_DIVIDENDS
columns:
  – name: GROSS_DIVIDEND_RECIVED_IN_FX
    tests:
      – dbt_utils.expression_is_true:
          expression: ">= 0"
```

This simple test demonstrates how to encode fundamental business assumptions directly into your dbt project, preventing unexpected or invalid data from propagating downstream.

Example 3: Enforcing a complex business invariant

When we are calculating positions from transactions, a key value is the cost basis of the position, as it tells how much the stock cost us (or paid us for short positions). We can validate that we have at least a cost basis with the correct sign with the following test.

```
# Model level test for model REFH_IB_POSITIONS_CALCULATED

      – dbt_utils.expression_is_true: # Cost basis sign
          expression: |
            CASE # the case code must be indented in the.yml file!
              WHEN TRANSACTION_TYPE = 'SPLIT'
                THEN COST_BASIS_CHANGE_FX = 0
              WHEN SIDE = 'Long' and OPEN_CLOSE_INDICATOR = 'O'
                THEN COST_BASIS_CHANGE_FX > 0
              WHEN SIDE = 'Long' and OPEN_CLOSE_INDICATOR = 'C'
                THEN COST_BASIS_CHANGE_FX < 0
              WHEN SIDE = 'Short' and OPEN_CLOSE_INDICATOR = 'O'
                THEN COST_BASIS_CHANGE_FX < 0
              WHEN SIDE = 'Short' and OPEN_CLOSE_INDICATOR = 'C'
                THEN COST_BASIS_CHANGE_FX > 0
              ELSE COST_BASIS_CHANGE_FX = 0
            END
```

This more advanced test demonstrates how you can precisely validate your data even against complex business rules or invariants. In the `ref_ib_positions_calculated` YAML file, you can find more examples of advanced tests like this.

Cross-model reconciliation with singular tests

Singular tests are the tool of choice for complex validations that span multiple models or require sophisticated SQL logic. They are perfect for reconciling data across different datasets. In our project, we now have two sources of position history: the snapshots from `refh_ib_reported_positions` and our more granular, event-sourced history from `ver_ib_positions_calculated`. As a critical sanity check, every position snapshot that exists in the reported history should also exist in our calculated history for that same point in time. A singular test is the perfect way to validate this:

```
-- tests/assert_calculated_positions_reconcile_with_reported.sql
WITH

reported AS (
SELECT *
, CASE
     WHEN VERSION_NUMBER = 1 THEN EXTRACTION_PERIOD_END
     ELSE EFFECTIVITY_DATE
   END as VALIDITY_DATE
FROM {{ ref('refh_ib_reported_positions') }}
),

calculated AS (
    SELECT POSITION_HKEY, VALID_FROM, VALID_TO
    FROM {{ ref('ver_ib_positions_calculated') }}
)

SELECT r.*
FROM reported r
LEFT JOIN calculated c
  ON r.POSITION_HKEY = c.POSITION_HKEY
  AND r.VALIDITY_DATE BETWEEN c.VALID_FROM AND c.VALID_TO
WHERE c.POSITION_HKEY IS NULL
```

This test performs a temporally constrained join to find any reported position snapshots that are "missing" from our calculated history. A test failure, which occurs when the query returns any rows, would indicate a significant discrepancy between our two position models, flagging a potential bug in our recursive logic.

Please note that we had to handle the first version of each reported position in a special way by calculating a `VALIDITY_DATE` that places these positions back at the end of the snapshot period. This is needed because the first transaction that establishes the positions does not necessarily occur on the first day of the snapshot period. Still, it is somewhere inside it, while the validity period of the calculated positions correctly starts when the transaction occurs, without any knowledge of when reported positions are extracted.

Isolating complex logic with unit tests

As discussed in Chapter 12, unit tests provide an incredibly fast feedback loop, isolate code from data, and are invaluable for testing complex logic or edge cases. The recursive CTE in `refh_ib_positions_calculated`, with its complex, stateful calculations, is the most complex piece of logic in our project. It would be an ideal candidate for a unit test, as we could feed it a specific sequence of transactions and assert that the resulting position state is correctly calculated. Unfortunately, at the time of writing, dbt's native unit testing framework does not support testing recursive models, so we must pick another example. Another good candidate is our `agg_ib_dividends` model, which is not recursive, and its `SUM(CASE WHEN...)` logic for pivoting transaction types into columns is a critical piece of business logic that we must validate.

We will write a unit test to confirm that our aggregation model correctly consolidates multiple raw transaction rows into a single, clean summary row. We can define this test in any `.yml` file. A good practice is to create a file to collect all unit tests for each model, naming it after the model itself with a `.yml` extension. The test will provide a mock input for `REFH_IB_DIVIDENDS` that simulates a single dividend event composed of three transactions: the main dividend payment, a tax withholding, and a fee. We can leave the input for the calendar empty, using `[]`. The expect block will then define the single aggregated row that the model should produce. Create the `AGG_IB_DIVIDENDS.yml` file with the following code:

```
unit_tests:
  - name: test_dividend_aggregation_and_pivot_logic
    model: AGG_IB_DIVIDENDS
    given:
      - input: ref('REFH_IB_DIVIDENDS')
        rows:
          - {POSITION_HKEY: 'div1',
             DIVIDEND_SETTLEMENT_DATE: '2024-06-10',
             TRANSACTION_TYPE: 'DIVIDEND',
             AMOUNT_IN_FX: 100.00}

          - {POSITION_HKEY: 'div1',
             DIVIDEND_SETTLEMENT_DATE: '2024-06-10',
             TRANSACTION_TYPE: 'Withholding Tax',
             AMOUNT_IN_FX: -15.00}

          - {POSITION_HKEY: 'div1',
             DIVIDEND_SETTLEMENT_DATE: '2024-06-10',
             TRANSACTION_TYPE: 'Other Fees',
             AMOUNT_IN_FX: -1.50}
      - input: ref('MDD_DATE_CALENDAR')
        rows: []

   expect:
     rows:
       - {GROSS_DIVIDEND_RECIVED_IN_FX: 100.00,
          TAX_PAID_IN_FX: 15.00,
          COSTS_PAID_IN_FX: 1.50,
          NET_CASH_RECIVED_IN_FX: 83.50}
```

Please note that, at the time of writing, the unit tests have a life of their own, and you need to reference the model they refer to using the `model` attribute. This unit test powerfully validates our business logic: the given block simulates the raw, multi-row data that our model ingests, and the expect block asserts that our pivoting logic correctly calculates each component and that the final net amount is accurate. You can run the new unit test with the following command line:

```
dbt test --select AGG_IB_DIVIDENDS,test_type:unit
```

(no space after the comma) or all unit tests in the project with this other command line:

```
dbt test --select test_type:unit
```

Even though we could not unit-test our recursive model, applying this pattern to other key models significantly increases our confidence in the correctness of our Refined Layer. For now, the best way to validate recursive models is to test what they produce for selected rows where you know the correct expected results. Eventually, you can add fake test data for this purpose, making it easy to filter it out from the model output in non-development environments. The RECORD_SOURCE column is very useful in this kind of situation.

Finalizing our models for the next layer

Our Refined Layer models are now logically complete and thoroughly tested. They represent trusted, reusable business concepts that constitute the core of our data platform.

In Chapter 12, we discussed several advanced Governance and dbt Mesh features, notably **model contracts and model versioning**. These features are essential to create formal "data products"—stable, reliable, and well-defined outputs intended for consumption by other teams, BI tools, or applications. Within the Pragmatic Data Platform architecture, these formal data products are typically built in the Delivery Layer. Using them between models in one project might make sense in very big, structured projects, but it limits flexibility. Similarly, it is common to use **groups and access modifiers** to organize big Refined layers; they also affect simplicity and flexibility, so weigh their use on the benefits they bring. Our sample project is too simple to use them.

We deliberately wait to implement model contracts and versioning in Chapter 14, when we build the Delivery Layer for the stonks project, specifically when creating data marts that require a strict, stable interface for their consumers, exactly like any API. There, we always use contracts.

Chapter review

You have successfully navigated the practical implementation of the Refined Layer, transforming the theoretical principles from Chapter 12 into a suite of powerful, working dbt models. You began by establishing a clean foundation, configuring the project structure with domain-driven folders and sensible defaults. You then tackled your first use case, applying a pragmatic Master Data Management pattern to create a unified and versioned "golden record" for the Security entity. Next, you dove into temporal analysis, building a valuable time-series model of daily position values. In the process, you mastered the declarative `time_join` macro to correctly handle point-in-time joins and saw how an incremental materialization strategy can be used to improve performance. You then moved on to address real-world complexity, improving data quality in our dividend data. You learned how to aggregate noisy, multi-row events into a clean, analysis-ready format and explored both the reversal and restatement patterns for correcting historical data without compromising auditability. The capstone of the chapter was implementing a powerful event-sourcing pattern, using a recursive CTE to reconstruct a complete position history from a stream of transactions. This demonstrated how to build a highly granular and auditable view of your data from the ground up. Finally, you put your work to the test, writing practical data tests and unit tests to validate your business logic and ensure your models are trustworthy.

You are now equipped with a powerful set of patterns and hands-on experience to build the logical core of any data platform. In the next chapter, the Delivery Layer, we will explore the principles of the final layer in our platform, where we will shape this refined data into optimized user-facing data marts for business intelligence, analytics, and other use cases.

Recommended resources

dbt Documentation

The official dbt documentation is the best source for up-to-date information on the testing and governance features we implemented.

- **Unit Tests**: For a deeper dive into the syntax and capabilities of dbt's native unit testing framework. https://docs.getdbt.com/docs/build/unit-tests.
- **dbt Seeds**: For more information on how to manage and use the static data we used for manual corporate actions. https://docs.getdbt.com/docs/build/seeds.

Snowflake Documentation

These resources from Snowflake provide more detail on the advanced SQL functions in our models.

- **ASOF JOIN**: The underlying technology for our time_join macro, essential for point-in-time analysis. https://docs.snowflake.com/en/sql-reference/constructs/asof-join.
- **Window Functions**: To better understand functions like `LAG()`, `LEAD()`, and `ROW_NUMBER()` that were used extensively in our models. https://docs.snowflake.com/en/sql-reference/functions-analytic.
- **Recursive CTEs**: For a deeper understanding of the syntax used to build our event-sourced position history. https://docs.snowflake.com/en/sql-reference/constructs/with-recursive.

CHAPTER 14

The Delivery Layer

Welcome to the final and most critical stage of our data platform journey: the Delivery Layer. This is the "last mile" of data engineering, where all our previous work culminates in tangible business value. It's here that the well-structured, integrated data from the Refined Layer is shaped into trusted, purpose-built, and user-friendly data products. In the previous layers, our focus was primarily technical. We built a faithful, historical record of our source systems in the Storage Layer and then transformed it into clean, reusable business concepts in the Refined Layer. Now, our mindset shifts from that of a data plumber to that of a product manager. The central question is no longer "What is the data?" but rather, "Who will use this data, and how can we make it as useful, reliable, and intuitive as possible for them?"

This chapter covers the principles, patterns, and engineering practices for building out our Data Product Repository. We will explore how to serve a wide variety of consumers by creating product categories ranging from traditional data marts for BI analysts to curated datasets for machine learning models and secure APIs for applications. We will start by outlining the pragmatic process for designing and building BI data marts, grounded in the timeless principles of dimensional modeling, which remain the bedrock of business intelligence. Then, we will introduce key software engineering principles, such as Design by Contract, and show how modern dbt features, like contracts and model versions, enable us to build data products with the rigor and reliability of production software. Finally, we will explore how a well-architected Delivery Layer serves as the foundation for advanced use cases and enables a decentralized Data Mesh architecture. By the end of this chapter, you will have a comprehensive framework for designing and building a Delivery Layer that not only meets today's needs but is also robust and flexible enough to evolve with your organization's future demands.

In this chapter, we will cover the following topics:

- **Structuring and Organizing the Delivery Layer**: Blueprint for our Data Product Repository.
- **Building Data Products for Business Intelligence**: A pragmatic process for building BI data marts and covering the timeless dimensional modeling patterns that power BI analytics.

- **Engineering Excellence in the Delivery Layer**: Software engineering principles, Design by Contract (DBC), and dbt features to build trustworthy and maintainable data products.
- **Data Products for Advanced Use Cases**: Serving data to applications, preparing features for AI/ML, securely sharing data, and enabling a decentralized Data Mesh architecture.

Sample project and code

The sample dbt project is available at: **https://github.com/pragmatic-data/stonks**. The code samples for this chapter are in the sub-folder `chapter_14`, under the `code_samples_by_chapter` folder. Please note that, to better fit the limited space on the printed page, we omit most comments and change the formatting of code blocks compared to the files.

The delivery layer in customer cases

The Delivery Layer is the final and most crucial stage of the Pragmatic Data Platform, representing the 'last mile' where technical effort translates directly into business value. The experiences of companies adopting the principles shared with the PDP architecture demonstrate their ability to address critical enterprise needs across three key areas: achieving unshakeable trust through continuous governance, enabling the creation of impactful dashboards, and fostering massive-scale self-service BI for hundreds of business users. The complete case studies for Rebtel, Stora Enso, and OutSystems are in Chapter 6.

- **Rebtel**: Good Data Quality and Governance are key to user acceptance. Rebtel embedded CI/CD, SQL code review, and SQLFluff into their BI workflows, turning every deployment into a quality checkpoint and ensuring dashboards always reflected a trusted state of data.

- **Stora Enso**: At Stora Enso, the Delivery Layer turned data into actionable insight. By modeling supply chain and production data into clear, business-aligned marts, they built dashboards that trace renewable material flows end to end — helping teams monitor emissions, optimize logistics, and make sustainability a measurable part of daily operations.

- **OutSystems**: At OutSystems, scale defined the challenge. A single set of wide, tested "gold" tables empowered 700+ BI users to explore data confidently, replacing ad-hoc reports with governed self-service analytics that still spoke a common business language.

The delivery layer as a data product repository

We have traveled a long way through the Pragmatic Data Platform architecture. We began by capturing a complete and faithful history of our source systems in the Storage Layer. We then moved to the Refined Layer, where we cleaned, integrated, and transformed that data into a set of reusable, business-oriented concepts. Now, we arrive at the final and most visible part of our platform: the Delivery Layer, the true "last mile" where data is served out to produce usable business value.

It is helpful to think of the Delivery Layer as a **Data Product Repository**. The Refined Layer provides us with high-quality, standardized materials—our integrated business concepts. The Delivery Layer is where we curate, assemble, and present these materials as finished goods, or **Data Products, designed for specific consumers**. These consumers are diverse:

- **Business Intelligence (BI) tools** like Tableau, Power BI, or Looker require proper Kimball fact and dimensions or wide, denormalized tables to allow analysts to slice and dice data.
- **Data analysts** who write ad-hoc SQL queries and need intuitive, well-documented models to explore data and answer novel business questions.
- **Data scientists** who require specifically structured datasets, or "feature tables," to train and run machine learning models.
- **Operational applications** that consume data via APIs to power customer-facing analytics or internal dashboards. Critically, they often require sub second response time.

Building this repository requires a fundamental shift in our mindset. In previous layers, we primarily acted as data technicians, focused on accuracy, integration, and historical accuracy. In the Delivery Layer, we must become data product managers: our focus shifts to the needs of our users. We must ask:

- Why are we serving this data?
- Who is the audience for this data?
- What business question are they trying to answer?
- What structure would be most intuitive for them and their tools?
- What guarantees of quality, freshness, and reliability do they need?

This user-centric approach is the hallmark of a successful Delivery Layer. The goal is no longer abstract and generic to build a well-organized repository of trusted, easy-to-use, and maintainable data products that empower the entire organization to make better decisions. The goal, now, is to make real colleagues to discover and use the data.

To simplify navigation, this repository can be structured into distinct **Categories** reflecting different use-case needs, such as BI, applications, or AI/ML. They contain curated **collections of data products**, called **Data Marts**, whose purpose is to simplify the lives of their users. Engage with them to understand how they think and what they need.

Every model we build in the Delivery layer is a direct interface with our stakeholders, and its design, quality, and stability will determine the success and adoption of our data platform. Do not guess, ask their evaluation.

Structuring and organizing the delivery layer

Before we write a single line of SQL for our data products, we must establish a clear and scalable structure for them. A well-organized Delivery Layer is intuitive to navigate, simple to maintain, and easy for consumers to trust. Without a consistent structure, this layer can quickly devolve into a confusing collection of tables, leading to duplicated logic, user uncertainty, and a brittle data platform.

The organizational principles we outline here are designed to support the "**Data Product Repository**" concept. We will organize our repository into distinct Categories based on the type of consumer, and within each Category, we will group related models into Data Marts, which are Collections of Data Products. The Data Mart structure broadly aligns with dbt folders and Snowflake schemas, and Data Products are composed of coherent, integrated dbt models.

This ensures that every model has a logical home and a name that clearly communicates its purpose, providing a navigable map for anyone exploring the repository to discover available data products. This helps all stakeholders, not just developers.

Folder and model organization

The first step is to create a clean separation between the Delivery Layer and the upstream layers. All models in this layer should reside within the `models/03_delivery/` directory in your dbt project. Within this directory, the top-level folders represent our product Categories.

Common **categories** include:

- **`marts/`**: For traditional BI data marts with facts and dimensions, or wide tables.
- **`apps/`**: For data marts with models specifically tailored to power applications.
- **`ml/`**: For data marts with feature tables designed for machine learning models.

Within each category folder, we create sub-folders for each specific model collection. In the Pragmatic Data Platform, a collection is a data mart. A data mart is a container for a cohesive set of related data products (dimensions, facts, reports). For example, all portfolio analysis models form one collection, while marketing models form another. In PDP, a data mart typically corresponds to a dedicated folder in dbt and a dedicated schema in Snowflake. This hierarchical structure provides immediate clarity:

```
models/
└── 03_delivery/                       # The Repository
    ├── marts/                      # The "BI Marts" Category
    │   ├── portfolio_analysis/     # "Portfolio Analysis" data mart
    │   │   ├── _portfolio_analysis.yml
    │   │   ├── dim_securities.sql
    │   │   └── rpt_total_return.sql
    │   └── marketing/              # "Marketing" data mart
    │       ├── dim_campaigns.sql
    │       └── fct_ad_spend.sql
    └── apps/                       # "Applications" Category
        └── current_portfolio/      # "Current Portfolio" data mart
            └── rpt_current_portfolio.sql
```

This folder-based organization is easy to understand and facilitates governance of each collection by assigning Snowflake schema access to different roles.

Naming conventions

Clear, consistent naming conventions serve as a cataloging system for our repository. A well-chosen name signals the type and purpose of a model at a glance. In the Delivery Layer, we use the following standard prefixes:

- **DIM_ (Dimension)**: Models containing descriptive attributes of business entities (the "who, what, where, when, and why"). They represent the current state only, e.g. `dim_customers`.
- **SCD_ (Slowly Changing Dimension)**: For historical dimensions that track changes over time (Type 2 SCD). They represents all versions, e.g. `scd_customers`.
- **FCT_ (Fact)**: Models containing numeric measures about business events or processes (the "how many" or "how much"). Examples: `fct_trades`, `fct_daily_sales`.
- **RPT_ (Report)**: The user-facing models, typically denormalized, created by joining facts and dimensions, and optimized for the specific use. E.g.: `rpt_marketing_kpis`.
- **FILTER_ (Filter)**: A useful pattern for creating simple models that contain a reusable set of filter conditions. Example: `filter_active_customers`.

Configuring deployment schemas

A key principle of a clean repository is that your database structure should mirror your project structure. We do this by configuring custom schemas in the `dbt_project.yml` file for the folders that contain our marts. This automatically places all models from a specific collection into a corresponding database schema. For our `portfolio_analysis` data mart, the configuration would look like this:

```
models:
  stonks:
    delivery:
      +materialized: table  # A possible default for direct queries
      marts:
        portfolio_analysis:                    # one BI data mart
          +schema: BI_PORTFOLIO_ANALYSIS       # its schema in Snowflake
        marketing:
          +schema: BI_MARKETING

      apps:
        current_portfolio:
          +schema: APP_CURRENT_PORTFOLIO
```

This configuration ensures that when you run `dbt build`, the models inside the `portfolio_analysis` folder are built into the `BI_PORTFOLIO_ANALYSIS` schema in Snowflake. Keeping the dbt and database structures aligned makes both governance and discovery simple.

Materialization strategy

The materialization directly impacts consumer query performance. In the Delivery Layer, the priority is speed:

- **table**: The default materialization for most core data products, especially `FCT_` and `RPT_` models if they are repeatedly hit by user queries. The computational work is done once during the dbt build, ensuring consumers enjoy fast, responsive queries.
- **view**: Views always provide up-to-date data without requiring a `dbt build,` but can be slow if the underlying logic is complex. Views are also perfect when your models are queried only once, because your

BI tool keeps the data in a long-term cache and performs a few refreshes. In such cases, it is better to use view flexibility, as the table speed is not used.
- **incremental**: This is rarely a good choice for the delivery layer, but can be used selectively for very large fact tables where a full rebuild is prohibitively slow.

Documentation as a product feature

Finally, a crucial step is to **treat documentation as a core feature of your data products.** A repository is only as good as its catalog. For every model in the Delivery Layer, you should:

- Provide a clear, business-oriented description of each model in YAML files. Use rich markdown format to provide complete and compelling information to your potential users. Use the `meta` config to name an onwer, provide a contact email/phone and point to extra documentation, where available.
- Document every column, explaining what it means. When in doubt, give examples. If you don't bother to document a column, it should not be in the data product.
- Define data tests to guarantee logical integrity and data contracts for physical integrity.

This metadata powers `dbt docs`, transforming it from a simple technical reference into a rich, searchable product catalog for your data repository. It empowers users to discover, understand, and trust the data products.

In the Delivery Layer, it is common that the same refined data is exposed multiple times in slightly different forms; this is encouraged to provide users with the best solution to their needs.
At the same time, it is imperative that the business logic is not repeated.
Write the logic once in the Refined layer, and present it multiple times in the Delivery layer.

Building data products for business intelligence

While our data platform must serve a variety of modern use cases, its most common and visible consumer is still Business Intelligence (BI). This is where analysts and decision-makers interact with data through dashboards, reports, and ad-hoc queries. To serve them effectively, we must present data not only accurately but also intuitively and quickly queryable. For this, we turn to the time-tested principles of dimensional modeling.

This section will explore how to build high-quality data products for BI within our Data Product Repository. We will revisit the core concepts of dimensional modeling, adapt them to the modern data stack, and show how they fit perfectly within the Pragmatic Data Platform's layered architecture.

Kimball revisited in the modern stack

For decades, **Ralph Kimball's dimensional modeling** and its signature **star schema** have been the gold standard for designing data warehouses for analytics. The concept is simple yet powerful: a central fact table containing numeric measurements, such as Position Daily Values, is linked to a set of surrounding dimension tables with descriptive context, such as Security, Calendar, and Portfolio.

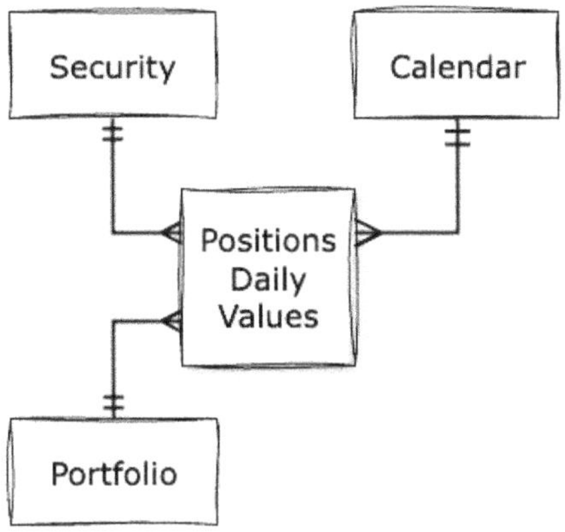

Figure 43: Example of a star schema, using entities from the Stonks sample project.

The resulting structure is exceptionally effective because it mirrors how business users think: "Show me Position Daily Value [fact] by Portfolio [dimension] and by Security [dimension] on this date [dimension]." This structure is highly optimized for the way BI tools work, making it easy to filter, group, slice, and dice data. Furthermore, the simple hub-and-spoke design of a *proper* star schema naturally avoids common SQL pitfalls like the fan traps and chasm traps we discussed in Chapter 1, which can arise from more complex join paths and lead to incorrect results.

Star schemas for presentation, not for data storage

Star schemas are great for providing easy-to-query data marts. However, we already saw in Chapter 1 that using them as the primary storage model for your entire data platform would not be a good idea, as that alone would cause significant limitations:

- **Brittleness**: Dimensional models are designed around specific business processes, and data is modified to fit that view. If a process changes, the data must be transformed to accommodate the new process, which can require costly rework. As we do not have the original data, the adaptation process must be careful not to lose or break the data, and sometimes it can be impossible, not just difficult and time-consuming, as star schemas are less representative by design than general relational models (to make them simple).
- **Difficult Integration**: Conforming data from different source systems into single, unified facts and dimensions is a notoriously manual, difficult process. If you store your data in star schemas, you store it after changing it and then you must keep changing your data every time you need to make a change in a conformed dimension or -potentially- one of its facts.

This is why the Pragmatic Data Platform separates data storage from business rule implementation and data presentation. We do not store our data directly in the fact and dimension tables. Instead, our Storage Layer provides a resilient, source-aligned historical record that absorbs source system changes and provides a rock-solid base for the other layers. The Refined Layer handles the complex work of integration and business logic. Finally, in the Delivery Layer, we assemble this clean, stable data into star schemas that we can change at will without impacting the previous layers or the stored data. This gives us the best of both worlds: a flexible, maintainable, and robust back end, with a user-friendly, high-performance, and easy-to-change front end optimized for BI.

A pragmatic process for building a data mart

Building a successful data mart is not just a technical exercise; it's a collaborative process that must be rooted in business needs. Rushing to write SQL without a clear plan is a recipe for a data product that no one uses. Based on our experience, we recommend a structured, four-step approach.

1. **Understand the Business Need**: The process always begins with a business question. This could be a high-level goal ("We need to understand our portfolio's performance") or a specific request ("I need a report of daily returns, including dividends, by security type"). Engage directly with the stakeholders to clarify the requirements. What are the key metrics (facts)? What are the key concepts/attributes they want to filter and group by (dimensions)?
2. **Create the Conceptual Data Model**: Before writing any code, sketch out the star schema on a whiteboard or in a diagramming tool. Identify your central business process (the fact table) and the relevant business concepts (the dimensions). This is the **bus matrix** design phase, where you identify the facts you need and the dimensions you use to analyze them. Update the matrix with the new findings. For our `portfolio_analysis` mart, the central process is the Daily Position Valuation, with Trades and Dividends completing the mart. The entities are Security, Portfolio, and Date (Calendar). The **bus matrix** would look like this:

Business Process (Fact Table)	Date	Security	Portfolio
Trades (FCT_TRADES)	X	X	X
Dividends (FCT_DIVIDENDS)	X	X	X
Daily Positions (FCT_POSITIONS_DAILY)	X	X	X

   This simple visual matrix, along with the star schema model, is a powerful communication tool to build, refine, and validate your understanding with business stakeholders.
3. **Identify and Prepare the Data**: With the conceptual model approved, map the required facts and dimensions back to the available data in your Refined Layer. Do the necessary models already exist? If not, what new transformations are needed? If you need to create new refined models, draw a data model to clarify and document what they contain and how they relate to the other models in the refined layer. This step ensures you map your needs to the reality of your data, add any missing entities to the Storage layer, and design high-quality refined components before you start building the final data products.
4. **Build and Test the Data Mart**: Finally, it's time to code the business rules and serve them through a data product. Build the reusable models that serve multiple data marts in the Refined layer, or build the highly specific ones directly in the individual data marts, then build the `FCT_` and `DIM_` or `SCD_` on top of them to extend your data product. If needed, assemble them into a final `RPT_` model. Throughout this process, add documentation and tests to ensure the output is correct, reliable, and understandable. Once built, present it to the stakeholders only the final products and iterate based on their feedback.

Please note that it is intentional that our process goes through our layers twice. First, start from the end to identify the result you need, and move backwards to see what you have and what you need to build or add to the data platform. Then, once you have a solid plan, you implement it from the sources, completing the work with the models in the delivery layer.

This structured process transforms data mart development from an ad-hoc art into a repeatable engineering discipline, ensuring the final product is well-designed, aligned with business needs, documented at the right level of abstraction and trusted by its users.

Dimensions

Dimension models are the **soul** of the data mart. They provide the context, the "who, what, where, when, why, and how" behind the numbers in our fact tables. A dimension table contains the descriptive, textual attributes that users will use to filter and group data in their reports. For our Stonks project, a `dim_securities` dimension would include columns such as symbol, security name, security type, listing exchange, and more.

Key characteristics of dimensions include:

- **Descriptive**: They are rich in textual attributes and should not have numbers to do math on.
- **Wide**: They often have many columns.
- **Shallow**: They have significantly fewer rows compared to the fact tables.

In a BI data mart, you will encounter several types of dimensions:

- **Standard Dimensions**: The most common type, representing core business entities "as of now," that is, only with their current values. Our `dim_securities` and `dim_portfolios` are perfect examples.

- **Time Dimension**: Calendar or date is an essential dimension with a row for every day, providing ready-to-use calculated fields like `year`, `month_name`, `day_of_week`, and `is_weekday`. It dramatically simplifies time-based analysis. You might have smaller granularities too, but a calendar with days is the most common and always present.

- **Slowly Changing Dimensions (SCDs)**: Business attributes change over time. An `SCD` dimension is a pattern for managing this history. Our VER models implement SCD Type 2, adding a new row for each change and handling its validity with `valid_from`, `valid_to`, and `is_current` columns. For instance, querying a full `SCD_Securities` dimension, we could see the time when **Barrick Gold** still had this name and **GOLD** as the symbol, and that now it's called **Barrick Mining Corporation** and has **B** as the symbol. The security's name and symbol have changed, but the security and its code have not.

There are many SCD types, with normal, current data, dimensions being SCD of Type 1. We encourage you to read about the other types, but discussing them here is beyond the scope of this book.

Advanced dimension patterns

Two other powerful patterns are worth knowing:

- **Role-Playing Dimensions**: A single dimension can be linked to a fact table multiple times, with each link representing a different "role." The classic example is a single `dim_date` table that is joined to a fact table on `order_date_key`, `ship_date_key`, and `delivery_date_key`. Each join defines a different role that the date dimension plays.

- **Junk Dimensions:** This pragmatic pattern groups miscellaneous low-cardinality flags or attributes from a source system into a single dimension. Instead of adding many small columns to a fact table (e.g., `trade_status`, `order_type`), you can combine them into a "junk" dimension with one row for each combination of the observed values and place only a key in the fact, to keep the fact table small. This used to be important for performance when using row-based databases, but with the advent of columnar databases like Snowflake, this is no longer a problem, and we can avoid the extra complexity and work.

Facts

Fact models are the **heart** of the data mart. They contain the numeric measurements of the business. A fact table consists of foreign keys that link to the surrounding dimension tables and the numeric measures themselves. In our `fct_trades` model, the measures would be columns like `quantity`, `trade_price`, and `commission_usd`.

Composite facts

A crucial rule of thumb when using a star schema is to **avoid joining a fact table to another fact table in a BI tool**, directly or indirectly through common dimensions. This operation is risky for business users, who may not be aware of the different grains of the tables and can easily create a join that produces disastrously incorrect results due to **fan or chasm traps**. To overcome this limitation, data engineers and analysts create safe, pre-joined models. Using their expertise, they can correctly join base facts to create **composite facts** or denormalized reports. This is a powerful pattern because:

- **It ensures correctness**: The potentially complex join logic is defined once by an expert and tested on real data with dbt tests, preventing end-user errors.
- **It improves performance**: The join is pre-computed during the `dbt build`, making queries in the BI tool much faster.
- **It simplifies the user experience**: The user is presented with a single, coherent table that is ready for analysis.

If a composite fact is a fundamental business concept that will be reused across many data marts, like our `fct_positions_daily`, it should be built in the Refined Layer. If it's a specific calculation needed for a single data mart, it can be built directly in that mart's collection. Thanks to the flexibility of dbt, you don't need a magic crystal ball. If you are unsure about reusing a composite fact or report, you can start implementing it in the data mart, and when you start to reuse it, move the model with the logic into the Refined layer and put a simple view in the data mart in its place.

Understanding the grain and additivity

Two fundamental concepts define a fact table:

- **The Grain**: This is the definition of what a single row represents. It is the most important piece of metadata for a fact table. The grain of our `fct_trades` is "one row per trade execution." The grain of `fct_positions_daily` is "one row per security, per portfolio, per day." A clearly stated grain prevents misinterpretation of the data.

- **Additivity**: This describes how numeric measures in a fact can be aggregated.
  - **Fully Additive**: Measures that can be summed across any and all dimensions. `trade_amount_usd` in our `fct_trades` is fully additive not considering currencies.
  - **Semi-Additive**: Measures that can be summed across some dimensions but not others. `position_value` in our `fct_positions_daily` is semi-additive; you can sum it across securities to get a total portfolio value for one day, but summing it across days makes no sense.
  - **Non-Additive**: Measures that cannot be summed, such as ratios, percentages, or temperatures. These must be calculated from their fully additive components.

While quite intuitive to most users, it is better to clarify these two concepts in the data product documentation, so that users of every level can use the data without doubts or oversights.

Denormalized reports (RPT)

While a well-structured set of `FCT_`, `DIM_`, and `SCD_` tables forms a complete and flexible BI data mart, it is not always the final step. For many common or performance-intensive analyses, it is highly practical to create **Denormalized Reports**, which we identify with the `RPT_` prefix.

An `RPT_` model is a wide table created by pre-joining a fact table (or multiple fact tables, as we discussed) with several of its most frequently used dimensions. It is important to understand that `RPT_` models do not replace the underlying facts and dimensions. Instead, they happily live alongside them within the data mart's collection.

The `FCT_` and `DIM_` tables provide flexibility for ad hoc exploration and for BI tools optimized for star schemas. The `RPT_` tables can provide a high-performance, easy-to-use shortcut for the most common and important reporting needs. For example, our `rpt_total_return` would pre-join `fct_positions_daily` and `fct_dividends` with `dim_securities`, creating a single table with columns like `report_date`, `symbol`, `market_value_change_usd`, `dividend_ income_usd`, and `total_return`. The PDP encourages providing both, offering your users the right tool for their specific task.

Engineering excellence in the delivery layer

As we build out our Data Product Repository, our responsibility shifts from simply providing data to **providing a reliable service**.

Downstream dashboards, critical business reports, applications, and machine learning models depend on the data products we create. An accidental change—a renamed column, an altered data type, a modified business rule—can break downstream consumers, eroding trust and causing disruption. To prevent this, we must treat our data products as the critical software components they are. Fortunately, software engineering has been solving these problems for decades through a set of design principles that promote robustness, maintainability, and scalability.

In this section, we will adapt three of the most impactful principles to data engineering and show how dbt provides the native tools to implement them, going from abstract theory into daily practice.

Design by Contract (DBC): The foundation of trust

In the real world, a contract is a formal agreement that clarifies expectations and sets boundaries. The principle of Design by Contract applies the idea to software and is the foundation of a trustworthy data product: **a data model's contract is its public promise to its consumers**. This promise guarantees the model's structure, or "shape." Specifically, it guarantees that:

- Columns will have specific names (e.g., `symbol`).
- Columns will have specific data types (e.g., `VARCHAR`, `NUMBER`).
- Data will adhere to specific constraints (e.g., `not null`).

Historically, these contracts were just implicit agreements or manual documentation.

With dbt, we can make them explicit and automatically enforced. dbt model contracts are a literal implementation of the DBC principle. By adding a contract to your model's YAML file and setting `enforced: true`, you are creating a binding agreement. The snippet shows how you can easily add data type and constraint information to the usual YAML files used to describe and test our models.

```
models:
  - name: rpt_total_return
    config:
      contract: {enforced: true}

    columns:
      - name: report_date
        data_type: date
        constraints:
          - type: not_null

      - name: symbol
        data_type: varchar

      - name: total_return_usd
        data_type: number(38, 6)
```

One key point is that a data contract covers the entire surface of a model; **you must describe all columns** with their names and data types. If your model's code ever produces an output that violates its contract, `dbt build` will fail. For example, if `total_return_usd` were cast as a `string` you would get an error. This prevents you from publishing a breaking change by accident. Model contracts are the single most important tool for ensuring that your data products are stable and reliable. You can always fix, extend and evolve contracts, with versioning as needed.

The Open/Closed Principle (OCP): Building for the future

The Open/Closed Principle states that
software entities should be open to extension but closed to modification.

This is a powerful guide for evolving your data products gracefully over time.

- **Closed for Modification**: Once a data product is published and in use, you should not change its existing structure or meaning. The existing interface is "closed," and no (breaking) changes are allowed. Renaming `total_return_usd` to `return_total_usd` or changing its data type would violate its contract and break downstream consumers.
- **Open for Extension**: Business requirements are never static. Your product must be "open" to being extended with new functionality, and support the old ones. You will inevitably need to add new columns or metrics to your data products. Your design must allow for this.

How do we add functionality, even compatibility-breaking ones, without abruptly modifying the existing product? The answer is **dbt model versions**.

Versioning lets you create a new, enhanced version of a model while the original remains stable. Both are live at the same time, and consumers can decide which to use, providing a controlled transition period. For example, if we need to add the currency conversion rate at the time of the position's last change to our report, we also need to rename the current exchange rate `fx_rate_to_base,` to make it clear it is the exchange rate on the day of the position value.

Instead of renaming it, which would break our clients, we create a new model for `v2` and define the new version in our YAML file. Existing dashboards can continue to use the current reference `ref('rpt_total_return')` (which defaults to `v1`), while new development can explicitly use `ref('rpt_total_return', version=2)` to access the enhanced model. This provides a safe, explicit path for evolution and prevents the common problem where "improving" a report for one team breaks it for another.

To further improve our process, the model versioning feature in dbt allows us to deprecate versions we want to phase out and pick a default version, allowing us, for example, to switch the default from v1 to v2 at some point. This would be a wake-up call for clients not yet migrated to `v2`. To avoid disruption, they could keep using `v1` until we keep it live, just by explicitly adding the version to their reference, so we can be sure they got the memo with minimal disruption.

The Interface Segregation Principle (ISP): Right-sized data products

---

The Interface Segregation Principle states that
no client should be forced to depend on methods it does not use.

When we translate this to data, a "client" is a data consumer (e.g., a BI dashboard), and an "interface" is our data product (e.g., a table or view). The principle becomes: **No data consumer should be forced to depend on a table that is larger or more complex than it needs.** This principle directly combats the temptation to serve a single, monolithic "god table" to serve every possible business need. These tables inevitably become slow to query, confusing to understand, and difficult to maintain.

A marketing dashboard that only needs three columns should not have to depend on a 200-column table that was primarily designed for the finance department's reporting. The ISP is the philosophical justification for the "Categories" and "Data Marts" structures we defined earlier. It guides us to build lean, purpose-built data products tailored to specific use cases. Our BI users have access to the `portfolio_analysis` collection and its rich reports. Our Streamlit application uses a lean, fast `app_current_portfolio` model that contains only the columns it needs to display. This approach leads to a system that is faster, easier to understand, secure, and simpler to maintain and evolve. By providing right-sized interfaces, we serve our users better and build a more resilient data repository.

Building data products for advanced use cases

While business intelligence is a primary consumer of our data products, its value does not end there. A truly modern data platform must serve a much wider and more diverse audience, including applications, machine learning models, and even other data teams. In this section, we explore how our data product repository can be extended to serve these advanced, often programmatic, consumers.

Data as a Service: Secure data sharing

> *The most elegant way to treat data as a service is to eliminate the need for data movement entirely, making data immediately available without writing any ETL.*

Snowflake Secure Data Sharing is the signature Snowflake feature that enables you to grant other Snowflake accounts secure, live, read-only access to your data products without ever copying or exporting the data. The consumer is granted a direct window into a specific "share" of your repository, meaning there are no data movement costs, no latency, and no risk of stale data. This pattern is far superior to traditional methods, especially older ones like emailing CSVs or maintaining SFTP sites, which are insecure, slow, and create data silos. With Secure Data Sharing, you retain complete control.

Example: Sharing a client's portfolio data

Imagine in our Stonks project that one of the brokerage portfolios belongs to a high-value client who also uses Snowflake. They want live access to their portfolio performance. We absolutely do not want to share our entire `rpt_total_return` table, which contains data for all portfolios. Instead, we can create a secure, version-controlled sharing solution in our dbt project.

Create a Secure View: First, we build a model that will become a secure view. The `sh_client_portfolio` model contains the SELECT logic, which uses Snowflake's row-level security features to ensure the consumer can only see rows corresponding to their specific `account_id`.

```
SELECT *
FROM {{ ref('rpt_total_return') }}
WHERE account_id = (
  SELECT account_id_for_share
  FROM {{ source('governance', 'share_recipients') }}
  WHERE snowflake_account_id = CURRENT_ACCOUNT()
)
```

The code above uses the `CURRENT_ACCOUNT()` function to filter the data, ensuring that each customer only sees their own data.

Only secure views and tables can be shared. We configure this model to be materialized as a **secure view**, by adding the `secure: true` configuration in a `{{config(...)}}` local block or in a.`yml` file (as shown below).

```
version: 2
models:
  - name: sh_client_portfolio
    config:
      materialized: view
      secure: true
```

Create and Manage the Share with dbt: We use dbt hooks or a macro called with the run-operation command, as we do for the ingestion, to manage the Snowflake `SHARE` object and grant privileges on the secure view. This keeps the entire sharing configuration version-controlled within our Git repository. The benefits of this approach are immense:

- **Unmatched Security and Governance**: The data never leaves our Snowflake account. We have granular, row-level control over what is shared, and we can revoke access instantly.
- **Live Data with Zero Latency**: The client is querying our live production model. The moment our dbt build completes, they see the updated data. No ETL delay.
- **No Engineering Overhead**: We completely eliminate the need to build, monitor, and maintain a separate data export pipeline for this client, saving significant engineering effort on both sides. No API calls, no orchestration, no new security risk.

Powering APIs and applications

The data products in our repository can also serve as the direct back end for data-intensive applications. That is what data products are designed for. However, interactive applications have much stricter latency requirements than traditional BI. While a dashboard might be acceptable with a response time of seconds and sometimes minutes, a user-facing application often requires sub-second query responses for tasks like point lookups (e.g., retrieving a single customer's profile). API calls are even more strict, sometimes requiring responses in the single-digit millisecond range. To meet these needs, we can build lean, application-specific models and leverage Snowflake's performance features, such as the Search Optimization Service. For even more demanding use cases, we can turn to specialized table types, such as Hybrid Tables.

Hybrid tables for transactional workloads

Hybrid Tables are a powerful feature in Snowflake designed for hybrid transactional and analytical processing (HTAP). Unlike standard Snowflake tables, which are column-optimized for large-scale analytical queries, Hybrid Tables are row-optimized.

This allows them to perform rapid single-row lookups, inserts, and updates typical of transactional (OLTP) databases such as PostgreSQL or MySQL. The problem they solve is the classic "two-database" issue, where companies must maintain a separate transactional database to power their applications or as an interface for high-speed APIs, and then build a complex ETL pipeline to move that data into Snowflake for analysis and enrichment, and back to the database for high-speed serving. This creates data silos, latency, and engineering overhead.

Hybrid Tables allow you to unify these workloads on a single platform. For example, our Stonks project could evolve into an application where users can add their own price targets to individual positions. We could create a `price_targets` Hybrid Table. The application would perform fast, transactional `INSERT`s and `UPDATE`s on this table as users add or edit their targets.

In Snowflake, you could even create the Price Target application with Streamlit, a lightweight platform that allows you to create rich UI based applications based on data residing in Snowflake and totally hosted inside your Snowflake account. This would create a UI on top of such a table and use Snowflake user and roles for access and authorization, solving another problem.

Our analytical models in the Delivery Layer could then perform a large-scale `JOIN` between our existing `fct_trades` or `fct_position_daily` tables and the `price_targets` Hybrid Table to create an enriched report estimating the volume of operations we expect based on customer targets or send out alerts to customers. This unified approach dramatically simplifies the architecture, eliminates data silos, and allows you to build rich, data-driven applications entirely within the Snowflake and dbt ecosystem.

Preparing data for AI/ML

Data scientists and machine learning engineers have a voracious appetite for clean, well-structured, and reliable data. Our Data Product Repository is the perfect source for their work, and with the right organization, it can function as a highly effective Feature Store.

A feature store is a centralized repository that enables data scientists to discover, share, and reuse features: the individual, measurable properties or characteristics used to train machine learning models. The goal is to accelerate the ML development lifecycle by avoiding teams' need to constantly rebuild the same features and ensuring that features are calculated consistently across projects. A good feature store provides several key capabilities, easily delivered with dbt and Snowflake:

- **Discoverability and documentation**: Data scientists need to find what features are available and understand what they mean. The dbt Catalog provides a searchable interface with clear descriptions, column definitions, data test results, and lineage graphs.
- **Versioning**: As a feature's logic evolves, it's critical not to break existing models that depend on it. dbt model versions allow us to safely introduce new versions of a feature while maintaining backward compatibility.
- **Governance and access control**: Not all features should be accessible to everyone. By organizing features into dedicated collections (e.g., `ml/finance_features`) that map to specific Snowflake schemas, we can use Snowflake roles to manage access with precision.
- **Consistency**: The feature's calculation must be consistent, whether it's used for training a model today or for generating predictions six months from now. dbt's declarative nature ensures this; the SQL code is the single, immutable definition of the feature.

Preparing features in the Pragmatic Data Platform

The process of creating models in our platform is, in itself, a form of feature engineering. The decision of where to create a feature depends on its reusability:

- **The Refined Layer**: This is the ideal place for foundational, business-oriented features that are likely to be reused across many different analytical use cases, not just a single ML model. For example, a model that calculates a `security_52week_max_price` metric is a core concept that could be used in BI reports as well as for ML.
- **The Delivery Layer (ml/ Category)**: This is where we assemble features for a specific ML project. We create a dedicated collection (e.g., `ml/trade_ forecasting/`) and build models that select foundational features from the Refined Layer and create new, model-specific ones. The final output is typically a single, wide, denormalized table where each row represents an instance to be predicted (e.g., a portfolio or a security in a given day, week, or month) and each column represents a feature to be used for the training/prediction.

Example: Building a feature table for trade forecasting

Let's imagine a data scientist wants to build a model to predict the number of trades a specific portfolio will execute in the upcoming week. This is a classic regression problem. To train this model, they need a feature table with one row per portfolio and per week. We can build this feature table in the Delivery Layer by aggregating historical trade data and creating time-based (or "lag") features that describe past behavior. We can create the model `ml_portfolio_weekly_features.sql` with the following code. Note: the following is some pseudo-code meant to show what a feature model would look like. You will not be able to run it, as the source tables and column names do not match those in the sample project, but you could build something close to it if you like the idea. The below dbt model (which could have dozens more features with multiple lags, built refactoring the SQL into our own macros called inside a loop… I hope you start seeing how the patterns connect) produces a clean, wide table that is perfectly structured to be passed to a regression model. It creates powerful features based on historical behavior, like `trades_last_week` and `avg_trades_last_4_ weeks`, which are essential for forecasting. This feature table is now a discoverable, versionable, and governed product in our repository, ready to accelerate our data science team's work.

```
WITH weekly_trades_by_portfolio AS (
  -- First, aggregate trade data to the portfolio-week
  SELECT
    portfolio_key,
    DATE_TRUNC('week', trade_timestamp) AS week_start_date,
    COUNT(*) AS weekly_trade_count,
    COUNT(DISTINCT security_key) AS weekly_dist_securities
  FROM {{ ref('fct_trades') }}
  GROUP BY 1, 2
),

final AS (
  -- Now, create lag features based on past weekly activity
  SELECT
    -- Keys
    portfolio_key,
    week_start_date,

   -- The target variable
    weekly_trade_count AS trades_in_week,

   -- Feature: N of trades in the prior week (lag feature)
    LAG(weekly_trade_count, 1, 0) OVER (
        PARTITION BY portfolio_key
        ORDER BY week_start_date
    ) AS trades_last_week,

   -- Feature: AVG trades in last four weeks (rolling agg)
    AVG(weekly_trade_count) OVER (
        PARTITION BY portfolio_key
        ORDER BY week_start_date
        ROWS BETWEEN 4 PRECEDING AND 1 PRECEDING
    ) AS avg_trades_last_4_weeks,

   -- Feature: N distinct securities traded in prior week
    LAG(weekly_distinct_securities, 1, 0) OVER (
        PARTITION BY portfolio_key
        ORDER BY week_start_date
    ) AS distinct_securities_last_week

 FROM weekly_trades_by_portfolio
)

SELECT * FROM final
```

From features to predictions: Training a model with snowflake cortex

Once the feature table is built, the next step would be to export this data to a separate workload for model training. However, with Snowflake Cortex, we can train and deploy our regression model directly in Snowflake using simple SQL and fully integrate the process into our dbt workflow.

Snowflake Cortex ML-Based Functions are a set of serverless tools that allow you to train models and generate predictions without moving data. We can use a `dbt post-hook` to automatically retrain our model every time its underlying feature table is updated.

We add the `post-hook` to our model's `.yml` configuration file, telling Snowflake to train a regression model on our feature table (`{{ this }}`) and specifying the column we want to predict (`trades_in_week`).

```
version: 2
models:
  - name: ml_portfolio_weekly_features
    config:
      post-hook:
       - |
         CREATE OR REPLACE SNOWFLAKE.ML.REGRESSION
         trade_forecasting_model(
           INPUT_DATA => SYSTEM$REFERENCE('TABLE', '{{ this }}'),
           TARGET_COLNAME = 'trades_in_week'
         );
```

Now, every time we run `dbt build`, the `ml_portfolio_weekly_features` model is created with updated features, and this `post-hook` immediately starts model training on the new data. The result is a new, usable Snowflake table-like object called `trade_forecasting_model` that encapsulates the trained model.

Once the model is trained and available, using it to generate predictions is as simple as a `SELECT` statement. We call the `PREDICT` method on our model object, passing in the features from the latest available week to forecast the next one.

```
-- Example of how to use the trained model
-- to forecast next week's trades

SELECT
    portfolio_key,
    trade_forecasting_model!PREDICT(
      OBJECT_CONSTRUCT(
        'trades_last_week', trades_last_week,
        'avg_trades_last_4_weeks', avg_trades_last_4_weeks,
        'dist_securities_last_week', dist_securities_last_week
      )
    ) AS predicted_trades_next_week

FROM {{ ref('ml_portfolio_weekly_features') }}

-- Use the latest week of available data to predict the next one
WHERE week_start_date = (
        SELECT MAX(week_start_date)
        FROM {{ ref('ml_portfolio_weekly_features') }}
      );
```

This query takes the latest week of features for each portfolio and passes them to the model to forecast the number of trades for the upcoming week. Just by using dbt models, a post-hook, and Snowflake ML functions, we have been able to create the features, train a model, and use it to make predictions. All inside our own dbt pipeline. No extra tools, no extra orchestration, no extra security… just simple.

This fully closes the ML lifecycle within our data platform, demonstrating how a SQL-first approach can democratize machine learning and allow the entire data team to participate in building and deploying predictive models.

The delivery layer as the key enabler for data mesh

Throughout this book, we've introduced the concept of Data Mesh, first as a modern architectural style in Chapter 1 and later as a governance paradigm in Chapter 3. A Data Mesh is a socio-technical approach that decentralizes data ownership, moving it from a central data team to the business domains that are true experts on their data.

Now, in the Delivery Layer, we move from theory to practice, as this is the architectural ground where the data products that a Data Mesh thrives on are made available to the public. The structure of our Data Product Repository is designed to enable this decentralized model. However, having multiple domain teams working in the same dbt project and sharing the same Refined Layer can make management complex. While a single, unified dbt project with a logical Mesh can work for smaller organizations, a Data Mesh approach usually evolves into a multi-project setup.

In this distributed operational model, each domain team can have its own dbt project or set of projects, managing the full lifecycle of its own data products. Also, teams publish their final data products (the models in their data marts) and can consume the trusted data products published by other teams. This creates a network of interconnected data products in which each team is both a producer and a consumer. For example, a team might produce two data marts for different audiences: one for internal finance and another, with different aggregations and security, for an external partner.

Key principles for a successful data mesh

A decentralized architecture only works if there are strong, automated guarantees that allow teams to trust and consume each other's products without fear of unexpected breaking changes.

This is where the engineering principles we established earlier become the essential technical pillars that make a Data Mesh functional and reliable:

- **Data as a Product with Guaranteed Contracts**: For a data product to be useful to other domains, it must come with a guarantee of its structure and quality. Design by Contract (DBC), implemented via dbt's enforced contracts, provides the guarantee of the product's shape and interoperability. It ensures the schema will not change unexpectedly.
- **Guaranteed Quality with Data Tests**: While contracts guarantee the shape, dbt data tests (e.g., unique, not_null, relationships, and custom generic and singular tests) ensure the correctness and quality of the data within that shape. A robust suite of data tests is a critical part of a data product's definition, ensuring consumers can trust the values it contains.

- **Safe Evolution with the Open/Closed Principle**: Domains must be able to evolve their data products without breaking downstream consumers across the organization. dbt model versions provide the mechanism for this safe, controlled evolution.
- **Federated Governance with Clear Ownership**: A Data Mesh requires decentralized governance. Deploying data marts to their own Snowflake schema, we can use Snowflake roles to govern access to them. The owner is granted WRITE access to the schema, while authorized consumers are granted READ-ONLY access through standardized processes.
- **A Discoverable Product Catalog**: In a decentralized world, you must be able to find what's available. The dbt Cloud Catalog serves as the federated data catalog for the Mesh, allowing developers to discover and understand the data products offered by different domains.

These principles are very well aligned with what we have discussed throughout the book, and they are ingrained in how we work in the Pragmatic Data Platform, making the evolution into a data Mesh a natural choice for larger projects without fundamentally changing the way we think and work.

Data mesh in practice: A multi-team example

Let's illustrate this with a practical scenario involving three distinct teams:

1. **The Source Team(s)**: This team owns the core ingestion and historization of source data. Their primary role is to produce foundational, trusted data assets. They ingest the source data and build the STG, HIST, and VER models. However, they do not expose the raw VER_ models directly. Instead, they build and publish a curated set of sparse data products on top of them to meet specific business needs. For example:

    - from `ver_securities`, they might publish two products: a simple `dim_securities` view, with current data only, and `scd_securities` with all the security changes.
    - from `ver_trades`, they could publish `trades_granular` with every transaction, and `trades_daily_summary` with pre-aggregated daily volumes by security and portfolio.
    - from `ver_cash_transactions`, they might publish a `dividends_aggregated` product to give the consumers a simpler picture that fully describes a dividend payment.

    Each of these data products is versioned, contracted, and thoroughly tested, forming the trusted base layer of the mesh.

2. **The BI & Analytics Team**: This team's goal is to serve business stakeholders with insightful reports and dashboards. They are consumers of the Source Team's curated products. In their own dbt project, they would source pre-aggregated models such as `trades_daily_ summary` and `dividends_aggregated`. This makes their work simpler and faster.
    They then build the `portfolio_analysis` data mart, including the final `rpt_total_ return` model for their users. They are both consumers of foundational products and producers of business-facing products.

3. **The Data Science Team**: This team focuses on building predictive models and requires maximum detail. They are also consumers of the Source Team's assets, but will choose the most granular products available, such as `trades_granular`. In their separate dbt project, they consume this feed to build the `ml_trade_forecasting` feature store we outlined previously, creating detailed lag features that

wouldn't be possible with the aggregated data. This, or the forecast result, could be a data product other teams can use.

In this data mesh scenario, **each team has autonomy and clear ownership**. The Source Team can evolve the underlying storage layer without breaking consumers, as long as they honor the contracts of their published data products. The BI and Data Science teams can work in parallel, selecting the products with the right level of granularity for their specific needs, while starting from the same trusted, centrally governed sources.

This is the power of a Data Mesh in action: a scalable, collaborative, and resilient way to deliver data value across an entire organization. With dbt and Snowflake you can scale it (almost) without limits, keeping overhead to a minimum, including data sharing with companies around your value chain.

Self-completing dimensions

A common and frustrating real-world problem is the late arrival of dimension values. This occurs when a fact record arrives in the warehouse before its corresponding dimension record. For example, a `fct_trades` record might arrive for a new security, but the `dim_securities` table has not yet been updated with the security's new code or symbol. The inner join between the two, done by the BI tool, would cause the trade to be dropped from the final report, leading to silent, incorrect analytics.

A common but low-quality fix is to replace the value of the dimension key in the fact with a default value like `-1`, which points to a generic "Unknown" record, when the original value is not found in the dimension. This approach should be avoided, as it loses the original business key. If you are rebuilding both the facts and the dimensions at each run, as is normal for all but the biggest tables, this is only a temporary loss, since the fact will start the next build with the correct key and keep it if the dimension is now complete. It is, instead, a big problem if you are building your facts incrementally, as the fact record will not be updated when the actual dimension data arrives.

The Self-completing Dimension pattern provides a robust solution, useful for large fact tables loaded incrementally. It leverages the strengths of columnar databases like Snowflake, where a `select distinct dim_key from fct_table` query is very efficient, reading only the table's metadata. Instead of fixing the fact, the goal becomes to ensure that the dimension has one entry for each key in the fact table, even if it's just a placeholder until the real data arrives in a future build.

These are the logical steps automatically performed by the `self_completing_dimension` macro that you can find in the delivery layer of the Pragmatic Data Platform package.

1. Identify the values of the fact's key that are missing in the dimension table.
2. Enrich the dimension table by adding a new row for each missing value. Each new row provides the default values (like 'Description Not Available') for all other attributes.

This is a clean, additive process. The fact table is never modified. The dimension table is simply "completed" with the necessary placeholder rows to ensure every join succeeds. When the full dimension data eventually arrives from its source, a subsequent dbt build will not generate the placeholder rows for the keys that are now available in the dimension.

The following snippet of code shows how you would use the macro to build a dynamic Security dimension connected to the position daily values and dividends facts:

```
{% set configuration %}
fact_defs:
  - 'model': 'TS_IB_REPORTED_POSITIONS_DAILY_VALUES'
    'key': 'SECURITY_HKEY'
  - 'model': 'AGG_IB_DIVIDENDS'
    'key': 'SECURITY_HKEY'
{% endset %}

{%- set cfg = fromyaml(configuration) -%}

{{ pragmatic_data.self_completing_dimension(
    dim_rel = ref('REFH_IB_SECURITIES'),
    dim_key_column   = 'SECURITY_HKEY',
    dim_default_key_value = '-1',
    ref_columns_to_exclude = ['SECURITY_HDIFF'],

    fact_defs = cfg.fact_defs
) }}
```

As usual, we have used a YAML-based configuration to specify the facts for which we want to make sure that the dimension contains all keys. Then we invoke the macro passing the needed parameters.

It is important to note that the dimension must contain a default record and that the value of its `dim_key_column` must be set in the `dim_default_key_value` parameter. This pattern makes our data pipelines resilient against the inevitable timing issues of real-world data sources, guaranteeing data integrity in our final reports without losing valuable business context.

Chapter review

Congratulations on completing your journey through the Delivery Layer! This is where the true value of the Pragmatic Data Platform becomes real, serving well-structured information to provide actionable insights and power services for the organization. In this chapter, you learned how to shift your mindset from a data technician to a data product manager, focusing on the needs of consumers.

We established a clear, scalable structure for a Data Product Repository, organizing models into categories and data marts with consistent naming conventions and schema configurations. We then delved into the practical, four-step process for building high-quality BI data marts, revisiting the principles of dimensional modeling to create intuitive facts, dimensions, and denormalized reports. You learned how to apply engineering excellence by using dbt features like data contracts and model versions to implement essential software principles, such as Design by Contract, ensuring your data products are reliable and easy to evolve. Finally, we explored the frontier of advanced use cases, discovering how our repository can securely serve data across account boundaries, build and use ML models with Snowflake Cortex, and provide the essential technical pillars for implementing a successful Data Mesh.

You are now equipped with the principles and patterns needed to build a robust, user-centric Delivery Layer that delivers tangible business value. In the next chapter, we will put all this theory into practice by building the Delivery Layer for our "Stonks" sample project.

Recommended resources

Dimensional Modeling

- **The Data Warehouse Toolkit by Ralph Kimball**: The definitive book on dimensional modeling. While many technical aspects are dated and were shaped by limits in legacy, row-oriented databases that do not apply to Snowflake and modern analytical databases, the core principles on how to design intuitive data models for business users remain timeless and essential.
- **Dimensional Modeling Techniques:** a brief description of all the "official" Kimball dimensional modeling techniques, by Kimball Group. Includes a 21-page handy PDF with the description of all the techniques. A lifesaver! https://www.kimballgroup.com/data-warehouse-business-intelligence-resources/kimball-techniques/dimensional-modeling-techniques/.

dbt Labs Documentation

The official dbt documentation is the best source for up-to-date information on the features discussed.

- **dbt Model Contracts**: https://docs.getdbt.com/docs/build/contracts.
- **dbt Model Versions**: https://docs.getdbt.com/docs/build/model-versions.
- **About** dbt **Mesh**: https://docs.getdbt.com/docs/use-dbt-mesh/about-dbt-mesh.

Snowflake Documentation

- **Snowflake Secure Data Sharing**: https://docs.snowflake.com/en/user-guide/data-sharing-intro.
- **Snowflake Cortex ML-Based Functions**: https://docs.snowflake.com/en/user-guide/ml-powered-functions.
- **Hybrid Tables:** https://docs.snowflake.com/en/user-guide/tables-hybrid.

Data Mesh Resources

- **Data Mesh by Zhamak Dehghani**: The original book that defined the principles and architecture of a Data Mesh.
- **How to Move Beyond a Monolithic Data Lake to a Distributed Data Mesh**, article by Zhamak Dehghani, the inventor of data mesh. https://martinfowler.com/articles/data-monolith-to-mesh.html.
- **Awesome Data Mesh Resources on GitHub**: A curated list of articles, videos, and tools related to Data Mesh. https://github.com/JacekMajchrzak/awesome-datamesh.

CHAPTER 15

Coding the Delivery Layer

In the previous chapter, we established the principles, patterns, and engineering practices for building a robust and user-centric Delivery Layer. We defined our goal as creating a Data Product Repository with well-structured, reliable, and easy-to-use data marts. Now is the time to put that theory into practice.

This chapter is a hands-on journey where we will build the `portfolio_analysis` data mart for our "Stonks" sample project. We will translate the architectural concepts from Chapter 14 into tangible, working dbt models that solve real-world analytical challenges. We will begin by setting up our project structure, then build each component of the data mart: dimensions, facts, and reports. We'll start by creating our conformed dimensions for portfolios, securities, and dates. Next, we will construct our core fact tables for position changes and dividends. Finally, we will assemble them into powerful, denormalized reports optimized for BI tools and even build a specialized, lean model to power a hypothetical application. Throughout this process, we will apply the engineering excellence principles we've learned, implementing data tests and dbt contracts to ensure our data products are trustworthy and maintainable. By the end of this chapter, you will have a complete, production-grade data mart and a clear, repeatable playbook for building one in your own projects.

The topics that we are going to cover in this chapter are:

- **Setup for the Portfolio Analysis Mart**: We'll set up the folder structure and configuration.
- **Creating the Core Dimensions**: We will develop the core dimensions, providing `DIM_SECURITIES` in both current and historical versions.
- **Building the Facts**: We build key facts from our polished sources in the Refined Layer.
- **Assembling the User-Facing Reports**: We will create the denormalized `RPT_` models, which are optimized for performance and ease of use in BI tools.
- **Applying Engineering Contracts and Governance**: We apply dbt contracts to our report models, turning implicit assumptions into explicit, automated guarantees.
- **Building a Data Product for a Streamlit Application**: We will create an API mart for our app and show how you can create a Streamlit app inside Snowflake.
- **Finalizing and Validating the Data Mart**: To conclude, we will build the project to validate the integrity of our new data mart and review the final lineage graph.

Sample project and code

The sample dbt project is available at: **https://github.com/pragmatic-data/stonks**. **All the code** we will write in this chapter **is in the dbt project folders**, mostly in the `refined` folder. The materials that do not belong in the project code will be in the sub-folder for this chapter, `chapter_15`, under the `code_samples_by_chapter` folder. Please note that, to better fit the limited space on the printed page, we omit most comments and change the formatting of code blocks compared to the files.

Setup for the Portfolio Analysis Mart

In the previous chapter, we laid out the principles for building the Delivery Layer, our user-facing Data Product Repository. We discussed how to structure the repository into categories and marts, the importance of dimensional modeling, and the engineering practices required to deliver trustworthy data. Now, it's time to put that theory into practice.

Project structure

As we established in our design principles, a well-organized project is crucial for maintainability. All the models we build in this chapter will reside within a dedicated folder structure that clearly identifies them as part of the Delivery Layer, specifically the `portfolio_analysis` data mart. All our dimension, fact, and report models for this chapter will be located in the `models/03_delivery/marts/portfolio_analysis/` directory. Following the "Repository > Category > Mart" analogy, our project structure will be:

- `models/03_delivery/`: The root directory for our Data Product Repository.
    - `marts/`: The category for our BI-oriented data marts.
        - `portfolio_analysis/`: The folder for the data mart we are building now.

Should we need to build data products for other purposes, we would create new category folders at the same level as `marts/`. For example:

- `03_delivery/apps/`: For lean models designed to power applications.
- `03_delivery/ml/`: For feature tables for machine learning.
- `03_delivery/shares/`: For secure views used for Snowflake Data Sharing.

This clean separation ensures our repository is easy to navigate and govern.

Naming conventions

To ensure clarity and consistency within our data mart, we will adhere to the naming conventions established in Chapter 14. A clear prefix on a model's name instantly communicates its purpose to anyone browsing the project. In this chapter, we will be building models with the following prefixes:

- DIM_: For standard dimension tables that represent the current state of a business entity (e.g., DIM_PORTFOLIOS and DIM_SECURITIES).
- SCD_: For Type 2 Slowly Changing Dimensions that capture the full history of an entity's attributes (e.g., SCD_SECURITIES).
- FCT_: For fact tables that record business events (e.g., FCT_DIVIDENDS). We use `FCT_` instead of `FACT_` because dbt Catalog, at this moment, does not recognize the latter and makes no sense
- to fight against the tool.
- RPT_: For denormalized, user-facing report models that are optimized for BI tools (e.g., RPT_POSITIONS_DAILY_VALUES).

Configuring dbt schemas

To ensure our physical database layout in Snowflake mirrors our project's logical structure, we will configure custom schemas in dbt_project.yml. This tells dbt to build all models from a specific folder into a dedicated database schema. For our portfolio_analysis mart, we will create a schema named MART_ PORTFOLIO_ANALYSIS. We can also set a default table materialization for the entire Delivery Layer, since most of our final models are tables, ensuring fast query performance for end-users. Add the following configuration to your dbt_project.yml file:

```
models:
  stonks: # Your project name

   03_delivery:
      +materialized: table # Useful for marts with direct queries
      marts:
        portfolio_analysis:
          +schema: MART_PORTFOLIO_ANALYSIS
```

In a similar way, you can add more categories and marts inside them:

```
      apps:
        app_name:
          +schema: APP_NAME_DATA
      ml:
        use_case_name:
          +schema: ML_USE_CASE_NAME
```

With this configuration in place, every time we run dbt build, all the models for our portfolio analysis data mart will be deployed in the MART_PORTFOLIO_ANALYSIS schema in Snowflake. Our project is now set up and ready for us to start building our dimensions.

Creating the core dimensions

With our project structure and schemas configured, we can now begin building the essential components of our portfolio_analysis data mart. The first and most important components are the **dimensions**. These models will provide the descriptive context—the "who, what, where, and when"—that allows analysts to name, understand, slice and dice the numeric measures in our fact tables. For our mart, we will build three core dimensions: one for securities, one for portfolios, and one for dates. Each serves a distinct purpose and demonstrates a different approach to effectively building and presenting data to your end users. We must ensure these dimensions are not only accurate but also thoroughly documented and tested, as they are the primary interface for our data consumers.

The data mart bus matrix

Before we write any code, it's best practice to create a data mart map. The bus matrix, a cornerstone of Kimball's methodology, is the perfect tool for this. It provides a high-level blueprint that maps our business processes (which will become fact tables) to the common, shared dimensions used to analyze them. This simple grid is an invaluable tool for planning our work and communicating the design to stakeholders. For our `portfolio_analysis` data mart, the bus matrix is as follows:

Business Process -Fact \ Dimensions	Date	Security	Portfolio
Position Transactions	X	X	X
Dividends	X	X	X
Daily Position Values	X	X	X

This matrix clearly shows that our core three business processes can be analyzed by the same three conformed dimensions, confirming a coherent design for our data mart. This matrix, along with the conceptual models presented in Chapters 5 and 14, provides the blueprints we need to start building our data mart.

Now, let's build it.

Building DIM_SECURITIES

The security dimension is arguably the most complex and valuable in our project. In this sample stonks project, we will build two versions of this dimension:

- `DIM_SECURITIES`: A Type 1 dimension, the standard type of dimension, showing only the most current attributes for each security.
- `SCD_SECURITIES`: A Type 2 dimension, called a Slowly Changing Dimension (SCD), showing the complete history of all attribute changes over time.

As we saw in the Storage and Refined layers, we have already done the heavy lifting of collecting fragmented security attributes from multiple sources (trades, positions, etc.) and creating a unified "golden record" in the `REFH_IB_SECURITIES` model.

Normally, we could simply create our SCD dimension model by reading from that REFH model, and the DIM out of the SCD by filtering on the current rows. However, for the purpose of this chapter, we will build them to demonstrate an important real-world pattern: the **Self-Completing Dimension**. As we discussed in Chapter 14, this pattern is designed to prevent data loss caused by "late-arriving dimensions," in which a fact record (such as a trade for a new security) arrives before its corresponding dimension record. The `pragmatic_data.self_completing_dimension` macro handles this by:

1. Scanning the connected fact tables for foreign keys that do not exist in the dimension.
2. Adding placeholder records for these missing keys to the dimension.
3. Using a default record as a template for these new placeholder rows.

This ensures that every join from the fact table will succeed, making our data mart more resilient. This will also be validated by `relationship` tests of the facts.

The code

Let's review the code of the `SCD_ SECURITIES` model. The first part is a now-familiar block of YAML that we put directly in the SQL file. This is a powerful dbt feature that makes it easy to manage complex configurations, such as a list of fact tables or columns to exclude, right alongside the code that uses them.

```
{% set configuration %}

fact_defs:        #  A list of facts with 'model' and 'key' values
  - 'model': 'TS_IB_REPORTED_POSITIONS_DAILY_VALUES'
    'key': 'SECURITY_HKEY'
  - 'model': 'AGG_IB_DIVIDENDS'
    'key': 'SECURITY_HKEY'

ref_columns_to_exclude:     # A list of column names to exclude

  - FILE_LAST_MODIFIED_TS_UTC
    ...
  - LOAD_BATCH

{% endset %}

{%- set cfg = fromyaml(configuration) -%}
```

We then pass this configuration to the `self_completing_dimension` macro, which generates the complete SQL for our final dimension.

```
{{ pragmatic_data.self_completing_dimension(
    dim_rel = ref('REFH_IB_SECURITIES'),
    dim_key_column   = 'SECURITY_HKEY',
    dim_default_key_value = '-1',
    ref_columns_to_exclude = cfg.ref_columns_to_exclude,
    fact_defs = cfg.fact_defs
) }}
```

As you can see, we can mix and match which parameters we fill in directly and which we define using a YAML block to improve readability.

The `DIM_SECURITIES` is simply derived from the `SCD` model by filtering on `IS_CURRENT`:

```
SELECT * FROM {{ ref('SCD_SECURITIES')}} WHERE IS_CURRENT
```

A one-liner is now enough to provide you with the current and most used dimension.

Building DIM_PORTFOLIOS

For our portfolio dimension, we take a different and minimalistic approach. Instead of extracting and historizing "portfolios" in the Storage Layer as we did for "securities", we create a light dimension by just listing the portfolios that appear in our transactional data, directly in the refined layer.

This approach has pros and cons. The advantage is that it's simple and fast to implement, as we don't build a historization pipeline, we just scavenge for data. The price is that we only know about portfolios that had activity. If a portfolio exists but has no transactions of the types we track, it won't appear in our dimension. Also, it's easy to get the "somehow" current values, not all the changes.

In the stonks project, this is perfectly fine for this secondary dimension. In your projects, this is a pragmatic trade-off you will have to decide on based on the use cases. It is often a first step for less important dimensions, before deciding to build a proper dimension, ingesting the relevant data (when becomes available) from the source.

Step 1: The refined layer: Collecting all portfolios

First, we create a model in the Refined Layer, `REF_PORTFOLIOS`, to produce a master list of all unique `PORTFOLIO_HKEY`s.

To do this efficiently and without repeating code, we use a Jinja loop. This is a perfect example of the DRY principle (Don't Repeat Yourself). Instead of writing a SELECT statement for each source, we list them once and let Jinja generate the full SQL. As usual, we start with some YAML for the configuration.

```
{% set configuration %}
source_models:
  - VER_IB_ALL_POSITIONS
  - REF_IB_POSITIONS_TRANSACTIONS
  - VER_IB_CASH_TRANSACTIONS
{% endset %}
{%- set cfg = fromyaml(configuration) -%}
```

Then we use it to generate one CTE per source model, without code repetitions, that extracts the data from each of the listed models, including eventual conditionals for each source model:

```
with
{% for model in cfg.source_models -%}
portfolios__{{model}} as (

   select...     -- getting the desired columns for the portfolios
    from {{ ref(model) }}
    qualify...
)
{% if not loop.last %}, {% endif -%}
{%- endfor %}
```

Finally, we bring them all together with another `for` loop.

```
, all_portfolios as (
{%- for model in cfg.source_models %}
    select * from portfolios__{{model}}
{% if not loop.last %}     UNION{% endif %}
{%- endfor -%}
)
```

In the last step, which you can find in the full model in the repository, we simply read from the `all_portfolios` CTE and we keep the most recent portfolio record.

Step 2: The delivery layer: Enriching with calculated columns

Now, in the Delivery Layer, we create our `DIM_PORTFOLIOS` model. This is where we can add value by creating calculated columns. These are new attributes derived from existing data to make analysis easier for our end-users. It's a best practice to put calculated columns in dimensions when they describe the dimension itself (like `is_active_last_30_days`). Calculated columns from multiple entities that are numeric measures typically belong in a **fact** or **report** model.

Let's have a walk through the `DIM_PORTFOLIOS` model. The first CTE gets the base columns of the dimension from the model in the REF layer.

```
With portfolio_base_dim as (
    select * from {{ ref('REF_IB_PORTFOLIOS') }}
)
```

The `portfolio_position_stats` CTE then calculates statistics on the portfolio's positions.

```
, portfolio_position_stats as (
    select
        portfolio_hkey
      , min(effectivity_date) as first_activity_date
      ...
    from {{ ref('VER_IB_POSITIONS_CALCULATED') }}
    group by portfolio_hkey
)
```

The `portfolio_daily_value_stats` CTE calculates metrics based on the position daily values. This is handy, but can be dangerous... and that's why Kimball advises against metrics in dimensions.

```
, portfolio_daily_value_stats as (
    select
        portfolio_hkey
      , round(sum(position_value), 2) as portfolio_value
      ...
 from {{ref('TS_IB_REPORTED_POSITIONS_DAILY_VALUES')}} as v
    where VALUE_IS_CURRENT and side != 'Closed'
    group by portfolio_hkey
)
```

Finally, we join the base data with the calculated columns. Good documentation for the calculated columns is essential because, no matter how good the names are, there's too much to clarify to fit in the name. An analyst can immediately use the `is_active_last_30_days` flag for filtering without having to write the date logic themselves, but he could also have a question about what "active" means. Does a dividend keep a portfolio active?

---

*It is common to include metrics, as we did with `portfolio_value`, in some dimensions to facilitate quick reporting, but this is risky. These numbers are usually out of context and not well defined (e.g., when were they last updated?), and, most importantly, users must refrain from applying math to them when working with multiple tables or **risk catastrophic data errors**.*
This topic, introduced in Chapter 1, is discussed in detail later, just after DIM_DATE.

Writing good documentation is important, but it does not need to be slow or tedious. We can use tools like dbt Copilot or other AI-based tools to help generate descriptions and basic tests, speeding up the development process.

Building DIM_DATE

The date dimension is the cornerstone of any time-series analysis.

Building it is simple because we are leveraging the Master Data Dimension (MDD) we created in the Refined Layer. Our `DIM_DATE` model is, in fact, a simple pass-through from the `MDD_DATE_ CALENDAR` model. This demonstrates the use of Master Data Dimensions. In a real project, you would likely have many more, such as `MDD_CUSTOMER_SEGMENTS` or `MDD_PRODUCTS`, which can be easily exposed in any data mart.

For our `DIM_DATE`, a valuable extension would be to integrate a local holiday calendar. We could join our `MDD_DATE_CALENDAR` to a seed file containing a list of stock exchange holidays. This would allow us to add a Boolean column `IS_TRADING_DAY`, enabling analysts to easily exclude non-trading days from their performance calculations, making our data mart even more useful.

Why are there no metrics in the dimensions?

In our `DIM_PORTFOLIOS` dimension, we have two metrics that should not be there, as a pretext to discuss the pros and cons of a too-common and risky shortcut. Besides the obvious reason that having metrics in a dimension exposes the data mart to the **Fan Trap**, as we have already covered in Chapter 1, let's have a deeper discussion.

The pros of putting metrics in a dimension

The primary reason developers place metrics like `portfolio_value` in a dimension table is for convenience and perceived simplicity, especially for end users.

- **Ease of Use in BI Tools**: It creates a "one-stop shop" for the user. An analyst can drag the "Portfolio" object into their report and immediately have access not only to descriptive attributes but also to the most recent portfolio value, without needing to understand or perform a join to a fact table.

- **Simplified Logic**: For simple use cases that only require the latest value (e.g., a list of portfolios and their current worth), this approach avoids a join and can make the BI tool's query logic simpler.

The dangers: Cons and risks

While the pros are tempting, the cons are significant and can lead to a data model that is misleading, incorrect, and difficult to maintain:

- **Grain Confusion (The Biggest Sin)**: This is the most critical issue. A dimension table should have a clear and simple grain. For `DIM_PORTFOLIOS`, the grain should be one row per portfolio. With a metric like `portfolio_value`, what is the grain now? Is it "one row per portfolio with its value as of the last data refresh"? This ambiguity is dangerous and violates the core principles of dimensional modeling.
- **Increased Risk of Bad Joins (Fan Traps):** A clean star schema, where facts join only to dimensions, is designed to prevent analytical errors such as Fan Traps. Adding a metric to a dimension encourages users to create dangerous join paths by using the metric in a join with a fact table. By design, facts have a different granularity than their dimensions, which creates the Fan Trap, leading to incorrectly multiplied results and flawed analysis.
- **Risk of Incorrect Aggregations**: BI tools are designed to aggregate numeric columns (usually SUM). If a user groups securities by country and drags the `portfolio_value` column into the tool, the tool will likely sum the value of the full portfolio for each security row, which is completely meaningless. Metrics like `portfolio_value` are semi-additive—they can be aggregated across some dimensions (like brokers) but not across others (like time). A fact table is designed to handle this, while a dimension is not. This can lead to silent, disastrous reporting errors.
- **Update Frequency Conflict**: Dimensions are typically designed to be slowly changing. Portfolios are created or closed infrequently. However, `portfolio_value` changes daily. Putting this metric in the dimension forces the entire dimension table to be updated as frequently as a fact table, which is inefficient and goes against the architectural purpose of separating stable, descriptive data from volatile, numeric data. This is less of a problem for modern analytical databases, but can add time and cost.
- **Scalability Issues**: The trick breaks down as soon as you need historical context. What if a user wants to see the portfolio value from last week? Or compare this month's value to last month's? You cannot keep adding columns like `portfolio_value_last_week`, etc. The model doesn't scale.

The best practice: The pragmatic approach ☑

The generally accepted best practice, and the one that aligns with the Pragmatic Data Platform, is to keep measures in fact tables.

- **Place Metrics in a Fact Table**: Metrics like `portfolio_value` belong in a fact table. In our stonks project, the `TS_IB_REPORTED_POSITIONS_DAILY_VALUES` model in the Refined Layer serves this purpose perfectly. Its grain is clear: "one row per position, per portfolio, per day." This structure correctly models the data, handles semi-additivity, and scales for any time-series analysis. If you need, add the portfolio (aggregate) snapshot (current only or fully historical) fact.

- **Use a Star Schema for Flexibility**: The correct way to analyze this data is to join `DIM_PORTFOLIOS` to this daily snapshot fact table. This is the clean, unambiguous, and scalable pattern that underlies star schema modeling. It gives analysts the flexibility to perform any kind of analysis without risk.
- **Create RPT_ Models for Convenience**: If you want to provide the convenience of a single, wide table for a specific, common use case, the correct place to do that is in a denormalized report (`RPT_`) model. You would create a model like `RPT_PORTFOLIOS_CURRENT_VALUES` that joins `DIM_PORTFOLIOS` with the aggregated snapshot from the position daily values fact. This is safe as it needs no more joins (you treat it like the fact it is).

This approach gives you the best of both worlds: the core dimensions and facts remain clean, scalable, and true to their purpose, while you can still provide a simple, denormalized, high-performance table for specific reports without corrupting your core data model. In summary, unless the distribution of your mart is limited to people who understand the risks of metrics in a dimension and know how to deal with them, it is much better to avoid them and stick to the recommended practice. The risks are too high compared to the tiny gain of not creating a fact.

Building the facts

After creating the dimensions that provide the descriptive context for our analysis, the next step is to build the fact tables. These models are the quantitative core of our data mart, containing the numeric measures and metrics about the business processes we want to analyze. They are the tables that users will use to answer questions like "How much?" and "How many?"

In dimensional modeling, there are several types of fact tables, each designed to model a different kind of business process. The two most common and important types are Transactional and Snapshot facts.

- **Transactional Facts**: These are the most granular and fundamental type. Each row in a transactional fact table represents a single event that occurred at a specific point in time. Examples include a single trade, a website click, or a single dividend payment. They are excellent for analyzing the details of a process.
- **Periodic Snapshot Facts**: These tables capture the state of something at the end of a regular, predictable period, such as the end of a day, week, or month. A classic example is a daily inventory snapshot that shows the quantity on hand for each product at the end of the day.

For our `portfolio_analysis` data mart, we will provide two transactional facts for core events (Transactions and Dividends) and one Snapshot fact (report) for the daily values of positions.

Transactional facts

We will create two transactional facts: one to capture every transaction that changes a position's quantity and another to capture every dividend payment.

FCT_POSITION_TRANSACTIONS

This is our primary transactional fact table. It's crucial to note that its grain is one row per position-altering transaction. This is more powerful than just a "trades" fact, as it includes not only trades but also transfers and corporate actions, giving us a complete view of what drives changes in our holdings.

We will build this model directly from REF_IB_POSITIONS_TRANSACTIONS model in our Refined Layer, which has already done the hard work of unifying these different event types into a single, consistent model. Looking at the code, you can see that most of the work is done in the Refined layer, so we can now just select the columns we want and eventually calculate a few extra metrics.

```
select
   -- Keys (PK and FKs)
     TRANSACTION_HKEY
   , POSITION_HKEY
   , PORTFOLIO_HKEY
   , SECURITY_HKEY
   , EFFECTIVITY_DATE

   -- Degenerate dimensions
   , TRANSACTION_TYPE
   , ASSET_CLASS
     ...

   -- Measures
   , QUANTITY
   , TX_MONEY_FX
   , CURRENCY_PRIMARY
   , FX_RATE_TO_BASE
     ...

   -- Calculated Measures
   , round(-TX_MONEY_FX / QUANTITY, 2) as TRADE_PRICE_FX
     ...

from {{ ref('REF_IB_POSITIONS_TRANSACTIONS') }}
```

The division of work between the Refined layer and the Delivery layer is important. In the Refined layer, you set the (lowest) granularity and specify the available columns, along with the calculations and aggregations considered of global interest. In the Delivery layer, you select the columns you need, aggregate at the desired level, and add the calculations that matter for the use case.

FCT_DIVIDENDS

This fact table will capture every dividend payment. Again, we will build it from the AGG_IB_DIVIDENDS model in the Refined Layer, which provides a clean, daily aggregation of dividends per security. You can find the code in the sample project, but it is just a simple SELECT from the model in the Refined layer, as it is common in the Pragmatic Data Platform.

Note that this fact provides both a SECURITY_HKEY column to join on the SCD1 DIM_SECURITIES and a SECURITY_SCD_HKEY column to join on the SCD2 dimension SCD_ SECURITIES. This is a powerful combination, as it allows users of the data mart to analyze facts in relation to both the current definition of the Security and the historical one that was in effect at the time the fact occurred.

With these two models, we now have a solid transactional foundation for our data mart, capturing the key events that drive our portfolio's performance.

Snapshot facts

A snapshot fact table records the state of an entity at regular intervals. In our case, a very useful snapshot fact would be one that records the quantity, market value, and cost basis of every position at the end of each day. This would allow for powerful time-series analysis of our portfolio's value.

The Refined layer model TS_IB_REPORTED_POSITIONS_DAILY_VALUES already calculates this data, producing a sparse time series of these daily values for the dates when we did an export. You can simply join it to the calendar to fill in the empty dates with the last known value. We have done it in RPT_POSITIONS_DAILY_VALUES, but given the already highly denormalized source, what we got feels more like a denormalized report model than a fact, so we named it accordingly. We will describe it in the next section.

Keeping denormalized columns is a common and effective pattern in the Pragmatic Data Platform: we avoid duplicate work (normalize first, join back later), improve performance, and simplify the user experience by keeping the denormalized columns in the models we get from our sources. As storage is cheap, we do not try to aggressively normalize our models unless there is a material advantage in doing so for storage, performance, governance, or any other reason. You can use the RPT model as a FACT, but you will find that the most common columns are already there, leaving us with little need to join the RPT to the dimensions. If you want to be super clear and apply the least surprise principle (LSP), you could create a view on top of the RPT with the fact name and expose only the columns that you see belong in the fact.

Assignment for the reader

As an exercise to solidify your understanding, you can create a "true" periodic snapshot fact table yourself. Try building a FCT_PORTFOLIO_WEEKLY_VALUES model. To do this, you would need to:

- Read from the TS_IB_REPORTED_POSITIONS_DAILY_VALUES model.
- Produce the portfolio value (market value), cost basis, and other metrics at a weekly cadence (e.g., taking the value for each position from the last *available* day of each week).
- The grain of your model must be one row per portfolio, per security, per week.

This exercise will give you hands-on experience creating a periodic snapshot fact table from a more granular time series, and experience firsthand common questions related to the design of such a model. As an example of design questions, you can decide to use week numbers, fixed days (like Fridays), or some other way to provide a complete fact with a predictable weekly schedule, even when one or more positions have no new value on a given date or week. Another interesting question is which currency to use and how to handle other non-additive metrics.

Assembling the user-facing reports

The final step in building our `portfolio_analysis` data mart is to create the reports. These are the denormalized, wide, and business-friendly models, prefixed with `RPT_`, that are specifically designed for consumption by BI tools and less senior analysts. While most analysts can join the fact and dimension tables themselves, creating pre-joined report models for the most common analytical paths provides significant benefits. It simplifies the user experience, as all the necessary data is in one place without the need for joins, and it dramatically improves query performance, as the complex joins are pre-calculated during our dbt build. For our mart, we will build one core report together and then design a more advanced one as an exercise for you, the reader.

Building RPT_POSITIONS_DAILY_VALUES

This report is the primary tool for analyzing the historical value of our portfolio over time. Its goal is to provide a single, easy-to-query table containing the daily valuation for every position, enriched with all descriptive attributes from our dimensions.

Logic and Benefits

The logic is straightforward: we take the sparse time series of daily values from the Refined Layer (`TS_IB_REPORTED_POSITIONS_DAILY_VALUES`) and we join it with our common dimensions (`DIM_DATE`, `DIM_SECURITIES`, and `DIM_ PORTFOLIOS`) to enrich the fact with useful descriptive info from the dimensions.

As we already said in the previous section, the TS_ model in the refined layer is already quite complete, as it was built by a time join between the position daily values, the positions, and the securities. It already contains the descriptive info as of the value date, so we just enrich it with calendar-based columns to simplify querying and reporting, and add a few calculated fields. Should you need more descriptive information, it comes complete with the HKEYs to both the current and historical tables for positions and securities, and the HKEY to the current Portfolios, making extensions to the report or through joins straightforward.

The key benefit of a report is that an analyst can now query this single table to perform powerful time-series analysis without writing any joins. They can easily group by security type, portfolio, or any attribute on the date dimension (like month or quarter) to see how the portfolio's value has evolved.

The Code

The code is quite simple, so let's go through its major points.

First, we get the data from the two base tables, calendar and daily values. Note that we limit the calendar forward to the last day of this month.

```
WITH
calendar as (
    select * RENAME (DATE_DAY as CALENDAR_DATE)
    from {{ ref('MDD_DATE_CALENDAR') }}
    where FIRST_DAY_OF_MONTH <=
                DATE_TRUNC('month', current_date())
)
, position_values as (
    select *
    from {{ ref('TS_IB_REPORTED_POSITIONS_DAILY_VALUES') }}
)
```

Think about the ingenious use of `FIRST_DAY_OF_MONTH` along with `DATE_TRUNC` to select all days of the current month and all the previous ones. Next, we have a quite long select that lists the columns from the TS_ model and the calendar dimensions, and adds a few calculations.

```
SELECT
    v.ACCOUNT_ALIAS
    ...

FROM calendar as c
JOIN position_values as v
    ON c.CALENDAR_DATE >= v.ADJ..._POSITION_VALUE_VALID_FROM
    and c.CALENDAR_DATE < v.POSITION_VALUE_VALID_TO
```

It is interesting to note the join: it is not a traditional equi-join, but a combination of two inequalities to achieve the effect of a between, without the equal on the `VALID_TO` side. It is also interesting to note the cardinalities in play, as the calendar has about 365 rows for every year of range, and the daily value table can also have about 250 rows for each position for each year of depth, so for a four-year period, even with just seven positions, these tables have thousands of rows.

While the current numbers are small, even for a Snowflake XS warehouse, in a real setting with hundreds or thousands of positions, it might be worth moving the report to an incremental load strategy. We suggest you do it as an exercise.

Example Usage

With this report in place, an analyst can now easily answer a question like, "What was the total market value of the stocks in each portfolio every day in 2024?" with a simple query:

```
SELECT
    ACCOUNT_ALIAS, YEAR, MONTH_NAME, CALENDAR_DATE,
    round(SUM(POSITION_VALUE_BASE), 2)  -- Value in base currency
    AS total_portfolio_value_base
FROM {{ ref('RPT_POSITIONS_DAILY_VALUES') }}
WHERE YEAR = 2024 AND ASSET_CLASS = 'STK'
GROUP BY 1, 2, 3, 4
ORDER BY 1, 4
```

This query is very simple; the most difficult part is using the portfolio's common base currency and not summing the values in the transaction currencies. That would be a big error in the report's logic.

```
and CALENDAR_DATE = LAST_DAY_OF_MONTH
```

By adding a simple extra line to the where clause, like the one above, you can limit the results to the values at the end of the month, week, or quarter.

Assignment: designing RPT_TOTAL_RETURN

Our current report is excellent for analyzing position values, but it's missing a key component of investment returns: **dividends**.

A more advanced and holistic report would calculate the daily total return by combining the change in market value with any dividend income. We leave the implementation of this `RPT_TOTAL_RETURN` model as a valuable exercise for you. At some point, you may even find it implemented in the final stonks repository for you to study.

Follow this design blueprint: Start with `RPT_POSITIONS_DAILY_VALUES`. This report provides the daily market value for each position. To calculate the change in market value, you will need to use the `LAG()` window function to get the prior day's market value for each position. Pay attention to changes in the quantity held in the position. Next, incorporate dividends. `LEFT JOIN` your result to the `FCT_DIVIDENDS` model on the position and date keys. This will attach any dividend payments to the day they were received. Finally, calculate total return: the final measure, `TOTAL_RETURN`, would be the sum of the daily capital gain and the dividend amount for that day. An alternative could be to look at daily value plus dividends received, less purcahse cost.

Building this model will give you hands-on experience creating a complex report that combines multiple data sources (a snapshot and a transactional fact) to produce a powerful, user-centric data product. The daily total return aligns well with the granularities of the facts we have, but it does not have a strong meaning. Monthly or quarterly returns have. Design how you would calculate them.

Applying engineering contracts and governance

Having coded our dimensions, facts, and reports, it might feel like our work is done. However, building the models is only half the battle. To ensure our data mart is reliable, maintainable, and trustworthy over the long term, we must apply the software engineering principles we discussed in Chapter 14. This is the crucial step that hardens our data products against unexpected changes and makes them safe for the entire organization to depend on.

In this section, we will demonstrate how to implement two of the most important software engineering principles—Design by Contract and the Open/Closed Principle— in our data platform using dbt's native features.

Implementing design by contract

As we learned, a dbt contract is an explicit guarantee about the shape of a model's output. It ensures that the column names, data types, and constraints will never change unexpectedly, protecting all downstream consumers from breaking changes.

We must add enforced contracts to all user-facing models: facts, dimensions, reports, ...
Everything exposed in the delivery layer should have a contract.

As an example, let's add an enforced contract to our `FCT_DIVIDENDS` model. We do this in the model's `FCT_DIVIDENDS.yml` file. Below is just a small, stripped-down extract of the full contract.

```
models:
  - name: FCT_DIVIDENDS
    config:
      contract:
        enforced: true

    columns:
      - name: DIVIDEND_SETTLEMENT_DATE
        data_type: date

      - name: PORTFOLIO_HKEY
        data_type: binary

      - name: SECURITY_NAME
        data_type: string

      - name: GROSS_DIVIDEND_RECIVED_IN_FX
        data_type: number(38,5)
```

The contract must describe all the columns of the model, specifying names and data types. The description must be there, but it is not part of the contract. With `enforced: true`, we activate the contract and dbt will now validate the output of our model during every dbt build. If a code change in an upstream model accidentally causes the dividend received column to be cast as a `VARCHAR`, instead of `NUMBER`, the build will fail with a clear error message. This prevents the incorrect data from ever reaching our BI tools, turning our implicit assumptions into explicit, automated guarantees.

Versioning for safe evolution

Business needs are never static. Sooner or later, a stakeholder will ask for a new column to be added to our report. In such cases, we can usually extend our model and contract to include the new column, as clients can just ignore the extra column. However, in some cases, this generally compatible schema evolution can also cause problems.

Other requests can arrive to change a column name, its type, or its semantics, or to remove a column, as it should no longer be available to the model's audience. In these cases, we cannot just make changes to the model and the contract. **We must explicitly evolve them.**

The Open/Closed Principle states that our existing report must be "closed" for (breaking) modification, but "open" for extension. dbt model versioning gives us a safe way to handle this.

Let's say the analytics team wants to remove or hash the `ACCOUNT_ALIAS` column from our `FCT_POSITION_TRANSACTIONS` model because it contains personally identifiable information that must not be exposed. That would break downstream data consumers that use that column. Instead of just altering the model and fixing the contract by removing the column, we better create a new version so the old and new versions can be both live for a period, allowing consumers to migrate to the new version. This is essential for semantic changes that would go unseen, like hashing the column content. We can do this in two easy steps:

1. **Create the v2 Model**: We create a new file named `FCT_POSITION_TRANSACTIONS_V2.sql`. The new model will be like the original, but without the column to be removed.
2. **Declare the New Version in YAML**: Next, in our `FCT....yml` file, we declare that this new version v2 under the "canonical" model name, as shown in the following block of YAML code.

```
– name: FCT_POSITION_TRANSACTIONS  # Canonical name
  latest_version: 1
  config:
    materialized: table
    contract: {enforced: true}

  columns:
    – name: TRANSACTION_TYPE
      description: The transaction type
      data_type: string
    #... existing config for the v1 model...

  versions:
    – v: 1  # v1 defined under the model name (no columns here)
      deprecation_date: 2999-01-01
    – v: 2
      columns:
        – include: all
          exclude: [ACCOUNT_ALIAS]
      # means all columns in v1 but the one to remove...
```

By using the standard dbt naming convention, we could add a second version just by creating the model with `_v2` and adding its configuration under `versions:`. Please note that while you could describe all the columns of both versions, it is much clearer to just describe the versions with the changes they apply.

Now, any existing dashboards that references `FCT_POSITION_TRANSACTIONS` will continue to run against the stable v1 model, completely unaffected. New projects that do not need the deprecated column or have migrated can ask for the new version by using `ref('FCT_POSITION_TRANSACTIONS', version=2)`.

This provides a safe, explicit, and maintainable path for evolving our data products without breaking anything. By also adding a deprecation date for version v1, we can both communicate the deadline and automatically enforce it for migrating to the new model.

The `deprecation_date` feature in dbt can be applied to any model, not just versioned models, and it is the best way to handle the retirement of models when having consumers outside the team managing the model.

Building a data product for a Streamlit application

Not all data products are destined for a BI tool, as we saw in Chapter 14. Increasingly, data teams are asked to power interactive web applications, and our Data Product Repository must serve these consumers effectively. This is a perfect opportunity to apply the **Interface Segregation Principle** (**ISP**), which we discussed in Chapter 14. The principle states that we should not force a consumer to depend on a model that is larger or more complex than it needs.

The `RPT_POSITIONS_DAILY_VALUES` report we built earlier is perfect for historical analysis, but it contains a large volume of historical data and many columns that a simple application doesn't require. Forcing an app that only needs to show current positions to query the entire history would be slow and inefficient. Instead, we will create a new, lean, and purpose-built model specifically for this use case, in a specific data mart for this application.

Creating an app-specific mart

The best practice for serving an application is to create a separate, app-specific data mart inside the application-specific `app/` folder. Just as we created a `portfolio_analysis` folder and deployed it to the corresponding `MART_PORTFOLIO_ANALYSIS` schema for our BI users, we would create a new folder, such as `03_delivery/apps/current_positions/`, and configure it to deploy to a dedicated `APP_CURRENT_POSITIONS` schema. This approach provides several key benefits:

- **Performance**: The application queries a small, optimized table containing only the data it needs, delivering a fast, responsive user experience.
- **Security**: We can grant the application's service role access to only its dedicated schema, following the principle of least privilege. The application has no access to the broader BI data mart or any other part of the data platform.
- **Maintainability**: The data model for the application is decoupled from our BI data marts. We can evolve the portfolio_analysis mart freely without risking breaking the application, and vice versa.

By now, you should know how to edit the `dbt_project.yml` file to apply this configuration, so try it. If you have any doubts, you can look it up in the sample project.

Coding the application's data model

Our goal is to create a simple report, `RPT_POSITIONS_CURRENT_VALUES`, that shows a snapshot of the most recent value for all currently held positions. This needs to contain exactly what a portfolio dashboard application would need to display. The logic is simple: we take the daily values report we have developed for our BI data mart, which includes the `IS_CURRENT` flag and all required columns, and filter it to keep only the latest record for each position. We then apply a contract to guarantee that the application will have a stable data source. The model's code is a simple select of the fields we want, with a `WHERE` clause to filter to the current date for open positions, as shown in the following snippet.

```
SELECT ...
FROM {{ ref('RPT_POSITIONS_DAILY_VALUES') }}
WHERE VALUE_IS_CURRENT
  and CALENDAR_DATE = CURRENT_DATE()
  and SIDE != 'Closed'
```

With our little model, we have created a small, fast, and efficient data product that is the perfect "interface" for our application. Materialized as a table, our Streamlit application queries it in milliseconds, providing a snappy user experience, without scanning through years of historical data.

While it is true that depending on the BI report is not ideal, it is, in any case, better than duplicating the logic to read from the `TS_` model in the refined layer. The right solution would be to move the logic to produce a dense report with values for all dates into the refined layer and use it from both marts. The reality is that time has value, and this solution is simpler, quicker, and good enough for the long term. It would make sense to mark this as technical debt to be improved when possible. Have the architecture in place, the new model, implement as needed, when needed.

Creating the Streamlit app in Snowflake

With our data product built, creating the application is very simple using Streamlit in Snowflake. It lets you build and host Python web applications directly in your Snowflake environment, leveraging its security and governance.

The high-level steps to create a Streamlit app in the Snowsight UI are

1. Go to the **Streamlit** section in the left navigation bar and click the "+ Streamlit App" button.
2. Give your application a name (e.g., `STONKS_POSITIONS`), choose a warehouse for it to run on, and select a database and schema to store the application object itself. Click Create.
3. Creating the app will open an in-browser code editor with a sample Python script file. Write or paste your Python code into the editor, click Run, and your application will be live.

You can share it with any other user or role in your account, with the usual Snowflake Governance based on roles. There is more work needed to have a DevOps process, but this shows the power of it.

The Streamlit application code

Here is a brief example of the Python code you would paste into the Streamlit editor. It connects to the active Snowflake session, queries our `RPT_POSITIONS_CURRENT_VALUES` model, and displays the data in a clean table. The first part is just the standard boilerplate code.

```
# streamlit_app.py
import streamlit as st
from snowflake.snowpark.context import get_active_session

# Set page title
st.set_page_config(layout="wide")
st.title("My Current Portfolio Holdings")

# Get the current Snowflake session
session = get_active_session()
```

Then we start defining the table we want to query and creating a Streamlit dataframe viewer, adjusting the visualization of some columns and hiding another one.

```
# Query our dbt model and convert to a Pandas DataFrame
target_table = "<db>.<schema>.RPT_POSITIONS_CURRENT_VALUES"
portfolio_df = session.table(target_table).to_pandas()

if not portfolio_df.empty:
    st.dataframe(
        portfolio_df,
        column_config={
            "GAIN_FX": st.column_config.NumberColumn(
                "Gain FX", format="%.2f"
            ),
            "GAIN_PCT_FX": st.column_config.NumberColumn(
                "Gain % FX", format="%.1f %%"
            ),
            "POSITION_CHANGE_DATE": None, # Hide the column
        },
        hide_index=True,
    )
else:
    st.write("No current positions found.")
```

In the sample project, under the chapter code samples, you can find the code for a slightly improved Streamlit app. You are welcome to play around and make it nicer!

This example shows how a well-designed data product in our Delivery Layer can be easily consumed by other applications, extending the reach of our data platform far beyond traditional BI.

Finalizing and validating the data mart

We have now coded all the individual components of our `portfolio_analysis` data mart, from the foundational dimensions to the transactional facts and the user-facing reports. The final and most satisfying step is to run everything together, validate its integrity with our tests, and review the complete data lineage we have created. This process turns our collection of individual models into a cohesive, production-ready data product.

Running the full mart

Thanks to dbt's powerful **node selection syntax**, we don't need to run our models one by one or the entire project; you can decide which models to build with a powerful selection syntax. With a single, elegant command that names our model with a + in front of it, we can build our report and all its upstream dependencies, including those in the Refined and Storage layers. Put the + after and you run all dependencies. No space between `+` and model name. Use your command line and run the following command:

```
dbt build --select +RPT_POSITIONS_CURRENT_VALUES
```

Alternatively, we can decide to build our entire `portfolio_analysis` data mart. By using the folder path as a selector, we instruct dbt to build everything within our mart.

```
dbt build -s models/03_delivery/marts/portfolio_analysis
```

This command tells dbt to find all models in the `portfolio_analysis` folder and execute them in the correct dependency order. Because we are using dbt build, it will also run all the data tests in our `.yml` files after the models are created. If you want to build the upstream models as well, add a + in front.

Validating with tests

This is the moment of truth. As the dbt build command finishes, you will see the output of the data tests. A successful run, with all tests passing, is our guarantee that the data mart is not only built but also correct, at least for the features that you have decided to test.

If you added the relevant tests, this automated validation confirms that all our keys (PORTFOLIO_HKEY, SECURITY_HKEY, etc.) are unique and not null in the dimension tables with current data. Also, that the relationships between our fact tables and dimension tables are intact, with no orphan records. Any custom business logic tests, like our singular test to reconcile calculated versus reported positions, are passing.

This step is what transforms our data from a collection of tables into a trusted, reliable data product that the business can depend on for critical decision-making.

Reviewing the docs and lineage graph

With a successful build, the final step is to visualize the fruits of our labor.

If you are on dbt Cloud, you can open the Catalog or Documentation, and if you have configured your jobs to build the docs, as we suggested at the end of Chapter 2, you should now see the documentation for your project, including the lineage.

If you are using dbt Core, generate the documentation and serve the documentation site to see the complete documentation and lineage graph for your new data mart using these commands:

```
dbt docs generate

dbt docs serve
```

You can also use these commands in dbt Cloud command line to generate the documentation based on the contents of your branch and DEV environment. When you open the dbt docs site and navigate to one of our final `RPT_` models, you will see a beautiful and complex Directed Acyclic Graph (DAG).

This graph is the architectural blueprint of our work. It shows the entire flow of data from the raw source tables on the far left, through the meticulous historization of the Storage Layer, the intelligent integration of the Refined Layer, and culminating in our new, user-focused Delivery Layer models on the far right.

This visualization is not just satisfying; it's a critical tool for data governance, debugging, and stakeholder communication, making our entire data platform transparent and understandable.

Chapter review

Congratulations on building a complete, production-grade data mart! This chapter was a hands-on journey that transformed the architectural theory from Chapter 14 into tangible, working dbt models that solve real-world analytical challenges.

We began by setting up the structure for our `portfolio_analysis` data mart, creating a dedicated folder and configuring a custom schema. From there, we built our core data products, piece by piece. You learned how to create conformed dimensions for portfolios, securities, and dates, applying different patterns, such as deriving a dimension from existing transactions and enriching it with powerful calculated columns.

Next, you built the quantitative heart of our mart: the transactional fact tables. You created `FCT_POSITION_TRANSACTIONS`, a useful, unified log of all position-altering events, and `FCT_DIVIDENDS`, a clean, analysis-ready model for dividends. We then assembled these foundational components into user-facing reports, denormalized the `RPT_POSITIONS_DAILY_ VALUES` for time-series analysis, and built a purpose-built model to power a Streamlit application, demonstrating the Interface Segregation Principle in action.

Finally, we elevated our models to production-grade data products by applying dbt contracts and discussing versioning, ensuring our mart is not just functional but also trustworthy and maintainable over time.

You are now equipped with a complete, repeatable playbook for building high-quality data marts and a full Pragmatic Data Platform in your own projects.

Recommended resources

The primary resource for this chapter is the stonks sample project itself, where you can find the complete source code for every model we have built.

- Stonks Sample Project: https://github.com/pragmatic-data/stonks.

The following materials offer more information on the specific dbt and Snowflake features we used.

dbt Documentation
The official dbt documentation is the best source for up-to-date information.

- **dbt Exposures**: Learn more about how to define and use exposures to document and track the downstream uses of your dbt models. https://docs.getdbt.com/docs/build/exposures.
- **Jinja and Macros**: For a deeper dive into using Jinja for control structures like the for loop we used to build our portfolio dimension. https://docs.getdbt.com/docs/build/jinja-macros.
- **dbt Model Contracts**: https://docs.getdbt.com/docs/build/contracts.

Snowflake Documentation

- **Streamlit in Snowflake**: The official QuickStart guide for getting started with building Streamlit applications directly in Snowsight. https://quickstarts.snowflake.com/guide/getting_started_with_streamlit/index.html.

Your Journey Continues

Thank you for joining us on this journey through the Pragmatic Data Platform.

We have traveled from the foundational principles of modern data engineering to the practical, line-by-line implementation of a complete, production-grade data platform with dbt and Snowflake. If you've followed along and built the stonks project, you have not only learned the theory but have put it into practice, tackling real-world challenges like data historization, time-series analysis, and creating user-centric data products.

Our goal for this book was not just to teach you the syntax of dbt or the features of Snowflake, but to share a philosophy for building data platforms that are simple, maintainable, testable, and, above all, valuable to the organization.

The specific tools and technologies in our field will undoubtedly evolve, but the core principles of the Pragmatic Data Platform—a layered architecture, a commitment to software engineering best practices, and a relentless focus on delivering trusted data to your users—will remain timeless.

The data world is vast and constantly changing, which makes it such an exciting field to be part of. The patterns and models you've learned here are a powerful toolkit, but they are a starting point, not an endpoint. We encourage you to take these concepts, apply them to your own unique challenges, adapt them, and improve upon them. We look forward to seeing where your ingenuity and vision lead the data community next and the lasting impact your work will have.

The conversation doesn't end on this page. For ongoing insights, new patterns, and updates on the ever-evolving world of data, please visit the official Pragmatic Data Platform blog at:

https://pragmatic-data.org/

It has been a privilege to share this journey with you. We wish you the very best of success in all your data endeavors. Go build great platforms, deliver incredible value, and make a lasting impact on your organization.

Roberto and Jakob

Index

www.ingramcontent.com/pod-product-compliance
Lightning Source LLC
LaVergne TN
LVHW060022210926
848481LV00013B/3765
* 9 7 9 8 8 9 8 1 6 0 4 9 4 *